Both Sides of the Sheets

Annie Armitage

Matador
5 Weir Road
Kibworth Beauchamp
Leicester LE8 0LQ, UK
Tel: (+44) 116 279 2299
Fax: (+44) 116 279 2277
Email: books@troubador.co.uk
Web: www.troubador.co.uk/matador

ISBN 978 1848764 866

British Library Cataloguing in Publication Data.
A catalogue record for this book is available from the British Library.

Typeset in 11pt Book Antiqua by Troubador Publishing Ltd, Leicester, UK
Printed and bound in the UK by TJ International Ltd, Padstow, Cornwall

Matador is an imprint of Troubador Publishing Ltd

For Ian.
For those caring for the sick.
For patients
For my profession.
For Lupus suffers.
(Lupus UK - Telephone number (044) (0) 1708 731251)

ACKNOWLEDGEMENTS

I wish to thank Ian for his love and compassion over all the years, for editing this book, and for encouraging me on numerous occasions when I was threatening to abandon my writing.

Thanks to all those that have read my chapters, contributed ideas, constructively criticised and encouraged me and particularly June Counsel, Anne Elphick, and Rebecca Duffey,

Thanks to my dear friends The Queen Elizabeth Nurses – Eileen Fortey (nee Anderson), Sylvia Williams (nee Edgington) Gill McGowan (Nee Bradbury) and for all the support from my other friends and relatives.

Some name changes are to protect the innocent and me from the guilty.

CONTENTS

CHAPTER 1

CRISIS

I opened my eyes.

"Are you all right?"a female voice asked gently. I tried to answer but couldn't make words of the thoughts inside my head. I wriggled, eventually managing to whine,

"I -I -I need a wee."

The voice said soothingly, "Don't worry, just do it… You're wearing an incontinence pad as a nappy, so it won't matter." I relaxed, feeling the damp warmth seeping between my legs. Then, opening my eyes again, I stared at the owner of the voice, but I couldn't make sense of what I saw. Then she was talking again, "You've been in a coma, so we're moving you from Peterborough District Hospital to Addenbrooke's Hospital in Cambridge."

I was finding the journey tedious in my damp nappy. The sun was streaming through the skylight in the roof of the ambulance. I thought, "Ah! I have it, perhaps we could break the journey and stop for a picnic." Somehow I would have to put my thoughts into words.

"C -c -c- could we stop for a picnic?"

The ambulance woman sounded incredulous, "It's January and it's freezing outside."

The warmth of the heating had protected me from the winter cold, and even the urine in my damp nappy had retained its warmth. I slept until, eventually, we reached

Cambridge and the ambulance doors were drawn back.

A male voice asked, "Has she been all right?"

"Yes, she's been fine," was the response.

Indignantly I thought, how can she say I'm fine when I'm in this state? But now they gently moved the stretcher down the ramp, out of the ambulance, into a lift and onto a ward. Two nurses appeared and transferred me into a bed. A warm hand took mine and the ambulance woman said,

"Take care, my love."

My education of life as a patient between the sheets had begun. Gradually, as the dimmer switch of consciousness increased in intensity, I became aware of my environment. Actually I'd lost only three weeks of my life and fortunately, at that stage, I didn't realise what was going or what was ahead of me.

Only a month before it had been Christmas, but a very different Christmas to those that had preceded it. Shortly before the day my blonde, twenty-year-old student daughter, Sarah, arrived anticipating the festive season. All the cards had been written and posted and the fridge and freezer stocked with food. Carefully wrapped presents had been retrieved from their secret hiding places and placed under the tree, which my husband, Ian, had brought in from the garden. I could still recall the evocative smell of pine filling the sitting room, as Ian, at six foot tall, had no difficulty in reaching up to the tree and various other places that needed decorations to transform our modern, four-bedroom house into something of a winter wonderland.

Then, at the most inconvenient moment, the oven broke down and refused to work. Spare parts were not available at such a late stage in the festive season. It was Christmas Eve, so Ian, who is always good in an emergency, nipped out to buy cold meat for our Christmas lunch. The turkey was relegated to the freezer. My breathing had begun to deteriorate since early December and despite visits to the GP, had continued to worsen. By this time I was so breathless I couldn't participate in the preparations in any useful way. After all the excitement of Christmas, it must've been a very disappointing time for everyone, as my relatively small frame lay gasping for breath on the sitting room sofa.

As soon as the Christmas holiday period was over, Ian drove me to see Don, the acupuncturist. Don felt for the four pulse levels of Chinese medicine, but didn't reach for the acupuncture needles. Instead he turned to Ian, saying,

"Anne needs to be in hospital. Take her straight to her GP, may I phone to say she is on her way?"

Ian must have agreed because when we arrived at the surgery we were shown straight into see Dr Doyle, my G.P. He stood up looking concerned and asked,

"Would you be happy to come into hospital under the care of my next-door-neighbour?"

Dr Doyle's gentle voice with its soft Irish accent immediately made me feel secure. His presence exuded warmth and he was holding my hand while waiting for my response.

Dr Doyle always looked as though he'd rushed out to a call during the night, hastily dressing in any clothes that came immediately to hand. On this occasion I felt so poorly that I would have accepted any suggestion with gratitude even if his next-door-neighbour had been an astrologist! In fact Dr Doyle lived next door to the consultant Dr Guttman, whose speciality was in heart and kidney medicine.

Ian drove me to Peterborough District Hospital and we were directed to Ward 2Y. I was shown to a bed in an eight-bed bay and Ian went home, relieved that I was in good hands. By that time I was out of it and quite unaware of what was going on. I presume the houseman must have admitted me. I lay in bed for a few days periodically coming round but becoming increasingly disorientated. This culminated one night in my going to the toilet and, on returning, climbing into the first unoccupied bed. The occupant had left it to meet her call of nature and was not best pleased to find my oporific body in her bed on her return.

My bad behaviour was reported to Ian the following day and I was moved into a single room; possibly as the result of my nocturnal wanderings, or maybe because my breathing had deteriorated into such a state of hyperventilation that it was disturbing the other occupants of the ward. Years later, I found out that my chief misdemeanour was masturbating during the night. The Ward Sister had confided in Carole, my friend, who at forty still maintained the appearance of a punk and, because of this, the Ward Sister felt able to share such delicate information with her.

As a further test of Dr Guttman's abilities, my breathing problems were exacerbated by partial heart and kidney failure.

"But not clitoris failure," Carole said later.

Clearly if left to my own devices I'd soon be dead.

Something had to be done. A very kind Ward Sister sat and held my hand for most of the day, handing over to a nurse when she went off duty. When Ian visited, he whispered in my ear,

"Just keep breathing Annie."

Ian heard the doctors discussing my chances of survival and my potential life expectancies after survival. A lengthy discourse ensued and eventually the doctors decided to take the plunge and offer me an intensive-care bed. I had my chance.

A case conference was held and Hilaire Belloc's poem, "The Death of Henry King", might have been written with just that event in mind;

Physicians of the utmost fame
were called at once,
But when they came
they answered as they took their fees;
"There is no cure for this disease
Henry will very soon be dead"

4

I knew the odds but I was not dead yet!

I was twenty-six when I was diagnosed with the auto-immune disease, Lupus. When I consulted my nursing textbooks, I'd read, "prognosis must be guarded and particularly where there is renal involvement, the outlook is bad, patients surviving just a year or two."

Once Lupus has been conclusively diagnosed there is no cure.

As for me, I was transferred to Intensive Care and my nearest and dearest relatives were called to my bedside from far-flung corners of the country, to potentially say goodbye. But at my greatest moment of melodrama, I was cerebrally absent.

Ian orchestrated the initial meeting between relatives and the medical team, who began to explain my state of health with the aid of matchstick-men type drawings. My relatives sat entranced, until Ian broke in with an explanation of the backgrounds of the audience, pointing out that there was a GP, a pharmacist, a senior accountant and company director, and two undergraduates, with himself an ex bank manager, all knowing that I was suffering from Lupus, some having known this for over twenty years. One of the doctors pointed out that I was in kidney failure, but I could always go on the list for a transplant. The audience realised that the outlook was bleak. Ian suggested,

"That really isn't feasible is it?"

"No, we are afraid it isn't. We are simply trying to comfort you with options," added a doctor.

That only emphasised a sad appreciation of my poor chances of a good recovery.

After the meeting, Ian told me that all the relatives retired to a local hostelry, to commiserate and discuss the dismal prognosis being forecast by the medical profession. Sarah, who is normally a tightly packed bundle of assertiveness, just sat and cried into her salad roll, whilst my son, John, six foot and every inch a Leo, entered a quiet, reflective state.

Amongst the sadness, jokes were resorted to and my brother, John, who was the doctor, thinking that this levity was upsetting Sarah, went across to hold her hand. There was much reassuring and cuddling for several days afterwards. All were dealing with their fears and anxieties as best they could.

For three days I was connected with tubes for feeding, hydration, medication and catheterisation. I responded to this treatment and, having stabilised me, the doctors proceeded to try to find out what had caused this crisis. So they added another tube to get blood samples whenever they wished, as my veins often retreated when under threat.

Over the next week these tubes were gradually removed but until then, my loved ones had to endure various unpleasant aromas and sights. Feeding tubes are notoriously smelly and nasty, and mine were no exception. The current nursing recruitment strategy seems to rely on entrants having a very poor sense of smell. The nursing staff seemed oblivious to my dishevelled state, leaving my visitors to clean me up as best they could. Fortunately, I was not aware of the putrid smell that my body was exuding, but when Don came to see how I was, he went straight to the sluice to collect the things he needed to give me a blanket-bath, so that my visitors didn't have to face me still smelling like a pole-cat.

Don Snuggs had worked at the local hospital as a Clinical Nurse Teacher but now was a registered acupuncturist, having spent three years training in London to obtain his qualifications. He had become particularly interested in achieving health improvements by holistic methods, during his work in the Far East as a nurse in the RAF.

Fortunately, I have very few memories about my care, or the absence of it, but I do remember the delicious feeling of being fresh and clean after the blanket-bath. I also have a vague memory of lying in a cot bed with my catheter, the balloon

inflated with water, hanging over the cot side. I must ha⸺
actually done it, although pulling it out would have been ⸺
mean feat with the balloon inflated. I don't suppose it did ⸺
great deal for my pelvic floor and hopes for future continence.

For the first time in my life, that anyone can recall, I lost my appetite. Not surprising, considering the wear and tear my throat and sensory perceptions had endured. Ian later reported with some amusement that when he was visiting me, a nurse came to take my blood pressure. Having carried out the task, she asked me what I would like to drink.

"I'll have a gin and tonic please!"

She exclaimed, "I meant a sip of water or similar! You won't be able to drink alcohol for a very long time."

To which I retorted, "You can fuck off then."

She responded, "That's not very nice, Annie."

I replied, "Isn't it? Oh no! I'm sorry."

Just before my transfer, friends, who run a small hotel and restaurant in Peterborough, came to tempt my taste buds. While Tony watched, Thomas, the chef, fed me with delicious fresh fruit salad. My taste buds, which had been so abused by tube feeding, suddenly woke up and I shouted,

"Oh! That was really delicious!"

The taste of fruit, eaten the previous day at Peterborough, sustained me throughout my ambulance journey to Addenbrooke's hospital in Cambridge and, comforted by the warmth of the ambulance woman's touch, I lay dozing and wondering about my new surroundings in Addenbrooke's Hospital. Long gone are the Nightingale wards of the old Addenbrooke's hospital, this has been replaced by a new hospital building covering a large site to the south of Cambridge. The wards having been built to the modern concept of eight-bed side wards.

My vision was very poor but my hearing was compensating and becoming more acute. So, it was lovely to hear Ian's soft Suffolk accent, introducing himself and Sarah, my daughter. He was asking which bed I was in and if it was

ght for them to visit me. I could hear the staff nurse, with
voice more appropriate for a Sergeant Major, or a guard at a
orstal, than for comforting distressed relatives, introducing
herself,

"I am staff nurse Williams. Your wife has had a
comfortable journey. She is in bay one, first bed. Please make
the visit brief; she is to have a scan this afternoon. "

It felt truly wonderful when Ian and Sarah trooped in. Ian
took my hand, asking,

"How are you?"

He leaned over and kissed me. I smiled, snuggling down.
I was feeling as cosy as a baby in its cot. Suddenly the
atmosphere of the cold formality of the ward was of no
consequence to me. Sarah wasted no time at all and began
busily filling my locker with cosmetics and toiletries. She
paused to say,

"We've sorted it all out, Mum. I'll come in each lunchtime
and feed you and Ian will be in each evening to give you
your supper, and settle you down for the night. We have put
a large jar of muesli in your locker for breakfast."

All too soon both were standing. Ian said,

"We've got to go because you've got to have an MRI scan
this afternoon." I bit my lip as he kissed me and, determined
to be brave, I lifted my left arm to try to wave goodbye.
Without thinking, I'd automatically compensated for the
complete lack of feeling in my right arm.

I heard a squeaky wheelchair coming and the porter
giving my name, then he and the Sergeant Major arrived at
my bedside. Together, they moved me into the wheelchair
without a word being spoken. Then, with the wheelchair
squeaking incessantly, the porter pushed me along a rabbit
warren of corridors. I wondered as we went along, "Isn't
there anyone with a can of oil in Addenbrooke's." The porter
seemed completely oblivious of me, or the noise. He went to
the reception desk, booked me in and left. Without the
continuous squeaking to keep me awake, my head lolled

onto my chest and I started snoring so loudly that even I was woken by the thunderous decibels. The duty nurse came and looked at me and then returned to her position behind the desk without comment. I felt sorry for the other patients who had to share the waiting room with barely conscious patients, such as myself.

In due course I was wheeled into the scanning room. Two pairs of arms lifted me onto a flat surface and a domed lid was fastened over me. A disembodied voice instructed me,

"Hold your breath". After what seemed an impossible length of time, and when I had quite given up hope of being rescued from this metal tomb (I was wondering if I would be left until I expired?), a voice came out of somewhere saying, "You can breathe normally now." With great relief, I took my first breath and I lay there gasping and thinking, "I hope metal coffins never catch on."

Eventually, I was returned to the wheelchair and taken back to the waiting room. Nobody spoke. The porter came back, retraced his route to the ward and still no one spoke to me. What information had they hoped to gain from the scan? I'd apparently achieved a state of total invisibility.

Once back on the ward, I was put into bed by two nurses. One said to the other,

"There is nothing of her is there?"

In fact, apparently I actually weighed just under six stone. I probably looked a bit like a stick insect. When they'd finished, the nurses drew the screens back, revealing the rest of the bay.

I was beginning to get used to this total lack of communication, when a cheery voice called out from the bed opposite,

"Hello! My name is Evelyn. How are you?"

I responded, "I-I-I'm Annie, I- I j-just feel exhausted!" and with that fell fast asleep.

Ian arrived that evening and, after feeding me with a pasta bake, held my hand in his, gently asking me how the scan had gone. He helped me to the toilet and, having cleaned my teeth, he kissed me and left me to sleep. I'm ashamed to say, I was unable to consider how Ian must have been feeling, fully preoccupied with thinking about my life on the ward. But Ian was going to have to face a regular journey to Peterborough and then a trip to Nottingham or environs for work as well as looking after Abbey, our nine year old golden retriever.

The night staff arrived, going around the ward and noting the state of any new admissions. Then the ward lights were turned off. No doubt I was soon asleep, only to be wakened by the need to wee. I lay there for a while but couldn't get anyone's attention, and then could hold it no longer. The urine trickled between my legs, soaked into my bottom sheet and I soon felt very cold. The tears began to run down my cheeks. Then, I became aware of a nurse asking,

"Why aren't you asleep?"

"I - I - I've wet the bed" I answered in a pathetic voice. The nurse said,

"Don't worry, we will soon sort you out." She disappeared to fetch her colleague. They returned and two highly competent pairs of hands changed the wet sheet for a dry one and re-made the bed, in what seemed to me only seconds, and without speaking. When they had finished, one of the nurses placed a bell at my right hand and left.

My right hand was completely without feeling, so there was no way on earth that I could summon help.

"How could nurses on a cerebral injuries ward just assume I could press that bell? Presumably, whenever Steven Hawking is ill he goes into Addenbrooke's, but they wouldn't give him a bell to call for help would they?" I lay there thinking this through until I dozed off. Fortunately, I woke in the morning with a dry bed. This process was to recur again and again during my time in Addenbrooke's, and at no time was I able to make them understand that I couldn't use the bell in my right hand and I couldn't coordinate my left hand sufficiently to lean over and work it with that hand. The night staff, having completed their task, always scurried off as quickly as they could.

My memory may be playing tricks, but I trained as a nurse during the 1960s and spent many of my nights sitting on patients' beds, holding their hands while we chatted, whispering so as not to wake the slumbering forms all around, until the insomniac sufferers felt able to go back to sleep. We were not actually allowed to sit on patient's beds, but at night the ward doors squeaked and alerted us to the night Sister's visits. So the absence of oil cans, or certainly the use of them is not new to the National Health Service.

Perhaps it was due to the whispering, but the conversations during the night always had a conspiratorial feel, and I certainly learnt a lot. I recalled the instance of a patient called Derek. He was an insomniac, probably because he wasn't used to sleeping in the comfort of a bed and had learnt to maintain a nightly watchfulness for his own security. He'd been admitted during the early hours of a freezing cold, winter night. He'd been sleeping rough and one of his shoes was leaking; frostbite and hypothermia were the result. Derek set out to educate me on the shortcomings of prison life. He'd experienced the dubious pleasures of many different prisons and shared the hierarchy of horrors, saying,

"Preston jail has got to be the worst. Bedford is only a bit better." It was like an alternative travel guide, as though I was intending to go there.

From the sublime to the ridiculous, I recalled another of my nightly conversations. This time with Mr Oddy, an asthmatic private patient. Somehow his breathing was always worse in the small hours of the night. To help him settle down to sleep, I'd sit on the side of his bed, and he'd talk about his son, the famous comedian who was part of 'The Goodies'. His conversation was about the juvenile comedian's escapades and his rise to fame.

"It's not that he was a malicious boy," his father explained, but he just loved to make people laugh. "One day he went into a local off-licence with a water-pistol and pointed the pistol at the owner saying, "Your whiskey or your wife!" Anxiously, the shopkeeper handed him a bottle of whiskey. At this, my son became completely baffled and said, "You were only supposed to laugh. I am only 16, I'm not allowed to drink alcohol."

Sharing the pleasure of his memories, we laughed together. He relaxed and was able to breathe normally. Shaking his head in amusement he continued,

"After that sort of start it is amazing that he made such a successful career."

We learnt about people when I trained to be a nurse. Where has this gone? Our training, where patients were people with a past and, hopefully a future. A training during which we were instructed to always hold a patient's hand while we were talking to them?

Now it seems as though the patients are the enemy, or at least just specimens on which to perform a task. A stethoscope casually worn around the neck being a badge of authority. Has empathetic care gone forever?

But wait! As the next morning dawned, a male nursing aid arrived with a trolley. He took my hand and in a broad Cambridgeshire accent said,

"Hello Annie, my name is Robert. Would you like me to freshen you up by washing your face, before breakfast?"

My eyes widened in disbelief,

"Y-y-yes p-please," I stammered.

I stared at Robert, realising for the first time that when I thought of the Addenbrooke's nurses I always thought of them as shadowy figures rushing off as quickly as they could when their tasks were accomplished. Robert was different. He stood still and close enough for my eyes to focus on his face, while he gently washed my face with his large, but very gentle hands. All the time he was smiling kindly at me. I watched him as he moved around the ward, cheerfully dispensing comfort. He limped, and one of his shoes was built up. Was his disability the reason why he was able to offer such sympathetic care?

Later, Robert returned and started feeding me with my breakfast muesli. He asked,

"Would you like a bath?"

To me it was almost a rhetorical question, as a bath seemed a distant memory, an unimaginable luxury. The sheer joy of a bath for a body that has been regularly soaked in wee is unimaginable. The gentleness of Robert, a man in his forties with the kindness and compassion of a saint, was truly wondrous. The delight of the warm, refreshing water with the Christian Dior Dune-perfumed bubble bath, was exquisite. "That's what Sarah was putting in my locker," I thought and remembered she'd bought it for me at Christmas.

Now smelling fragrant and refreshed, I was returned to rest back in bed. Robert turned his attention to Evelyn, while I luxuriated. Suddenly a flurry of white coats, like ferral pigeons descending on Trafalgar Square, broke the peace. They arrived at my bedside first; Dr Caine, the consultant, relaxed and confident as the melee of his entourage danced around him like mayflies in summer. A young and anxious Ward Sister was nervously introducing me before handing over to the housewoman. The teaching registrar sat on my bed and took my hand, lulling me into a false sense of security while the conversation went on around me, but not to me, with lots of discussions about my blue toes, suggestions of biopsies and such things. Then they moved on to Evelyn's bed.

With the screens drawn around Evelyn, I started to focus on the commotion going on in a third bed. The lady of about 40 years old was becoming increasingly agitated. As the medical entourage emerged from Evelyn's screens and started pushing the note trolley towards the third lady, she started a high-pitched wailing. What must have happened in the past to cause such an extreme reaction? I wondered.

When the medical troop moved off, we compared notes.

"I'm having a lumbar puncture tomorrow," I announced.

"So am I," Evelyn said quietly.

I was suddenly deflated. I'd been feeling that I'd achieved a certain status of interest. By now the wailing coming from the third bed was gradually subsiding. I quickly grasped the opportunity for a chat.

"My name's Annie... Are you alright?" I thought, now I'm doing it too. Why is the conversation so limited to asking about being alright? Clearly we're in here because we're not. Eventually a quivering voice came from the bed, "Evelyn"

"My name is Evelyn. What is your name?" She answered,

"Wendy." I tried to soothe, "Perhaps you will feel better soon." After that, silence reigned, as we were all lost in our own thoughts.

Then Sarah arrived to feed me with lunch.

"Did you have a good night, Mum?"

"Oh, yes," I responded, thoughtfully. Somehow starting a conversation with tales of urinary incontinence didn't seem quite the right thing before eating. Sarah was talking

"I'll just go and sort out your food. There's some lasagne. Be back in a minute."

The time went by until Sarah eventually came back carrying a tray with a delicious smelling dish on it. Previously unaware of aromas, the perfumed bath must have jolted my olfactory nerve into action. Sarah moved me into a comfortable position, seated herself, placed a napkin on my tummy, filled a spoon full of food and started towards my mouth.

"Open Mum, here comes the train. Swallow and down the tunnel it goes, "she sang.

"Oh! Sarah," I chuckled.

Life in Addenbrooke's suddenly seemed very comfortable, Sarah appeared to appreciate the opportunity to reap revenge on her Mum for those years of my spoon-feeding her as a baby. I slept until Ian arrived to give me supper and settle me down for the night. Ian left me feeling very cosy, when like the soft wings of a butterfly he gently brushed my cheek on kissing me goodnight.

Our night's sleep was disturbed by Wendy. She was banging on the window. A nurse rushed in and said,

"What's the matter, Wendy?"

"I've killed my baby. I'm going to throw it out of the window," she shouted.

The nurse tried to pacify Wendy, whilst steering her back to bed and pressing the bell to summon assistance. Help soon arrived, one nurse stayed with Wendy and the other rushed off, soon to reappear with a hypodermic and administered an injection. Apart from Wendy's snoring, peace was soon restored.

The next morning, the feeling of calm was quickly shattered. We were disturbed by the Sergeant Major's military style. She sorted out the breakfast and somehow even made the drinking of tea through a straw feel rushed. It became a race against time and I would choke if I didn't swallow quickly. After that, she started on the bathing routine. The whole procedure was brutal in comparison with the luxury of the previous day. It was conducted more like a sheep-dip! (Though, as I have never operated a sheep-dip, I may be doing a great injustice to the likes of Bert Fry of the Archers.) At least it felt good to be clean again.

All too soon, I was back in bed.

"I think it's today we are having the lumbar puncture," said Evelyn.

"Oh, yes," I agreed. With that, Wendy started wailing. "Don't worry Wendy, it's only Evelyn and me who are having that done. You'll be alright."

While we were talking, the coffee trolley arrived on the scene and the catering assistant carefully helped me to drink through the straw. No sooner had she finished than a porter-propelled wheelchair arrived, accompanied by the Sergeant Major, instructing as she hauled me out of bed,

"You are going to occupational therapy."

Unseen hands pushed me along, again without communication.

When we arrived in the department the therapist, a gentle, charming woman in her thirties, gave me a comforting pat on my arm and started to assess my competence. She picked up my right hand and it fell like a dead weight back onto the table. She lifted my left hand, and when she released it I was able to hold it in the air. She said,

"Now Annie, what I want you to do is take a cone in your left hand and place it on a pin of the same colour."

I grasped a cone and, with uncoordinated movements, I moved it onto the target.

"That is very good," she urged, "but, unfortunately you moved a green cone onto a yellow pin."

Only then did I realise that I couldn't tell the difference.

Back in the ward, Sarah arrived.

"Did you have a good night, Mum?" she asked.

"Yes, but I'm afraid Wendy disturbed us, trying to dispatch a baby through a window," I whispered. Sarah shook her head saying,

"Oh no! When I went to fetch your lunch yesterday, the reason I was ages before coming back with it was because I met Wendy, who was looking for a tooth she said she'd lost. Fortunately, a nurse came along as I was busy searching for it under cushions, or I would probably still be there. Poor Wendy." Then Sarah smiled and, changing the subject, said, "Mum. There is this wonderful cheesecake shop I bet you'd go a bundle on. I'll buy some for tomorrow." She must have known that it was a rhetorical comment but, just in case, I answered enthusiastically,

"Ooh yes please!"

As soon as lunch was over and Sarah had helped me to and from the lavatory, a nurse and the housewoman came in pushing a trolley. The housewoman was a small, slim, mousey slip of femininity but moved very purposefully. The lumbar punctures were about to begin.

"I bet she hasn't done many of these," I thought and I started to worry, perhaps with good reason. Wendy began wailing again and, because we'd spent every spare moment that morning reassuring her that it was only Evelyn and me that were involved, I started to reassure Wendy that she would be alright.

"Who is to have it done?" asked Evelyn.

"You all are," said the housewoman.

At this point the wailing from Wendy reached a crescendo. It must have dawned on the housewoman that the only way to stop the racket was to start with Wendy herself. Businesslike, they got on with the job. No doubt they also gave Wendy something to cause unconsciousness, because peace was restored. Next it was my turn. The housewoman, together with the staff nurse, turned me onto my face and then one of them began cleaning my lower back with spirit.

"What is your daughter reading, English language or literature?" the housewoman asked conversationally.

I mumbled, "English literature," though I couldn't quite believe her question was serious? Surely a graduate who'd presumably been rubbing shoulders with fellow students for at least five or six years, would know that for the last 400 hundred years it was English literature that was taught at Oxbridge? Well, at least since they moved from Latin to English, I thought. "Chaucer would be turning in his grave!"

On second thoughts perhaps she was joking, although I had never heard her crack jokes before! No, I concluded she was not joking.

We were told that we were to stay on bed rest for three days. We were only to get up to visit the lavatory, though perhaps that's why the Sergeant Major did the bathing routine with so much brusqueness. It was to stop us being miserable about three days without baths. While I was musing about this, two nurses and a porter arrived with a trolley. They drew the screens around Wendy's bed and took her away, never to be seen again.

We lay resting, trying not to think about the slight headache, pain and soreness from the needle site. I felt relieved that Ian didn't come that evening and feed me, because I felt sick. Instead, a student nurse came to wash our faces.

She exclaimed," Clinique soap! How lovely." With that, she loaded a face flannel with the soap and wiped it over my face and into my eyes. I lay there waiting for her to rinse it off. I waited and waited, but it didn't happen. I had to keep my eyes tightly screwed up, because when I opened them I couldn't see. "She must have moved on," I thought eventually. I called out to Evelyn,

"Have you got soap in your eyes?" Evelyn was unusually monosyllabic:

"Yes," she said. "There's nothing else for it, we'll have to wait for the night staff to come around and appeal to them to rinse the soap off." I sighed. It seemed such a small thing, but being incapacitated and unable to open your eyes without them stinging, seemed like torture. Time passed slowly, but eventually the night shift came to our rescue. They took some persuading, but grudgingly sorted us out and we settled down for the night.

Over the next two days of enforced bed rest, we lay in bed watching the staff as they rushed backwards and forwards about their tasks. We kept ourselves amused by discussing their individual characteristics and mannerisms. Suddenly, the Sergeant Major appeared from behind screens. We weren't sure whether she'd heard us or not. She was scowling, but then she normally did look grim. As the nurse left the ward, I said,

"Oh dear, she doesn't exactly dispense comfort does she? I think we'd better work out nick-names for them so we won't get caught out again."

"Eva Braun," said Evelyn immediately.

"Yes," I agreed heartily. We chuckled conspiratorially.

It seemed to us that we lay in bed simply as objects, which the nursing staff visited reluctantly to conduct various tasks, and not human beings requiring empathetic care. We felt we were facing a hostile environment and consequently we retreated to a school girl, dormitory-style humour, with the nursing staff as the enemy. I felt bemused about how these nurses had been recruited. They never seemed to pause in their officiousness, neither to offer comfort or care, but always dashed off to get the next task done, returning to safety in the company of their colleagues at ward control.

I wondered how they developed the notion that patients, rather than their ailments, are the enemy. I couldn't believe the claims that staff shortages caused this behaviour, because we could see nurses spending an inordinate amount of time chatting with the other staff once back at ward control. I wondered if they started out with a compassionate side to their nature and a wish to care? If so, where has it all gone?

Evelyn's sigh of boredom brought me out of my reverie.

"How did you end up in here?" I asked her.

Evelyn frowned, as though trying to recall a previous life.

"I'd been shopping in Cambridge as usual but, when I started for home, somehow it was later than usual; nearly evening. Perhaps I'm just being poetical, but I'm sure I could picture the sun sinking behind the gleaming spires of Kings as I started on the cycle path for Grantchester. As I joined the road, a passing lorry clipped my bicycle. He just carried on, leaving me sprawled in the road, (and with that she started to giggle).

"Apparently I was detached from my bike and surrounded by broken eggs, butter, bread, cucumber, and a smashed jar with a sticky substance oozing from it onto the road. There was to be no honey for tea that day in Grantchester! Another motorist must have stopped and phoned an ambulance and here I am! I'm sorry but I feel tired out with all this talking," and with that Evelyn went to sleep, leaving me pondering about how quickly our lives can change.

I was thinking this through when another nurse came in and woke Evelyn. We watched, entranced at the nurse's waddling splay footed gait. It was as if the illustrators of the cartoon Pingu had based their character precisely on that nurse.

"Penguin," I said. We both grinned, united in our child-like humour.

The ward doors opened to reveal the housewoman and Eva Braun. The housewoman said,

"We're going to put a drip up. You'll be having 100 grams of steroids over 8 hours every three days when I've got it running. In the meantime, I'm going to give you an intelligence test."

I thought, well that'll be interesting. The last one I had was by a university psychologist. Anyway, I didn't seem to have any choice but to give it a go. She sat down and started with, "Can you tell me what year it is?"

I didn't have a clue, and simply said,

"No." I felt disappointed with my answer. She went on,

"What month is it?" The questions were depressing me and, suddenly aware of the pain in my back, I answered,

"Lumbar puncture month." She continued with,

"What day of the week is it?" This time I'd better have an answer, though only two days ago I hadn't realized it was winter, and in the closed portals of a hospital I had little chance of knowing. I thought long and hard. Then I answered triumphantly,

"The day after yesterday, and the day before tomorrow."

Sadly, not even a flicker of amusement or wonderment for my clever reply crossed her stern gaze. She simply asked,

"Who is the Prime Minister?"

Again I thought for a long time and then recalled a poster

that my friend Jilly had bought me, now hanging in my study at home, of Ronald Reagan carrying Margaret Thatcher, above which is written in large type;

The film to end all films.
The most explosive love story ever,
Gone with the wind!
She promised to follow him to the end of the world.
He promised to organise it.
Now showing worldwide!

"Margaret Thatcher!" I exclaimed, very pleased with myself.

"Who is the President of America? "She asked, as though primed.

"Ronald Reagan!" I responded gleefully. I was delighted that I'd been able to recall the poster. The trip into creativity tired me and I felt crushed by her dismissive attitude. To the subsequent questions I just said,

"I don't know."

When Ian came to visit in the evening he told me that the housewoman drew him aside and said, "I have done an IQ test on your wife and been getting some very strange answers. Does she seem normal to you?"

Ian responded, "It depends upon where you start and your definition of normality."

The housewoman shrugged with incomprehension and walked off obviously thinking, dear me, here is another one.

Ian arrived at my bedside, grinning and asked,, "What have you been saying, to the Housewoman? She obviously thinks you're bonkers," and recounted the conversation. I explained, "I'm afraid I was playing games with her and she made me cross. Just because doctors have a medical qualification, they think it qualifies them to do anything. Honestly, an intelligence test, I ask you. She could do with an intelligence test herself."

Ian laughed saying, "Well she thinks I'm insane too."

He continued with the business of feeding me, settled me down for the night, kissed me and left me to sleep.

I thought I'd died during the night and ascended into a celestial world. The heavens were bright, illuminating an angel. Or was it merely that the ward lights were switched on? A spectre arrived at my bedside, inquiring,

"Would you like me to freshen you up?" Then the pain in my back, with its attendant headache, brought me back to reality.

"Yes please," I said gratefully. The angel was collecting things from my locker saying,

"I'm looking after you today. My name is Ruth. I hope you slept well."

She gently washed my face, carefully removing all the soap from my eyes. Ruth returned later to feed me with breakfast. She was Robert' s opposite number. I suddenly remembered the intelligence test and asked,

"What day is it today?"

"It's Saturday, so there won't be the usual commotion. It's usually much more peaceful at weekends."

Throughout the morning I rested, until Sarah arrived at lunchtime.

She asked, "How are you feeling now?"

"Still a bit sore," I answered honestly.

"I've got something to make you feel better. Wonderful lemon cheesecake for pudding. But you don't get your pudding unless you eat up your meat," she said triumphantly.

And she was right, the cheesecake certainly was scrumptious!

Saturday meant more visitors and after lunch there was much collecting of chairs. No sooner had Ian arrived than the ward doors opened to reveal my ebullient friend, Val, with her quieter husband, Geoff, and her normally docile father, Harold. They were virtually obscured by the enormous bunch of flowers, carried by Geoff. After greeting me warmly, Val went into the sluice room in search of vases. As the catering manager for Peterborough hospital, and knowing her way around ward storage, she had no problem, and the flowers were soon arranged and displayed. When Val returned, they settled around my bedside and all started talking at once. I felt confused and incredibly stressed by the cacophony, and shouted,

"Fuck off!"

Immediately, four faces turned towards me in astonishment. Ian moved over and grasped my hand,

"It's all right," he soothed.

Val was the next to recover and asked,

"Aren't they looking after you properly?" Calm again, I was able to recount the stories of Eva Braun, and the visit continued happily.

Heaven forbid, how could I treat such good friends so rudely? Yet I chuckled to myself, recalling their astounded expressions. Then I was taken back to memories of my late grandfather, Jack Armitage. As a steam train driver of many years experience, an article in *The Stephenson's Locomotive Society Journal* (December 1971) referred to him; "But this record would not be complete without reference to perhaps the most noteworthy of all, Jack Armitage. A quiet, serious looking man, he became the Mayor of Huddersfield and a very senior alderman. Pre-eminently, the [train] driver for the occasion, he was reputed to know every main "Road" on the old North Western... he was the automatic choice for Wembley specials and the odds were that whether the occasion was a football trip to Villa Park or a works outing to the Lakes, Jack Armitage would be in charge."

Grandad suffered a stroke aged 87. As a result, even he was so stressed by his incapacity that he used swear words previously unheard of in his vocabulary. My outburst made me at one with all the people under great stress from the past. Here, after all these years, I suddenly realised why my grandfather had been driven to using Anglo Saxon terminology. Sadly he didn't recover, and I was never to see him again.

"There's no cheesecake treat after lunch, the shop's closed on Sundays," Sarah explained the next day.

"Val, Geoff and Harold came yesterday afternoon," I told her.

"Did you enjoy the visit?" she asked.

"Yes, it was super to see them all," I answered.

I was thinking, "Best not go into details, it seems so ungrateful."

My son, John, arrived from Birmingham after lunch.

"How are you Mum?" he asked. He took my hand and kissed me. I couldn't answer. My eyes filled with tears and I started to cry. It was such a delight to see him. Eventually I regained my self-control and we chatted about how his degree course was going. After a while, I realised I needed to spend a penny.

"Please could you ring for a nurse, John?" I asked.

"Why?"

"I need a wee."

John said, "I'll take you Mum."

I wasn't ready for that. Allowing my six-foot, blonde teenage son to sit me on the toilet and wipe my bottom, wasn't right.

"No, please ring for a nurse," I repeated slightly indignantly, though not enough to offend him, I hoped.

Reluctantly, he rang the bell. It had been such a joy to see him and I felt very sad when he took his leave.

Ian wasn't able to come that evening. Consequently the Penguin came to feed me supper. Returning later to wash my face and hands and clean my teeth, she asked,

"Where is your tooth brush?"

"I've got an electric toothbrush in my locker," I said.

She rummaged about and found it. Then, on investigating it, she said,

24

"I have never seen one of these before. I don't know how to use one."

I was speechless with contempt, thinking this is getting silly. It's yet another example of the absence of basic nursing care. During my first year of nurse training I was on a cerebral injuries ward. The ward sister impressed on us that if our patients recovered, the last thing they'd want would be having all their teeth extracted due to decay. So the very least we could do was to ensure that, by using an electric toothbrush, we kept their teeth thoroughly clean. This was the practice thirty years ago! So much for progress!

I wouldn't want to give the impression that I considered nurse training in the 1960s some kind of nirvana, and I was always troubled by some of the silliness. For instance, going from bed to bed, waking each patient and inserting a thermometer under the tongue of the soporific patients. On its removal, we asked, "Have you had your bowels open?" Then we ticked, or otherwise, the chart. Surely it was ridiculous to expect a newly wakened patient to be immediately preoccupied with the state of their bowels? But it does seem that in bringing in "patient-centred care," in its present form, the baby has been thrown out with the bath water! Basic patient care seems to have been completely overlooked. We were trained to believe that the responsibility for the care of the patient was ours. Doctors couldn't be trusted with it, well at least until they had achieved the level of consultant, or Professor. By that time, all but the most arrogant medical staff would have been made aware that patients are people, and must be considered as people. If patient-centred care is being implemented by nursing staff whose time is mostly taken up at ward control, and presence at the bed side appears to be as a last resort reluctantly undertaken, then inevitably patients feel they are being looked after by the uncaring. Well we did anyway.

At the end of the Second World, the elections of 1947 saw the Tory government replaced by a Labour Government. They set out to establish the ideas of "health care for all" that had been outlined by the 'Tories White Paper' and that, in turn, had been borne from the hardships of the war and the coalition that governed during those traumatic and difficult years.

The doctors were against the formation of the National Health Service but the Minister for Health, Nye Bevan, achieved it in 1948, in his own words, "By stuffing their mouths with gold." Effectively the Labour Government sold out to the doctors. It seems that it took nurses another 30 years to sell out their caring role (this time to a Tory government), in favour of becoming "doctor's technicians".

The next morning dawned happily, as Ruth woke us, inquiring whether we'd like baths. My response was ecstatic after being denied the luxury since the lumbar puncture. Newly refreshed and anticipating coffee, I relaxed, only to be disturbed by the arrival of a porter propelling a wheelchair in my direction. Apparently I had an outpatient appointment and the longed-for coffee was not to be. Requesting refreshment before going seemed as inappropriate as asking for a trip to the shops.

The consultant bent over and examined my blue toes, discussing with junior doctors the pros and cons of biopsy. I sat shaking my head. I'd only just recovered from the discomfort in my back; the last thing I wanted was sore toes. Eventually, the consultant noticed my reaction and said to his staff,

"I don't think this merits intervention."

I wondered where I stood regarding any suggestion of my consent being given.

Needless to say, when I arrived back on the ward, any hope of coffee was well past. Sarah arrived,

"I've bought rum and raisin cheesecake as a treat for you today Mum," she said triumphantly.

Sarah went to sort things out, returning with a tray of food. She got me into position and as she moved the spoon towards my mouth, she started talking about the weekend.

"John called on me before coming to visit you. He was very anxious about how you would be. Was he happy when he saw you?"

"Oh dear, I hope I didn't make him feel worse I cried. I just couldn't help it. It was so lovely to see him," I said between mouthfuls. "Sarah, this cheesecake has got to be my very favourite! But do you know, John suggested he took me to the toilet." Sarah laughed,

"When John goes for a wee he doesn't wipe his willy, so he wouldn't expect to wipe your bottom," she explained, as if I had forgotten the arrangements of the male anatomy.

During the afternoon, the housewoman, who must have been looking through my notes, came to see me. Out of the blue, she asked,

"Which arm did you have your malignant melanoma on?"

Then she rephrased it, "The skin cancer, right or left?"

"Left," I said decisively. Of course, I didn't know my left from my right, so I was picking up the last word she used. She searched my left arm, but drew a blank. When Ian came in the evening, I recounted the examination. Ian said,

"It was on your right arm. When the doctor couldn't find it, why didn't she check the other arm? It isn't as if you are a spider, with eight arms." We laughed together. Ian's visit was always reassuring. When he left I soon settled down to sleep.

The next morning, we were woken by the student nurse of face-wash notoriety. After breakfast she started on the bathing routines, with a brusqueness that was reminiscent of Eva Braun. Fortunately, she was more empathetic with coffee drinking, and I was able to swallow my drink without fear of choking. When she'd finished and left the ward, we discussed bathing routines.

"I think that in future, before agreeing to have a bath, I will ask who is on bathing duties that day," I asserted.

"Well it might protect us from feeling as though we had been through the mangle," Evelyn said. Conversation was again interrupted by the arrival of a wheelchair for me. At least today I have had my coffee, I thought gratefully, as I was taken up to Nuclear Physics. A nurse explained,

"We'll take a sample of your blood today, tag it and return it into a vein tomorrow."

Whilst attempting to take the blood from my recalcitrant vein, she noticed my eternity ring and called to her colleague,

"Hey Sylvia, come and look at this lovely ring."

"Oh yes, I'd love one like that," cried Sylvia.

"It won't come off," I said defensively. To which the nurse said,

"Don't worry we can soon sort that out, we can cut your finger off." I smiled.

My veins were proving even more reluctant than usual and a doctor had to be summoned. He managed to find a vein and get a blood sample. By the time this was finally achieved, Sarah arrived. She was instructed where to find a wheelchair and started to take me back to the ward for lunch. Her attempts to manoeuvre along the corridors left permanent marks along the hospital walls. Whatever she did, the chair was determined to collide with the plasterwork. It was like the worst ever supermarket trolley.

When I was taken to Nuclear Physics the following day, I tried to put the hand that I wore my ring on behind me.

"What are you doing?" asked the nurse.

"Hiding my finger with the ring on it so they can't cut it off," I replied jokingly.

"We didn't mean it, you'll be alright," she soothed.

Oh dear, I thought, why can't I manage to be on the same wavelength? Of course I knew they wouldn't cut my finger off, or anything else for that matter!

I was disappointed at the gap between myself and the staff and our inability for sharing humour for the situation I was in. So, I felt very grateful when Sarah arrived with a wheelchair, to take me back to the ward for lunch. This time she towed the chair behind her.

"I've been taking lessons in how to steer these things," she smiled. I said,

"That's a good job, I don't think Addenbrooke's walls get refurbished very often.

No doubt those scars will be there for posterity!"

At last someone was on my wavelength, I thought. Consequently, I felt warm and content.

We were woken by Robert the next morning.

"Who's on bathing duties this morning?" I asked him.

"I am," he answered smiling. Robert was feeding me with breakfast.

When he'd finished and had left the ward, I turned to Evelyn saying,

"Well that's all right then." I'd expected her to overjoyed.

But instead Evelyn frowned, "I'm a bit worried…. Don't you think that it might look a bit odd and peculiar me wanting Robert to bath me, but saying no to some of the female nurses."

After thinking about it for a bit, I said,

"I don't think so. Anyway we're all in the same boat, and I for one am not prepared to be dumped in the bath by someone who clearly doesn't want to be bothered by my bathing routine. If we say no to them, they will just be pleased to be relieved of another job." Evelyn smiled,

"Yes that's true. I wouldn't want to forego the delights of a lovely bath….I suppose they will just have to think what they like."

After we'd had our baths excellently supervised by Robert, it was time for coffee. Then, with what was becoming monotonous regularity, the inevitable wheelchair arrived for me.

"You're going to occupational therapy (we shortened it to OT)" the Penguin announced as she, together with the porter, helped me into the chair.

I thought, "Wow! Nobody usually thinks to say where we're going." Generally things just happened to us. No-one ever seemed to think that we'd need to know. I was really chuffed to be going back to therapy again as, due to the bed rest after the lumbar puncture, I'd missed it for over a week, including a weekend.

On my arrival, the therapist greeted me enthusiastically.

"How've ye bin?" she said in her Scots accent, smiling.

"I've been busy with tests and investigations, but I'd rather have been coming here," I replied. What a sycophant! I thought. But it was true and anyway, the therapist didn't appear to notice.

"Well, let's see what we can do to make up for lost time today," she said cheerfully.

We'd only just made a start when another porter arrived with a chair.

"I've come to take this lady to the Medical School," he announced to the therapist, and together they helped me into the chair.

"I'm afraid today isn't going to be your day for therapy," she said sadly.

As the porter pushed, heading towards the Medical School, I was even more aware of my powerlessness. I wondered how the therapist must be feeling. She was offering an expensive and, in my case, a valued service, but she was having to put her schedule on hold again.

I was wheeled into a room in the Medical School and placed in front of the same registrar who I'd remembered holding my hand on that first meeting at the medical ward round. Gathered around him were about half a dozen medical students, all wearing scruffy white coats. The registrar produced his tie from his waistcoat, with a theatrical gesture that would have done justice to Laurence Olivier. Then, turning towards me, he asked,

"What colour is it?" I was already getting quite good at covering up my disabilities, so I thought for a while. The tie was clearly a tartan mixture. Struggling to remember the likely predominant colour of tartans, I ventured to make a guess.

"Green," I stated.

"No it's blue!" he asserted smugly.

Although I knew that I was on weak ground, I felt very irritated.

"It's green! I repeated decisively. He looked at his tie, as though seeing it for the first time, and showed it around his gathered audience, and then said,

"It isn't a very good choice is it?" I felt as though I'd had a minor triumph and sat back, pleased with myself.

I got lost in memories of my first ward of my nursing training in the 1960s. The Ward Sister was a lady of very generous proportions and her office chair was a Victorian gentleman's smoking chair, which seemed tailored to fit her. When medical students came onto her ward for a teaching round, they had to stand in line and wait outside her office. When she was ready, she carried out an inspection. They had to hold out their hands, so she could ensure they were clean on both sides.

"I won't have those dirty finger nails touching my patients." She might say, "They look as though you've been servicing your car. Leave the ward immediately and don't come back until they are scrupulously clean and I will see them when you come back."

The Sister would also check that the medical students were properly dressed, then, and only then were they allowed into her domain. Sartorial elegance wasn't her major concern but she'd probably have accepted the registrar's tartan tie. It would have been better for me if she hadn't, I mused. Also, she'd never allow a member of the medical fraternity to approach her patients unsupervised.

But while I was lost in my thoughts, the Registrar had moved on. He'd taken some coins out of his trouser pocket, showed them to the students and then turning to me he asked,

"How many coins have I in my hand?"

I didn't have a clue, and guessed, "Five."

He then turned back to his audience and showed them the result again. He didn't consider me. I felt incensed. I said, "I-I-if I-I-I'm wrong w-w-wouldn't it be helpful to tell me the result?"

He looked astounded, as if nobody had ever had the audacity to say such a thing before, and the examination was concluded. I felt humiliated, and arrived back on the ward in a distressed state.

"N-not only have I been taken away from my therapy session without a b-by your leave, b-but I feel abused," I sobbed to Sarah.

She'd been waiting to feed me lunch and had been inconvenienced as well because she was late for an afternoon lecture. Robert took over from her and I gave way to all my pent-up emotion.

Robert was still consoling me and wiping away my tears when Trish and Pam, neighbours from Peterborough, arrived. They stared at me, surprised at my distressed condition. Robert tried to explain why I was so upset, and then left me to my visitors. Pam had brought a beautiful perfumed rose from her garden and a vase to put it in. She went in search of water and returned, placing the vase on my locker so I could enjoy the fragrance. They chatted on about things at home and I began to recover.

"The nurse in charge of the ward is very kind, isn't he?" Pam said.

Realising she meant Robert, I answered,

"No, he isn't in charge, he's too good for that. Robert is a nursing auxiliary and he's fabulous."

All too soon, it seemed, it was time for them to go home and they left me enjoying the lovely smell of the rose.

By the time of Ian's visit, I was crying again. "These people are destroying me. How could a Registrar, who'd seemed so understanding when he held my hand, be so arrogant in front of his students?"

"Let's hope one day they'll be patients themselves and perhaps that will teach them a thing or two," Ian suggested, and we both smiled.

After a supper of delicious pasta-bake, Ian went in search of a mouthwash for me. He went to the ward control but there was no one there. After a considerable wait, the Ward Sister, a woman of approximately 50, arrived at the nursing station. As there were no other nurses available, Ian asked,

"Can I have a mouthwash for my wife please?"

"What does she normally have?" the sister asked.

"They usually put a tablet in a glass of water," Ian answered. The sister headed towards the sluice, with Ian following on behind. She started rummaging in the cupboards and eventually produced a very large bottle of dark purple liquid. She dispensed a glassful and handed it to Ian, saying,

"Here it is."

Ian asked, "How much should I dilute it?" Without looking at the label she replied,

"As it is."

Ian poured a little into another glass, thinking there is no way this is meant to be neat. It would destroy someone's taste buds. So he guessed the dilution rate and gingerly tested it before giving it to me.

"This is very strong," I criticised.

"You ought to have tried it to start with. The sister told me to give it to you undiluted. I don't know what she thought it would do to you, perhaps she wanted to destroy your ability to speak!" Ian retorted. We both giggled.

The next day was Friday and the Penguin was on bathing duty. Both Evelyn and I stuck to our guns and said, "No thank you," when she asked if we'd like a bath. Just after we'd had coffee, a porter turned up with the wheelchair to take me to occupational therapy again. Although I'd spent what seemed like hours in the company of a porter, being pushed around the labyrinth of corridors of the hospital, somehow porters always maintained a shadowy presence.

Anyway, it was great to be back at therapy again, and this time with no interruptions.

When I'd been returned to the ward, Sarah arrived for lunch. She seemed distracted. Were lunchtimes becoming tedious, I wondered.

"Is this getting too much for you, Sarah?" I asked.

"Oh, sorry Mum. The lecture I left to go to yesterday was given by Germaine Greer and she was brilliant, but I've got to write an essay on the role of silence in Othello and I'm struggling with it." I lay desperately trying to recall the play. I asked,

"What is the main female part in Othello?"

"Desdemona," she answered.

Unfortunately, Sarah was on a loser if she was thinking that her Mum might be able to provide valuable insight. "Keeping quiet is not one of my strong points," I thought. She sighed and smiled. After lunch, she scurried off to tackle her essay.

"Best of luck, Sarah," I encouraged.

When Ian arrived that evening, he said,

"I was intercepted by the housewoman, who asked where you had your skin cancer? I said Annie had a melanoma removed from just above her right elbow about six or so years ago. That's about right isn't it?"

I frowned and said, "Yes, it must be because I was followed up for five years and it's well over a year since I saw the consultant."

Ian added, "I thought she was very patronising when she saw me, so I'm afraid I was a bit indignant."

"I think she's just very tired. I mean it's not much of an issue is it? And she must have been thinking about it for days," I was suddenly feeling very sympathetic.

"Well it's the weekend now," said Ian wearily.

He fed me and settled me down for the night.

"Have a good rest, love," I said, anxiously.

I was hoping he'd get the benefit from a short break from work, as I settled down for the night.

34

I was woken by my elbow being gently shaken to announce the arrival of a steaming mug of tea complete with a drinking straw. I lay there for a moment luxuriating in the realisation that Ruth was on duty today. All would be well. She would be regularly providing me with tasty beverages and I would also have a lovely bath. What pleasure! I was feeling pampered.

Suddenly my musings were shattered by the screens being hurriedly pulled around my bed, heralding the arrival of the housewoman and an unknown male doctor. He remained unknown to me. Whilst I awaited an introduction to this grey, dull, little man, it wasn't forthcoming. Without making comment, the housewoman pulled up my pyjama sleeve, revealing my upper arm. I was still feeling bruised by the Medical School incident and I attempted to communicate my indignation at this discourteous behaviour by giving each one of them a hostile stare. This proved rather fruitless as they totally avoided any eye contact. I felt like a medical exhibit! Still ignoring me, the doctor produced a metal ruler from the pocket of his crumpled white coat and proceeded to measure something on my arm. He turned to the house officer saying,

"There's a subcutaneous scar measuring seven millimetres by four."

I thought, Aha! I have it, they're discussing my old skin cancer scar! The housewoman who was smiling ingratiatingly at him, said,

"Do you think there's any biceps involvement?"

Again I thought, "Aha! I've got it! The reason why the ruler is so cold and freezing my arm is that he must have come from the mortuary. Inviting him to see her exhibits is probably the only way she can think of to chat him up. An apology for the chilled state of his ruler would help," I thought irritably.

Voluntary participation in proceedings was apparently irrelevant. I supposed I'd have to forgive him if he was a mortician and only used to dealing with cadavers who didn't feel the cold. Whilst I was lost in my speculation, they wandered off without comment, flinging back the screens as they departed.

What was all that fuss about? The diagnosis of a malignant melanoma was something I'd rather forgotten about. It had been over six years ago when I'd noticed a small black mole on my arm. I'd been terrified at the time. Now I'd rather dispatched the thought to history. Not long after it had been chopped off, a male colleague drew me aside, ashen faced, saying,

"I've had a malignant melanoma removed." I was dismissive,

"Oh! Don't worry, I've had one of those too. It'll be all right, you'll see!"

It was almost the last thing I said to him. He was dead within two years.

I was still remorsefully remembering my inappropriate comments when Sarah arrived. It was lunchtime. She was looking very tired.

"How's the essay going, sweetheart?" I asked. Sarah sighed.

"Don't ask, Mum, I think it's the hardest one I've ever attempted."

She seemed distracted while she was feeding me, and lunch was an unusually quiet affair. Afterwards, Sarah set off to fight with her assignment. I was desperately wanting to help but just felt totally useless. I said sadly,

"Best of luck Sarah! I'll be thinking of you. I'm sorry that I can't offer you any more than that."

Sarah said, with the 'Wisdom of Solomon', "You think these things are crucial at the time but really what does it matter, compared to your Mum being so poorly."

My eyes filled with tears as I watched her leave the ward, "like a snail creeping unwillingly to school," I thought, wishing that I could have done more to help. I suppose you never stop feeling like a mother, even when your child is mothering you!

I was roused from my reverie by the commotion of collecting chairs. It was the Saturday visitors arriving. My brother and sister-in-law walked into the ward: John, my brother, tall, thin, watchful and concerned, his wife Hilary, bright, smiling, and carrying flowers.

"What a delight to see you!" I exclaimed ecstatically.

"How are you?" Hil asked, while bending over to kiss me. When John started asking what tests and investigations I was having, I turned to Hil, whilst saying petulantly to John,

"I'm not talking to you, I'm only talking to Hil, she's my friend."

John looked crestfallen and immediately got up and left the ward. I enjoyed a girlish chat with Hill and we giggled together companionably.

I'd always thought of Hil as a good friend, although five years my senior. We used to sing together in the Methodist Church choir. Initially Hil went out with the minister's son who I thought was creepy and obsequious. I was glad that it ended when John arrived back from studying tropical medicine in Africa. I couldn't understand how Hil could possibly have kissed the minister's son without being physically sick. Mind you, I couldn't quite imagine anyone wanting to kiss my brother either. Anyway, when John and Hil started going out together they had me as a little chaperone, following them everywhere on my little red bike, little legs and pedals getting faster and faster as they hurried to try and find some privacy. John was always kind and tolerant with his irritating little sister, and certainly didn't deserve to be treated like that now. How could I behave so childishly, again? It turned out that when John had left the ward he'd gone in search of the housewoman, who'd had little chance of withholding information from interrogation by my brother.

Later that afternoon, after the visitors had all left, Dr Caine and the housewoman appeared at my bedside. Dr Caine asked,

"Is it alright for us to give information about your state of health to your brother?"

"Yes, of course, whatever he wants to know will be okay with me," I said, and smiled at the expression of relief on the housewoman' s face as they left.

Turning to Evelyn, to share the amusement of the incident with her, I realised she was lost in thought.

" Are you alright?" I asked.

She responded immediately, "My visitors were my sister and brother-in-law, and they want me to give up my house and live near them in Dorset."

She sounded very sad.

"Do you get on well with them both?" I asked.

"Yes, but I would be sorry to leave Cambridge, though it is a long way for them to come and visit me. As they said, we aren't getting any younger and may all need help of one kind, or another. Dorset is a very pretty part of the country apparently, and they have found some sheltered housing nearby," she added.

I said, "I suppose the upheaval is always going to be hard, and it won't get any easier the longer you put off a decision. But then again, you have got to be confident that it's the right thing to do. Don't rush into anything."

Evelyn said, "They are spending the night in Cambridge and coming back tomorrow, so at least I can sleep on it overnight."

When Ian came that evening, I was relieved that he looked rested.

"What have you been up to and how is Abbey?" I asked.

"I'm afraid Abbey is wondering where you are. I haven't had time for anything exciting, just washing and ironing, and answering the phone to report how you are."

We gossiped about my brother John and the housewoman and Ian said,

"I do feel sympathy for her."

He settled me down for the night and kissed me. The sensation of the kiss lingered on my lips as I gave myself up to sleep.

The next morning we were lucky once more, as Ruth was on the early shift again. I was feeling comforted and cosseted, though I suspected Evelyn was considering issues surrounding the move to Dorset. We discussed the pros and cons but she was mostly anxious about being dependent and a nuisance to her sister and brother-in-law. She remained undecided.

Sarah arrived, looking happier.

"How is the essay shaping up?" I asked, as Sarah began the business of feeding me. She smiled,

"It is shaping up nicely, thank goodness." Then Sarah added,

"John and Corrine will be calling to see me before they visit you."

I was concerned, "Don't tell them what I said about the wee," I urged. Sarah grinned,

"No, I wouldn't let you down, but shall we go to the lavatory just before I leave."

She sorted me out, and left.

When John and Corrine arrived they were quite relaxed and the visit was very pleasant. I was particularly happy that I managed not to cry this time.

When all the visitors had gone, Evelyn said,

"Well, I've agreed that when I'm fit enough to sort out buying and selling, I'll go to Dorset to live near them. I feel relieved now I've decided."

Ian wasn't coming that evening and so the Penguin fed me and cleaned my teeth. She managed exceptionally well with the electric toothbrush.

I thought, "Well, at least I've made some small contribution to nurse-training during my stay in Addenbrooke's!"

Monday morning heralded the usual weekday bustle. We

were woken by the "face-wash" student nurse. Feeling cautious about her method of bathing I asked, "Who is on bathing duties?"

She answered,

"I am…Do you want a bath?"

"No thank you," was my immediate response.

Just after breakfast an unfamiliar male doctor arrived at my bedside. He said by way of explanation,

"I'm standing in for the housewoman, she's on holiday." Then, without further ado, he drew the screens around my bed and began to examine me. I said thoughtfully, and by way of conversation,

"My ear is aching a bit, but not much." With the skill of a magician he produced an auriscope from his pocket, and used it to look into both my ears in turn,

"The right eardrum has collapsed," he announced confidently. I was surprised, as I'd never had anything wrong with my ears. I looked at him quizzically and, to give him his due, he actually seemed to notice my response. Then he added,

"Dr Caine will be doing a ward round, this afternoon. We will see what he thinks." I sighed, thinking: "Well, the housewoman has gone on holiday, so I suppose he has come in as a new broom, sweeping clean. Come to think of it, he does have a look of Sweep (of Sooty and Sweep fame), with sagging jowls reminiscent of a Bassett hound.

After he'd left and we'd had coffee, the inevitable wheelchair arrived to take me to therapy. The student nurse dumped me unceremoniously into the wheelchair and the porter wheeled me away. I was musing gratefully about having made the right decision regarding a bath as we went towards occupational therapy. The therapist greeted me warmly, "I have some polystyrene holders for you to use with a spoon in your left hand. Let's see how you get on." I picked up the spoon, and with shaking movements was able to move it towards my mouth. At the same time I opened my lips, thus allowing me to put it inside. I felt exhausted by this feat of coordination and I looked for the therapist's response. She smiled, saying,

"That's very good," I was worn out, but exhilarated and thinking, now I'll be able to start to feed myself. The porter arrived and, after lifting me into the chair, she put a few holders in my lap saying cheerfully,

"See you tomorrow."

"Yes, I'll look forward to it," I said, grinning with pleasure.

On reaching the ward, I was met by a beaming Sarah,

"I've finished the essay," she said.

"Yes, I had a feeling that you'd done it," I smiled. She went on, "It's not the best one I've ever written, but anyway how are you? Still thinking about the essay?" I said. "Well, you don't know, sometimes when you've agonised over something it may mean that you've done it in more depth. You may be surprised." And with that, I moved onto Sarah's enquiry about how I was.

"I have been given some spoon holders so I can feed myself." She sorted the food out and handed me the improvised spoon. I tried to feed myself but I couldn't find my mouth. Instead, with jerky attempts, I was spilling the pasta bake off the spoon all over the table. Sarah soon intervened and I subsided into despair. Before I started sobbing she soothed,

"Don't worry Mum, you're probably very tired."

I felt sad. "But tomorrow I'll do better," I thought, as Sarah left, still smiling.

The ward round was the next event. After a discussion with the consultant about my ears, they decided to make sure by sending me for an outpatient appointment in the Ear, Nose, and Throat Department.

"If nothing is amiss you can go back to Peterborough," Dr Caine said.

Then they moved on to Evelyn's bedside. I thought, "I'm sure there won't be anything wrong, but it was good of him not to undermine his houseman in front of me."

When the ward round had left, Evelyn said, "I am going to theatre on Thursday for spinal surgery."

"How do you feel about that?" I asked.

"A bit frightened, but hopefully they'll sort me out," she added.

Realising that my transfer relied on the houseman making a phone call to make the appointment, and suspecting he may have more important things on his mind, I hung about near ward control. Suddenly he looked up, and gasped on noting my presence. He reached for the phone. Shortly afterwards, he came to tell me my appointment was for Wednesday afternoon.

When Ian arrived later we both had lots of news.

"I had to go for a meeting with the Professor on Sunday evening so I decided to stay overnight on the boat. Only this time I couldn't because, although I could see it at its moorings, happily and peacefully floating, the Trent had completely flooded the marina and I couldn't get anywhere near it. I spent the night at Hoskins Wharf and had a bit too much to drink. I felt gruesome, in the morning."

"Serves you right," I chuckled. Then I told all my news about my possible return to Peterborough District Hospital. Ian sorted me out and, contented, I snuggled down to sleep remembering happily the times we'd spent on our sixty two foot traditional canal boat, chugging along the cut.

Fortunately, we were woken on Tuesday morning by Robert. Breakfast, bath and coffee were gently supervised. Then the wheelchair arrived for occupational therapy. The therapist started with a question,

"How's it going with the spoon holders?" I sighed,

"I'm gradually managing to feed myself, but I'm afraid it's a slow process."

"You'll find that it will become easier the more you persevere." I became reflective,

"I think I'll be going back to Peterborough on Thursday, could you do holders for a razor so I could shave my legs?" For some reason she found this suggestion hilarious, saying "No, if you tried to use a razor there'd be a blood-bath!"

Over the next two days we continued with working on the movements of my left hand. Wednesday saw my appointment with the Ear, Nose and Throat Consultant who gave me the all clear. I was very relieved because I knew that I would be cleared for transfer back to Peterborough.

When Ian came that evening, he and the houseman discussed the arrangements for my return to Peterborough. Coincidentally it was the same day that Evelyn was down for theatre. By the time Ian arrived on the following day, Evelyn had been, returned from theatre, and, although she was still in an anesthetized state, she was doing her finger exercises. I was sad at the prospect of leaving Evelyn. I'd valued her company. I'd miss Sarah tremendously as well; although I was glad that this would relieve some of the stress that she was under. It was also a relief that Ian wouldn't have to travel to Cambridge each day, as well as all the other working journeys he had to make.

Sarah arrived to give me my lunch on her final day of responsibility, saying brightly,

"I've brought you, rum and raison cheesecake for your lunch today. It will be the last chance for the cheesecake shop". I grinned saying, "Yummy." And she went to put things together.

After lunch we said goodbye. I couldn't express the depth of gratitude that I felt towards her. Instead, we simply kissed. Sarah, having packed up the things, left the ward now able to continue her studies uninhibited.

Ian arrived smiling,

"Are you ready to go?" he asked. I returned his smile,

"Yes. How good it will be to get back to Peterborough."

He went to collect my notes, as he'd previously arranged with the ward staff. In a moment he came back.

"As the notes aren't ready, I'm going to get myself some lunch from the cafe in the concourse." I sighed in resignation and lay back on my pillows to rest before the journey.

Shortly after, Robert came to take me to the toilet, dressing me in plastic pants containing an incontinence pad. Next, he wrapped me in a thick towelling dressing gown and helped me into a wheelchair. Ian came back and we headed out into the corridor, pausing at ward control for Ian to collect a heavy envelope holding my medical records. Then Robert took over control of the wheelchair, wheeling me to the lift, through the concourse and waiting with me, while Ian went to bring the car to the hospital entrance. Then they helped me into the car together with my belongings and the all-important notes! I was sorry to say goodbye to Robert and Sarah, but not realising, at that stage, how much I would miss their kindness and gentleness.

CHAPTER 2

BACK HOME

We started the journey to Peterborough Hospital, leaving Cambridge and Addenbrooke's behind. My vision was still very poor. Regaining any spatial awareness would be a long time coming. I didn't have a clue about the route we were taking. Although I'd made many trips to Cambridge in the past, it was as if my previous life had happened to someone else!

The car's heating protected me from the cold outside. I was transfixed by the late winter landscape. Ian asked, "Do you remember the last time you were in Peterborough?" I answered sadly, "No, I'm afraid my mind's a complete blank."

"They were particularly kind to you, especially the Ward Sister," said Ian. I smiled, saying, "It'll be great to be nearer home, 'specially as you won't have to travel quite so far and Sarah will be free to get on with student life, rather than caring for me."

"She was only too pleased she could help out," Ian soothed. At that I dozed, until we reached Peterborough Hospital.

Ian's voice roused me.

"Wake up, we're here!" Ian was gently taking my hand.

"I'll leave you here, for just a moment, while I fetch a

chair." In seconds, it seemed, he was back with an assistant nurse and a wheelchair. They carefully helped me into the chair and transferred my belongings. After handing a gigantic bundle of notes to the nurse, Ian went to park the car. Taking my hand, the nurse asked in a Peterborough accent, "You don't remember me, do you?" I gazed at her without recognition, although I thought that she was the image of Polly (of Faulty Towers fame). I answered, "No, I'm afraid I don't." She squeezed my hand and comforted, I awaited Ian's return. I was thinking that all would be well now I'm back here in the kindness of this nurse's care. When Ian came back we went to the ward. It was where I'd been before, I remembered, but this time I was taken to the bay furthest from ward control. I thought, "That's a good sign, because they know I won't need so much looking after". Polly drew the screens around my bed and then helped me out of the wheelchair and into the bed. She left Ian to settle me in and unpack my things, taking the notes to ward control. Ian started unpacking my belongings.

"Is there anything you need?" he asked.

"No thanks, I'll be fine now," I answered thoughtfully. Kissing me goodbye, he opened the screens, and said, "I'll be back this evening," and, using my left hand, I returned his wave.

I turned to the matter in hand and my new surroundings. It was an eight-bed bay and was fully occupied. Turning to the other ladies I said,

"My name is Annie. I'm just back from Addenbrooke's."

"I came from there yesterday," a young lady opposite responded, and with that she turned away. No-one else spoke. I settled to rest, thinking it doesn't seem that we'll be in for long chats here.

A white coated, tall figure with a kind smile came up to my bed carrying a folder of notes. He drew the screens around and sat on the side of my bed.

"How have you been?" He had a Scandinavian accent.

I studied him. He had a kindly manner but with a jutting purposeful chin.

"I've been slowly improving," I responded cautiously. He was talking again, "I'm Sven, Dr Gutman's Registrar. Do you remember me?" he asked rhetorically.

Taking the shaking of my head as an answer he continued, "It's nice to see you back…. I'll just check you over." He then listened to my heart and took my pulse. When he'd finished, he left. I smiled to myself, thinking it's great to have a quiet, personal examination, rather than under the scrutiny of hoards of students.

Polly arrived.

"Would you like me to take you to the toilet?" she asked. On my answering, "Yes, please." She helped me out of bed and, linking arms, we walked to the lavatory.

She took off my waterproof pants, disposing of the (dry) nappy inside. I weed, she wiped my bottom and we washed our hands, companionably. On the way back we met another patient, on a similar mission. She introduced us.

"Jayne seems nice and friendly" I said, as she helped me back to bed, and she agreed.

Ian came in the evening and, having fed me, he cleaned my teeth and left me to sleep. I settled down, optimistically. Unfortunately, the disadvantage of being at the far end of the ward was that the bedpan washer was unbelievably noisy. It seemed to be in constant use throughout the night. Also, there was a howling gale sending a freezing draught through ill-fitting windows. I woke the next morning feeling as if I'd slept badly.

I was grateful that Friday morning had eventually arrived. Polly appeared with a trolley of sheets and mouth wash equipment. She drew the screens around my fortunately dry bed and helped me out of it.

"Can you manage to get to the toilet on your own?" she asked. I responded enthusiastically, "Yes, I can!" I toddled off and, on meeting other ladies, received their help with flushing the lavatory and running water into the wash basin. By the time I got back breakfast was in full swing. A catering assistant was getting everything organised. She approached my bed, "'Ello, mi name's Dawn, what would ye lyke te eat fer breakfast?" she asked kindly, in a broad West-Indian accent. Immediately at ease I explained, in a weak and halting voice that I had a jar of my own muesli in my locker, together with some drinking straws. She went in search of a cereal bowl, fed me and helped me to drink the tea through the straw (I needed someone to guide the straw to my mouth). Presumably she hadn't been trained for the task, but she seemed to know instinctively that I needed to be in an upright position and had to be relaxed in order to swallow both my food and drink.

No sooner had she finished than Val arrived, asking, "How are you, Annie?"

"It's great to be back, in Peterborough," I replied.

After a few minutes of chat, Val said breathlessly, "I must go and get on with the mountain of work on my desk." She rushed off and I lay back on my pillows of the newly made bed, relieved that work was not on my agenda, for today.

Dawn returned, helping me to drink my coffee. She'd only just finished when the wheelchair arrived. A student nurse accompanied the porter and together they helped me into the chair.

"You're going for occupational therapy," she explained.

They haven't wasted any time, I thought, as the porter pushed me along. We arrived at occupational therapy and I sat next to Jayne, waiting to be seen. The intensely bright fluorescent lights burned my eyes. I was in great pain and I started to sob, tears ran down my cheeks and snot was trailing from my nose. "Do you want to go back to the ward?" a therapist asked.

I struggled to reply, "N-n-no," I sobbed.

She made no attempt to wipe my nose or ask me what

was wrong, and after a while a porter took me back to the ward.

The pain was intense. I was put back into bed, feeling nauseous and very sorry for myself. Gradually the agony subsided and the feeling of sickness passed. I was grateful when Dawn came with my lunch. She fed me and settled me down for a nap. In spite of my feeling very frustrated with the therapist, I dozed, asking myself, "Why couldn't she see my problem? Would the intensity of the lighting prevent me from having occupational therapy in the future?"

Then, before I knew it, it was afternoon and visiting time. Carole arrived.

"Heard you were back in Peterborough," she said cheerfully.

We chatted. I wasn't much company but I did feel relaxed and content after my snooze. When Ian came that evening I was obsessed about the lighting in occupational therapy and related my experiences. I didn't think to ask him about what sort of day he had had. He fed me and settled me for the night.

On Saturday morning a student nurse gently woke us all up. I was pleased with myself, as I was able to get out of bed myself and walk off to the toilet. On my return the nurse asked, "Would you like a bath after breakfast?"

"Yes please," I said gratefully, although cautious. She was tall, slim and business-like. I hoped she would be gentle. I explained about the muesli and drinking straws in my locker. She sorted out the breakfasts and then helped me to the bathroom. Sitting me on a chair while she ran the bath, she unpacked my sponge bag. I asked, "Were you here before, when I was sent to Addenbrooke's?"

She replied kindly, "No, I only came here last month."

The nurse concentrated on the job in hand and that was the limit to the conversation. After my bath she took me back and helped me into bed. Coffee had arrived. She helped me to drink it, but she held the drinking straw at the wrong angle and I kept choking. I looked around my neighbours, but as they didn't appear to be interested in my gurgles or seem to want conversation I dozed for the rest of the morning.

At lunchtime, Ian arrived carrying a carrier bag.

"Look what I've bought," he said, flourishing a baseball cap. He put the cap on my head and said, "That will cut out the intensity of the fluorescent lights, and look, it says the A's, it's made 'specially for you," he claimed, triumphantly. It was of course a baseball cap bearing the logo of the famous American baseball team. Ian went to prepare my lunch and returned to feed me. I lay there with the cap pulled over my eyes.

"Do you think I might look a bit silly in this?" I asked.

"No, you're keeping up with the trend."

After lunch, he left to walk Abbey and do the chores, such as washing and ironing. I settled down for a snooze.

Very soon, Val and Geoff walked in, Val kissing me on the cheek,

"Sorry I had to rush off yesterday and I didn't have chance to see you again before going home. How've you been?" she gasped, without stopping for breath. Geoff just smiled and collected two chairs for them both. Val took my hand,

"We are leaving for Greece tomorrow. Will you be alright? You see, I've always wanted to see the Agropolis." I grinned, thinking warmly about Val's delightful malapropisms. I didn't want to correct her by saying Acropolis but went on to tell her about the wonderful catering assistant, saying, "I'll be fine while she's here to look after me."

We chatted generally about Peterborough and my stunning baseball cap.

"Have a super holiday," I said, and they rushed off to do last-minute packing. I smiled to myself at being able to recall times when Val had used the word gorgettes for courgettes, thinking that gorgettes is really a more appropriate word for courgettes anyway!

50

Ian arrived in the evening to feed me.

"Is the cap helping with the lights?" he asked.

"Yes it is, but do you really think I don't look very silly in it?" I asked cautiously.

"No, it's made for you, it says on the front A's team and it's up to the minute; you look really cool," he tried to reassure me again.

"That's what I'm afraid of," I retorted ungratefully. He fed me, cleaned my teeth, settled me down and left me to sleep, saying, "See you tomorrow."

Sunday morning dawned with a sense of peace. A man came around with the papers. I listened intently; although my sight was still very poor I could tell by his familiar Yorkshire accent that it was the paperman, who'd been there for years. Of course papers were of no interest to me. There was no way that I could read, let alone comprehend what was written, or manage to turn the pages. "Another pleasure that I have lost," I mused sadly. Then it was breakfast, which was a pleasant interruption to my thoughts, before ablutions. There remained an air of depression in the ward. I'd felt that when I first. But still, I could rest undisturbed. Ian came at lunch-time and explained, "I won't be able to come in again today, will you be alright?"

"Yes," I asserted, hopefully with the confidence I didn't feel.

When the afternoon shift came on, an auxiliary nurse came to my bedside and asked, "Is your husband coming in this evening?"

"No, I'm afraid he has to go to a meeting early in the afternoon, in Nottingham."

"Did you know, it's Valentine's day tomorrow?"

"No I didn't."

"Shall we go down to the shop and buy something for him? I'll be back in a minute." I smiled, feeling warmed by her thoughtfulness.

The visitors arrived. The young patient in the bed opposite, who'd also come back from Addenbrooke's, had a group of visitors collected around her bed. One of them was a young girl of eight or nine, but even she didn't manage to cheer her up. Soon I had something to take my mind off that, when the nurse returned. She helped me into a wheelchair and we set off to the shop. Once there, she helped me choose a little Valentine's cake for Ian. She took the money out of my purse and paid for it, then we went back to the ward; another unsung act of kindness that means so much to a patient. These touches seem to come purely from a generosity of spirit but I don't suppose those selecting candidates for nurse training consider these to be of any importance.

After tea I walked to the toilet, meeting Jayne again.

"Have you got any visitors this evening?" she asked.

I explained that Ian couldn't come in and I wasn't expecting anyone else. She suggested going back to her single room for a chat and I accepted gladly. We went into her room and she climbed onto the bed. I sat on the chair.

"I'm glad I'm in here on my own, I've got multiple sclerosis," she explained.

"Oh I'm so sorry," I said inadequately. She sighed, "I can't deal with anyone else's despair at the moment." I took that as a signal to find something amusing and told her about our silliness in Addenbrooke's and what a tonic that had been. We chatted about life as it had been before we were in here.

The nursing auxiliary returned to feed me and clean my teeth. The electric toothbrush presented no problem to her.

"When your husband comes in tomorrow, don't forget that it's Valentine' s day," she smiled.

I too smiled in agreement and appreciation,

"Thank you very much for your thoughtfulness. What is your name?" I asked as an afterthought.

"Sally," she responded. I couldn't express how much that act of kindness had meant to me and realised, for the first time, that I wasn't automatically told the name of practically any member of staff. I realised that knowing the staff member's name was an indicator of their importance to me.

I settled down blissfully to sleep.

The next morning was a rude awakening. The student nurse who had been kind and gentle two days previously was in a dreadful mood. Dawn wasn't on duty. When it was time for breakfast, the student nurse sent the bowl away which had been put in preparation for my muesli. As a result, I had no breakfast. I couldn't imagine why there was such a change of heart in someone who'd been so considerate so recently. I wondered what had happened in her life over the weekend to engender such a reaction. I was roused from my reverie by Don, my acupuncturist.

"It's good to see you looking a bit better," he said. I laughed, "Don't you mean, it's good to see you're still on this earth?" I asked.

"No, I think you've still got lots of fighting spirit left in you," he responded. I grinned, feeling pleased with myself.

In the afternoon Carole came to visit. We settled down for a good chat about my time in Cambridge.

"What have you been doing with yourself while I've been there?" I asked. Carole sighed, saying, "Don't ask. I've been laid off from my temporary job at the passport office. But the good thing is that I'll be around to see you." As if on cue, the nurse arrived with a porter pushing a wheelchair.

"You're going to physiotherapy," she said.

I turned to Carole, "Would you like to come with me?" I asked. I was chuffed by Carole's response,

"Yes, I'll come along and see what they do to you."

I couldn't quite believe my luck. Having left Sarah in Cambridge, suddenly I'd gained a very close friend to help me in Peterborough. Carole trailed behind the wheelchair to physiotherapy.

We arrived in procession. Physiotherapy departments

always appear as a hive of activity. I'm sure they appoint physiotherapists on the basis that they appear disgustingly healthy. I wonder if when they arrive in the morning they have a workout session together to build up their sense of fitness, all aimed at distinguishing them from the sad specimens of humanity that they are presented with throughout the day. Today was no exception. A therapist rushed over to us, hand extended.

"Hello, I'm Jack, we'll work out what you can do and take it from there."

There you are, you see, he immediately said work-out!

With Carole standing behind him looking sceptical, arms folded like a prison-warder, Jack set about assessing my strengths and weaknesses. This process involved getting me to run upstairs, well at least getting upstairs as best I could. We then returned to sitting, whilst he worked out what my hands could do. My right arm just hung from my shoulder, like a chicken hanging with its neck broken, but I did have some movement in my left hand.

When we got back to the ward, I said to Carole, "Phew, I'm exhausted, but you just looked sceptical. Is that how you felt?" Carole chuckled,

"I was sceptical, but with that lithe body you'd be bound to try hard to please him wouldn't you?" We giggled together like two teenage girls. I relaxed, happy in the warmth and the comfort that comes from good companionship.

Ian arrived in the early evening, carrying a parcel. I said,

"Look, I've got something for you in my locker, and Happy Valentine' s day."

Ian opened my locker and took out the cake. He smiled,

"Thank you, and here is something for my Valentine. Shall I open it for you?" I smiled, "Yes please."

As he unwrapped the package he'd being carrying, I thought he sounded very tired.

"They're lovely!" I exclaimed. I was fingering the soft silk of the pyjamas he'd just bought me.

"Are you alright?" I asked. Then Ian started to chuckle.

"Well, where shall I begin... I noticed during the week that the flood waters had subsided in the Trent. So I had a word with Gerry about him helping me to move the boat from Hoskins Warf. With Gerry being seventy, I was a bit wary, but he was very enthusiastic. So, we drove over yesterday. While I was at my weekly meeting, I left him to familiarize himself with the route on foot. I dropped him at Cox' s marina to check it out and follow the river onto the canal we were to take, ending up in the bar at the Wharf, where I'd meet up with him," he paused for breath, before carrying on, "Well you can imagine the rest, can't you? The weather was lovely, sunny and warm. He called in at the Malt Shovel for a pint or two on the way. By the time I arrived at Hoskins, Gerry was enthusing about the real ale and saying we'd better get the job done so we can get back to the serious business of drinking. I was dreading the force of the water still in the Trent and turning 62 feet of narrow boat across the current and into the marina. But it went like a dream and we moored without problem. Gerry didn't seem any worse for wear due to the beer." I was laughing as I imagined the scene. Ian carried on with his tale.

"After a delicious meal of duck, followed by sampling several more pints of real ale, we went back to the boat and, climbing onboard, Gerry fell into the well on the front deck, lying with his legs waving in the air like a dead budgie. Then he went through and sat on our bed, said 'this is nice and cosy' and immediately fell fast asleep, leaving me to go and make up the bed in the boatman's cabin for myself. In the morning one of the local white ducks had laid an egg and abandoned it. Gerry was very sad to see it lying there unclaimed. I said, "well you've eaten its mother, last night, so what do you expect?" Ian was laughing all the way through the story. When he finished he went to get my food organized, fed me, cleaned my teeth and kissed me.

"Thanks for the cake," he said. I replied, "It's great to see you so relaxed. I hope Gerry is recovering from the inevitable hang-over." Ian responded, "Gerry claimed he went on lots of flying missions during the war, chasing the Germans in a worse state than that." Ian went home, leaving me marvelling about how the allies ever won the war, as I settled to sleep.

The following morning we were woken by Sally, who attended to our needs in her normal and compassionate style.

"Do you need help to go to the lavatory?" she asked.

"No, thanks, I only need a wee," I responded.

I'd become very adept at asking other patients for help with flushing the toilet and turning on the taps. I could manage to wipe my bottom with lavatory paper if I'd only done a wee. A poo was a different matter to deal with. When I got back, Dawn was also around preparing for breakfast, so the morning was very pleasant.

Dawn deserved a medal for her patience and skill. How she achieved the ability to hold the coffee and straw in just the right position so that I could suck the coffee through the straw without feeling rushed and I could manage to swallow the coffee, I don't know. I was still finding that it took a lot of concentration to swallow and, if I felt irritated or stressed by the member of staff, I was unable to coordinate the action of sucking and swallowing. I suppose some staff-members considered holding a drink rather below their skill level. From my point of view it was a vital one. I felt all the more grateful to Sarah again. The effect of using the train-loaded-with-food analogy, encouraged me to relax. Consequently, my swallowing returned to almost automatic.

During the morning a physiotherapist came to see the other lady who'd come back from Addenbrooke's. She drew the screens around the bed, saying, "Now June, can you lift your left leg against my hand?"

"That's it!" she said enthusiastically,

"Now I want you to do this ten times every two hours." June didn't respond and in the end the physiotherapist walked away. I watched June over the next few days, and at no time did she even attempt to try the movements that the physiotherapist had recommended. I wondered why she wouldn't assist her own recuperation. Was it apathy due to despair or was she suffering from depression and required medication? No-one could blame her in the situation she found herself. Unfortunately, nobody seemed to tackle that as a problem, or had they tried and failed? It seemed so sad with a small child at home. (I was to learn later that she'd had a stroke following the birth of her daughter and had had a subsequent stroke after the birth of her second child.) Tragically, June had given up all hope and only did exercises to placate the physiotherapist when she was present.

Shortly after lunch, Heather, a friend who was also my hairdresser, came in.

"Hi, Anne, how are you now?" she said, taking my hand and bending over to kiss me.

I started to weep, silently. Heather sat quietly, waiting for me to compose myself. It was the beginning of something, which would recur for years, whenever I met someone who'd known me before this crisis. The emotion took over and I had an overwhelming sense of grief at being seen in such a sorry state. Heather was talking,

"If you feel well enough, I've come to wash your hair." Suddenly aware that my hair hadn't been washed since December (and it was now February), I responded,

"Ooh Yes please!" very gratefully. Heather said, "Won't be a moment" and went off to prepare the washbasin. Carrying her bag of hairdressing implements, she returned and helped me into the chair. The bag contained all she needed. She washed, cut and dried my hair, styling it, as best she could. Quietly, she concentrated on the task in hand; later I was to realize that we didn't have much of a conversation and so she was saved from the usual babble of chitchat, that always goes on in hairdressing in salons. Heather took me back to bed leaving me exhausted. She cleared up her things, packed her bag and left. I watched her go, impressed by her competence. In fact, my eyesight was quite poor, it was like looking through a thick fog and it was to remain that way for the next two years. I thought, "It's just like the fogs of my childhood when I lived in Birmingham in the early 1960s". In those days we frequently had to walk home from school when the buses weren't able to run. We walked the five miles from school in Erdington, round the outer-circle Number 11 bus route to Handsworth Wood, where we lived. Hardly able to work out where we were, we had to feel our way across the large traffic island at Stockland Green by holding onto the metal railings. We used to say, "At least no-one will drive by and run us over!"

When I was roused from my reveries, I was suddenly aware of a deliciously clean scalp. I ran my tongue around my top lip, horrified on realising for the first time that it was covered by facial hair. I thought, I must ask Ian for some tweezers. Suddenly I heard the student nurse's voice, she was introducing a new staff-nurse to the patients in the bay. She scoffed, "Look at that ridiculous hat, and she's a vegetarian." She spat out the word venomously as if she'd said I was a cannibal, or someone who made a habit of biting the heads off hamsters. Anyway, I wasn't a vegetarian, but in 1970 when Lupus was first diagnosed, I discovered that eating meat only twice a week helped to keep the level of uric acid low, and consequently I had fewer inflammatory problems in my joints. I tried to shrug off the nurse's disparaging remarks, concentrating on the delights of having clean hair.

I was feeling cheerful by the time Ian came in that evening. I recounted Heather's visit and asked him to bring in some tweezers next time. I recounted the student nurse's comments. Ian said, "She sounds like Miss Moneypenny, from the James Bond films."

"Yes, and she'd be very accomplished at torture, perhaps more like someone with a Soviet background. A woman from the KGB," I said. Ian was inspired by that, "'Eva Krol'," he responded. We grinned together in agreement. He settled me gently and I was soon asleep. However I was upset at the ridicule and I felt quite vulnerable.

Fortunately 'Eva Krol' wasn't on duty the next day. My good friend and neighbour, Pam, came to visit. I'd been to her birthday party and retirement from infant teaching just before Christmas and my admittance to hospital. She smiled,

"It's good to see you back in Peterborough."

"Yes, in a way, but I'm having great trouble with the lights, hence the baseball cap," I said. After thinking a while she said,

"Perhaps sunglasses could be the answer." Pam was on the case and went for sunglasses. She was soon back.

"Here you are, try these," she said.

They helped tremendously. When Ian came that evening, he asked, "Where did the sunglasses come from?"

"Pam came to visit and went to buy them for me."

"How much were they? Did you offer to pay for them?"

It simply hadn't occurred to me. The idea of money felt a lifetime away.

"No, I didn't, I never thought of money," I answered.

"I'll see her and sort it out," he said. Then I remembered my moustache,

"Did you bring in the tweezers?" I asked, as he went about the business of preparing my food and feeding me.

"No, sorry, I forgot. I'll definitely bring them in tomorrow," he said.

I was usually ready for sleep when Ian left in the evening, but I was wide-awake this night. When the lady from the next bay walked by on her way back from the toilet she noticed that I was awake and asked,

"Would you like to come next door for a chat? "

"Yes please." She waited while I climbed out of bed and put on my slippers.

I walked back with her.

"Where've you come from?" the lady asked.

I explained about Addenbrooke's and that I'd found some lovely satin pyjamas in my locker.

"They must have been for laying me out in if I died," I said in amusement.

"No, I shouldn't think so. My family run a funeral directors and we usually put the body in a paper shroud with a slit up the back so we can get it in easily," she explained.

"I don't fancy that either. I'm glad I survived in that case," I responded. We had a pleasant chat until we were sent off to our beds by the night staff.

Thursday morning went well. Not only was Dawn on duty, but also Polly. After lunch, Carole arrived and we went to physiotherapy. I was having some problems with my joints, Jack said, "Before we do anything more to you I think you'd better be seen by the doctor."

We went back to the ward. I was feeling that I'd won a reprieve from all the exertions, I'd found them very exhausting. We chatted a bit until Carole had to go. When Ian arrived, he was brandishing the requested tweezers. I asked,

"I found these lovely pyjamas in my locker, there are not the ones that you bought me. Do you know where they came from?" Ian looked serious.

"Don't you remember Eileen and Gill coming to see you before you went to Addenbrooke's?"

"No, I've no memory of that. What a shame. It must have been a long journey for them from Birmingham."

"I don't know about a long journey. I'd describe it as more of an epic trip. Eileen was driving and they got totally lost around the roundabouts and islands in Peterborough. When Eileen arrived home, she rang to say she was back. Gill phoned later, giggling about poor Eileen and her navigation skills."

"I bet they were a real pair, between the two of them." I said, "It's really sad that they came all this way and I've no recollection of it." When Ian went to sort out my supper, I reflected on Eileen and Gill' s friendship. We had all been together during nurse-training, and that was over twenty five years ago. Ian had been thinking too, and he said when he came back,

"Yes, and you had lots of flowers delivered during that time. How sad you weren't able to appreciate everyone's concern for you." I could only sigh sadly.

Dr Guttman and his houseman came to examine me the next morning. It was Friday. Dr Guttman said, "I think that your joint problems are pseudo gout. Are they causing you a lot of pain?" I said, "No not really, and I don't want to start taking pain killers."

"I won't prescribe anything in that case, but if you need to take something we can easily prescribe something for you. Don't just suffer in silence."

Sister came onto the ward during the morning, on her drug round with the cruel student nurse. I watched critically. Later, someone left a banana for me to eat, thinking that the nourishment would do me good. It would have done but there was no way that I could peel it and, without enquiry it was cleared away, so I remained hungry once more.

Next day, Sister was back on the ward.

"Did that nurse pass her drug assessment?" I asked, suspecting that she was being tested.

Sister said,

"Yes she did." I thought, "How could someone so uncaring be let loose on the vulnerable. It was horrific," but Sister was talking to me, "Do you think that you'd be able to manage at home?"

"Yes," I said confidently.

"Then I'll arrange for your discharge, probably Tuesday," she said.

She put the wheels in motion for my going home. As it was Sunday, Ian was busy with his meeting and didn't visit that evening. I was itching to tell him all the next day. Carole came on Monday afternoon and we went to physiotherapy together. When we arrived back on the ward I said to her,

"Ian brought some tweezers in last night. I want to get rid of the moustache on my top lip." Carole looked worried,

"What do you want me to do about it?" she asked.

"Could you draw the screens around, and pluck out any stray hairs?"

With the bed hidden from view, she started. Every time she pulled out a hair I groaned. I was groaning most of the afternoon.

As soon as Ian arrived in the evening, I burst out, "I'm coming home tomorrow!" Ian was incredulous,

"How can you possibly manage at home?" he asked.

"I can't stay here for ever," I said petulantly. Ian reluctantly went to see Sister and arranged the time to come and collect me. Not that he wanted me to stay but he was very concerned as to whether I could cope with home life whilst he was at work.

Tuesday morning, Ian arrived with some chocolates as a 'thank you' for the nurses. I thought, "If that horrible nurse eats any I hope she gets tooth ache!" I said goodbye to everyone while Ian was getting all my things together. The horrid nurse fetched the wheelchair and Ian took me to the car.

"Just leave the chair in the discharge area," she instructed.

Ian drove the three miles home and helped me out of the car. We walked towards the front door and I took a deep breath, luxuriating in the unaccustomed softness of the fresh spring air. As soon as the front door was open Abbey greeted me effusively. There was much tail wagging.

"At last I'm home," I sighed as I sank into my chair in the sitting room and patted Abbey.

The morning after my hospital discharge the doorbell rang. Ian had just got me up, washed, dressed and fed. Three occupational therapists stood on the doorstep. They rushed in and, using something like a soldering iron, they constructed and fitted plastic extension levers to the toilet flush handles in the toilet and upstairs bathroom. Mission completed, they left as quickly as they'd come.

A routine was established. After getting me sorted each morning, Ian would rush off to work. Shortly after he had left, Carole would arrive to help with my care. We'd walk Abbey, with me dragging my left leg along behind and, after lunch, a hospital car would arrive to take us both to physiotherapy. During one of the initial visits the, therapist pointed out that the cuticles on my left hand were green.

"You'd better telephone the surgery and arrange for a doctor to look at these,"she said.

I knew what had caused it, but I felt too ashamed to admit to it. Consequently, I said nothing. I was thinking: "When I'd been to the toilet, opened my bowels and tried to wipe my bottom, I'd covered my fingers with poo. Unable to turn on taps, my fingers had to stay in a contaminated state. That's why they'd become infected!"

The physiotherapist was talking to Carole. She said, "Can you try to get her to use that right arm?" I still hadn't any feeling in my right arm and it hung uselessly from my shoulder. She left me feeling completely overlooked. Carole made a doctor's appointment for the next day. She drew Ian's attention to my fingers. He washed them and applied Germolene. The next day, together with Carole, we went in a taxi to the doctors. Carole managed to shut my arm in the taxi door.

"They said I'd got to get you to use it! Instead I'm shutting it in the door!" she laughed. "It doesn't matter at all. It feels as dead as a Dodo" I assured her. The doctor arranged for the district nurse to visit weekly. I think he knew jolly well how my fingers had become infected but if so, he thought it kinder not to embarrass me.

The next day was Friday and I had another appointment at physiotherapy. The physiotherapists appeared to be very busy and were chasing about like startled goldfish after seeing the cat. A senior therapist, whilst still ignoring me, out of the blue said to Carole, "I'm sorry, we can't help your friend anymore."

I went home in a daze. The joy of arriving home had subsided into despair.

It had been so lovely to be sleeping in a double bed with Ian again. However, during my time in hospital I had adopted the unfortunate habit of sleeping in the starfish position, arms at right angles to my body, trying to occupy all the bed at once. Ian was unable to get a decent night's sleep, so the only solution was for me to move into a bed in another room.

Having settled in a spare bedroom I was now frequently disturbed by nightmares. I often awoke thrashing about in bed, fighting off an unseen assailant. I was suffering from the long forgotten nightmares that had caused my old post-traumatic stress disorder. My solution was to get out of bed, put on the radio and listen to the BBC world service, until eventually the panic attack eased and I could drift back to sleep. I thought, "How cruel it is that whilst I'm living with the brain of a toddler, the traumatic experiences of long ago are still coming back to haunt me."

But I did have something to look forward to. Brother John's daughter was shortly to get married. Ian and I rummaged in the wardrobe and found an appropriate suit. I went to a beautician for my legs to be waxed, and Ian packed everything we needed for the Saturday wedding of Fiona and Douglas. We were to meet up in the Raven Hotel in Droitwich and stay the weekend. Ian drove and, arriving at the Raven, helped me out of the car and took me to sit down in the reception area of the hotel. My second cousin Pat, who had never met Ian, was sitting there whilst her husband Edmund was checking them in.

"Pat, meet Ian," I said. Pat stood up and they shook hands. Then Ian said, "I'll leave Annie in your care while I get checked in. "

Pat resumed her position and, turning to me, asked, "How are you feeling after your journey?"

"J-just a b-b-bit tired," I was stuttering then I heard my mother's voice. She and Dad had arrived in a taxi and, having paid off the taxi, Dad went to check in whilst Mum came towards Pat and me. Pat stood up to greet her. I remained seated, then Mum turned to Pat and said, "Aren't you going to introduce me to your friend?" Pat said, "It's Anne." Mum came towards me, arm extended to shake hands. Pat added quickly, "Your daughter, Anne!"

Mum backed away and sat down.

The wedding lived up to expectations. We had a delightful time. Sadly, the helplessness of my position subsumed me as soon as we got home. A letter from Carole was waiting. Ian opened and read,

'I can't help you any more! Please don't contact me again. It's signed Carole,'

I felt even more sorry for myself. I thought, I must have looked so poorly that even my own mother didn't recognise me. The physiotherapy department has written me off and now even Carole had given up on me. I'd never felt so desolate, not even when I was first diagnosed as suffering from Systemic Lupus Erythematosis and thought that I only had two years to live, and that was bad enough. On that occasion my response was to go straight home and look up the diagnosis in my copy of *A Short Textbook of Medicine by Houston, Joiner, and Trounce*. I read, "Prognosis must be guarded. There is much to commend the division of the cases into benign and malignant.... Benign cases may progress very slowly for many years but once the malignant phase begins..... the outlook is bad, patients usually only surviving a year or two."

I had been devastated. I had a one year-old child and somehow I had to survive. Now that one-year-old was 20, her brother 18. The determination to survive had become ingrained but it was now under threat.

A week after we'd arrived home from the wedding I had an outpatients appointment with Doctor Guttman. He shook my left hand warmly. I felt flustered and confused. I was unable to get my eyes in focus. My left leg dragged and my right arm was totally useless. My friend Val had said to me, "All the time you were in Intensive Care, Doctor Guttman slept in the hospital. That was in spite of his wife being poorly at home. My first job upon getting to work was to make his breakfast."

Indirectly, I probably have Hitler to thank for my survival. Dr Guttman' s father was the late Lord Guttman. When the Guttmans were escaping persecution by the Nazis, Britain offered them sanctuary. Lord Guttman repaid the offer by devoting his life to the care of patients at Stoke Mandeville, later his son to medical care in Peterborough. I thought, "I mustn't repay all his efforts by not playing my part at working hard on my recovery." But I was in a sorry state; my sight was very poor and I could only recognise people from their voices rather than their faces, my speech was hesitant, my vocabulary stunted and I'd forget what I was saying mid-sentence. When walking I dragged my left leg, I soon became breathless with even modest exercise and Ian had to supply my basic needs, bathing, taking me to the lavatory and wiping my bottom. The occupational therapist's addition of the levers to the toilet handles meant that I could flush the toilet but I wasn't able to turn the water taps on or off. I was still living with the constant threat of the nightmares of my post-traumatic stress disorder left by the trauma of my first marriage.

All in all it led me to thinking that, *I'd rather be dead than disabled.*

CHAPTER 3

CHILDHOOD

It was Easter Sunday when I arrived, naked and crimson faced, in Huddersfield. I filled my lungs with air and started to yell when the midwife smacked my bottom. I was six pounds and furious at being ejected from the security of my mother's womb. It was an untimely arrival at the Princess Alice Nursing Home because the slumbering giant of the National Health Service was due to be implemented but was still in its embryo. Were my own embryonic seeds of Lupus present at my birth, lying dormant and waiting to make an untimely entrance? There are many gaps in the knowledge of this complex disease, Systemic Lupus Erethematosis, now commonly called Lupus. Despite research, even in this twenty-first century, how or why it starts is unknown. As early as 1949 great strides were being made in the development of a drug which was to save my life, some forty-two years later. It was quite by chance that Doctor Hench, an American Rheumatologist at the Mayo Clinic, recorded his discovery of the amazing power of steroids over inflammatory diseases.

But to return to my birth in 1948, being born in Huddersfield made me a member of the Brigantes tribe and, since our family records began, my ancestors had lived in Yorkshire. But before I'd mastered the lingo of 'God' s own county', we left our semi detached home in Mayfield Avenue in Huddersfield and headed south for Dad to seek his fortune. I gather that he was driving when we were packed into his plum-red Hillman Minx and took the Great North Road. Dad had a military bearing, no doubt gained from his experience as a Major in the wartime army. His hair was ginger and he had a matching military moustache. Seated next to him was my Mother, a dark-haired, small, neat and pretty woman. We, the children, were in the back. My assertive eight-year-old sister Elizabeth, known to me as Bid and my brother John aged six, bespectacled and serious, were squeezed alongside my carrycot. Father, as he always did when he was driving, was puffing out sickly sweet smelling St Julian' s Empire blend tobacco smoke from his pipe. Somehow, despite the copious clouds of smoke, Dad found the A43 to Kettering and we eventually arrived at what was to be our new home; a 1930s semi-detached house in Pytchly Road, Kettering.

The culture of the times was focused on putting the war, with all its deprivations, into the past. Gradually the restrictions of food rationing ended, although the wartime children' s dietary supplements were still in use. Children were given Ministry of Health Cod Liver Oil, which tasted disgusting. When my mother took the yellow Cod Liver Oil bottle out of the cupboard, it was a signal for us all to disappear. On the other hand, the Ministry of Health Orange Juice was sweet and nice, and we would gladly assemble for this to be dispensed. Mum soon learnt to brandish the orange juice to tempt us into the open, substituting the cod liver oil as soon as we arrived. Tricked, we would each complain in turn, as we wrinkled up our noses in disgust.

Kettering was a great place for a child. We lived near to Wickstead Park, with all its amusements. I still have a photo of myself riding a pony in the Park. I, as a little girl of eighteen months, had blonde hair, all tangled at the back from my habit of rocking backwards and forwards perpetually, in my bed or chair. The photo shows Dad trying to hold me astride a plump, piebald pony of some ten hands. I'm trying to push Dad away and have a look of grim determination, clearly wanting to take control of the reins myself. The pony looks bored and resigned to her fate.

All too soon we were on the move again. This time it was to live in a flat above the Co-op shop in Coopers Road, Handsworth Wood, Birmingham. I discovered that the great thing about living above a row of shops was the proximity of sweets. Even better when the rationing of sugar and two ounces of sweets was just about to end, and I was considered old enough to go as far as the shops on my own. On one of these early sorties for sweeties, I bumped straight into my double. She also had bobbed blonde hair and was bent on the same errand. She stood back, eyeing me up and down and said, "I'm KayKay. I'm freee."

I'd just had my birthday, so replied with an air of seniority, "'Ello, I'm Annie, I'm four."

Instantly, a life time close bond of friendship was formed.

Although the flat suited me admirably, my mother was keen to be upwardly mobile. Or perhaps downwardly is more accurate on this occasion, as she wanted to live in a house rather than a second floor flat. So within the year we moved half a mile away into a three-storey, semi-detached house in Somerset Road. These properties were built during the nineteenth century in warm red brick. There were about thirty solidly built houses occupying both sides of a hill and stretching up the road to a sweet shop. Running up the road to reach the shop meant passing a large, imposing, red brick Methodist Church, on the other side of the road. The church, with its ancillary buildings, must have covered at least half an acre. These included a two-storey building used for social activities. However, I was bent on my mission of the day. The small corner shop selling sweets was one hundred yards away, uphill. It presented quite a challenge for little legs. I can remember rushing to the shop with a threepenny piece firmly gripped in my fist.

"Liquorice laces please, Mrs. Foxhall," I panted.

"Four laces a penny, mi luve," Mrs Foxhall, a lady of diminutive stature, replied, smiling. I'd got tuppence left to spend, and I didn't need anyone to teach me that.

Though I'd been happily getting my life organised, it seemed that other people had different priorities. Both Kay Kay and I were approaching five years old and the education system beckoned. We graced Cherry Orchard School with our presence as part of the post-war bulge, fifty children with no pre-school experience! It must have been like trying to put fifty white mice into a box, in our classroom. So I suppose Mrs Fleming, the warm and cosy reception class teacher, could have managed without me around, but she wasn't given the option of avoiding my continuous chatter. Morning break- time seemed to start just after the register was taken. We were all given a third of a pint bottle of free milk, which we drank through a paper straw before going out to play.

It was here that my education was broadened by extra-curricular activities, courtesy of Michael Jones. A fat spotty little boy, he said, "I've got some fink to show you, it's in mi trousers. "

We gathered around a drainpipe in the playground, giggling in anticipation. His scarred knees showed below his grey serge shorts. He had grey, woolen, knee length socks with the left one wrinkled around his ankle. Scuffed black school shoes completed his ensemble. He fumbled to undo the buttons on his flies, eventually Michael achieved his goal and said, "This is my winkle. Do you want to stroke it?"

"Yes," Kay Kay, Margaret, another friend and I all said with varying degrees of enthusiasm.

We all had a feel.

Who was the keenest? My lips are sealed. We still argue about it.

"Urrg, it feels all soft, wrinkly and squashy," Margaret said.

We were all complicit in something we knew was naughty, and so shared a guilty secret. Margaret and I had first met in the reception class with her long, blonde hair secured by a rubber band. We shared the same birthday, the 18th April, so we felt like twins.

Mrs. Fleming was saved from my regular attendance at school by my frequent bouts of tonsillitis. I understand that the newly formed NHS already had a two-year waiting list for a tonsillectomy. So for what was to become the first of many hospital experiences, I was booked into a private hospital in Birmingham. This way my parents ensured that I didn't miss too much school due to illness. The hospital was in a large, Victorian detached house and by chance, our next-door neighbour, Barbara Black, was admitted for a tonsillectomy at the same time. I hadn't had a lot to do with Barbara before that time, other than our families getting together when the Black family kindly invited us all to watch Queen Elizabeth II's Coronation on their television, in June 1953. The size of the television screen was only ten inches. The five of us joined the four members of the Black family and all crammed into the Black's breakfast room to peer at the television in its brown, wooden cabinet made of Bakelite. We felt very 'with it'.

Later when we returned home, I asked Dad,

"Why can't we have a television?"

"Because it would interfere with your brother and sister's homework," Dad replied decisively.

So that was the end of that conversation and we didn't get one for several years to come.

Going into hospital with someone I knew did help a bit but Barbara was a year older than me, and I didn't count her as one of my real friends. She lived with her grandmother as well as her parents and they seemed so self-contained. She had never joined me on the dash for sweets. Barbara, her parents, my parents and I all walked into the hospital together. It was scary and smelt funny. A nurse showed us all into a room with four beds. Her chin and her upper lip had black hairs growing on them.

The nurse spoke to Mum and Dad in what I thought was a foreign language, whilst I sat on the bed, screens pulled round me and a glass thermometer under my tongue for what seemed like forever. It enforced my silence, while I marvelled at the traces of the black moustache, thinking "I've never seen such a thing as a moustache on a lady before". The nurse eventually withdrew and read the thermometer, drew back the screens and went over to where Barbara was waiting with her parents. She left without saying anything to me. Dad squeezed my hand, and Mum and Dad left. I sat on my bed feeling frightened.

Shortly, the nurse returned. This time it was with a man all dressed in green, and the odd smell was even stronger.

"Lie down on your bed," the nurse commanded.

Then he pulled a weird glass thing over his eyes. Lying down obediently, I stared up into it. It was like looking at those funny mirrors in a fun fair. He looked grotesque, was he really going to do anything to me? I was scared at the very thought of it!

Despite having had nothing to eat or drink all night, I was lifted onto a trolley and taken away into a room that had the same funny smell, though even stronger. Next, I awoke with blood running from my mouth onto a green cotton pillowcase. I was feeling as if I'd had my throat cut.

Another nurse I couldn't see properly took my hand and asked,

"How are you feeling, dear?"

"Urrgh," I gurgled with blood in my throat, determined not to cry.

After squeezing my hand gently, she carefully changed

the blood-soaked linen, smiling soothingly. She made me feel secure and peaceful, inspite of my aching and painful throat. I thought, "Never mind, the good thing about this is that I've been promised ice-cream to cool my aches and pains. I hope it comes very soon!"

Being young and healthy I soon recovered from the tonsillectomy, especially as we were due to go on holiday to Cornwall. We packed into our new black Rover 90 and headed out of Birmingham on the A38, playing 'I spy with my little eye' in a desperate attempt to alleviate the boredom of the journey.

John said, "I spy with my little eye, something beginning with T! "

Bid cried out, "Tarmacadam!"

"That's not fair." I whined.

I had spent so much time being ill that my vocabulary and spelling was poor and, anyway I didn't have a clue what Tarmacadam was.

To get a break from my constant complaining, or maybe to emphasise still further her and her brothers' superiority, Bid tried a different approach.

She started singing, "There were ten in the bed and the little one said, roll over, roll over. They all rolled over and one fell out. There were nine in the bed, and the little one said…

With that, I started to cry. I couldn't count backwards.

John said, "Well, when I am in assembly, because my singing is so off key I've been told just to mouth the words, so I can't sing either! So I don't know why you're making such a fuss! "

Apparently John was considered to be tone-deaf and ordered not to attempt singing in assemblies, as his enthusiastic shouting out of the melody destroyed everyone else's attempts at the pitch. Unfortunately, with an age gap of five and eight years, finding an entertainment in which we could all share on our journeys was a lost cause.

During all this time, Dad' s priority was to keep his pipe alight and Mum's was to find a 4 star hotel for lunch and a similar place later for tea. There weren't such places as McDonald's or Burger King in those days so, reaching Cheltenham, we pulled in at a hotel for lunch. The receptionist directed us to the dining room, where a black-suited headwaiter showed us to a vacant table, bowing to my father (I'd have called him obsequious, if I'd known such a word).

"May I help you sir? he asked Dad.

"We'd like lunch for five," Dad responded.

The headwaiter raised his arm and, after clicking his fingers a white-coated underling arrived, providing menus for each of us. He left us to decide. Importantly, I opened the red leather-bound volume. I could read enough to work out that I wasn't impressed.

The waiter returned for the order and starting with my mother asked, "What would Madame like?"

My mother replied, "Roast beef with Yorkshire pudding and vegetables."

He continued through the rest of the family, getting the same response each time, until he reached me. I didn't know why I didn't like roast beef, but the prospect of rendering the vegetables tasteless by boiling them to a pulp didn't appeal.

I asked, "Do you have sausages for breakfast?"

He raised his eyebrows and replied, "Yes, we do."

"Then could I have sausages and chips, please?" I asked triumphantly.

Spotting a problem, head-waiter arrived.

"May I help you, Modom?" he asked me.

"Please may I have sausages and chips?" I said, sticking to my guns.

"We do not have chips, Modom... we have sauté potatoes," he sighed.

Eventually our food was brought in, I looked at my sauté potatoes, and asked, and "May I have tomato ketchup with it, please?"

Disdainfully he returned, tomato ketchup in hand, and I relished the taste.

I'd achieved sausages and sauté potatoes, despite them not being on the menu, and jolly good they were too. I followed it with ice cream. It was a much better alternative to the apple-pie, drowned with tasteless custard that had been chosen by everyone else. When we left, I was feeling particularly pleased with myself.

"The lunch wasn't very nice," Mum said irritably.

"Mine was jolly good. Perhaps you should have all asked for sausage and chips," I said in a triumphant tone. We departed in dead silence and it remained so for several minutes.

The combination of single-carriageway A roads, the breaks for food, and my Dad' s preoccupation with keeping his pipe alight, resulted in a twelve hour journey. Eventually we arrived at The Saint Catherine's Hotel at Fowey; my bucket and spade was ready. The next day I couldn't wait to get busy on the beach. The sun burnt my eyes so I wore my bright pink plastic sunglasses. Wearing a blue, ruffled stitched one-piece bathing suit, I spent the day happily digging in the sand and building sandcastles. In the evening I apparently had a fit.

On becoming conscious, I heard a voice that I didn't immediately recognise. I kept my eyes shut and listened. I thought, "It can't be Mum asking if I am alright." The voice was warm and concerned. My mother always spoke in an irascible and irritated manner, as though everything was too much trouble. Eventually I made up my mind. Yes it was her, so I kept my eyes closed, basking in the novelty of this unexpected kindness. After a while I looked at her. She smiled briefly, and then returned to her usual style.

"Too much sun," she said dismissing the subject.

I was put to bed without further attention and left alone to sleep it off. It wasn't mentioned again during the holiday, and it appeared to have been completely forgotten. As usual, I felt that I was being treated as a nuisance and that I had put on the fit for my own selfish reasons. I thought, "Oh well! Perhaps they are right about that, as well as everything else. They seem to know more than I do about everything."

All too soon the holiday was over and we had to return home. Although only six, I was expected to get myself bathed and ready for bed. Then, clad in my nightie, I was allowed downstairs to sit on Dad' s knee. He smelt of Old Spice as he gave me a cuddle and it reminded me of the bottle in the bathroom, bearing the distinctive old sailing ship label. I became lost in the strong but comforting aroma that I associated with my Dad. All too soon the cuddle would come to an end and Dad would say,

"Time for bed."

Then, I'd climb reluctantly off his knee, kiss Mum on her proffered cheek, transiently catching the scent of her Coty' Laitmant and climb the stairs. Getting into bed, I would rock myself backwards and forwards until sleep took over.

My attempts at my ablutions didn't quite measure up to the expected standard of my parents. One day, Dad took me to have a haircut at the Central Co-operative. He was an accountant and Secretary of the Birmingham Cooperative Society and was treated with obvious respect for his position of seniority. On returning home, Mum was furious,

"You could grow potatoes in the filth on your neck, what did they think?"

With my hair now an inch or two shorter, a tidemark was revealed. I felt triumphant, I had survived until I was ten before they had caught me out for my cursory attention to my ablutions. However, they made me feel ashamed and I commenced a lifetime's habit of scrubbing my neck extra hard before trips to the hairdressers.

It seemed that there was a rivalry between children born during the Second World War and postwar babies.

"Oh! It's alright for you, you've bin spoilt. When I was seven we could only get two ounces of butter and that had to last a month," Bid said irritably.

I'd come into the breakfast room from the kitchen with my breakfast. Bid was already eating her toast and I commenced spreading copious amounts of butter onto mine.

She went on, "And you could only get two ounces of soap each week."

I giggled about the very thought of that saying, "I wouldn't care about that…Anyway, you wouldn't be so long in the bathroom if there wasn't so much soap about." I thought I'd made a good point and felt smug. Bid had recently become interested in boys.

She retorted very quickly, "Yes, you would. It included washing clothes, and the state your dress is in…" she tailed off.

I took the opportunity of returning to the attack, "You're just in a bad mood because your boyfriend has been called up for National Service!"

At that point John walked into the breakfast room with his cornflakes. He rose to Bid's defence immediately, "At least she's got a boy-friend, with your disgusting habit of biting your nails, nobody will ever ask you to go out with them!"

With that, John tucked into his breakfast. I carried on eating indignantly, butter and strawberry jam smeared all over my plump cheeks. I was thinking, "It isn't my fault that I wasn't even alive in the War. As a ten year old, what could I do about it?" Anyway, I'd heard these stories so many times before. I put it down to Bid being seventeen and having a boyfriend and John, at fifteen not having (to my knowledge anyway) a girlfriend.

In the nineteen fifties fresh food, and particularly fresh meat, was highly prized by those who'd lived through the Wartime shortages. Our family seemed set upon making up this deficit. Mum, as the queen of the kitchen, didn't want to be disturbed when she was cooking, but all this changed on Sunday mornings. Dad would get dressed and take Mum a cup of tea in bed. Then he would return to the kitchen and fry breakfast for the two of us, as my other siblings, being of teenage years, would slumber on. I would sit waiting in the adjoining breakfast-room, rocking backwards and forwards in a brown upholstered Parker knoll chair. Dad, having completed his cooking task of the week, would carry the two plates of scrumptious smelling bacon and eggs and ceremoniously place them on the table for us to tuck into and share in his culinary delights. I luxuriated in the opportunity to have Dad all to myself and talk over such things as how I was getting on at school. All too soon the breakfast would be over and we prepared for the short walk up to the Methodist Church for the 11 o'clock Sunday service.

Being Methodist meant that we always went to church on Sundays. We still didn't have a television, so the Church tended to form the focal point of companionship and entertainment for me. Alcohol was a topic of horrified gossip.

"The Church of England have asked for us to join them in Communion," the Reverend Goodacre announced from the pulpit one Sunday.

He was a short, plump, bald man, with a bulbous nose and ruddy complexion. I thought he looked ridiculous in his flowing cassock. Nevertheless, when he was leaning over the mahogany pulpit, berating us for some sin or another, he became an awesome spectacle. He looked down from on high, his congregation stretching before him seated on rows of hard wooden chairs, their holders for hymn books in their backs and the rows seeming to stretch for miles.

After this particular service Mr. Wright, a tall imposing chorister, was enraged,

"Their Communion wine has alcohol in it," he said accusingly.

As far as he was concerned, that was the end of the matter. I wondered how he'd known that their Communion wine contained alcohol. Had he been to their Communion Service and taken part? That was surely heresy? But the answers to my musings were not forthcoming as the voices were lowered. Such a thing was not a fit topic for discussion within the vicinity of young ears.

I was told that abstinence was a big issue in the Methodist Church. John Wesley, the founder of the Methodists, was born in the eighteenth century and reached the great age of ninety years despite the average life expectancy being just over thirty years of age. He extolled the virtues of temperance and condemned what he considered to be the depravity of the English Churches, both the established Church of England and the Papal Catholic Church. Disgusted, he sailed to America but only found a guilty and useless humanity in the New World. The Reverend Goodacre felt obliged to continue John Wesley' s mission. He continually bombarded us with the message, "Your only value is in being of service to others. God will judge you on what you've done in this world, before you enter the next. He will know your every thought."

Guilt seemed the order of the day and I started to attempt to assuage mine by collecting for the overseas missions. Collecting book in hand, I approached a lady after the service.

"Mrs. Wright, would you like to help starving children?" I asked boldly.

It was a very brave gesture as Mrs. Wright was even more fearsome than her chorister husband. She looked very severe with her grey hair scraped back from her face and secured firmly with a grip.

"Yes, I'll give a shilling a week," smiled Mrs Wright to my surprise.

So I began charity work, signing up people to donate a few pence each week.

Mum would be at home cooking Sunday lunch when we arrived back. This always consisted of a first course of a rather flat Yorkshire pudding, which I ate with sugar, whilst the rest of the family consumed it with gravy. Then there was roast beef and vegetables and a pudding course of something like apple pie and custard, with tap water to drink. Then it was washing up and, not long after, preparing for a tea that usually consisted of cold ham, salad, bread-and-butter, and a fruit trifle, followed by sponge cake. Thus more than fortified, we all attended the 6 o'clock service.

But my life wasn't totally taken up with Church and good works. For myself as the youngest of three, school holidays tended to drag. Evidently, I drove Bid to distraction with my teasing. The boyfriend she'd met at the Church youth club had now been called up for compulsory military service and she was permanently miserable. Playing Frank Sinatra's "Dreams are made of this" over and over again, she would weep and mumble, "The way you wear your hat, they can't take that away from me.... The way you hold your knife, they can't take that away from me" This became something else to her insensitive little sister.

I sang, "The way you blow your nose, they can't take that away from me.... The way you shave under your arms, they can't...

"Shut up!" she interrupted my flow.

Fortunately, Bid had a holiday job to distract her from the sadness and, leaving a trail of scent, she walked up the road a hundred yards beyond the Church to a parade of shops, where she worked for Mrs. Bell in her pharmacy, which was to become her future career. Later she obtained her degree in pharmacy. John, in the meantime, was fully committed to Boy Scout activities.

From time to time there were intermissions in my boredom. Since then I have discovered that all youngsters, and particularly teenagers, claim to have the affliction of boredom. One time I lost a tooth, and in the night a tooth fairy brought me a silver sixpence. The very next morning I ran to the sweetshop.

Mr. Foxhall was serving. Unlike his tiny wife, he was so big; he seemed to fill the shop.

After waiting impatiently for my turn, I said, "The tooth fairy has brought me a silver sixpence. I've come to spend it on some sweets, please Mr. Foxhall."

"What wuld ye lyioke," he smiled.

"A threepenny stick of liquorice and six aniseed balls, please," I said decisively.

I put the sweets safely in the pocket of my gingham dress and wandered across the road to the Church, looking for a quiet place to indulge myself. In the grounds behind the Church were some tennis courts so I sat down, took the liquorice out of my pocket and starting eating it. Then I noticed a hole in the fence that I hadn't noticed before. The fence separated the tennis courts from The Wesleyan and General Sports ground. I'd never been there before. "I'll explore," I thought and I crawled through the hole. As I started to cross the cricket pitch I noticed the grounds-man and he noticed me. He whistled his Alsatian, "After her, after her!"

Immediately, I ran for the gap as fast as my legs would carry me. Just at the point where I had to bend to get through the hole, the Alsatian reached me and sank his teeth into my bottom. Then he returned to his master, wagging his tail, pleased with completing his security responsibilities. I headed for home feeling sore but was consoled when I felt in my pocket, and the aniseed balls were still there. It was some time before I could sit down in comfort. My bottom was very sore and, knowing that I shouldn't have been there in the first place, made me brazen it out while it was healing. I had to sit down carefully, but running around wasn't a problem

Another intermission in my boredom was one afternoon when Dad asked, "Shall we go to go to Barr Beacon with Barbara this evening?"

I cried, "Yes, great!" and began collecting bats and a ball before we called for Barbara.

Barr Beacon was an uncultivated area five miles to the north of our home and is the highest point in the area. It was a popular recreational area that provided an open space for us to run around in. For Dad, it allowed him to take a break from the responsibilities of work. Its name is said to be derived from the adjacent Great Barr and the beacon that, in previous centuries, had been lit to signify a pending attack or for a celebratory event. Barbara was keen to come so, well equipped with bats and balls, we jumped into the car and Mum and Dad were ready to take us. Once there, Barbara and I began knocking a ball to each other. Mum and Dad sat down on the rug they'd brought with them. Sitting on a rug nearby there was another couple enjoying the early evening sunshine. They had a small baby crawling about on the grass. Suddenly the man grasped his forehead and shouted out,

"Argh!!"

He fell onto his back. I could clearly see blood oozing between his fingers. Mum led Barbara and I away. Dad went and took his hand. A police car, its siren blaring away, was soon on the scene, closely followed by an ambulance. Dad joined us; we quietly collected our things and left the scene in a shocked and subdued state.

"The man had been shot… He was already dead…. Killed by a bullet to the head," Dad said.

I was very impressed by his immediate command of the situation. "Dad must have learnt all that in the war," I thought, feeling very proud.

Dad took Barbara home to explain what had happened. I went indoors with Mum, she simply said, "Go and get yourself into bed."

I lay in bed feeling haunted by the man's blood-curdling cry, as I tried to get to sleep. But the land of nod eluded me. Eventually I must have gone to sleep because I woke up in the morning, though still feeling shocked. (Later I was told that two boys were shooting rabbits in a nearby field and a ricochet off a stone had hit the man).

The five churches in our local group were referred to as the 'Church Circuit' and it was decided that they would hold a competition, which they called the "Circuit Eisteddfod".

"Annie is ten now, isn't she? So could she read a poem?" Mrs Wright asked.

"Yes, of course she will," my mother replied confidently.

I took the choice of material very seriously and though not consciously aware of it at the time, perhaps the experience that day on Barr Beacon affected my choice.

On Saturday afternoon, as usual, Dad and I changed our books at the Little Endwood library sub-branch. In addition, I was trying to decide what I should read at the 'Eisteddfod'. I was an avid but discerning reader. I rejected Enid Blyton's Famous Five, because George's dog "Timmy "was nondescript. I considered The Secret Seven because their dog "Scamper," a golden spaniel, was vividly described and really came to life. However, Enid Blyton didn't offer a resource for poetry. I looked elsewhere.

The recital day dawned and I sat clutching my chosen poem. I had to endure such renditions as "They're changing guard at Buckingham Palace", "The Charcoal Burner", and "King John's Christmas."

Then the judge asked, "Are you ready, Annie?"

I took my place and started earnestly,

"I remember, I remember, the house where I was born,

The little window where the sun came peeping in at morn,
It never came a wink too soon, or brought too long a day
But now I often wish, that night had borne my breath away."

The pathos of a little girl, so ardently wishing for death, was not missed by the judges. They awarded me first prize!

I may have been precocious at speaking in public but due to the tonsillitis, I was behind with maths. The 'Eleven Plus' was approaching and Dad started to focus on my academic requirements.

At the schools parent's evening Dad asked, "What are Annie' s chances of passing for Grammar School?"

Mr. Grisewood replied decisively, "Annie hasn't the first idea about arithmetic."

Then the battle commenced. Dad arrived home with a book of tables. We struggled each evening to make up the deficit. Addition, subtraction and multiplication, grudgingly were to form my entertainment before bedtime until the date of the Eleven plus arrived.

It said a tremendous amount for my Dad's patience that I passed for Erdington Grammar School. My friends Kay and Margaret were to go there too.

Just before I left Cherry Orchard Primary School, Dad said, "We're buying a house in Hinstock Road, so we'll be moving."

"That's super, we'll be near school" Bid and John said in chorus.

"What about me?" I whined.

"It will mean you'll only have to catch one bus, instead of two, so it'll be better for you too,"Dad added reassuringly.

Bid and John were both at Handsworth Grammar School and Bid was Head Girl. In those days grammar school boys and girls were separated. Both schools had very good reputations, which I assumed they didn't want me to spoil, hence my relegation to Erdington Grammar, I thought. So after breakfast every school day I left home in Hinstock Road and headed a hundred yards up the road, past the park to the bus stop. As I looked back at the house I felt pleased about the move, despite it only being about a mile from our previous home in Somerset Road. The new home had been built in the nineteen thirties. It was a large, five bedroomed detached "chalet style" house, directly opposite Handsworth Park and it had a beautiful magnolia tree in the front garden. To get to school I had to catch the Number 11 Outer Circle bus. Kay, on the other hand, initially caught the Number 16 from her home before changing to the Number 11. Most mornings we met on the bus and Margaret joined us a stop later for the six-mile trip.

For me, school was largely a social experience. Work tended to be incidental to the proceedings. Nevertheless every afternoon on leaving school I filled my satchel with my homework, fully resolved to tackle the work once I arrived home. Inevitably, other arrangements decided on the journey home, meant that my good intentions were forgotten and I returned the next day, satchel unopened.

However, this routine was to save me from a potentially nasty event. One evening as I was walking home from the bus stop, two boys ran across from the park side of the road and grabbed me by the belt on my gabardine mac.

I swung my heavy satchel repeatedly, hitting one then the other.

"Argh," cried the first, beaten off by the impact.

"Ooof," said the other and they both ran off.

I ran home like the wind, rang the doorbell frantically and fell into the door as Mum opened it. Then began a tedious business of the police meeting me off the bus, seeking to identify my assailants. The boys never came that way again and I still kept packing my satchel with books. After this Mum must have worried about my lonely walk alongside the park in the dark evenings.

"I think you need to learn judo to learn protect yourself," she suggested.

There had been an advert in the Birmingham Post advertising classes. I discussed it with Kay and we decided to go and give judo a try.

We arrived for the first lesson and changed into our white judo suits, paid our fees and, following the others, presented ourselves barefoot on the mat in the hall. We commenced with a series of stretching exercises to loosen up our ligaments and muscles. It all seemed very boring, so the next week we timed our arrival to skip the preparation. No one checked to see that we were properly prepared before we walked on to the judo mat. We entered and took up positions on the judo mat. Suddenly, someone took hold of my white judo suit collar, and I was thrown onto the mat with a resounding crash. I thought "I must have broken my neck at the very least," as I had landed so heavily on my shoulders. I struggled to my feet and moved my head from side to side. A grating noise came from the ligaments in my neck. The grating noise was still there on the next Saturday, so I said to Kay, "I can't see much point in turning up just to be thrown about onto a hard mat. That's not my idea of fun. It is more dangerous than walking home!"

Kay responded, "No, I'm sure there are better ways of spending Saturday afternoon!"

So that was the end of our Judo experience. For some time after that we spent our Saturday afternoons just wasting time, messing about and doing nothing in particular.

Frequently I had wondered about our next-door neighbour. Apart from the milkman calling each morning, there were very few signs of life coming from the dover grey fortress-like house. Then one evening our doorbell rang. Dad went to answer it and, always inquisitive, I followed. Standing on our doorstep was a very ill kept, small and plump, distressed, middle-aged lady, apparently from the house next door. In what I took to be a marked German accent she said, "My Auntie has fallen... I can't lift her"

As she spoke, she revealed a huge gap between her front teeth.

Dad said, "I'll just go and change out of my slippers."

I was left smiling nervously at her, whilst staring at the huge sagging breasts clearly showing beneath her well-worn jumper. In no time Dad was back and went with her to help deal with her problem. I was left to speculate about the situation. I thought, "So that's who lives in the fortress."

Dad soon returned home. He said to Mum, "It wasn't too difficult to get her Auntie into her bed as there is a hospital bed in the middle of the breakfast-room."

Then turning to me, he said, "I've arranged for the lady to deliver a shopping list here each Friday and for you to get some things for them on Saturday morning from the Grove Lane shops…It's not far."

I wasn't at all pleased, thinking, "Huh! What if I don't want to? What if I've got other things to do?"

But I couldn't wriggle out of it. Next Saturday found me, shopping list in hand, walking the five hundred yards to the small parade of Grove Lane shops. This short journey meant that I had to pass the swimming pool. As I walked along, I thought, "I must ask Kay if she'd like to go swimming? "

In the meantime I was committed to the weekly shopping trip. When I returned with the groceries I would knock on the heavy front door and a small portcullis type grill was drawn back, revealing a small window, so that I could be identified. The door was opened, and I went in with my carrier bag. They always asked me in for an orange squash, and a chocolate finger or two, my favourite. As I ate, they talked and our relationship developed. I discovered that the lady was called Miss Borges and her Auntie was Mrs. Shilling. They were Austrian Jews who had fled to England with Auntie's husband just before the war had started. He had been a doctor but sadly died, leaving the two lonely ladies living together in England.

With a hankering for the old pre-war days, Miss Borges and Mrs. Shilling talked of Austria with much fondness and as an idyllic place in which to have lived. Through their stories they transported me into a dreamlike world. They told me romantic stories about Princess Eugenie's balls and parties as though they'd been frequent guests. It all seemed very incongruous to their present surroundings, with Auntie sitting in the hospital bed with its iron bedstead in the middle of the breakfast-room and Miss Borges, looking as though she had been dragged through the hedge backwards, her ample bosom hanging loose, and, in my opinion, lacking the support of a much-needed bra. Nonetheless, the room was filled with what even I could see were valuable antiques. My favourite was an unbelievably lifelike porcelain duck and drake. I was often transfixed by its beauty as I sat next to Auntie's hospital iron bedstead, sipping my orange squash from a delicately cut glass. I would start saying my goodbyes when I thought that it was a polite time to leave the Austrian fantasy world.

After my chores for the neighbours I was free to spend Saturday as I wanted and one day I said to Kay,

"How about going swimming on Saturday afternoons?"

"Yes, let's give it a try," she said enthusiastically.

We equipped ourselves with swimming costumes and towels and headed to the baths. We paid to go in and headed to the female changing rooms, which were upstairs in a gallery running along above the pool. As I climbed up the metal staircase, I became aware of a strong smell of chlorine and the echoes from the cold white floor tiles sounded strange. Once changed, we made our way down the stairs to the water, coming out alongside the deep end. By the pool sat two middle-aged, female lifeguards concentrating on their knitting. They took little notice of what was going on in the water, and as I walked past the life-guards en-route to the shallow end, Paula Jones, a nasty girl from primary school, was standing, hands behind her back, propped up against the wall. As I started past her, she moved her leg and pushed me into the deep water. I came back up and went under again and then a man swam over, took hold of my hand and pulled me to the side. I climbed up the ladder and took my injured pride past Paula as she laughed. With all the dignity I could muster, I walked to the shallow end, climbed down the steps and joined Kay. Looking at my bedraggled state, Kay laughed and said, "Paula's just jealous because she's failed her Eleven plus."

Feeling reassured by Kay's explanation, we messed about in the water happily. But it wouldn't do: somehow, I'd got to learn to swim.

I was lucky because the minister's children had come home on holidays from their boarding schools and were also at a loose end. There was a daughter of about my age and brother called Nigel and he was two years older than me. They didn't have friends in the area. Nigel was pleased at being asked to take over as my swimming coach. However his initial approach was rather unorthodox. Nigel waited for me to come down the steps from the changing rooms. Then he said, "You climb up to the top diving board!"

He followed me blocking my escape, and said, "Go on, I'll stand here till you jump."

I was impressed with Nigel. I thought him to be tall, dark and handsome, and authoritative. Consequently I couldn't lose face, and a queue was beginning to form. There was nothing else for it. I jumped into the water off the top board and into the deep end.

"Weeeee!" I called out, as I went through the air.

Then *splash*, as I hit the water and into the uncanny subterranean world, until I naturally rose to the surface with adrenalin coursing through my veins. As I started to sink again, Nigel jumped.

After he'd surfaced, he grabbed the costume of my now sinking body, towing me to the side. Then he grabbed my hand, putting it on to the steps leading out of the deep end. I climbed out and we repeated the performances over and over again until gradually, oh so gradually, I was began to learn how to swim. Unfortunately, before the end of the holidays Nigel went off to stay with his friend, before going back to his boarding school, leaving me feeling sad and bored. Until we were back at school too.

Then one Friday on the bus home, we were chatting about what to do.

Kay said, "How about going skating? We could catch the bus to the ice-rink."

My response was immediate, "That would be fabulous."

So Saturday mornings Kay and I were to be found at the Number 16 bus stop waiting for the bus to the ice-rink and skating became a regular appointment. We skated as fast as we could and learned to shrug-off the inevitable bruises; our speed was usually greater than our skill. One Saturday, skating-boots tied nonchalantly around our necks, we went to catch the Number 32 bus home from the rink to Hinstock Road. Approaching our stop opposite the swimming baths, Kay and I stood on the platform, unnoticed by the conductor. As the driver started to pick up speed to climb the hill, "Jump," I called to Kay.

Simultaneously we both jumped, falling over and lying like two skittles on the pavement, ice skates still attached to our necks. The bus stopped. The black bus conductor walked back and stood over us. He was very cross.

"You never do dat agin, on mi bus," he instructed.

"We rang the bell, and you ignored us," I retorted indignantly.

It was no use, he was already back on his bus.

Growing up in Birmingham in the Fifties, I had been totally surrounded by white faces and had hardly ever seen a black-faced person, and yet West Indian migration to England had started in the year I was born. It was then that the boat, The Windrush, left Bermuda, setting sail for Tilbury. The cost of the crossing was £12. The Caribbean people had been living in extreme poverty. America had shut its doors and so England seemed an attractive alternative to escape the ravages of their economic situation. The West Midlands' engineering businesses were calling for more labour and the Government began offering assisted passages. Staff shortages on the buses drove London transport into opening a recruitment centre in Jamaica. Or, as Lenny Henry declared later on, "Nowadays people are travelling for their holidays to the West Indies. Whereas my parents, facing financial hardship, said, I know, shall we go to Dudley?"

It is difficult to imagine the dislocation Lenny' s parents must have felt on arrival in England in the cold foggy days, lost, lonely and facing racial prejudice.

As we travelled on the Outer-circle bus route taking us to and from the school I remember that we passed signs on boarding houses proclaiming, "Room to let. No blacks." Perhaps it was easier for that first generation because they had nothing to lose and were determined to succeed. For me, growing up in our post-war, middle-class, white family life was anything but tough. And of course we were not subject to racial prejudice.

Summer holidays were spent indulging our youthful pursuits. One day Kay suggested a new adventure,

"There's a great outdoor lido in Droitwich. It's about 25 miles, do you think we could make it there and back on our bikes?"

It sounded fun, although Kay was, by now, over two inches taller than I was, so she had a much larger bike. Mine was a 14-inch frame with four gears; Kay' s was a 16-inch racing bike with seven gears.

I said, "I'm game, if you are."

We studied the map and agreed we'd give it a try. The next morning we set off cycling three miles into the centre of Birmingham to our first arranged rendezvous, Lyon' s city centre coffee house in Colmore Road, Birmingham.

We propped our bikes up outside and walked into the café.

Kay ordered, "Two cups of tea please."

Behind the counter stood two ladies, one of whom was holding a gigantic, aluminium teapot. She started pouring tea into a row of cups on a tray which the other lady had just delivered to her.

"E kep arskin," she said to her colleague with a shrug.

Not looking at us, she put two cups full of mahogany fluid onto Kay's tray.

"Two'n tuppence," she said.

Kay handed over the money whilst I was stirring three teaspoons of sugar into each cup.

We carried the tea over to a table and studied our route as we drank our syrupy sweet tea.

"What was she saying?" I asked.

"I haven't a clue, but come on we've got to work out where we're going."

Refreshed by the stewed tea, we set off on the Hagley road, then on to the A38. Finding the swimming pool easily and the weather warm, we had a great time playing about for three hours.

But cycling the 25 miles home with only a packet of Spangles for sustenance, I was exhausted. I started to cry silently, as I followed Kay's bike, my eyes anxiously glued to her disappearing back wheel. Was it that I was already suffering from the debilitating effects of Lupus, which diminished my stamina, or possibly my smaller vehicle? Whichever it was, when I arrived home I felt absolutely drained.

"You shouldn't have gone swimming while it's weeping," Mum said.

"I had a plaster over it," I replied defensively.

I'd had TB vaccination at school just before we had broken up for our summer holidays. Now it had gone septic. We had been told to keep the wound dry until it healed but my interests lay elsewhere and I had just forgotten that the injection site was still weeping. "Anyway, chlorinated water couldn't do it any harm, could it?" I thought. However the vaccination site became well and truly septic. It was only the size of a ping-pong ball, but it smelt like rotten eggs. I was put on antibiotics and the swimming baths were banned until my wound was totally healed. Was this complication another early sign of my Lupus?

"I'm bored. What can I do?" I whined to Mum.

"I'll ring Auntie Kath and see what Angela's doing," Mum was fed up with my moaning.

Their telephone conservation ended with, "Yes you drive round here with Angela, then we'll go together."

I beamed with success. An embargo had been put on my meeting Angela, since Auntie Kath and Uncle Bill had taken us to a Point to Point race meeting. When I got home I'd bragged about my winnings. Good Methodists do not gamble and Mum and Dad reacted as though I'd supped with the devil himself. As a consequence they had put a stop to all contact with them.

I was glad that my whinging had weakened Mum's resolution, as Auntie Kath was fun. She was a tall, sporty type and the shorter Uncle Bill had previously been our close friend from church. In fact we were not related but as was common in those days we called them Uncle and Aunt as a matter of courtesy. The alternative was to call them Mr and Mrs but this seemed too formal for such a nice family. Their daughter, Angela, was the same age as me. Blonde, tight curly hair and eyes with the brightness of the super fit, she was a very keen and able tennis player. Though we had a grass court in the garden, tennis wasn't suggested, and instead Angela and I soaped the red oilcloth floor in the kitchen to make an exciting slide, we had great fun until Mum arrived home. She was furious,

"It will take Mrs. Giles hours to get the red back into that floor."

Again, Angela and I were not allowed to play together. Whatever we did was never acceptable to Methodist teaching, and the subsequent embargo was a long one.

Dad did what he could to help out and alleviate the boredom that I regularly claimed as an affliction. Wednesday was his half-day and he had started playing golf in the afternoon at the Belfry. During my holidays he took me along to get me out of the house and from under Mum's feet. Both he and his golf partner demonstrated great patience with me whilst I hacked my way round the course, using a half set of cut down clubs.

I was growing up, and I often reminisced about the years when Dad took me and Bid to New Street station to go on our Easter holidays. We travelled first class and Dad would instruct the smart, blue suited guard to ensure that we changed trains at Crewe. It felt as though we were the wartime evacuees that I had seen on the documentaries about the war. I was seven when this first occurred and I can remember sitting on the train clutching my new copy of Enid Blyton's Secret Seven, waiting for our arrival into Crewe. When we arrived the guard said, "Have you got all your possessions with you?" and with that the porter carried our bags and supervised us until we were safely aboard the train for Rhyl. The excitement of the train journey with the compartment door closed, and the scenery passing by. The clickety-clack of the train building up speed and the anticipation of simple pleasures for us to share.

As the train drew into Rhyl station the small, neat figure of Aunt Mary would be waiting, waving and smiling. She usually wore a brown felt hat and brown woollen coat, with highly polished black-laced shoes. Aunt Mary was actually our Great-Aunt Mary and had been widowed in the First World War, before she'd had children. Then we waited for the bus, it would be a bus ride to the home she shared with her older sister, Sarah, in Llysfaen. Their mother had died in early life leaving Aunt Sarah as a teenager, and caring for her father, three brothers and two sisters. When the rest of the family moved on it left the two sisters alone in Huddersfield so they decided to leave Yorkshire and run a boarding house in Rhyl. Eventually, they retired and moved to a smaller property in nearby Llysfaen. Their semi-detached house had been built towards the end of the 19ᵗʰ century, and one hundred yards down the hill was a row of shops, which in those days was the shopping centre for the village. For several years I stayed for a week during my Easter holidays.

Aunt Sarah was a great cook and produced some wonderful meals for us.

Aunt Mary was more of an outdoor type, and we shared the delights of nature walks together, collecting primroses and cowslips.

"Are the primroses ready yet?" I'd ask in anticipation.

"I haven't seen them, but the lambs are in the field, so that's a good sign. We'll check them tomorrow," Aunt Mary would reply kindly.

The Aunts were Baptist, and the time that Aunt Sarah fractured her hip I was amused to see a brandy bottle being decanted into a medicine bottle for her to surreptitiously drink to ease her pain.

They were a stoic pair, accepting what life had in store for them. For us they provided many happy memories.

CHAPTER 4

TEENAGE YEARS

I was fourteen going on fifteen, with the simple pleasures of childhood behind me but the fun of adolescent life ahead.

Kay asked, "Mi mum goes Old Time dancing, shall we go too?"

With no hesitation I replied, "Yeah, that would be jolly good."

Weekly trips to the dancing studio were added to the social calendar. Both Kay and I were enthusiastic novices. After just a few weeks we were thoroughly prepared, due to the instruction of Mrs Rafferty, for Modern as well as Old-Time ballroom dancing. Being the shorter of the two of us was to my advantage. Kay had to take the male part and I the lady's; that was to cause Kay problems at real dances in the future. Mrs. Rafferty was a lady of ample proportions. Taking hold of me to demonstrate where we were going wrong, she'd cry out, "Oh fer sure, you got tree left feet, between the both of ye!"

"Dat's de way we do it!" With her gigantic bosoms crashing into my adolescent frame.

"Well, we might not have much idea, but at least we can get close to each other." I whispered.

Kay giggled. Mrs Rafferty looked sternly at us and we looked as though butter wouldn't melt in our mouths. A look perfected at school, which probably didn't convince Mrs Rafferty any more than our school mistresses.

Anyway we had a great time and Kay's Mum, Nora, was great fun to be with and she remained that way all her life. When she was in her eighties and living in a sheltered housing complex, she went with group of the residents on holiday to Majorca. Nora was demonstrating some dancing techniques on a table and fell off breaking her hip.

I spent many afternoons in the School holidays at Kay' s, laughing a lot and testing out the feeling of being grown-up. We pilfered her sister Ann's, make-up. Our faces garishly coloured and giggling, with eyelashes plastered so thickly they looked like massive spiders. Ann also had a good supply of nail-varnish but that was no use to me, still with nails bitten down to the quick. We continued to experiment with adult things. We cycled to a pub where Kay drank a half pint of lager and lime, and I opted for cider. There were plenty of options in those days for two fourteen year-olds to avoid compliance with the drinking laws. Life for us could be daring and exciting.

School made the dreadful mistake of putting us both in the same class and was simply an extension of opportunities for amusement to us. We arrived at school each morning, full of enthusiasm and giggling. Any idea that we might be there to work passed us by.

Miss Nottman struggled to teach me German.

"Sprechen sie Deutsch?"

I replied,"Wert Ich zink zo."

Miss Nottman sighed and turned to the blackboard to write the correct response. She must have just been to the lav as her gray pleated skirt was caught up in her white cotton knickers. We fell about in paroxysms of laughter at the sight of her bloomers. She turned to face us, then back to the board and the laughing started again. Nobody explained but eventually our diaphragms ached and we went quiet.

How she managed to avoid having a nervous breakdown must be attributable to her strong German character!

I really should have been encouraged to take my learning of German more seriously following the family holiday that summer. We travelled to Igles, via Innsbruck, and stayed in this beautiful winter skiing resort. Even in winter, skiers were able to relax in the warm pool. During the summer we lay on benches, enjoying the sunshine. It was here that the peace was suddenly shattered by a woman's screams. Four, or so, macho young men dived in to save her. Her screams intensified, "My husband is under the water," she managed to gasp.

They clearly had no understanding of English. I went to the poolside, "Es ist der Heren unter vasser," I shouted as loud as possible.

My knowledge of German was sufficient for them to comprehend. They left the lady and started diving under the water, retrieving the husband's body. It was too late, he was dead. I watched in horror and shock as two young men carried the body out of the water and laid him beside the pool.

The rest of our holiday was rather over shadowed by this tragedy. It transpired that the pair were on their honeymoon, and we were the only other English in the hotel. In the Fifties most holiday companies were not set up for such eventualities and as we were travelling with Thomas Cook, Dad contacted them to arrange help. Again Mum treated me like a complete nuisance, and I was left trying to deal with the shock of the experience and having disturbed sleep. Sadly, the experience didn't engender in me the awareness that foreign languages could be of great value.

When I returned to school, I treated language studies as even more of an opportunity for comedy relief. This was much to the frustration of the French mistress, the more she struggled to perfect my French accent, the harder I tried with a Black Country accented response.

She wrote the number 3 on the blackboard and asked, "Combien des centimes avez vous?"

"Truzz"

"Annie, the answer is trois"

"Tats's wat Oi said Miss," feigning the accent.

This was much to the amusement of my classmates, but to the annoyance of the French mistress.

Whilst speaking foreign languages was an entertainment, maths was a very different matter. I was terrified of Miss Gauley, the maths Mistress. She was a severe, tall lady with long grey hair plaited and coiled up, secured by grips to the back of her head to look like two "ear-phones." I worked hard at maths.

The school was of traditional design for a grammar school, set out in two quadrangles and windows all around the corridors. Miss Gauley's room was directly opposite the French classroom. If there was a noise in the French lesson, even if I was innocent, which was rare, I was dismissed to stand in the corridor. If I saw Miss Gauley's classroom door beginning to open and her coming out of her office (I'd have been mortified if she knew I'd been misbehaving), I'd crawl around the quadrangle, making sure she didn't see me. Despite French O' level being compulsory I was not allowed to sit the French paper. I suppose that they didn't want to waste the exam entrance fee. I passed maths.

Bid and John on the other hand, acted much more seriously than me, applying themselves to academic pursuits with alacrity. John was put in the express class. In addition he involved himself with scouting and photography, making his bedroom into a dark room for processing films. Inevitably, though uninvited, he was aided by me whenever I could creep into his room.

Bid had been taking maths and physics with chemistry, but for pharmacy she also needed biology. She had to stay on an extra year at school to do it and, as many of her friends had left the previous year, she was lonely and generally irritable.

Bid and Mum argued continuously. One day something had happened at school and, returning home, Bid was furious. Bang went the door as she crashed in.

"That bloody school, d'y know what they've done now?"

Mum said indignantly, "You shouldn't use the word bloody, bloody is swearing."

"Well, you've used it twice, so there!"

She went out and, "Bang!" went the door, showering plaster from the lintel. She stomped off up stairs.

Realising that both Bid and John would be leaving me for university within a year of each other, I began my campaign for a dog for company.

"Any dog would do," I begged.

Then I noticed a *Birmingham Evening Mail* advertisement: 'For Sale, Gun-shy Golden Retriever would suit inner-city home'.

Then my pleading started, "Please, can we have it, Dad pleeease?"

After suffering my pleading for several hours Dad phoned the number. "Come and see him," the lady said.

So, one Saturday afternoon in April, Mum, Dad and me arrived at Miss Evans' deep in the Leicestershire countryside. As the car approached the kennels, we could hear dogs barking. The owners of the kennels were two slightly eccentric sisters, clad in Wellington boots and dressed with no thought for fashion, they opened the gate to reveal about ten Golden Retrievers. Both sisters led us to a kennel where there was the young male dog on his own.

"He is a lovely dog, but terrified of guns," one said.

The other Miss Evans was opening the kennel to an enthusiastic retriever who rushed out to greet us. I was captivated. Her sister explained, "You see, our business is to breed and train gundogs for local shoots. It is very sad when a dog with such a nature panics at the sound of guns."

Dad said, "We live near a park, but it is in the centre of Birmingham. So there's no fear of him having to suffer gun fire there."

Everyone was smiling; I couldn't quite believe my eyes, or ears. It seemed that somehow the decision had already been made and we were to own a beautiful Golden Retriever. Dad went off with the vocal Miss Evans.

She said to her sister, "You collect a bed and a lead, and I'll get the vaccination certificate and information on feeding."

The quiet Miss Evans returned with the lead, put it around his neck and handed it to me. A feeling of joy overwhelmed me, my dreams had come true. Dad emerged with the paperwork and a bag of dog food. We set off home, leaving the two Misses Evans looking quite sad. As we started home, Mum suddenly declared,

"Sandy!"

So Sandy was his name.

I woke early next morning. Had it been a dream? I jumped up and went into the breakfast-room. There was Sandy on his bed. I hugged him tight, falling in love with him forever. Now I wouldn't be alone, I'd have a soul mate to hug and sob the tears of adolescent anxiety into his ever-patient fur. He always responded with a comforting licking, as though he fully understood exactly what I was going through, in whatever was my current state of despair.

Bid was accepted to read pharmacy by the University of Nottingham. I missed her terribly, particularly as she always had time to tell me stories. One of them, the elephant and the chip, was an ongoing saga that had lasted for years. But having Sandy as a companion was a tremendous compensation. A decision was taken that, before leaving for Nottingham, she was to come on holiday with us for the last time. "We'll head north instead of south and go to Scotland," Dad announced.

It was the summer of 1961 and the Portuguese had

invaded the Cornish coast in the form of Portuguese Man o'
War. The winds had been in such a direction that a plethora
of jellyfish was washed up on the Cornish beaches. I had
seen a few the year before and they had appeared to me as
iridescent Cornish pasties, with long stinging tentacles trailing
below them in the sea. We hadn't so much been put off by
this but rather we'd all had enough of the twelve-hour
journeys to Cornwall. After taking Sandy for his holiday to
the Misses Evans, we took the road north, making Manchester
for lunch, Penrith for tea, and eventually arriving at Oban.

Of course, the journey to Scotland was also tedious and
we didn't save on holiday journey time. In addition, I was
bitten by some very ferocious mosquitoes and my legs were
swollen, itchy and painful.

"They have powerful insects in Scotland," I complained.

"It's always you who's in trouble on holidays," Mum
retorted unsympathetically.

I wasn't sorry to get back home, particularly as it was
wonderful to get back and collect Sandy.

The next year John was accepted to read Medicine at
Edinburgh. How I'd miss his gentle companionship. By now
I'd joined the Church Choir and my position as a first soprano,
standing next to a small, petite blonde, pretty girl called
Hilary Jones.

She asked wistfully, "How's your brother getting on?"

I shrugged my shoulders and responded, "He's alright, I
suppose."

But I was thinking, "Why does she want to know? She's
going out with Mr Goodacre's son."

It was a mystery that was solved in due course.

I awoke one morning some seven months later, thinking,
"Oh no, it's Sunday again." It was after a brilliant Saturday
night at the Plaza with Kay. We'd been frantically doing the
twist to the likes of Chubby Checker records. Now it was
early morning communion at 8am. I couldn't make it. So
instead I had breakfast, already feeling guilty about missing

the first service, I put my collection in my pocket, and shouted, "Goodbye, see you later."

I headed for the Church, going in through the vestry door.

I was met by a melee of people chatting while they donned their choral gowns. Hilary smiled warmly. Mr Wright raised his eyebrows in his permanently severe face, the others all turned to look at me. It was if they'd known I was dancing last night and inevitably guilt was written all over my face.

I thought, "Huh, what a sanctimonious selection of humanity", but meekly put on my chorister's gown and obediently practiced my scales, attempting to reach the top 'C' for the anthem. This was to be Jonathan Rutter' s setting of the 23rd psalm and I hoped the communal singing of John Wesley' s hymns wouldn't be too loud and raucous for my delicate senses.

Lent arrived and I struggled to find a pleasure to forego. Gone were the days when I gave up chocolate and sweets for Lent so I decided to give up biting my nails!

We filed into church for morning service. I had the good fortune to miss out on the sermon, as I had to leave to teach the Sunday School. But at evening service at 6pm there was no escape from it and I felt Mr Goodacre's message was aimed at me personally, "The value of Lent is in abstinence." We reflect on what God has given up for us and it strengthens the weakness in our character."

He could have said it all in two minutes and he took half an hour!

I slunk out after the service, heading for the youth club.

"What have you given up for Lent, Louise?" asked Rick.

"Nothing," Louise replied.

They were friends. I felt grateful for Louise's response, but noted that Rick didn't feel the need to ask me. "They all know that Mr Goodacre was addressing his sermon at me", I thought.

103

Changing the subject Rick turned to me, "We're going to Guernsey for our holidays in the summer, have you been there?"

With surprise, I responded, "Funnily enough, we're going there too, my Dad is fed-up with driving long distances so we're flying from Birmingham Airport."

The holiday in Guernsey nearly didn't happen. Mum discovered a lump in her breast two weeks before we were due to fly to the Channel Isles. Grandma had died of breast cancer. Mum wouldn't confide in me, but she must have asked herself, "Is history repeating itself?" What a tremendous relief when the growth was removed and it was benign.

However we were delayed and too late, the flight had gone. So Dad arranged for George, his driver, to take us to Southampton to catch the ferry to Guernsey instead (George was really Dad's chauffeur but with the Co-op being a socialist organisation, chauffeurs were called drivers). When we sailed into St Peterport a car was waiting to drive us to the Chalet Hotel in Fermaine Bay.

It was well named, just like a Swiss chalet, except that it was set on a hill, isolated and a hundred yards above the beach, just what Mum needed for her recuperation. There was a large terrace with a view of the bay, perfect for a leisurely read with a good book. The chef was French and the food a great improvement on the early Sixties British hotels of our previous holidays. It was very peaceful but I was bored and missed the companionship of Bid and John.

"There's nothing to do," was my frequent complaint.

Despite this, I satisfied myself with trying to obtain a tan by lying daily on a wooden beach bench in my bikini, whilst Mum lay next to me recuperating. Dad spent the daytime wearing his normal holiday gear. This involved a short-sleeved shirt, knee length shorts, sandals and socks pulled up to his knees, leaving his bony kneecaps on display. His apparel was probably based on his Major's uniform that he wore during his wartime in the Middle East. Dad was able to change into his swimming costume in changing rooms at Fermaine Bay and join me in the sea for a swim and play with me on the wooden raft that he had hired. Mum had, and never would, learnt to swim, but surprisingly she did trust us enough for us to take her out to sea on the raft on a few occasions.

Nevertheless, I felt mainly bored and fed up. I must have made this abundantly clear to my parents with frequent complaints of, "I'm bored!"

At the end of holiday, Mum presented me with "The power of positive thinking for young people", written by Norman Vincent Peale. I read, "Perhaps you have an older brother, who is a brilliant student and you never hear the last of it. So you believe you can never succeed …then fill your mind with overflowing faith. Develop a tremendous faith in God…Acquiring faith is accomplished by lots of prayer."

I devoured the book and the brainwashing techniques began. I was re-energised when we eventually caught the plane from Guernsey Airport. We arrived just an hour later at Birmingham Airport, and I was very anxious to be re-united with Sandy.

John had been at home, looking after him.

"Has Sandy missed me?" I asked.

"No, not really, he's had lots of long walks, and I'm now calling him Fang, because I feel silly shouting out Sandy," said John.

"Well I'm not calling him fang and, by the way, I know, you've started going out with Hilary Jones, haven't you?"

"Yes, I have, as a matter of fact. How did you know?"

"It's obvious; she kept asking how you were getting on in Edinburgh, in a soppy way. She's lovely and I think you're better than her previous boyfriend, anyway."

When planning the next summer holiday, Dad said, "Shall we go to Guernsey again next year?"

"I was bored to death there," I said, engaging my mouth before my brain.

Dad continued without reacting, "I wonder if Kay would like to come next year, and we'll stay in St Peter Port, where there's more for youngsters to do."

"Dad, that would be superb!"

Then he said, "I' ll have a word with her mother, and in the meantime young lady, you'd better work out which A levels you'll be doing, and apply yourself to your books."

"I'm not going to do 'A levels'," I said.

"You'll be staying on in the 6th form and working out what you're going to do with the rest of

your life." he said decisively.

"I'll stay at school for the rest of my life!" I said, and stomped out of the room.

When the holidays were over, and we were back on the bus to school,

I turned to Kay, asking, "Kay, what are you going to do next year?"

"That's easy, I'm going to the School of Domestic Arts to do a catering course, I shall be applying for a place now I've decided that's what I want to do. What are you going to do?"

"I dunno, Dad says I've got to stay at school until I've decided."

Life resumed as normal, with study regularly interrupted by the rock and roll dances at the Church youth club. Dancing with Kay, we put in plenty of practice. One Sunday evening Louise, a friend from the year below me at school, came with her friend Rick. He just stood and stared at me as we danced. Rick was unnerving.

But the school year continued in much the same vein as always, though Kay applied and was awarded a place at the College. The tedious business of O level examinations had hardly started, when early one evening the telephone rang. Dad went into the hall to answer it. He came back into the sitting- room. He was looking shocked and slumped heavily into his armchair.

He said, "Your grandmother died rather suddenly early today. The funeral has already been arranged."

Mum came back from the kitchen and, with her usual sarcastic style, knowing the right words, at the right time said,

"Grandad didn't waste much time, did he?"

Used to it, Dad went on, "It's in Huddersfield crematorium, of course."

The choice of venue was inevitable because Grandad was a confirmed atheist. When he was Mayor of Huddersfield he'd been responsible for ensuring that the crematorium was built.

Dad said to me later, "You're Grandmother's funeral is on Wednesday afternoon at 2pm. You can't go, of course."

Although I wasn't close to my grandmother, and her broad Yorkshire accent meant I couldn't understand anything she said, I felt that I should be there.

"I want to go," I asserted to Mum.

She replied, "You can't go, it's your English literature paper that day…you are not making that an excuse not to sit the exam."

She had decided, there was to be no further discussion. The exam started at the same time as the funeral. I stared at the paper. It was half past two when I took up my pen to start. My thoughts were in Huddersfield. Then I started writing. It was my best subject but I failed.

John had come down from Edinburgh to the funeral, and afterwards he said to Mum and Dad, "I've asked Hilary Jones to marry me. She has said yes."

Mum said, "You've spoiled the happiest day of my life."

No further comment was made, but Mum arrived back from the funeral in a very angry mood. Dad looked resigned.

I was wondering what had happened and asked Dad.

He explained, "Mum is cross because John has asked Hilary to marry him."

"That's really good news," I said enthusiastically.

"Anyway, how did your English exam go?" Dad asked changing the subject.

I was embarrassed but answered, "I couldn't concentrate."

Mum, entering the breakfast room, was quick to respond,

"Don't go using the funeral as an excuse for not having done your revision."

I just kept quiet, not knowing what to say. I thought that I was well prepared and I'd enjoyed the syllabus, so I couldn't understand why I couldn't start answering the questions until l thought that the funeral service was over. How could I find the words to explain my feelings of sadness and confusion? No one seemed to understand, that is, apart from Sandy. I knew that at least he understood! I'd told him all about it as soon as I came home, and we went for a walk in the park, which we both enjoyed.

The exams were over, and there was a holiday in Guernsey with Kay to look forward to.

Then Dad dropped the bombshell, he said,

"We'll ask Grandad and Auntie Mary to come to Guernsey with us, it'll be good for Grandad to have a break. You can share with Auntie Mary."

"But I was going to share my room with Kay!" I called out in indignation.

"I will discuss it with Kay's Mum."

As much as I'd enjoyed those springtimes with my Aunts, my heart sank into my boots at the thought of losing the holiday with Kay. Was my self-sacrifice going to have to be the inevitable result? The thought of the holiday with Kay had kept me going through my O levels, and I'd clung onto the anticipation of it, like a drowning man clinging onto driftwood.

Struggling to hide my disappointment, I said reluctantly,

"Yes, Dad, it would be lovely for Auntie Mary to come, but what about Kay?"

Dad talked it over with Nora and arrangements were made. I was to share a room with Auntie Mary and a room was found for Grandad in a hotel nearby. We'd still be staying in St Peter port.

Kay was to come two days later with her mother and sister, Ann, as they'd managed to get a later flight and accommodation in the same hotel as us. Kay and Nora were always full of fun, whereas Ann was rather taciturn.

Before Kay was due to arrive, I'd already got a start of two days with my tan. I dedicated myself to the task and I felt that I'd made a good start by the time they arrived. We had then become a group of eight and had lots of fun. Nora had a knack with Grandad, who'd always seemed so austere to me. He relaxed in Nora's company. One evening we all gathered together to discuss what we would do next day. A majority decision was taken that we'd all go to Sark.

"Well we want to go to the Fermaine beach," I said, speaking for Kay as well.

While the others queued for the boat to Sark, Kay and I waited for the Ferry to Fermaine.

Arriving on the beach, Kay and I concentrated on tanning ourselves throughout the day. We lay under the beating sun, simply turning over to cook the other side from time to time. We caught the last ferry back from Fermaine, meeting up with the Sark explorers in the early evening.

"Your back looks like raw-steak, doesn't it hurt?" Mum asked. Her voice giving away what she was thinking, "Annie's causing trouble as usual."

"Yes, it is very painful and I feel shivery and quite ill," I reluctantly admitted.

She raised her eyes to the ceiling and let out a sigh.

A summit meeting was held and it was decided, "It's hospital for you, my girl," Dad said.

Following discussion with the Hotel proprietors, a taxi was called. Mum packed a bag of things she thought I'd need. The taxi duly arrived, Dad picked up my bag and we climbed into the back of the red saloon car.

Dad said, "The casualty unit at the Princess Elizabeth hospital, please."

"Dear me! What's happened to you?" said the wizened taxi driver, his skin like a wrinkled prune.

"She's burnt all the skin off her back from lying too long in the sun," Dad said. Mum said nothing.

They shared a look in the car mirror, as though they were in mutual agreement about my stupidity.

I thought, "Well you can talk, you look as though your skin has been baked to the consistency of leather," I was feeling irritated.

The taxi driver was still talking, he said,

"I'll drive slowly, so as not to make it any worse."

To give him his due, he went carefully and dropped us at the casualty entrance of Princess Elizabeth Hospital.

We walked in, Dad carrying my bag. It was seven o'clock.

He said to me, "You have a seat. I'll check you in."

I sat down gingerly on a long plastic covered bench, leaning forward to avoid any pain from contact between the bench and the burns on my back.

After what seemed like an eternity, Dad came and sat next to me. We waited for what felt like forever, time seemed to have stopped, but the clock on the wall only said half past seven. Nothing seemed to be happening.

Eventually, a voice rang out, "Annie Armitage!"

Dad picked up my bag and, following the direction of the sound, we walked together through a doorway. There we were met by a pretty blonde nurse. A vision in white starch. With a swish, she drew back a screen revealing a small cubical containing a trolley covered by a white sheet and adorned with the standard grey plastic chair alongside.

Mum had stayed outside. In a voice which oozed

sympathy, the nurse said kindly, "You lie down, dear. The Doctor will be with you shortly."

I sighed, feeling quite depressed and low. I managed to manoeuvre myself, so that I lay on a trolley facedown, without causing too much pain. Dad sat down on the chair. The nurse left, and again we waited. Then there was a swish of screens, and the pretty vision in white starch returned with the Doctor, clutching a buff coloured cardboard folder.

The Doctor looked tired and exasperated, as he examined my back.

In a supercilious voice he asked, "Is the rest of your body just as burnt?"

I answered, "No, it's only my back that hurts, it's very sore."

I was trying to be brave. I felt pleased that he seemed to be relieved by my answer. I thought, "You can't be any more grateful than I that it's simply my back." But he was talking again, "Um, second degree burns, I think you'd better stay in until it starts to heal."

Turning to the nurse, he smiled as their eyes met, I thought "Ah! Is a romance in the air?"

"Can you clean it and dress it please, nurse?"

"Yes doctor," she said, returning his smile.

I felt like crying, but didn't, "You've brought this on yourself," my thoughts returning to my predicament.

Dad had a look of sadness as he turned to me and said, "Have a good night love, I'll phone tomorrow to see how you are."

Dad kissed me gently on the cheek and left.

It wasn't long before the nurse returned, "We'll pop you into a bed, then I'll clean your back, and put some dressings on your wounds."

She gently helped me off the trolley and, picking up my bag, led me into a side-room off the main ward.

Helping me into bed she said, "I'll only be a minute."

She was soon back, pushing a trolley covered by a green cotton towel.

111

"I will try to be as gentle as I can be, but I'm afraid it may hurt."

I kept biting my lip, determined not to cry. As the nurse wiped solution over my back, I marvelled at her tenderness. I watched as she dropped each used swab into a paper bag fastened onto the trolley with a large bulldog clip. She kept asking, "Are you alright, Annie?"

Then I'd have to stop biting my lip to answer, "Yes."

When she'd finished cleaning the burns, she put dressings on them.

Then she said, "I'm leaving you to rest for a short while, but I'll be back with a drink later on."

I thought, "Now my lip hurts as well as my back! Oh well! So much for a sun-tan"

Surprisingly, I managed to sleep well throughout the night. I was woken by another nurse. She was dark haired, but just as pretty and caring as the blond one had been on the previous evening.

She asked, perhaps rhetorically, "How are you?"

Then, without waiting for answer, "I'm going to take your temperature."

She put the thermometer under my tongue. Then having removed and read it said, "That's fine, I'll get you your breakfast now."

After two days of tender loving care by all the nurses, the Doctor came back with a dark haired nurse. He removed one of my dressings. It felt as though he'd torn my skin off. I bit my still sore lip even harder.

He then said, "That's alright, she can leave when you've taken the rest off,"

He smiled conspiratorially at the dark haired nurse.

I thought, "You cheeky flirt!" but as she tossed her head as they left, I could see she wasn't as impressed as the blonde nurse had been.

Pushing a trolley, the dark haired nurse came back. "I'll

112

try to hurt you as little as possible, but I'm afraid it will hurt, my dear."

The gentle sympathy for my predicament was so touching, that I cried.

She held my hand, saying softly,

"Tell me when you're ready for me to start, there's no hurry."

She was very careful as she removed the remaining dressings. When she'd finished, she asked,"Are you feeling alright?"

"Yes, thanks," I answered through my tears.

"You're father is coming to collect you in half an hour, just time for a cup of coffee, would you like one?" she smiled.

"Yes please," I replied, and smiled.

While I sipped the coffee, I wondered about the nurses. They seemed to move about their tasks with a gentle and graceful cheerfulness. It was as though they were totally at one with their tasks. I thought, "I've never felt that confident about anything I've ever done."

My thoughts were interrupted when Dad arrived to take me back to the hotel to resume the holiday.

I felt a bit delicate during the next week or so and, when we finally arrived home, I was the one without the suntan. I was so affected by the loving care that I was shown in hospital that I'd made a decision for my future.

"I'm going to train to be a nurse," I told John proudly when we arrived to home.

He was looking after Sandy. As usual his favourite retort was, "You'll have to stop biting your nails, they won't accept you with disgusting bitten nails,"

"We're going to sell the house and move to Shenstone," Dad announced when we arrived back from holiday.

I was indignant, "What am I gonna do?"

But there was no hope of insurrection. Dad had it all worked out.

"It'll be alright, Shenstone is on the railway line from Lichfield stopping at Erdington station. This house is far too big for the three of us. It's a lovely bungalow in Shenstone. I'll take you over so you can see for yourself."

We went. I didn't like it. I didn't want to move house, but there was already a "sold" sign outside. It was a fait accompli!

Of course, at a stage when you're about to lose the house that has been your home, you realize how much you've taken for granted and you start to look at things afresh. The beautiful magnolia tree in the front garden, the enormous back garden with its grass tennis court, the spare bedroom with its table tennis table. To lose all this to live in a small bungalow, it just didn't seem fair.

Kay started at the Catering College and I went back to school with Margaret.

"I'm going to do the pre-nursing course, what have you decided to do, Margaret?" I asked.

"I'm doing the pre-nursing course, too. But Dad is against me doing that, he says nursing will always be second rate to doctors and I'd be better off doing teacher training, so I've got to do two A levels as well."

Louise was on the bus.

"I'm not staying for the 6th form, after my 'O levels'. I'm going to Lucy Clayton's finishing school," she announced, rather arrogantly.

I couldn't quite see it really, Louise wasn't exactly pretty. Like me, she'd got bitten fingernails, and I'd equated finishing school with modelling and debutantes.

When we arrived at school the business of sorting out our subjects took over. Because of the failed English Literature paper, I couldn't look Miss Brown in the face, and she avoided me. I arranged to do the pre-nursing course with general studies. I was told to go to the Headmistress's study.

"Annie, Erdington Grammar School are pleased to offer you the role of a prefect."

"Thank you, Miss Hill," I gasped in astonishment.

As for me, school that year wasn't exactly arduous! I just suppose they just wanted to keep me out of mischief by giving me some responsibility to occupy my mind.

All too soon, I arrived home to a "house sold" sign and was told to put my belongings together into various boxes. Moving day arrived and I caught the bus to school. Dad explained to me, "It's quite simple, walk from school, into the centre of Erdington, and catch the train for Shenstone. Here's the ticket and a map of how to get to the bungalow from Shenstone Station."

It was really quite exciting, as I stood on the station, waiting for the train. It was only a five-mile train journey from Erdington to Shenstone Station. Then a five-minute walk to the bungalow. Dad opened the door and I walked in to tea and cakes laid out on the table in the conservatory.

I suppose I should have been happy with the situation, but I missed my life in Handsworth and it quickly seemed like a world away. I felt totally cut off and I missed the vibrancy of city life. Out of school, contact with friends was now only by phone. The village of Shenstone was dominated by a prominently positioned large Church of England, built on top of the hill. As I went down the hill, I passed large houses in their own ground, and then newer developments. Our bungalow, in Footherly Road, was one of these. There were hardly any people of my age. Even walking Sandy wasn't as easy. We'd lived just opposite the park in Handsworth, whereas Shenstone was surrounded by fields of sheep, and obviously dogs were not allowed to run free. Sandy and I felt fed up. I couldn't work out how to help Sandy, but I regularly read Norman Vincent Peale's *Power of Positive Thinking*. I was particularly struck by the statement, "A sense of inferiority and inadequacy interferes with the attainment of your hopes... whenever a negative thought concerning your personal powers comes to mind, deliberately voice a positive thought to cancel it out." I kept trying to work on my inferiority, and there wasn't much in the way of distraction in Shenstone. Whilst there was a small Methodist Chapel, it did not have a youth-club or a choir.

Most mornings, I went to school by car and Dad would drop me off before proceeding to work at Birmingham Cooperative Society. But on Thursdays George, Dad's driver, would arrive smartly dressed in his uniform so that he could take the car for valeting. If Dad was away, it was the Devil's own job persuading George not to go anywhere near to school. I'd die of embarrassment getting out of a chauffeur driven car.

"Please drop me here; there's no need to go out of your way past the school gates," I'd say.

After school, I'd usually dawdle into Erdington to catch the train, stopping at the grocers, "Could I have a hazelnut yogurt please."

Then, fashioning the lid into an impromptu spoon, I'd start eating it as I walked up the ramp to the station and often the train would be waiting. That meant that I'd have to run through the passenger arrivals and, taking hold of the door handle, I'd throw myself bodily into the departing train. Trying to keep the yogurt intact took all my concentration. Inevitably, I'd have to re-form my spoon and I would continue eating nonchalantly. The Great British train passengers just ignored me and looked elsewhere. Now I grow cold remembering the risks that I took. I can just imagine the headlines, *"Death of a school girl. Annie was dragged along by the 4:30 from Erdington station."*

At last! I'd reached my 17th birthday and driving lessons were on the agenda. Dad's driver, George, was now recruited to teach me to drive. I enjoyed these lessons, but when the examiner grabbed the hand brake and told me that I had failed, I was rather upset and felt incompetent once more. Everyone that I told about my failure seemed to have expected it.

Although driving had been the most important thing on

my agenda at the time, I turned my attention to an alternative, the Student Christian Movement. They visited the school on a recruiting mission for Voluntary Service Overseas and The Community Service Volunteers. A bearded man called Mr James spoke very enthusiastically about the opportunities offered by voluntary work. I felt committed and spoke to him afterwards.

"I really want to join up, but my Dad won't let me leave school," I complained.

"If you're seventeen, he can't stop you," he explained.

He gave me the application forms and left in the company of Miss Jones, the careers Mistress.

I was called to see Miss Jones the following week.

"Now Annie, have you made any decisions about your future and particularly VSO?"

Incredulously, I looked into her lined face and whiskery chin, as she stared intently at me.

I was thinking, "Could she really be that stupid, she knows I'm on the pre-nursing course and that I took the application forms for voluntary work." I defiantly met her gaze, "I want to be a nurse." I simply said.

"You'll need to be eighteen to enter nurse training. Do you intend to stay in the sixth form until then?"

"Heaven forbid", I thought, feeling increasingly irritated, but I said, "If I finish the first year, it'll be six months before I'm eighteen. I'd like to spend that doing Community Service Voluntary work. I have read the application form that Mr James left."

She didn't appear to be listening, and was rummaging in a drawer. She produced an application form, and thrust it at me, with an air of triumph.

I took it and read 'Queen Elizabeth Hospital, Birmingham, Application for Training. I was delighted and said, "Thank you." And left her office. I met Margaret in the sixth form common room.

"Are you really going to leave school next year?" she asked.

My response was immediate, "Yes, I have decided. The best thing for me to do is a fill in six months in community service and then start nurse training at the Birmingham Queen Elizabeth Hospital when I'm eighteen."

Margaret was sceptical, "Are you sure you are doing the right thing?" she asked.

"Yes," I said, decisively.

If my friend Margaret was unsure what would Mum and Dad say? I suspected that they would need some convincing.

I arrived home carrying the two application forms and was amazed by my parents' reaction. Perhaps Mum wanted to get rid of me? Showing no surprise, Dad helped me complete the applications.

"They both want two references," I said.

Dad said straight away, "Miss Hill the Headmistress, and try the Minister for the second. Have a word with him at Church on Sunday."

I felt wary, but was amazed when Dad seemed enthusiastic. I'd seen the Minister as grey, dull and very boring. "Oh, well", I thought," Nothing ventured, nothing gained."

Then the phone rang; it was Louise.

She said, "Rick has offered to drive me over to see you for an evening, in his Dad's car. Would you like that?"

"That would be great Louise, I'm dying of boredom here." I said.

The evening went well, as Louise and I chatted about our plans. Rick took part in the girly talk, but he did say that he was leaving King Edward's high school at the end of the year. He also said that he hoped to take an engineering degree at Oxford University; I thought rather arrogantly. I felt unnerved by him, and remembered that it was exactly like the time when he came to the youth club dance, and stared at me as I danced with Kay. I seldom saw Kay now that she was settled on her catering course, so our times together seemed a lifetime away

A few days later I arrived home from school, and Mum said, "There's an envelope addressed to you on the hall table."

Retracing my steps, I collected the buff coloured envelope. It was franked, *Queen Elizabeth School of nursing*. I felt a bit nauseas as I opened it and read, "Would the candidate, together with her mother, attend for interview at Priorsfield at two o'clock on Wednesday 24th. Map attached."

My nausea left me immediately and excitedly I rushed back into the conservatory to show it to Mum, asking,

"Can you come with me, Mum?"

"Yes of course," she said in a rather patronizing tone.

Then I thought, "That's strange. When Bid and John went for their interviews for university I am sure that they went on their own. Why would they want to see Mum, I wonder? I hope she doesn't put them off." Then my thoughts started to race.

"Oh that's great, I'll need the day off school!" I said.

Then added anxiously, "What shall I wear?"

"Your yellow lambs-wool twinset and plaid skirt," Mum replied without hesitation.

I thought, "How boring?" though I thought it was better not to say anything.

On the appointed day, both of us soberly attired, we climbed into her black Morris Minor and proceeded to the interview. We parked in the driveway of a large half-timbered house and walked into the entrance hall. It was grand, and I could imagine the debutantes and their mothers waiting patiently to be presented at Queen Charlotte's Ball. But back to reality. I felt quite sick as I saw a lady wearing a drab, grey uniform seeking names and directing us hopefuls into a waiting room. A badge on the uniform identified her as "Warden".

Mum gave our names and we went into the waiting room, taking the last two vacant hard, wooden chairs. The room was full of thirty or so prospective trainees and mothers. A nervous hush hung over the room.

Soon, two ladies wearing uniforms of dove-grey marched in and stood in front of us. The fidgeting stopped and everyone was giving these ladies their undivided attention. As they stood surveying us, I thought, "It might be dove-grey, but their manner doesn't suggest the dove of peace." I felt grateful for Mum's suggestion regarding my dress. I certainly didn't stand out alongside everyone else. One of the ladies moved forward. She looked as though she was held together by starch, her hair was tightly scraped back, leaving a gaunt face bereft of make-up. She almost spat out her introductory talk. "Welcome. I'm senior sister-tutor Briggs. My colleague here is sister-tutor Abbott."

She indicated the equally plain and glum tutor standing behind her.

"Good afternoon." Sister Abbott' s heavy jowls creased into an apology of a smile.

Sister Briggs continued, explaining about the Queen Elizabeth's nurse training. She finished by saying that the prospective nurses should follow sister Abbott, proceeding upstairs where they'd be interviewed individually. Meanwhile the mothers, should remain to be addressed by Sister Briggs.

We trooped up the wide, curved stairs to another sitting room. We were invited to sit down and wait our turn. Too nervous to speak, we awaited our turn. Eventually Sister Abbott appeared and called out my name. I followed her into a room where another formal and equally starched figure rose, hand extended. I noticed her vice-like grip as we shook hands. She was dressed in a uniform of a darker grey.

"Take a seat," She instructed, continuing with, "I'm Miss Dodwell, Principal of the nurse training school. Now, tell me why do you want to become a nurse?" Her piggy eyes seemed to bore straight into my soul.

"I've recently been in hospital and I want to give the tender loving care that I was shown there," I blurted out nervously. After a few more questions I was dismissed. I didn't feel very confident. I thought, "I must just keep my fingers crossed."

I found Mum waiting for me and without asking me how I had got on, we started for home. She wouldn't say what they'd been told while we were being interviewed, and I was glad when we got home. Surprisingly, it must have been satisfactory because I received an acceptance in the post during the following week.

The very next week, after my acceptance at the nurse training school, a letter came asking me to an interview in London with The Community Service Volunteers. It said,

"Miss Hoodless will be pleased to see you for an interview in her London office at 9:30am."

"I can't get to an interview in London at that time in the morning," I said to Mum.

"Of course you can, I'll phone Uncle Philip, I'm sure you can stay with him and Aunt Kath."

Uncle Philip and Aunt Kath were Mum's brother and sister-in-law, and they lived in London. It was all arranged; I stayed overnight and went on to my interview. I enjoyed the visit, and the week after arriving home from the interview, an envelope arrived, accepting me and outlining details of my placement at Blachington Court. It was a school for partially sighted boys in Seaford, Sussex.

Within a week, Aunt Kath had phoned to say that she had a very good friend living near Seaford, called Sadie. She had talked to Sadie, and I was to phone her when I arrived in Seaford. I was feeling pleased with myself as the last year at school drew to a close. I'd sorted my future out and was even awarded the sixth form prize for English.

I felt excited, a new beginning and a new adventure living away from home, The Community Service Volunteers for six months and then on to start my nurse training.

The remainder of the summer seemed tedious as I excitedly awaited my trip to Sussex. Dad drove Mum and me to Seaford in early September. We found the school, parked

121

and walked across the gravel path to the front door. I rang the bell push. Strangely enough, the building was very similar in size and layout to Priorsfield School of Nursing. I was musing on this when, after a few minutes, a middle-aged lady emerged from the doorway.

She said, "Good afternoon, I'm Barbara, the Headmaster's Secretary. Would you be Annie Armitage?" I confirmed this and she continued, "Would you like to follow me to meet Mr Pugh in his office? I'll make some tea and then show you to your room. Then you can unload her things from the car. The boys will be arriving tomorrow."

We trailed along a corridor until she knocked at a door, and, in response to a softly spoken command, "Enter."

The three of us went in. Mr. Pugh stood up, hand extended, "I'm the Headmaster, Mr Pugh Please take a seat."

We sat down, and he continued, without drawing breath, "Now, Annie will be paid thirty shillings a week. She needs to come to my office on Friday mornings to collect it. Annie, your day off will be on a Tuesday, with Thursday as a half day. Barbara will take her around and will show her to her room." He was delivering his monologue to Dad, without looking at me.

Barbara arrived with our tea and, as we drank it, the usual polite small talk about the quality of our journey ensued. Then the three of us followed Barbara around as she showed us all the rooms on the ground floor, including a modern single-storey extension of classrooms. The building seemed to be deserted. Then she climbed three flights of stairs to an attic bedroom. In her sensible flat shoes she mounted each staircase quickly. I arrived, gasping for breath. We were shown the bathroom and toilet then a tiny bedroom with a hand basin in the corner, which she indicated was to be mine. Mum sat on the bed getting her breath back whilst Dad and I collected my belongings from the car. After stowing them away in my bedroom descended to the car park together and said our good-byes.

As Mum and Dad drove away I had a sinking feeling. I walked back from the car park and took stock of the building. It was a large, nineteen-thirties, redbrick detached property, though solid it did have a slightly forbidding feel to it. I went and unpacked. Soon I heard the commotion of other people arriving, so I went down to the staffroom to see what was going on. The housemothers had started to gather and were chattering about their summer activities since they had last met. As I entered the room they went quiet and turned to stare at me. A tall, emaciated looking woman introduced herself, "I'm matron." she said and then introduced me to her five colleagues. All quite formal. I was overwhelmed by a foreboding feeling, "This is an unhappy place to fetch up in!" I thought when I settled down to sleep in my little attic room.

The next day, thirty partially sighted boys aged between 6 and seventeen years old arrived. Somehow they seemed sad. I was introduced to the lady I was to work with, Mrs Johnson. She was a kindly, middle-aged lady with a warm smile. For the first time I felt comfortable. Together we were to take care of the seven to nine year old boys after breakfast, during break times and at weekends. The teaching staff weren't residential and arrived daily. They undertook the supervisory duties of the older boys.

There was a wide range of intelligences and a variety of reasons for their partial sightedness. Some of the children were albino and others had such disorders as Cerebral Palsy or Downs Syndrome.

I soon settled into the routine. Tuesday came around and I decided to ring Aunt Kath's friend.

"Hello, Sadie here. How may I be of assistance?"

I explained.

"It would be superb to see you Annie and do call me Sadie. Now what are you doing on Thursdays?" Sadie asked.

"Its my half-day." I replied.

"That's ideal. I run a Cub pack on Thursday evenings.

Would you like to come for tea and then help me with the Cubs?"

Very soon I became a teacher of knots to the Cub pack.

On my first full day off I wandered into Seaford and bought a map of the area. In a nearby café sipping my espresso coffee, I studied the map. "I know, I'll go to Eastbourne." I found the bus stop and caught the Eastbourne bus. Setting off through the Cuckmere Valley, the scenery was enchanting. We reached Eastbourne and I got off the bus. Wandering along the high Street I spotted a café with 'The Bondolfi' boldly proclaimed above the door. It was lunchtime and hunger pangs were starting so I went in and chose Welsh rarebit. It was delicious. Despite the other clientele having an average age of about eighty, it was all very pleasant and friendly. I felt content and it wasn't the last time that I enjoyed Bondolfi's cuisine.

Arriving back in Seaford, I spotted an advertisement in the Post Office window, which read, "Driving lessons, 1 pound, Contact Mr. B. Reynolds, qualified driving instructor."

"Would I be able to afford it?" I wondered. But then on Saturday, a letter arrived from Dad with good wishes and a brown ten-shilling note. One came every week. That made my income two pounds a week. I rang to arrange a driving lesson. The next Tuesday Mr Reynolds drew up in his green Ford Anglia. He opened the passenger door and I climbed in. He drove away, saying," I'll just drive round the corner, then you can take over and we'll see how you get on."

I enjoyed the thrill of driving around Seaford. Back at the school he said,

"Pull up here and we'll exchange seats." I did as instructed.

Then he said, "Your driving is very positive, but have you read the Highway Code?"

"No, what's that?"

"It's the rules of the road. So before the next lesson I want you to buy a copy from the Post Office and study it. I'll expect you to be word perfect by your next lesson."

I did as I was instructed and found it very illuminating.

The most friendly of the masters, Mr Jones, heard about my driving lessons, said, "I've got a small plastic model of an engine, would you like to borrow it so you can see how an engine works?"

"Yes please," I said.

He went to fetch it and the system of pistons and cylinders made the complexity of a piston engine easy to understand.

The following evening there was a governors meeting which we were all expected to attend.

Mr Jones decided to introduce me to everyone saying, "Meet Anne our new recruit. She was at school at Rodene."

Then he moved on leaving me to bluff my way through the ensuing conversation.

"You really dropped me in it," I said when I caught up with him later.

"I knew you'd be able to cope," he grinned.

"The atmosphere is awful. What's wrong?" I asked.

"I thought you'd notice. The deputy head has been suspended on suspicion of interfering with the older boys. Everyone seems to blame themselves, thinking they should have been aware of what was going on." He looked sad.

A few weeks later I was woken by someone knocking at my door. I tried to sit up but couldn't lift my head from the pillow.

"Come in," I croaked.

The figure of matron was standing by my bed.

She started to say, "You are late..." but left the sentence unfinished and went out.

Then Miss Bradley her assistant arrived. She proceeded to place a jug of water and a glass on my locker. Producing a thermometer she said, "Put this under your tongue Annie."

The next two weeks went by in a blur. A doctor was called and he diagnosed 'Glandular Fever'. When I was judged fit enough to travel, Miss Bradley contacted my parents and packed my suitcase, pending the arrival of Mum and Dad.

Dad helped me down the three flights of stairs into the car and Miss Bradley carried my case. We drove home to Shenstone and I slept the entire journey.

There followed several weeks of rest and recuperation. I couldn't eat and I got so thin that I resembled a stick insect. Mum tried to encourage me with nutritious food but Christmas came and went and I was still quite poorly. It was time for me to return. I didn't want to go back. I just didn't feel well enough. But did Mum take pity on me? No, the prospect of my not returning was never mentioned and I was taken back to Blachington Court.

My life in Seaford resumed as before. I'm sure that the staff thought that I was malingering until they discovered that I still had a slight temperature and it was 99 degrees. I gradually recovered, though I was still very weak for several days after.

Eventually I re-started driving lessons. Mr Reynolds said, "You are nearly ready to take your test. As the test centre is in Eastbourne you'll need a double lesson to get enough experience of driving there."

"I'm afraid I'll have to miss a week as I can't afford to pay £2 in one week." So I had my awareness drive in Eastbourne and the date for my test was set for two weeks later.

The day of my driving test arrived and I drove Mr Reynolds to the test centre in Eastbourne.

The examiner took his seat beside me.

"Good luck," said Mr Reynolds. The examiner then gave me various instructions, including when he wanted me to perform an emergency braking. Off we went round the test route that he had selected. Back at the test centre I applied the brake, and turned off the engine to await his decision.

"Congratulations, you've passed your driving test," he said. I was delighted and relieved all at the same time. He filled in the certificate and I gratefully took it from his outstretched hand. Mr Reynolds returned to the car. "Well?"

he said. "I've passed, I've passed," I repeated,

"Well done, I can see you're pleased," he said.

"Yes! I feel so excited. Thank you so much for your help," I said.

"See, I said I could get you through! Do you want to drive or shall I?" he asked.

As I drove he chatted away, clearly feeling he'd finished his task. As we made our way along the dual carriageway I was truly conscious for the first time of the dramatic scenery. Climbing up over the heights of Beachy Head, and then as the land fell away to the cliffs down to the sea so far below; making a slight mistake with the wheel could be fatal. In spite of Mr. Reynolds talking I was aware, driving amid such scenery, of my sudden power and responsibility.

Eventually, the time for me to leave Seaford came. As I packed my case, I knocked the model of the engine off my dressing table. It broke. Why hadn't I given it back to Mr Jones? I couldn't face him to apologise. I simply left it behind without saying anything. I was left feeling guilty and was still feeling guilty and cowardly when Mum and Dad came to collect me. The greeting from Sandy was truly great and Mum said, "Someone called Rick has been on the phone for you. He wants you to ring him when you get home."

I wasn't sure what to do about that, but then again, I did feel lonely. "Don't suppose it will do any harm," I thought, as I unpacked, then considered the requirement for repacking and the next stage of my future.

127

CHAPTER 5

NURSE TRAINING

I bought some pink suede shoes for my eighteenth birthday. They had only an inch high heel, quite a departure from the white two inch stiletto shoes, which every girl teetered about on in the Sixties. So I packed my trunk, put on my new suede shoes and said to Mum, "I'm all packed up and ready to go."

I gave Sandy a tearful hug and we humped my large blue trunk, with my name boldly stenciled on it, into the car. From then on my trunk was in the hands of the porters and it was their responsibility to see that it was transported around the various accommodation that I was to occupy during my training. I was feeling very nervous, but proud and up to the minute in my new shoes. We climbed into Mum's black Morris Minor and drove away to begin my new life. I was clutching the directions as we headed for Edgbaston.

"Here's the road," I called out, a little too loudly.

"There's no need to shout! I'm not deaf!"

Mum' s voice showed distinct irritation as she turned at the Nurse Training School sign, and we returned to Priorsfield. This time the car park was busy with girls arriving. A short man wearing brown overalls was waiting with a trolley and, no sooner had Mum parked the car, than he had pushed the trolley alongside to await the contents of

128

the car's boot. Mum opened it and he manhandled my trunk onto the trolley. I'd turned to say goodbye but she simply said, "Good luck," and with that she drove away. I stood watching the departing car feeling desperately unwanted, until it disappeared between the trees. The porter pushed his trolley into the hallway. I trailed alongside trying to look nonchalant and cool.

It was chaos. Girls were milling around and a very stressed, plump, dark-haired lady, clad in a pink overall, was trying to sort them out. She had a dark damp patch showing under each armhole and a badge on her lapel identified her as 'Mrs Jackson - House keeper'. On the wall behind her was a large chart noting our names and room numbers. When it came to my turn, I stammered out my name, and Mrs Jackson directed me to my bedroom.

She said in a voice which didn't invite a response, "John will have delivered your trunks to your rooms, if they are clearly marked. If not you will have to wait until we sort it out later."

I went up the wide oak staircase leading up from the blue and white tiled hallway floor. As I climbed the stairs, my senses were assailed by an intoxicating aroma of furniture-polish and disinfectant.

Struggling for breath, I found my room, turned the large brass door handle and fell into a bright room with six beds in it. The sun streamed in through three large windows, with bright yellow curtains adding to the lightness. Three other girls were already unpacking.

I said, "Hello, my name' s Annie."

A Julie Andrews look alike stood up, arm extended and with a warm smile said in melodic tones, "Hi, I'm Eileen, this is Gill, and this is Sylvia."

Two girls broke off from what they were doing and we all shook hands, exchanging nervous smiles. The others were blonde, like me. Gill was about my height and both Sylvia and Eileen were tall. They all had kind, warm smiles and I immediately felt at home.

Sylvia said, "Hey, I like your shoes."

Gill said, "There's a kitchen downstairs, where we can do our own toast and drinks, Sue from one of the other beds told us."

Eileen explained, "The other two girls, Sue and Bonnie, have been her before and already done some of their training, they are out looking for any old friends that may be back."

I sat on my bed, admiring the view. Looking out through the trees, I could see another large house about fifty yards away. Gill noticed me looking. She said, "Sue pointed that out earlier and said that's another accommodation block for nurse training its called Southfield. I think they have gone over there to look for their friends." She went on, "Evidently it's like Priorsfield with another twenty student nurses. It's where we go for our food, lectures and training."

Sylvia said gently, "It's nearly half-past four. We are due in the sitting room for a meeting."

We all trooped downstairs to assemble in the sitting room, where the other new recruits were collecting together. Mrs Jackson was standing at the front of a semi-circle of easy chairs. Mrs Jackson introduced Miss Alan. She was a plump woman in a dull grey uniform and was peering at us sternly over her horn-rimmed spectacles. I recognized her as one of the tutors at my interview. Together they outlined the house rules and explained what would be covered during our eight week Preliminary Training. We were to wear yellow check dresses for our practical and ward experience. The ladies from the linen room would supply the check dresses when they came to measure us up for our first year nursing uniforms. We were to wear our own clothes (which someone referred to as Mufti, using the army slang for civilian clothes). Miss Alan's voice echoed around the room, "Are there any questions?"

Silence reigned.

"In that case, it's tea time. It is being served in Southfield."

As we all started shuffling towards the door, two other girls came over.

Eileen said, "This is Annie, and Annie this is Sue and Bonnie."

We shook hands as we kept up with the others on our way to Southfield. Sue, a blonde with a strong Somerset accent had already achieved her Orthopaedic Nursing Qualification. She had previously nursed a Birmingham research student when she was in Bristol and he had persuaded her to do her complete her training in Birmingham. Bonnie was also partly trained, having already obtained her Opthalmic certificate. She was small, dark, very pretty and had a soft local accent.

During the next few days we all had to be examined by the chiropodist. We were to have six monthly referrals for chiropody throughout our training, at no charge to us personally. Clearly our feet were regarded as a very precious asset and needed regular attention. I tried to remember whether the tutor had sneaked a look at my feet during the interview. A few days after the chiropody the work-wear suppliers came to fit our statutory brown lace-ups. Miss Alan was present throughout, though not Mrs Jackson. Miss Alan maintained her stern observation of every movement, her glasses catching the light as she tilted her head this way and that, with the now customary air of disapproval, but she did say, "I advise you to change into Scholl exercise sandals after ward duty. They will rejuvenate your tired feet."

Desperate to make a good impression, I bought the Scholl exercise sandals and also chose some Kay Skips, as they looked sensible and sturdy. Later I regretted this decision, as they were totally lacking in glamour and looked rather frumpy. But at the time, making a good impression on Miss Alan was all that mattered.

"They give me the appearance of 'Mini Mouse'," I whined later.

"You'll always be very feminine, Mini Mouse isn't!" Gill said conclusively.

I couldn't make any more mistakes on my limited budget. The only other item of clothing that we were advised to buy, a brown woollen cardigan to wear over our dresses in class and to keep us warm on night-duty. After buying a fob watch to pin to our uniform breast pocket the ensemble was complete, and I felt like a proper nurse.

The spending spree ended with having to buy textbooks. The van from the old-fashioned, oak-floored bookshop in Colmore Road arrived. The bookshop staff of three bespectacled ladies with identical and unflattering tight buns perched on top of their heads stood next to their small, metal cash-boxes. I thought, "Its like a scene from a Dickens novel." They had placed heaps of textbooks on trestle tables, which groaned under the strain of the heavy texts. I bought Winifred Hector's *Book of Modern Nursing*, *The Principles and Practice of Surgical Nursing*, *Toohey's Medicine for Nurses* and *The nurses Aid to Arithmetic in Nursing*. I had to invade my purse once more, was relieved of the princely sum of £6.10d and struggled away with my heavy load.

We were told to report to the school demonstration room wearing our uniform dresses. At the top of the stairs some of the girls were examining themselves in the enormous mirror.

"I just look like a lanky banana," Gill said.

She was nearly six feet tall and her skirts seemed to almost touch the floor. There was lots of giggling and excited chatter as we walked in. The Southfield classroom and demonstration room was just like the one that I had left in Seaford.

We were to have a demonstration on how to lift patients. We took our seats in a semi-circle and Miss Alan and Miss Rogers, another tutor, stood at the front ready to commence the demonstration.

Miss Rogers said, "We will now demonstrate how to lift and turn patients. This is a crucial activity for you to learn so you won't injure your backs."

It seemed that if a nurse's feet were regarded as a vital part of her anatomy, the nurse's back was also to be protected. Miss Alan and Miss Rogers, using a life-size dummy, went through the aspects of safe lifting. Then we divided into groups of three, nominating one to climb onto the bed and be lifted by the other two. Taking turns, we all had the experience of lifting and being lifted. The inevitable giggling was greeted by a stern frown of disapproval from the supervising tutors. They stood observing every movement, like a pair of grey wood pigeons, their eyes darting about and their necks twitching backwards and forwards.

In the next demonstration room session we were taught to make beds and how it was always important to have two nurses to do this, because with one nurse it took two and a half times as long. Wasting time was regarded as a dreadful sin. I was intrigued by the addition of a draw-sheet. The draw-sheet was a strip of doubled cotton, two feet wide, which went across the bed under the patient's bottom. It was some three feet longer than necessary, so that it could be easily moved across by the patient raising their bottom, allowing the bed to be easily refreshed without having to completely re-make the bed. Another cunning feature of bed making, was for the nurse on the left hand side of the bed to make a tuck in the sheets and blankets, to make room for the toes. The bed was finished off by a perfectly mitred corner to the counterpane.

Practical demonstrations were interspersed with such lectures as "The Theoretical Aspects of Nursing" which emphasised the importance that food has in restoring good health and the need for the nurse to monitor diet. We learnt about Diabetic and other special diets, finishing with the Ethics of Nursing. It reminded me of the little booklet that I had been given at interview which started, "The Queen Elizabeth School of Nursing – Training for a Noble Profession".

She opened her lecture saying, "Nurses must maintain

the highest ethical standards. The fundamental responsibility of the Nurse is three fold: to conserve life, to alleviate suffering and to promote health." Miss Alan introduced the fourteen points of code of the International Council of Nurses, whilst watching us with her eagle eyes she built us up into a state of Messianic zeal.

During the next week we concentrated on the need for clinical observations. It fell to Miss Rogers to talk about the patient's toilet.

Miss Rogers said, "Scrupulous attention to the cleanliness of the skin is much appreciated. It raises the standard of morale and is a good index to the efficiency of the nursing staff."

Then, to demonstrate, Miss Rogers and Miss Alan blanket-bathed the dummy, and we all had to show that we were competent to do the same. On reflection, perhaps it would have been better to blanket-bath each other, it certainly would have been more fun! Mouth care was covered, before we were let loose on the wards. We were taught to clean a patient' s tongue by swabbing the tongue with a dilute solution of sodium bicarbonate and finishing by applying glycerine to re- hydrate the mouth.

After the first four weeks we commenced weekly afternoon visits to the wards. Two coaches arrived outside Southfield. One coach was to take nurses to the General Hospital, the other to the Queen Elizabeth Hospital. The more experienced and worldly-wise nurses, including Sue and Bonnie, went to the General whilst Gill, Eileen, Sylvia and I went in The Queen Elizabeth coach. We had to arrive in time for the two o'clock ward report. Both Eileen and I were allocated West Ward 1. Arriving at the first floor we pushed open the doors to be greeted by four proper nurses, who were obviously waiting for us.

The dark haired Nurse said, "Just follow us."

We followed them into a cloakroom, where they took off

their red cloaks, hung them on hooks and began buttoning on aprons, which they shook out from a neatly starched square bundle that each one carried under their cloaks. The starched aprons crackled as they encased the skirts of the nurses' dresses completely. They were wearing simple cardboard caps. Eileen and I just stood, not knowing what to do.

The nurse who'd spoken before said, "Hang your cardigans up and follow us."

So we did and then hurried along the ward corridor trying to keep up with them. They moved quickly, pausing briefly to push open a heavy large glass door, with a sign above it declaring "Sister's Office".

A very fat Sister, with a long frilly cap over her hair sat behind a desk writing and ignoring the nurses' arrival. I thought, "She may have been pretty once long ago, but she's not much to look at now." The nurses remained standing, lifted one side of their aprons, to take out their notebooks from their dress pockets and pens from their right breast pockets.

Then Sister Matthews spoke, "Nurses please welcome our new colleagues and make sure that you help them with anything that they don't understand."

Then she started to discuss the patients. I was baffled by the jargon. "Were they speaking English?"

'Two hourly turns' was difficult enough; Mr Jones still needs his dressing replaced was understandable but TLC didn't make any sense at all. Sister Matthews was still talking, "Nurse Taylor, you take one PTS (Preliminary Training School) nurse and start on the main ward."

I was standing next to Nurse Taylor as the nurses began putting their notebooks and pens back into their pockets.

She turned to me, saying enthusiastically, "Come to the sluice with me."

Off she went at break neck speed. I was almost running to keep up with her.

Catching my breath, I gasped, "What does TLC mean?"

"Tender Loving Care. That patient, Mr Jones, is in a single room. His prostrate cancer has progressed so far that all we can do is look after him with loving tender care, and increase the doses of morphine until he dies."

I thought, "I bet that's why I was accepted. It just happened to be the words I used on interview."

I'd hoped Nurse Taylor might slow down but she delivered the explanation on the run and we arrived in the sluice. If the jargon had seemed like another language, the sluice was a different world. A large container, the size of a modern chest-freezer, was bubbling away at one side of the room with huge windows above it. Nurse Taylor moved to the opposite wall and pressed a lever at waist height, a hinged door came down revealing a bizarre internal structure, a cross between a small dishwasher and a lavatory set deep into the wall.

"This is the bed-pan and bottle washer. You put the bedpan onto this framework to empty the contents, close the door and press this lever to flush it. Urine bottle fits onto this nozzle then they go into the steriliser."

She pointed to the various parts in the sluice. The she went to the bubbling thing, the steriliser,

"Good, it's already full."

She took hold of the handles of an intriguing contraption that looked like a milkman's crate with two layers of urinals and removed it from the steriliser, placing them on the bottle trolley ready for use.

Over her shoulder she called, "Come on let's get going." Then she said, "We'll go and load a trolley with fresh sheets."

After loading the trolley, we went back to the ward. Approaching the first bed we drew the screens round and taking the patient's hand, Nurse Taylor said,

"I've brought a new nurse to see you today, Mr Jones."

Mr Jones was sitting up in bed wearing a pink and white striped pyjama top and, drawing back the sheets, Nurse

Taylor, revealed a man, naked from the waist down. A plastic tube extended from his penis. My eyes came out like organ stops! The only penis I'd ever seen was Michael Jones' five-year-old appendage. I didn't know where to look. Mr Jones and the nurse chatted about the weather. It didn't take long before I recovered from my embarrassment, and from that time onwards I took nudity in my stride. My first big lesson of life as a nurse had occurred.

Back at the training home we shared our stories. Sylvia kept a supply of Marmite which we spread on toast to revive us as we sat together talking and laughing, sometimes crying, about our afternoons on the wards.

Sylvia said, "I had to give a lady a bed pan. I was so embarrassed because I had to ask which way round does it go?"

Gill said, "Somehow, I knew."

"We were all right, weren't we, Eileen? "I said. Eileen had a similar time with another nurse.

We started training in May and it wasn't long before we discovered that the May set were called the Debs and Dotties, as we were the girls who had left school before taking A levels. Throughout our training, any hint of stupidity by us was met with a shaking of the Sister's head, as she sighed, "May set, you know."

At one of the toast and Marmite sessions, Sylvia said, "Do those Sister tutors wear whale-boned corsets to keep them standing so stiffly?"

Gill laughed, "I bet they wear Harvest Festival knickers too."

We looked confused.

Gill explained, "You know, like my Nan says, all is safely gathered in."

Eileen laughed, "I've never heard that before, but I'd like to know where they buy their shoes, so I could avoid that shop."

I smiled, "My Great Aunties still wear identical lace-up

shoes with that little heel, they regularly eat spam and they're in their eighties! So perhaps they're trying to tell us something. That good shoes and a perpetual diet of battered Spam is the key to a long life."

The staple food of the Preliminary Training School seemed to be Spam, and despite good appetites we were soon fed up with it.

The mood soon changed, when Sylvia said anxiously, "I've seen a man with half his face eaten away by a rodent ulcer. I was fascinated, because I could see his tongue through the side of his cheek. They said I'd feel sick or faint, but I was just fascinated. Do you think I'm emotionally stunted?"

Then we all dived in discussing our anxieties. It was the start of the mutual emotional support that we gave each other. The modern terminology is 'counselling' and it would be conducted by a trained and certified counsellor. I wondered about the surprises that were in store for us and how we would react to them. What had I let myself in for? I'd been amazed by the sight of a naked male organ, and Sylvia was shocked by the horrifying rodent ulcer.

I said, "Well Miss Alan said we'd be thoroughly prepared for our ward visits. But I wasn't in any way ready for the appearance of fully grown male genitalia!"

"It's just a load of old cock," Gill said.

We all dissolved into laughter. Our original group of four are still close friends.

I wondered whether Sue had been put into our room to help us because she had previous experience. She must have thought that we were very naive, so I was amazed when she asked, "Would you and Eileen like to come down to Cheddar for a week's holiday before we start at the other hospitals?"

Sue lived with her parents, who were strawberry-farmers in Cheddar. We discussed the question of transport to Cheddar.

Eileen said, "Shall I ask if my boyfriend Peter can take us?"

I chuckled, "Peter' s car is a two seater soft top Morgan, we wouldn't all fit in!"

I'd been tremendously impressed seeing Peter sweep majestically into the drive at Priorsfield, hood down in his British Racing Green Morgan. That sight was etched indelibly on my memory.

I said, "I've passed my driving test. I'll have a word with Mum to see if she'll lend me her car."

I did and to my amazement Mum said, "Yes."

So the three of us set off to Cheddar for our week' s holiday before we started full time training on the wards. Sue' s parents were warm and welcoming and we helped to pick strawberries occasionally, eating them frequently! To my surprise I found my knees became very inflamed. Many years later I discovered that strawberries are high in uric acid, which causes problems for joints, one of my problems now associated with Lupus. But even inflamed joints didn't spoil the holiday and we returned feeling ready to face whatever was in store for us!

I returned the car all in one piece with no dents or scratches. Mum was waiting for me when I arrived.

"Rick phoned the day you left. I told him you'd be back today."

"OK," I said, with a nonchalant shrug.

I was hoping she didn't notice my heart pounding beneath my blouse.

Mum brewed a pot of tea, and I sat on the Ercol wooden kitchen chair sipping my tea and chatting. The telephone rang. Mum went to answer it, "Yes, she's just arrived. I'll call her."

As I went into the hall to take the black bakelite telephone receiver, I was feeling excited and breathless.

"Yes, I'm free. I have to report to the hospital tomorrow afternoon, but I can come for a drink this evening."

I went back to the kitchen to finish my cup of tea, and said in response to Mum' s raised eyebrows, "Rick is picking me up at eight o'clock this evening."

Rick arrived with unnerving punctuality, and at the sound of his green Ford Cortina approaching, I rushed out of the house, my stomach filled with butterflies. As I climbed into the passenger seat beside him, he asked,

"Will the local pub be OK?"

I shrugged, "Yes, that's fine with me."

With that he drove the hundred yards to the Railway Arms in Shenstone village, parking the car outside the red brick, two storey building. We went inside and sat down on a wooden bench.

Rick turned to me, saying, "What would you like to drink?"

"Half of cider, please."

He went to the bar, returning with two half-pint glasses, and set them down. As I self- consciously sipped my cider I gabbled on about Nursing. Rick didn't speak but just kept sipping his drink and staring at me with an unsettling cold stare. It made me feel nervous so I just talked faster. Eventually, when I paused for breath, he asked, "When will your know duty roster?"

I replied, "Apparently we'll find out tomorrow. If you like, I'll phone to let you know when I'm free... But how's life in Oxford?" I asked as an afterthought.

"It's fine," was all he said.

Obviously he didn't want to talk about himself. I already knew he was in his second year of an Oxford Mechanical Engineering degree.

When he drove me home, he kissed me with hard hungry lips, leaving my mouth feeling bruised, and me excited but disturbed.

The next day I put all my things together, said another tearful goodbye to Sandy and took my case to the car. Mum now familiar with the route, drove straight to The Queen Elizabeth Hospital. Busy with my thoughts, we didn't talk during the journey. I was wondering whether the spirit of self-sacrifice, which had driven young women flocking to join a nunnery in service to God centuries before, had now been replaced by nurse training in the secular society of the 1960s. Mum turned into a parking space in front of Nuffield House, the Nurses' Home directly opposite the five-storey Queen Elizabeth Hospital. Both buildings had presumably been built at the same time and kept to the same solid square style.

I collected my case from the boot and together we started to climb the wide flight of eight stone steps, leading into the Nurses' Home. A short stout porter, with Downs Syndrome, came down the steps with hand outstretched. He clearly expected to take my case from me.

"J-just th-.these?" he stuttered.

"Yes, please," I said as I handed my case to him.

As we followed him up the steps, I whispered to Mum, "Employing a man with Downs Syndrome means there's no risk of pregnancy for the nurses."

Mum looked astounded. I said goodbye and she hurried to the safety of her car. I turned and followed the porter up the steps and into the Nurses' Home.

The foyer had all the ambience of a 1930' s hotel. There was an oak checking-in desk under a large oak canopy, with heavy Art-Deco styling but with little of its niceties.

The porter placed my case gently by the desk. A severe looking lady with a well worn face was standing behind the desk. She looked up enquiringly.

"Annie Armitage," I announced, almost apologetically.

Before I could draw breath to say anymore, "Thank you Michael," she said dismissively.

Then turning to me continued, "I'm Miss Pritchard, the home's warden. On your right is a blackboard indicating your room number. The lifts are directly behind you. Your case and trunk will be in your room by now. Then we'll meet together in the nurses sitting room at four o'clock. It's situated further along this corridor to your left. Here is the key to your room," and I felt I'd been dismissed as well.

I took the heavy brass key from her outstretched hand without speaking. The unspoken words, "And I won't take any nonsense from you, my girl!" hung in the air.

I consulted the chart; I was delighted, as I was sharing with Eileen. I called the lift, stepped in and pressed the brass button for the third floor. I unlocked my door and went in. I found two narrow beds made with hospital linen, a built-in wardrobe and a bureau for our clothes. There was a wash hand-basin in the corner next to the long, tall, narrow window overlooking the hospital building opposite. I unpacked my things, putting them on a bed. I didn't want to make a choice until Eileen arrived. Then the door shot open and Eileen burst in gasping, "Nearly didn't make it in time!"

It was to become Eileen's catch phrase. She was invariably late.

Giggling nervously we sorted ourselves out and at four o'clock headed to the Nurse's sitting room.

The room was set out with easy chairs placed in a semi-circle. At the back of the room were trestle tables heaped with bundles of uniform dresses of buttercup yellow with white aprons. The bundles were tied together with remnants of the yellow cotton. Silently standing behind the trestle tables were two plump ladies, wearing pink overalls.

Miss Pritchard was standing at the front.

She called out to the ten gathered new recruits, "Quiet please! The front door will be locked at eleven 'o'clock precisely. Any nurse who has not arrived by then must go into the hospital and report to the night porter. He will accept one late pass until twelve thirty each week but this has to be issued by me in advance. You will be allocated supper shifts. First supper is at seven, second supper at half past seven and breakfasts are served from seven o'clock each morning. There is a small kitchen on each floor, which is supplied daily with milk for nurses to make hot drinks. Two sheets will be put into your rooms on Monday morning and you are to change your bottom sheet only. The top floor of the nurses' home is reserved for nurses to use when on night duty. During the day please remember that nurses on night-duty are sleeping and may easily be disturbed. Be considerate."

Without drawing breath, she continued, "You will be expected to be on duty in your wards at 8am tomorrow. The duty rota is displayed in Sister's office on each ward. If there aren't any questions we'll split the group in half to give you a tour of the building, and when you report back we'll equip you with your uniforms. Are there any questions?"

Silence reigned.

Then as if by magic, two uniformed student nurses appeared and, dividing us into two groups, set off to show us around Nuffield House. Student Nurse Jones, our guide, was tall and slim, but very thin and clearly bored by the task in hand. She scuttled around at a great speed and had obviously been press-ganged, rather than a willing volunteer. As she rushed us around, she'd open the door to a room saying, for example, "This is the library. Do you see?"

Then quickly closing the library door after we'd had the briefest look, it was immediately off to the next destination, without pausing to offer us the chance of questions or gaining additional information. Our whistle stop tour finished at the sitting room, and our motley crew was left panting. We quickly recovered from the dashing about and gave our names to the two plump pink ladies, who'd maintained their station behind the pile of uniforms. They handed over our packs; each bundle contained four primrose yellow linen dresses with short sleeves, a dozen cotton aprons and a separate parcel containing a navy woollen cloak, with a red woollen lining. Alongside the stacks of uniforms was a pile of paper caps in the form of self-assembly sheets, some collar studs and packets of white hairgrips. One of the plump ladies explained how to fashion the cutout sheets into a cap, secure it with the collar stud and how to use the grips.

She kindly warned, "Make sure that as you grip the hat on, your hair is secure so if you shake your head from side-to side it doesn't move. It spreads infection," she said confidently.

We arranged to meet up in the Nurse's dining room for our supper at half past seven and then went excitedly up to our rooms to try out our uniforms. Eileen and I sat on our bed, opposite each other, both attempting to fold our caps and emulate the dexterity of the plump lady who had demonstrated the art of cap making. We struggled and giggled. Eventually Eileen placed her cap on the bed and admired it, I nodded enthusiastically as Eileen said, "I think that that's not a bad effort!"

The Nurse's dining room was in the basement and had the atmosphere of an underground bunker. It was buzzing with activity as uniformed nurses arrived for their supper. They were obviously in a rush as they whizzed their trays along the stainless steel counters. Not feeling a part of the frenetic activity, we stood back, waiting for a lull. Then taking wooden trays from a huge pile by the door, we followed in their footsteps, passing slowly along the servery. The pink clad, middle-aged catering ladies plated up each wholesome, though unimaginative first course. We moved along and another lady handed over a bowl of pudding. We proceeded to the next lady who then drowned our pudding in custard. There was no eye contact or conversation, as far as the catering staff were concerned we could have been red, white and blue aliens.

As we tucked into slices of incinerated roast lamb, with vegetables boiled to a pulp and glutinous gravy, followed by treacle sponge with custard, Sylvia said, "At least it isn't those Spam fritters!"

It broke the tension and we all chuckled. This unappetizing though sustaining type of food was to become our staple fare over the next three years. It was, of course, essential to fuel us for the amount of exhausting work that we undertook and surprisingly, despite the state of the food, our appetites increased dramatically.

Our meals finished, we met up for coffee. Eileen and I collected our mugs from our room, before going to Sylvia and Gill' s room. We all sat chattering and chuckling until bedtime. But none of us would let on how nervous we felt. So we discussed our seniors.

I said," All the Sisters and Tutors look so ugly, do you suppose it's an omen for our future?"

Eileen smiled, "Helena Rubenstein said, there's no such thing as an ugly woman. Just a lazy woman."

"How profound," I thought

We looked at Eileen, in amazement. Eileen used the least make-up of any of us, relying instead on her lovely complexion and personality. Amongst us, I was the one who used the most make-up. My skin was not bad but I felt that I needed to cover the minor blemishes that I did have. Was this Lupus already rearing its ugly head? Feeling the need for a barrier of war paint, I faced the outside world. While I was contemplating this, the conversation had moved on.

Gill was saying, "There's an old Russian saying, 'There's no such thing as an ugly woman, just not enough vodka'."

The companionship fortified our confidence, and eventually we went to bed.

Promptly, at seven thirty the next morning, we were in the dining room for our breakfast of fruit juice, cereal and bacon and eggs. I didn't have much of an appetite but realising the potentially heavy day ahead, I did my best to tackle it. After breakfast, we joined the chattering gaggle of nurses making their way along the tunnel connecting the nurse's home to the hospital. Each nurse was carrying a bundle, which contained her starched apron, under her cloak. Someone pressed the lift button and we proceeded to the first floor for Ward West 1, where Eileen and I were to work, and joined the other nurses on duty that morning. We hung up our cloaks in the cloakroom and shook out and buttoned on our aprons. With our three layers of linen and cotton in place, we were ready for action.

All the nurses collected in Sister's office and the senior night duty nurse gave her report before going off-duty. The junior nurse stayed on the ward looking after any patient's needs whilst this hand-over was taking place. The senior nurse on our shift then went through the day's activities and how we were expected to participate. I spied the off-duty rota hanging above Sister's desk. I didn't have the nerve to request a look at it, and we filed out of the office. Eileen and I trailed after the other nurses who were checking that the patients were ready for breakfast. Feeding patients was considered a crucial activity. At mealtimes the most senior nurse on the ward dished out the food from a gigantic heated trolley.

Together with the others, Eileen and I gathered around the trolley with trays and then took them to our respective patient. It was reiterated that monitoring how much food each patient ate was a most important job. In addition, there was a ward maid whose duties included preparing the trolley, making drinks for staff and patients and changing the patients' water jugs. She cleared away breakfast and pushed the heated trolley back to the lift, ready for collection by the kitchen porter.

"Ah! Nurse Armitage, you're working with me," a second-year smiled broadly at me.

I could tell she was in the second year by her blue epaulettes on her yellow dress.

"Come with me and we'll get the linen trolley ready."

As we loaded a stainless steel two-tier trolley with clean sheets, I asked tentatively, "When will we find out what duties we will be working?"

"Best thing is to look during report time after lunch. There's usually a bit of a lull then," she reassured me, as we headed to the first bed. She drew the screens around the bed occupied by a gaunt middle-aged man, whilst saying,

"Now Mr Jeffreys, I have a new nurse with me today, Nurse Armitage… Did you have a good night?"

"No, I'm afraid I've bled all over this sheet again, and it's only just been changed, Nurse Jacobs."

"I'll go and get a dressing, you stay with Mr Jeffreys," she said, turning to me and scurried off.

Not sure what to do, I started stripping the bed. Suddenly, '*Swish!*' went the screens, revealing the Staff-nurse.

"On your own, what do you think you're doing, Nurse?"

Of course, I knew I wasn't supposed to make beds alone, but what was I supposed to do in this circumstance? As I stood silent and forlorn, a hand slid under the sheet and took mine. I felt something hard. It was a wrapped sweet. My eyes prickled with tears and I swallowed hard. The Staff- nurse disappeared as quickly as she'd arrived.

"Don't worry mi duck, she's a bit of a tartar," Mr Jeffreys said kindly.

It was to be the first of many times when, in trouble with my seniors, I felt a patient's warmth and compassion.

The rest of the day passed without incident. During the morning the Red Cross volunteer ladies arrived and pushed around a trolley full of goodies for the patients. They went about their good works, bestowing benevolence, selling postage stamps and collecting letters for posting.

At lunchtime I checked the duty roster. The following day Eileen and I were on the late shift and the day after I was on an early and Eileen was on a late. As soon as I came off duty I phoned Rick.

"I'm off at four o'clock on Wednesday, so I could see you at half-past, if you like?"

"Yes, that's fine," was all he said. In great excitement I joined the others to chat over our day.

We were all on our first late shift from two o'clock until ten fifteen. Eileen and I arrived on the ward for ward-report at two o'clock, just as we had done during our preliminary training, only this time we wouldn't be leaving at four! Five student nurses collected in Sister's office for report. Sister Matthews stretched out her right hand and, drawing back some curtains

147

that I hadn't noticed before, we looked through her window onto a two-bedded bay. A lady lay in one of the beds surrounded by tubes and technology. She was being attended by a nurse clothed in theatre-greens. They seemed quite unaware of being watched (I was to find out later that the observation window was a one-way mirror to the kidney transplant unit).

Sister Matthews said," Nurse Jones, I want you to take over from Staff-Nurse Brown."

"Yes, Sister," Nurse Jones, one of the third year students, answered and went off to change into theatre-greens.

Then Sister Matthews turned to the rest of us with a summation of the morning' s developments and instructions for our contributions to the evening shift.

"Nurse Smith and Nurse Anderson will be on the main ward, and Nurse James and Nurse Armitage will do the rest."

The wards at the Queen Elizabeth included a main ward of sixteen beds, with another sixteen beds in single and four bedded rooms. The sluice and the linen room lay between the two arms of the ward.

Eileen and I made our way to the focal point for every junior nurse, the sluice. The steriliser was bubbling away ferociously and the large glass egg timer was indicating that it was sterile. Our, marginally, senior colleagues arrived, each with a trolley of sheets, and we began our rounds preparing the patients for the afternoon visiting hours between three and four. If any patients had been discharged, visiting time provided the opportunity to strip their beds. Working in pairs, we wiped the mattress with spirit of chlorohexidine then, turning it, one nurse wiped out the locker, removing the fruit bowl, whilst the other nurse returned with clean bedding to remake the bed.

After tea, we repeated the performance of tidying beds, plumping pillows and offering bottles and bedpans. Then it was a question of feeding patients with their evening meal and getting ready for the second visiting hour at seven pm. The evening shift was allowed into the dining-room, taking turns for a thirty-minute tea break, whilst the visitors were with the patients.

On Wednesdays the 'WRVS flower-ladies' used this time to remove wilting flowers and collect the newly arrived flowers for arranging in their vases. They saved any flowers that they could, rather than throwing them out, returning later with the visitors' fresh flowers and any rescued flowers re-arranged. Visiting times were brought to a close by the tinkling of a bell wielded by the Sister.

The visitors departed obediently at the sound of the bell and we settled the patients down for the night.

After the night-staff received the report, we removed our aprons, screwed them up and took them with us to the nurse's home laundry shoot, with a sense of relief, finality and tiredness. We collected in each other's rooms for winding-down with a cup of coffee. It became a custom. If our friends were not around we would to knock on any door, where the light was shining under the closed door, to share the wind-down with someone, rather than to be alone.

One evening Sylvia related, "I was asked to get a sample of urine and sputum from a patient yesterday and when I labeled them, I'm sure I mixed them up. When I went back today, I was convinced I'd killed her."

"Oh no! How dreadful," Eileen cried out.

Sylvia laughed, "No, she was fine. I hadn't killed her at all!"

We laughed, then Gill said, "One patient was given two pots and told to wee into one and cough into the other. When the nurse went to collect the specimens, they both seemed to have urine in them. So the nurse asked the patient about it and he said, "I did as you asked, I weed into the first. Later, I coughed when I weed into the second."

We thought that was hysterically funny.

Eileen was on a late again the next day, so she just turned over, sighed, and went back to sleep, as I made my lonely way down to breakfast to meet the others.

Sylvia laughed, "Gill, I don't believe what you said about the urine specimens last night. I bet you were just trying to cheer me up."

"No, honestly, Sandra told me, "Gill protested.

"That shows it is just a story," I put in.

"Well, it worked didn't it?"

We agreed, giggling as we walked along the underground tunnel to the hospital. We were reinforcing the group identity, using humour. What a weapon!

Gradually, I was feeling more confident.

"I bet Sister's bottom has spread to fit into that chair," I said rashly to the second year Nurse, who was preparing the bottle-trolley with me.

She was nodding and smiling in agreement, when a crackling noise started and Sister Matthews's voice said out of a hidden speaker, "Come and see me in the office, Nurse Armitage."

My heart sank like a stone as I went to face the music. Nervously, I knocked on the office door.

"Come," Sister's voice rang out. I went in, knees shaking.

"Now Nurse, I want you to collect a specimen of urine from Mr Jones. Do you know how?"

"Y-yes, Sister," I stuttered, hardly able to hide the relief in my voice. I shall never know whether she had heard me or not.

It seemed that not only the ears but also the eyes of the Sister were everywhere. Although the cleaning staff were not directly under her control, they too seemed very aware that she would not tolerate shoddiness. They moved around the ward with a quiet diligence as they shifted the furniture and mopped the floors. The only thing that was allowed to interrupt their endeavours was a medical ward round.

The day passed quickly and uneventfully for me and I was excited at the thought of meeting Rick after the shift. I did manage to remember to warn Eileen about the inter-com in the sluice, so I felt relieved I'd done that as I rushed to meet Rick. As I bathed and changed into my pink mini-dress, I looked out of the window and saw Rick sitting outside in his Cortina! Breathlessly, I ran to get the lift, then down the stone steps and opened the car door. I climbed in, bursting with all my news and felt the cold hard plastic of the seats on my bare legs.

Rick said, "There isn't anyone at home. So, shall we go to my house?"

"Yes, that would be great, "I said.

We drove there, with me still chattering on. When we arrived, we entered a poorly furnished house. I stood in the hall, expecting to be offered a chair.

But instead he said, "Would you like to see the photographs of the holiday we had in Guernsey...you know, the year when you'd have been there too."

"Yes, "I said.

"They are in my bedroom. Shall we go upstairs?"

He started to climb the dingy staircase. I followed.

He opened a door, "This is my bedroom."

We entered the drably furnished room. I sat on the bed, the rough counter-pane scratching the backs of my legs.

He pulled down the lid of a bureau, saying, "Here they are."

My attention was drawn to the bureau. It was smart and new, in stark contrast to the shabby furniture in the rest of the room.

"That's nice," I said, pointing.

"My Auntie bought it for me to do my homework on. Mind you, she's not my real Auntie."

He sat down next to me on the bed and started going through the photographs.

151

"Yes, that's Fermaine Bay," I recognised the view.

He continued turning over the photographs. Then there was someone I didn't recognise, though I knew the answer I asked, "Who's that?"

"That's my Dad, just before he died."

I sat there. I didn't know what to say. He put the photographs on the floor and pushed me over into a lying position, undoing his trousers and my clothes.

We had sex there on the rough counter-pane. I felt aroused and excited. I didn't resist. It hurt as he rammed his way through and I bled. The whole process was hurried, forceful and demeaning. I felt sore and confused.

Rick said, "My mother and sister are due home soon so we had better hurry up and get dressed."

We dressed and left. I didn't speak as he drove me back to the Nurses' Home. I felt dampness in my knickers and wondered, was I bleeding? He kissed me hard on the mouth, but didn't speak and left. I was shaking and upset. I felt tremendously guilty, dirty and defiled. Still shaking, I went to my room and looked into my knickers. The dampness was clear fluid. I ran a bath and sat in it for some while, contemplating the large brass taps in despair. I put my pyjamas on and climbed into bed. When Eileen came in, her stories of her late shift drove me out my desolation.

In the morning, the enormity of what had taken place started to dawn on me. In horror, I thought, "What if I am pregnant?" I had three weeks to wait for my period. It was the longest three weeks of my life! And then, tremendous relief! My period came. But, then I thought, "What if it happens again?"

I didn't dare tell anyone. I didn't realize at the time that Rick's forcefulness would lead to his increasing forcefulness, culminating in his desire to force me into an increasing state of humiliation whenever he could. I was in turmoil and the silliness of Kenny Everett's voice on Radio Caroline started to irritate me. I retuned to Radio London where John Peel was talking about contraception. I listened entranced. He said that the Family Planning Clinics would only offer birth control to girls who were engaged or had a wedding date fixed. But the newly opened Brook Street clinic in London was offering birth control to unmarried girls. He gave their phone number and in desperation I rang the number from a local phone box, grateful that nobody could overhear the conversation. I explained that I was calling from Birmingham and an enthusiastic voice at the other end responded, "There's a Brook Street clinic in Birmingham as well. Would you like their number?"

"Yes, please."

What a relief when I rang and was given an appointment.

I was treated with a consideration and courtesy that I didn't feel I deserved. I was put on the contraceptive pill. Somehow, I managed to take the pill each evening, without Eileen finding out. I never told anyone else. I felt an overwhelming sense of guilt and sadness. Could the stress caused by the guilt have triggered the start of my Lupus? Again, research is inconclusive.

Although obsessed by my guilty secret, I put it aside to cope with the day-to-day experiences in the hospital. There were so many mistakes that we made, such as carrying a drink without using a tray.

"Are you all right, Mr. Jones?" Eileen was taking the hand of a silently weeping man.

He sniffed. "I'd love a cup of tea," he said suddenly smiling through his tears.

"Won't be a minute, I'll get you one," she said and drew the screens around the bed.

She nipped off to get the tea, and was rushing back to Mr Jones, when the figure of Sister loomed over her, "What do you think you're doing, Nurse? Go and fetch a tray from the kitchen immediately!"

Sister Matthews' booming voice could have woken the dead.

"Mr Jones had just been told he'd got cancer of the prostrate. So, I went to get him a cup of tea and forgot the tray," Eileen explained as we went off duty.

I said, "I know, I expect everybody in Birmingham knows as well, the way Sister's voice carries."

We giggled.

The reason that a tray must be used is very logical. Its to prevent spills that would be a slipping hazard and require mopping up as soon as possible. But reasoned discussion and explanation was not the way of nursing in the Sixties. Practices and procedures were to be followed blindly and without question. Transgressions were met with orders barked out in a manner that would have done justice to a military parade ground. Avoiding these sort of responses became a vital aspect of surviving a shift, with nerves intact.

Another experience, which concentrated the mind, was how to cope with working night shifts. Day shift meant working 8am until four, afternoon shift was 4pm until 10pm and night shift was 10pm until 8am. We had a day and half off before working nights so we would finish at four, have a day off and then report for duty at 10 pm. We were quite worried about our first night shift. Both Sylvia and I were on the roster to start our night duty at the same time.

"It can't be too bad, because the night-staff looked all right when we arrived in the morning," I tried to reassure Sylvia.

We were allowed to wear our brown uniform cardigans for night-duty. Even so, I felt extremely cold by about three o'clock in the morning on my first set of nights. It may have been the lack of sleep, or have resulted from all the sitting still, or it could be that the heat was turned down during the night. Even the brown woollen cardigan wasn't enough to keep out the chill. Nurse Johnson, a skeletally thin, third year senior nurse was sitting in the main ward. She went and fetched her cloak. With it wrapped snugly wrapped around her she passed me, saying,

154

"I should get yours too, but don't let sister catch you. Its not officially allowed!"

I had to sit in the corridor to keep an eye on the side rooms. Although it was only autumn, there was a strong draught that felt as if it was blowing straight from the North Pole. Fortunately, the ward door squeaked, announcing night sister's visits, so I was able to take off my cloak, before she arrived. We took it in turns for our breaks and when the senior nurse left for three-quarters of an hour, I sat in the luxury of the draught free main ward. "Well, this is a bit warmer anyway," I thought.

Sylvia was on the cerebral-injuries ward, and we met at the junior nurses' break time.

"How's it going? I asked. Sylvia answered, "I just thought I'd seen a ghost! I was terrified. I was sitting in the main ward when a white figure floated by. Then I realised it was Mohammed, the theatre porter. He was dressed in white and wearing white wellington boots. As I recovered from the shock, I noticed his brown face, with gleaming white teeth. Then, thinking that ghosts have ghostly white faces rather than brown ones, I didn't know whether to laugh or cry!"

"What was he doing there?" I asked.

"No idea, I think he'd just come to frighten me, and it worked!"

We laughed in relief, whilst I stifled a yawn.

Time passed at a snail' s pace during the night, making me much more aware of ward routines than in the daytime. We had started at ten o'clock and after the report from the day staff, we took the drugs trolley round. After that we settled the patients for the night. If patients became disturbed during the night, we would creep quietly to their bedside carrying our torches and see to their needs. Eventually, the morning would arrive and, just before six o'clock, I would make a large pot of tea, equipping a trolley with sufficient cups and saucers, sugar and milk and the teapot for all the patients.

155

Punctually at 6 am the ward lights were switched on. Taking the tea trolley rattling into the main ward, I announced our arrival to the soporific patients, with a cheery, "Good morning!"

As I woke each patient, I took the thermometer from the little holder next to the bed and put it under their tongue generally asking, "Did you have a good night?" This was really rhetorical but sometimes we had an amusing or interesting response.

After returning to take and record pulse and temperature my next question was, "Have you had your bowels open?" before rewarding them with a cup of tea and writing up the results on their charts.

My senior colleague meanwhile, was busy replenishing the trolley for the morning drugs round. Next I loaded a trolley with clean sheets, collected the bottle trolley from the sluice and, heading for the main ward again, started stripping the beds of the patients who were up and about. We left the patients that were due for a blanket-bath as that would be done when the day staff came on duty. Working together, the senior nurse and I stripped and remade all the beds. We put the bottom sheet into the dirty laundry trolley and made the bed. The old top sheet was used as the bottom sheet and then the remade bed looked fresh and comfortable. With the ward of 34 patients now all clean and tidy, the senior nurse went to give the night report to the day staff. I was left very tired, but supervising until it was time for us both to go for our breakfast and later, very gratefully, to bed.

As we were starting to get used to things and making patients comfortable, plumping pillows, etc, the cheering word came more naturally and we changed wards. The sister' s idiosyncrasies tended to vary with each individual ward. Eileen replaced Sylvia.

Eileen said," It's awful, when he's doing a round Professor Smith won't allow any sound at all; patients can't even talk. I don't think that's caring, do you?"

"No," I said absent mindedly, as sadly I'd got my own problems.

I was on a medical ward, and the sister, Sister Stewart, was a martinet who considered it of great importance that the bed wheels must all be pointing towards the nearest wall. My previous ward sister, Sister Matthews, hadn't bothered about bed wheels, but it was the first thing Sister Stewart examined whenever she entered the ward. She was glum, plain and dumpy and with a gruff Scottish accent, which always made you feel that you were in trouble. Arriving each morning, Sister Stewart took the night report from the senior nurse and headed for the sluice. Arming herself with a wooden tongue de-presser, she thoroughly examined the products in the bedpan and expected the junior nurse to be as engrossed in the procedure as she was.

I was exhausted from a busy night, the smell of faeces made me feel nauseous.

Sister Stewart would ask, "What time did you say this was passed, Nurse?"

"Seven o'clock, Sister."

"Was it the only time in the night that she opened her bowels, nurse?"

"Yes, Sister." I learnt to be a good liar.

The horror of erroneously disposing bedpan contents, at about three in the morning, lives with me still. The bed pan washer merrily churning away and suddenly thinking, "Oh no, I was meant to save that!"

Peering closely into someone's faeces isn't the best way to stimulate an appetite for breakfast.

Sister Stewart was a Presbyterian and she ran the medical liver ward as though all the patients were there as a result of alcohol abuse. I worked night duty that New Year's Eve and the able patients were seeing in the New Year in the day-room, watching television. One of the patients produced a bottle of whisky.

157

She said, "Come on, get your glasses!"

The senior nurse' s eyes widened, "Perhaps a little drop, in a medicine pot, wouldn't do any harm."

We all linked arms, singing "Auld Lang Syne".

When the patients finally went to be and were snoring soundly, the senior nurse said, "Well, if it is their last New Year, at least they've enjoyed it."

Then it was down to me to scrub the smell of whisky out of the medicine pots. It seemed to take most of the night. I was terrified that in the morning Sister would be able to detect the smell and discover our dreadful crime. Fortunately, she didn't.

My next change of ward couldn't come soon enough. Eileen was pleased too. By now the next PTS set had begun working on the wards. We were due to go on just one more ward before our first year block of study.

Gill was pleased with her next ward, she was laughing as we went for tea.

"You'll never guess what happened. One of the September set was asked to clean all the false teeth. So she collected them all up in a bowl and went to scrub them. It wasn't until she'd finished that she realised she didn't know who they belonged to." I could just imagine them trying them all on to see which ones fitted. Gill continued, "This September lot are not very bright even with their with their A levels."

"I don't believe you, "I said spluttering over my Battenburg cake.

"God's honest truth," Gill said, as she wiped cake crumbs from my mouth with her napkin.

She went on, "I'm relieved to be off tomorrow, I'm not sure what's going on at home."

When Gill came to our room for coffee two days later she had been crying. We asked how things were at home and with that she began to cry again.

Eileen passed her a box of tissues and Gill removed her spectacles to wipe her eyes and sobbed. She didn't seem to be the same Gill whose easy chuckle had filled our evening with joy only two days earlier.

"Mum' s got the flu, Nana's stuck in bed after her stroke, Dad's desperately busy at work, and I hated leaving them in that state."

"What about Alison?" I asked.

Gill had a younger sister, "She's only twelve."

We sat having coffee, all feeling sad. We were used to Eileen crying, she was often overwrought at the end of duty. Holding her hand whilst someone said something funny always did the trick and comforted her but this didn't work quite so well on Gill.

At breakfast next morning Gill looked as if she hadn't slept. When I met Sylvia at lunchtime she told me that Gill had gone home.

I asked, "How come?"

Sylvia was bursting to tell someone, "The staff-nurse told Gill to stay behind after the morning report and asked whether anything was wrong. Gill explained and her heart sank when she was told to go and start work. But, not long afterwards The Beanpole, Assistant Matron, arrived and took Gill into the office. Beanpole said that Gill could have compassionate leave for two weeks to look after her mother and grandmother. Gill is to phone The Beanpole before she returns, to tell her that everything is OK."

"What a relief," I said smiling.

The two weeks passed quickly, and Gill was soon back at work. There were two Assistant Matrons at the QE. Now one of them had achieved the status of a saint in Gill' s eyes. Miss Jones was nearly six feet tall and very thin, so we unimaginatively called her, "Beanpole". The other, Miss Griffiths, was barely five feet and plump, so she was called, "Dumpling". The hems of their dresses were appropriate to their height, whilst ours had to be the statutory fourteen inches from the floor. They were clearly exempt from the rule, which governed us. We looked silly and were indignant but Gill wouldn't hear a word said against the Assistant Matrons.

Soon it was time for our first year block and we had to spend three weeks, full time, at the School of Nursing in Nuffield House. During the block we were prepared and studied for theatre work, casualty and The Children's Hospital. Apart from theoretical instruction we were given practical experience such as taking stitches out of a sausage shaped pillow. It helped with the procedure but, as it didn't feel a thing, it was far removed from pulling a stitch through someone's skin.

Sandra said, "When we meet a massive sausage, suture removal will be easy!"

Then the next day, as we went into the demonstration room the top half of a torso was facing us, with Miss Alan and Miss Rogers standing alongside.

Miss Alan started to speak, "Today you'll learn heart massage and mouth to mouth resuscitation."

We were amazed. Together they demonstrated what to do when a patient's heart stopped beating, and breathing ceased. We felt proud and powerful as we all took turns breathing into the hapless torso, thus bringing the dead back to life. No one could possibly die under our care. The next day we spent injecting oranges with sterile water. Again, it was far removed from puncturing the skin of a real patient, and it was a long time before we gained the skill and confidence for the quick stabbing motion that we were told would ensure almost painless injections.

We felt like top year primary school children breaking up for school holidays when we returned from our first block and attached the powder blue epaulettes. I was then transferred to the Birmingham Children's' Hospital in Iknield Street.

I'd survived the first year and now proudly wore the epaulettes denoting my seniority. All the anxiety I'd had about the mixing up of specimens and such things belonged to my past. I now had a single bedroom, and I was able to take the contraceptive pill in the privacy of my own room. Although I'd managed to take the pill all that time without Eileen finding out, it still made me feel guilty and ashamed. My sexual contact with Rick continued. It wasn't making love but simply carnal lust; despite this I was a willing participant.

The Children's Hospital was a pretty design, it made me think of the style of art-nouveau. It had probably been built in the 19th century and its architecture reflected that period. The wards had twelve beds in long rows on each side, with Sister's office and the kitchen at the beginning of the ward. The sluice was at the farthest end. I was allocated The Ears, Nose and Throat (ENT) ward. It had a claustrophobic atmosphere and I was glad that I was only required to work on one of the wards in the hospital. I remembered my own experience when I was seven and had my tonsils removed. But at least there wasn't the dreadful smell of ether, the memory of which had lingered on since. Fortunately, anaesthetics had improved but little mites lying in the recovery position, blood oozing from their mouths onto the sheets as they whimpered, tugged at my heartstrings.

"I could never be a children's nurse," I said to Sylvia, as we walked towards the dining room for breakfast.

She said, "Yes, but the smell of freshly squeezed oranges here is truly wondrous, couldn't that change your mind?"

We opened the door to the dining room and the smell of stale cigarette smoke assailed our tired nostrils.

I said, "So far it's the only place where the nurses smoke. Obviously it's their only crutch for coping with the stress of poorly children."

"Yes," she sighed.

Both Sylvia and I had just finished a night on duty. The ENT ward I'd just left, shared a kitchen with Intensive care.

I said, "Do you know, when I go into the kitchen at night, I have to put the light on with the door ajar and wait for the

161

scurrying of cockroaches to stop before venturing across the floor."

"Ugh," Sylvia wrinkled her nose.

"I was told that they are not common cockroaches you know, but oriental cockroaches."

Sylvia said, "That doesn't seem to make it any better, does it?"

"No not really. Hospitals have Crown immunity, no one else could get away with such unhygienic conditions, could they?"

We finished our breakfast in silence, each lost in our own thoughts and really too tired to say anymore.

I was relieved when we finished at The Children's hospital. Rick arrived in his car to collect me, and as we drove away he asked, "Will you marry me?"

It came out of the blue, and I was astonished.

"Yes," I gasped breathlessly.

Back at home, I said to Dad, "Dad, Rick has asked me to marry him, so he's coming to ask you. Do you think you could arrange an engagement ring, Dad, as Rick hasn't much money?" Dad arranged for some engagement rings to be available in the Co-operative Central premises, one evening. I met Rick there to try them on. I chose a Diamond Solitaire, with platinum shoulders. Dad drove us home. I was not only feeling excited, but also very trendy as I'd had a 'Sandy Shaw haircut', my ears pierced, and I had bought a red woolen mini dress. Mum didn't make any comment about the ring. She just said, "That dress is too short, it's disgusting, you'll catch your death wearing that."

I shrugged my shoulders, thinking, "What a put down!"

Two weeks later it was December and the end of Rick's term. We went to Oxford and got officially engaged at Chris Barber's Jazz Ball at the Oxford Union. Thanks to Kay's Mum, Nora, I'd been well prepared for dancing old time, modern jazz and popular. I felt great. My escort, although as cold as ice, was tall, dark and handsome. Sexual activity

162

remained clinical and efficient. I accepted it as normal, not knowing anything else. Rick booked me into a bed and breakfast accommodation. With money at a premium, we dined on cheese omelettes and chips at a cafe in The High. I felt happy.

After the break I was due to start at The Birmingham General Hospital, another Victorian style hospital. This time the hospital was Art Deco with its straight lines and cubic in character. Our Nurses' Home, Musson House, overlooked The Steel House Lane Police Station and Eileen and I were on the top floor. We often watched the Police as they walked up and down Steel House Lane, going on the beat or to The Law Courts.

Meanwhile, Eileen was on a busy medical ward. She kept getting into trouble for taking too much time with the patients particularly when she helped them to eat. She would say, "I've always been told to eat everything off my plate. That poor dear was too thin and needed her food." Sometimes she was crying as she came off duty.

"That's alright, Eileen, but you can't take hours on one patient when there's everyone else as well."

I was looking out of the window, as I tried to comfort her. It clearly wasn't working, I'd have to try something else.

I said, "I know, let's put the fire hose out of the window and give that policeman a shower"

She cheered, "Yes, good idea" she said enthusiastically.

The unsuspecting policeman was walking in a dream. Suddenly a shower of water came from nowhere, he looked up at the sky. It was cloudless, he carried on looking up and then he walked straight into a lamppost. It was just like a Charlie Chaplin film and we fell on the floor convulsed with laughter. Eileen forgot her despair.

Officially we were not allowed to have pierced ears. "Infection," they claimed. Anyway, I'd had mine pierced three weeks before, and I had to keep my sleepers in for six weeks to prevent the holes healing over. I cut out tiny squares of Elastoplast to cover them, and bought a hairpiece. I gripped this onto my head, my sidepieces over my ears, and placed my cap on the top. It must have made me about two inches taller but I was never challenged about my ears. However in retrospect I'm sure that they knew about it and it had probably been the subject of discussion in the Sister's Dining Room. I could imagine them saying, "And do you know what Nurse Armitage has been up to this time?"

I was allocated duty in casualty. The bespectacled staff nurse was looking over her glasses at me and I was pondering about the dark moustache on her upper lip. It was so stiff I was wondering if she waxed it to emphasise the unbecoming feature to put people off, when, suddenly I was woken from my reverie.

She was saying, "Mr Blenkinsop in cubical three, has two stitches in his abdomen from a stabbing last week. They're ready to come out. Could you do it, Nurse?"

Embarrassed about my thoughts, I rushed to prepare my trolley and entered the screens. A man was standing beside the trolley. He had taken off his cap and was twisting it round and round in his hands, as though he was trying to wash it. He had a blonde crew cut and sported large tattoos on each arm, one in a heart shape "I love Mum" the other a large Eagle, his fat tummy hanging over his trouser belt. I was fascinated but managed to drag my eyes away, and concentrate on the job in hand.

I said, "Would you like to sit on the trolley, Mr Blenkinsop? I'm going to take out your stitches."

He put down his hat and climbed onto the trolley, lifting his shirt and revealing two tiny stitches. I cleaned the wound, snipped the stitch and started to draw it through the skin. He fainted and started falling towards me. Fortunately, I don't know how but I managed to push him back on the trolley and laid him down before he squashed me flat. I finished the job. How strange that someone so tough could faint having a tiny stitch removed, when the week before he had been fighting with knives.

When I'd finished, I said, "Would you like to stay lying down for a little while?"

"Nope," was the irritated response, as he regained his composure, replaced his cap and left.

I was amused but realised that I could have easily been crushed by his heavy frame crashing on top of me. I never assumed toughness again. It was a lesson well learned.

Gill was on the gynaecology ward and all was not well.

"The Sister wants the ward lights switched out at eight thirty precisely, and she actually asked me this morning what time the ward lights went out. When I replied half past eight, she answered, no nurse it was quarter to nine."

I said, "How crazy. I suppose she knew because she can see the ward from her bedroom window. I'd have thought she'd got better things to do with her time!"

"Exactly and, anyway, most of the beds have got prostitutes in them. It must be like being on nights, for them to settle down to sleep at half past eight," Gill was exasperated.

Sister Greaves on gynaecology was a tall, co-coordinated woman with grey hair coiled up under her cap that always looked as though it was trying to escape. She lived in a flat in the Nurses Home, where she entertained a stocky gentleman caller with a limp. He carried a stick. We were fascinated by the idea of them together.

After the next duty, Gill was laughing, "I've just heard one patient saying to another that she'd had her womb out and a cafeteria inserted."

The next evening, Gill was laughing so much she could hardly get her words out, "Sister told a student nurse to put the flowers on the balcony, and the student thought she said flannels."

We were all laughing as Sylvia said, "Can you imagine someone walking along Steel House Lane, looking up to see

165

the balcony decorated with different coloured face- flannels."?

When I had my turn on gynaecology I was well prepared for Sister' s ways, after hearing Gill's stories. But she was not always predictable. A nurse came to report to her, "I've tried to take a high vaginal swab from Miss Scott, Sister, but I can't get the speculum to pass the swab high enough."

I had the misfortune to be standing next to Sister and suddenly I was nearly knocked off my feet by her elbow. I could swear that she used a pencil-sharpener to sharpen her elbows.

"You can't get it up, nurse? You can drive a double-decker bus up there!"

Our learning curve started to get steeper. During training at The General we'd injected oranges, now it was for real. I took my loaded syringe to Miss Scott, the unsuspecting patient, with an air of false confidence, hoping that I looked confident and professional. Of course, prostitutes can see through ineptitude but, nevertheless, she rolled up her sleeve willingly. I'd been giving injections in casualty but with her eyes firmly fixed on my face I was nervous, and introduced the needle as though it were a corkscrew.

"Oww, core blimey that hurt," she yelled.

I had learnt the stabbing method of giving injections by watching darts on television. After a little practice in the gynaecology ward I thought that I had become quite good at it. Being so young and inexperienced I'm sad to say that although we tried, we didn't offer the Birmingham prostitutes the truly caring and empathetic service that they deserved.

Gill was working in casualty on nights, and the next day I was on a late and sleeping in, when she knocked on the door.

"Come in," I mumbled.

She slumped into a chair, "What a night I've just had! Two gorgeous policemen brought in a tiny fifteen-year-old girl. She'd apparently gone for an abortion at a local back-street abortionist, but, when she left the abortionist, she'd collapsed on the pavement. The Staff-nurse took the policemen into Sister's office and I helped the girl onto a trolley, where she promptly delivered a live baby.

The Night Sister was called, and christened the baby boy 'John', after one of the policemen.

Then, she wrapped the baby in cotton wool and placed him in a shoebox. He died a few minutes later. The Mum was ashen faced, in shock."

"Gill, how awful, couldn't anyone resuscitate him?"

"No, the houseman was cross with the nursing staff, and said, 'Nurses just couldn't accept the fact that the little mite wasn't considered viable.'"

Gill started crying, "Then because he was christened he had to have a funeral, which had to be paid for. No one wanted to fund the funeral."

"I'll make you a cup of tea, Gill," now I was crying too.

Next, we left the General to begin our training in theatres at the Queen Elizabeth. Both Eileen and I were allocated Theatre 5. The theatres were built as a tower block in which each theatre generally served the ward on the same floor. Theatre 5 specialised in Open-heart surgery, with Gastric surgery, and a General surgical day on Wednesdays. Greeting us on our arrival, Sister Hutton said, "You have one of the most important jobs in theatres. It is holding the patient's hand and talking gently to them, while the anaesthetic takes effect."

It was another world. Sister's office contained the green gowns and white plimsolls, which we had to wear. Qualified staff wore white clogs. It was also the base for coffee making apart from the poor theatre porter. When everybody else retreated to drink coffee, his duties were to mop the floors. The doctors had their own changing rooms, emerging when green clad to partake in coffee drinking.

Meanwhile, as the junior nurse, I was sent to take over the anxious patient from the porter and ward nurse while continuing a relaxing type of chat and getting the patient onto the theatre trolley, and into the anaesthetic room. Here the gowned and masked anaesthetist, after asking his patients health-related questions, asked them to count from ten backwards, whilst administering the anaesthetic. We then rushed the unconscious patient into the theatre, where a more senior member of the theatre staff had prepared a trolley with the appropriate sterilised instruments, and covered them with a green theatre cloth.

Then with the patient ready to undergo the surgery and the anaesthetist maintaining the patient's soporific state, the role of the junior nurse was to assist as required. That usually meant providing such things as extra sterile pads for collecting the blood and hanging the used ones on a frame for counting before the patient was sewn up, thus ensuring that none were missing.

I enjoyed the drama of theatres and I stayed there until it was time for my second year block. This focused on preparing us for the responsibility of checking drugs and checking that we had grasped the basic requirements of patient care. We revised blanket bathing and, for bedridden patients, the two hourly turns and the need to massage the patient's buttocks. All this, despite the fact that even in those days severely ill patients could lay on special mattresses with the air regularly pumped into appropriate parts of the mattresses by an electric pump. Oral hygiene was another important factor. We were shown how to use an electric toothbrush.

"The last the thing that a patient needs if they survive this is to have their teeth extracted," was the mantra that was firmly reiterated by the nurse tutor.

During this time we were also prepared to take our state finals. We'd already been helping with drugs rounds but, with the third year and moving to become a short-cap blue, we were well on the way to qualification. But with this came responsibility!

"I've had enough of this, I'm going to get married," Gill announced to us all.

We'd come back after the holiday, and were astonished.

Sylvia was the first to respond, "You can't be married as a student nurse and live in a nurses home."

"Not at The QE!" Gill agreed triumphantly.

"What are you going to do then?" Eileen asked.

Gill continued, "Well, I went to see Miss Griffiths and she confirmed that I couldn't stay on if I was married and nobody else would be interested in a partly trained nurse. I phoned Stafford Hospital and yesterday on my day off and I went for an interview. They said, when would I like to make the transfer?"

We were speechless; it seemed to be a fait accompli.

Again recovering first, Sylvia asked, "When are you going?"

"In two weeks," Gill said triumphantly.

I puzzled over it. After all our dreams, how could Gill just walk away as a short-cap blue before qualification for a long-cap status? But she did, and very shortly we received our wedding invitations. We all went to the wedding. Tim was standing nervously at the door of the Handsacre Church but he greeted us cheerfully. Gill looked lovely in white as she walked down the aisle with her sister Alison as her bridesmaid.

The Vicar asked, "Raymond Darren Michael, do you take this woman…" And we looked at each other in surprise.

At the reception, I asked Gill, "I thought his name was Tim?"

Gill grinned, "So did I, when I first saw him. It was only later when I got to know him that I found out his name wasn't Tim at all."

We all laughed. Eileen said, "Isn't that just typical of Gill!"

"Yes, we'll really miss her dreadfully," Sylvia said sadly.

Gill and Tim made a delightful couple, and it seemed that Gill was happy with the transition to Stafford hospital for the rest of her training. They bought a new home, in Handsacre, and Gill coped with the travel back and forth to Stafford hospital. The rest of us stayed in the Nurses' Home and carried on with our training at the Queen Elizabeth, before taking our finals for State Registration.

I went to West 3, a general surgical ward. It was to be my last ward at the Queen Elizabeth as a short-cap blue and I was now able to undertake the drug rounds, although I was not qualified to give "dangerous or control drugs", such as diamorphine and barbiturates. When I was the most senior nurse on the ward I carried the drug cupboard keys and felt very important. It was customary to work in pairs. Placing the prescriptions in the document-holder on the drug trolley we would take the trolley from bed to bed, with both of us checking the prescribed drug and dose. I would take the appropriate bottle from the trolley, tip the tablet into the bottle-cap to avoid building up drug resistance from skin contact and put it into the medicine pot saying, for example, "Mr McDougall is taking Ampicillin for a chest infection. Is that correct, Nurse Jackson?"

"Yes," Nurse Jackson would agree before moving to Mr. McDougall, checking his name on his hospital bracelet and making sure that he took the prescribed medicine.

Then Nurse Jackson, in her first year, would return the empty drug pot to the trolley and we would proceed to the next bed. The next patient's drug chart would be collected and the process repeated until all our patients had had their prescriptions. The drug rounds were normally scheduled for six and ten am and two, six and ten pm.

Being a general surgical ward, West 3 had several patients suffering from cancer. One four-bedded bay was perpetually full of mastectomy ladies.

"Can you do the dressings, Nurse?" Sister asked.

I trembled as I prepared my first trolley. I dreaded revealing the mutilated chests as I went into the four-bedded ward. The ladies, all in their forties with carefully applied make-up, were sharing a joke. They went quiet as I introduced myself and explained what I was doing. I drew the screens around Mrs Williams, the first lady, and she unbuttoned her emerald-green satin nightdress. I needn't have worried. She made my task easy, though there was a drawn expression in her sad chestnut eyes as she looked calmly at her wound. I cleaned and re-dressed as gently as I could and she smiled reassuringly. I was thinking, "It's me that should be supporting you, not the other way round." I went from bed to bed carrying out my task and, just as I left, a raucous peel of laughter rent the air. I was amazed how these women were able to support each other despite their horrendous mutilation, loss of femininity and attractiveness. I felt overawed by their cheerfulness. Could I cope with having my breast removed with such optimism, or losing my femininity and sexuality?

My next task was to give Mrs Williams a specimen pot. She was in the bathroom and I knocked on the door, carrying the specimen pot. I found her sitting on a chair, convulsed in tears, so I sat on the side of the bath holding her hand, quite unable to do anything other than be quietly supportive. I looked into her tear-stained face and waited. After a while, she wiped away her tears and smiled at me.

"Thank you, I'm alright now."

Then she went back to her bed and I heard her laughing and saying to the other ladies, "Wouldn't you like to know what I've been doing with Nurse Armitage!"?

Sadly, in the Sixties cancer usually progressed on its destructive path until there was no hope. Then, at ward-report Sister would resignedly say, "It's carcinomatosis. TLC is all that is left. Gently as you can."

The gathered nurses would write TLC alongside the patient' s name, in their notebooks.

Whilst TLC meant tender loving care, it felt more like rest in peace. The patient was usually moved into a single room where we offered what solace we could, giving them a gentle blanket bath each day to refresh them. Inevitably, injections of diamorphine commenced, with increasing doses so that the inevitable death wasn't racked by pain, or so I believed.

Sometimes, the phone rang on night duty, "Hello, Nurse Armitage speaking."

Night Sister's voice, "Can you come to check some diamorphine on Ward West 4, Nurse?"

As I hurried along, I could foresee the situation that would be about to face me. A nurse would be refusing to give her permission for an increased dose in the belief that it would hasten the patient' s death. As I entered the ward I could understand the feelings of the nurse in question. She may regard me as a murderer, whereas I could consider her to be heartless and sanctimonious and the hapless patient would be calling out in agony. A difficult decision and a dilemma that is with us to this day. "If death is inevitable should I stand by watching someone suffering in agony?" I thought not.

My doubts about marriage and my relationship with Rick increased. I was trapped by my soiled state, the absence of my maidenhead and consequently resigned to my fate. After another squalid sexual experience and Rick's off -hand treatment of me, I threw the engagement ring back at him. It hit the wall; he picked it up and put it in his pocket. In silence, he took me back to the hospital. The next day Rick's car was waiting outside the hospital when I came off duty. I climbed in, and he calmly handed the slightly bent ring back to me. I took it and placed it on my finger, and life continued as before. I felt my impure state left me with no choice.

Rick had been sponsored throughout his degree by The Atomic Energy Authority and, as part of the deal, he worked for them each summer, while continuing to study. The understanding was that he was to be employed by them on a full time basis once he'd taken his degree. But when his results arrived, in the summer of 1968, he'd been awarded a First class degree.

He said, "I've been offered the opportunity to do a research degree. I'm thinking of going back to Oxford in September 1969. You would be qualified by then, so we could get married and you could get a job in Oxford. When I get married, my aunt has left me £3000."

There was a lot to think about. I didn't respond for several days.

Now was the time for decisions for the three of us. We had to take our state finals, and then Eileen, Sylvia and I had to decide where we would like to become Staff-nurses.

Sylvia said, "I'd like to go back to be a Staff Nurse at The General."

I said pensively, "I liked it there, but I loved it on theatres. What about you Eileen?"

Eileen responded immediately, "I didn't like the pressure at The General, it's theatres for me."

It was the mixture of drama and excitement interspersed with periods of quiet concentration during surgery that appealed to both Eileen and me. Much of our theatre preference was due to the tremendous confidence and admiration that we had for Sister Hallett. She ruled theatres and the medical staff with a rod of iron. She was warm but firm with us and so both Eileen and I felt confidence in her leadership. We were summoned to see the assistant Matron, who we had nicknamed Pumpkin, to make our requests, and later Eileen and I heard we'd been accepted. Sylvia was successful in requesting The General, as well.

CHAPTER 6

NURSING AND MARRIAGE

Autumn was turning into winter. By the time we were all back at The General I was suffering from toothache after a lifetime of neglect and too many sweets.

"Oww!" I howled as I bit into treacle tart.

A nurse in the dining room said, "The dental hospital don't charge for treatment and the students are dishy, why don't you try there?"

Anything was better than toothache, even lying in a dental chair with my mouth wide open. I didn't care what the dental student looked like. In the event, the student under the supervision of his tutor drilled and drilled for what seemed like hours. He then filled the tooth and I gratefully staggered back to the nurse's home for a sleep, thinking, "Well that was a daft thing to do. I wouldn't trust my body in the hands of a medical student, I wish I hadn't trusted a dental student with my teeth!"

At least when I woke the next morning I didn't have toothache.

Towards the end of 1968 and during a particularly cold night, a policeman on his city centre beat came across the half frozen body of a tramp in a doorway. The tramp, Mr Philpott,

174

was admitted with hypothermia. I put him in a theatre gown and gently cleaned his very thin, small body after which I placed a single sheet over him so that he didn't re- heat too quickly and put additional strain on his weakened body. Unused to the luxury of a bed and years of being alert to danger, meant that he usually slept badly. Some nights he would talk to me about his experiences and particularly about the weaknesses of the many prisons that he tried whilst being kept "At Her Majesty' s pleasure". He was quite astute, during one of our night's whispered conversations he said, 'You've got t' have a good matron.'

I replied, "I'm not sure. I don't really see much of her but I think she was trained by Florence Nightingale. Mind you, the Ward sister is scary enough."

Sadly, one of his legs had to be amputated below the knee. It turned out that one of his badly fitting shoes leaked, the water froze and he got severe frostbite. The leg couldn't be saved.

During one of my night duties, when the junior nurse was having her tea break, I felt a peculiar cold feeling and, convinced that something was wrong, I picked up my torch and checked all the patients. They were still asleep. Nothing to worry about, I thought, "I must be imagining it." We started our morning routine at 6am and I went to dispense the drugs. When I got to the third bed on the left the patient didn't stir. I shook him; he was stiff. I drew the curtains round the bed. I then knew that my earlier premonition had been correct and that the spirit of death had passed through the ward. Composing myself I said to the junior nurse,

"I'm afraid that Mr Jones died in the night, I'll phone the houseman."

I rang. He wasn't long coming to examine the patient. He went to Sister's office to write the death certificate. After covering the patient's face with his sheet, I followed the doctor.

"What time will you put as the time of death?"

He didn't look up, but said, "I'll say that I was called to the ward at 6:30, and found the patient had been dead some time."

My heart sank, then he started to laugh, "The look on your face is one of total horror, of course I won't," he said smiling.

At first I didn't find it easy to see the joke, then we both had a chuckle together. I continued with my morning routine, still wondering about how I'd felt so conscious of the patient's death. I hadn't checked his bed because I had seen him get up to go to the lo, and return to his bed just a few minutes before.

Mr Philpott was starting to recover from his surgery and the Ward Sister decided to sort him out. She took him to the bathroom and washed his hair. It stood up on end as if in shock from being clean and was a surprising rich chestnut-brown in colour. She wheeled him back to his bed wearing brand-new pyjamas. I don't know where the pyjamas came from they certainly were not NHS issue. When Mr Jones, the barber, came to shave Mr Philpott the next day, he wasn't in the least surprised by Mr Philpott' s smart pyjamas.

Mr. Jones said to me, "In spite of herself, Sister's an old softie at heart, when it comes to life 's down and-outs."

I looked at Sister Faulkner in a new light. She'd always seemed a rather tough old bird but now I realised that there was a lot to learn from the likes of Sister Faulkner. I was sad to leave her, The General and Sylvia behind.

But it was now time for Eileen and me to go back to Theatre 5 at The Queen Elizabeth.

I thought, "With Eileen's tremendously high level of empathetic care, surely she would be better placed with someone like sister Faulkner at The General, rather than theatres."

But Eileen had another surprise for me.

"I'm going to marry Peter in June," Eileen announced.

"That's before we get our exam results." I was surprised.

"Well, when are you and Rick thinking of getting married?"

"I'm not sure. He hasn't said, and if he's going back to Oxford…" I left the sentence unfinished.

Suddenly the cosy sheltered life I knew was coming to an end. When I had previously discussed it with Rick, we had settled on July the 12th, but somehow things were still undecided.

Life in theatres was exhilarating and I was enjoying the excitement. The Queen Elizabeth theatres were a Reception Centre for heart surgery cases from as far away as Wales. Frequently a helicopter would arrive carrying a patient needing emergency chest surgery. A field adjacent to the hospital had been designated as a landing zone and the traumatised patient would be rushed in, whilst I was busily boiling up the theatre instruments. I would wait for the instructions to receive the patient in the anaesthetic room. While the anaesthetist evaluated the patient I would be cheerfully chatting away.

"Have you been on your holidays yet?" Was the summer-time opener and, if Christmas was approaching, "What will you be doing for Christmas?"

These two questions never failed to get a response. The anaesthetist usually reported that the patient's blood pressure responded to this considerate treatment and showed a healthy reduction. Then, as soon as the patient was asleep, it was all systems go on the operating table.

As a senior-student nurse I was learning my trade and I was now the scrub-nurse for minor operations. I could approach the elbow-taps with confidence; I would turn on the water, invert the five-minute egg timer and scrub away for my allotted time. After that, I applied sterile talcum powder, donned my sterile gloves and then checked that all the required surgical instruments were correctly and conveniently set out for the operation. On Wednesdays we normally did the list for suspected breast tumours. Sometimes I felt worried because the doctors didn't always show the appropriate respect of an unconscious patient.

I remember one of the doctors saying, "She's a bit of all right."

They were all grinning when suddenly Sister appeared at the foot of the table and, suitably chastened, the medical staff continued with the operation in silence. Patients would have a small sample of the dubious tissue removed and sent to the laboratory for confirmation of cancer. While we waited for the results I would cover the instruments on the trolley wait with the team.

On another occasion, in Sister's absence, "Look at these pendulous breasts," grinned the Registrar, lifting one breast by the nipple.

The assisting medical staff giggled.

I was appalled, knowing that if Sister were present they'd never have dared to abuse a patient in front of her. I started pushing the instrument trolley towards the sluice, saying over my shoulder as I went, "If you intend to be so callous about the patient in your care, you can continue to operate without the scrub nurse."

Silence reigned, then, "I'm very sorry," the Registrar called to me.

I returned and we resumed the surgery.

I explained what had happened later to Eileen.

"Good for you," she said, smiling.

Eileen was leaving to start her wedding preparations.

"Now I'll be all on my own," I complained to Rick.

He said, "I've got some news. I've been accepted to do a PhD at my old college in Oxford. I think that it would be much more sensible if we delay our wedding until I start in September."

I shrugged my shoulders, my opinion was, as usual, ignored.

He went on, "I've been talking to someone at work whose wife is a Health Visitor. That would be a good thing for you to do and Oxford pay a full salary during training."

I thought, "If we are intending to have any children, that would at least give me some confidence in how to bring them up, I don't feel that I got any knowledge about that from my mother."

So I wrote to Oxford City Health Department and the Chief Nursing Officer replied that I would need some community experience, together with an obstetrics certificate. I replied requesting that Oxford offered me that experience and I received an acceptance shortly afterwards.

At last, the long awaited State Registration results arrived. I'd passed, and I went on duty wearing a broad grin. I was met by Sister, who said, "Matron wants to see you straight away."

For the first time ever, I knocked on Matron' s door.

A voice rang out, "Come."

In trepidation, I entered. Matron was seated at an enormous antique desk, which accentuated her tiny stature. She was a bespectacled vision of starched white lace with a well-creased face. A sister stood by the desk to attend to Matron's needs. I approached the desk and gave my name. It seemed like I was facing Queen Victoria. She smiled as she handed me a set of long cap and said,

"We'll hear more of this nurse."

"Thank you, Matron," I said, accepting the proffered lace trimmed, linen caps.

But I was thinking to myself, "The old soul, does she not know that I'm leaving to become a health visitor! Though at the same time, I was so much in awe of her I felt I should walk out backwards.

When I went back to theatres, Sister said, "Can you report for major injuries training tomorrow?"

"Yes Sister."

So the following day found me wearing a white tracksuit with fluorescent QEH NURSE emblazoned on the back, white hard hat with flashlight, and a battery box strapped around my waist. One of the training routines was to run up the five flights of stairs that ran at the back of the theatre block to connect the theatres, to keep fit. The training was to deal with severely injured patients from a major disaster. At the time, New Street station had been amalgamated with the Snow Hill station and the railway authorities were concerned that, should trains crash whilst in the numerous tunnels, there would be many casualties needing rescue. Fortunately a Railway disaster didn't happen, and when the tragedy of the Birmingham pub bomb occurred I was married and living in Oxford. So I didn't use this major disaster training in a live situation.

I was now on my own. Eileen, like Gill, had left to get married, and Sylvia was enjoying life at The General. I felt so alone with all my closest nursing friends gone, but I did have wedding arrangements to make and bookings to organise. Rick and I worked separately on our guest lists and, when we put them together, it seemed that the Methodist Chapel would be far too small for the number of guests.

"See what the Shenstone Church of England Vicar thinks," Dad suggested.

"Yes, St. John' s could accommodate you on that date, and I'd be happy to conduct the service," said the Vicar, his smile bringing warmth into his otherwise grey and gloomy face. There was no mention that his church was in conflict with the Methodists about alcohol in communion wine.

"It doesn't matter, because we won't be taking communion during the marriage service, will we Dad?"

But it was a different story about the proposed venue for the wedding reception, originally planned at the Belfrey.

"It's not available for the September date," Dad announced.

Eventually, he did manage to book the 'Bowling Green' in Lichfield.

It was usual for Dad to take the lion's share when it came

to making arrangements. Mum and I were left to organise the clothes and write the wedding invitations.

Mum sighed and appeared to be bored with everything.

I asked, "Was it because I was the youngest, that you didn't want me?"

Without hesitation she replied, "No, I didn't want any of you."

Suddenly my paranoia was put into perspective.

Mum and Dad thought that Rick was a man with good prospects and a very suitable husband. However, in my heart of hearts I knew that things were not alright and when I threw my engagement ring back at Rick, it was an indication of my severe doubts and trepidation.

"I don't have to put up with this. It's over!" I'd shouted at the time.

But I still felt that the only way I could reclaim my decency would be by marrying the man who took it from me. Rick shrugged off my confusion and qualms as simply due to my being female. He'd arrive for each date and sit in his car at the Nurses' Home. I'd climb in meekly, feeling completely trapped and that I'd burnt my bridges. But I was an incurable optimist and hoped our marriage, just like Cinderella's, would have a fairy tale ending and we would live "happily ever after".

In fact I was destined to follow Isabelle Archer in *Portrait of a Lady*. I'd read the Henry James book at school and spent valuable time discussing Isabelle's lack of self worth and how she had in the depth of her nature an unquenchable desire to please, which was to be her undoing. Isabelle's husband, Ralph Touchett, began with being a young man of promise. At Oxford he distinguished himself. Ralph was a very dark character and Rick held unnerving similarities to him and, like Isabelle, I now had no self worth. I felt degraded by having lost my virginity and it had left me with an overwhelming sense of guilt. "Marriage is my only way out. Then I will be absolved from this great weight of tremendous guilt," I thought.

Having graduated, Rick was working with the company that had sponsored him through his first degree. I went to spend my days off with him in his rented flat-share in St. Anne's. There were two other engineers staying there. Gerald Wise; short, dark and as skinny as a rake, and his social skills were about as exciting as a cold, damp tea bag; but he had one saving grace, his car. He drove a white Mini Cooper S, although the sole topic of his conversation was cars and their engines.

"It's to do with the highly tuned carburettors and the amazing differential in the gearbox," he'd say to Rick.

Rick said, "You know Martin, the bloke I work with, was telling me about buying and restoring a 1937 Morris 8. He's asked us all to go and see it this evening, is that OK?"

"Yes," Gerald agreed, his face lighting up.

We were all sitting at the table, tucking into a dish of spaghetti bolognaise, cooked by their other flat-mate, Steve.

Steve said, "I've got to do the washing-up first."

"I'll help with that," I said enthusiastically.

Steve was a tall, sandy haired, charming man, who seemed to be equipped with the entire sum of good humour for the three of them. He just laughed at their complete lack of empathy with anything other than engines.

We chatted amicably as we did the washing-up.

"I'm only here for six weeks, then it's back to St Catherine's for my final year," Steve told me.

I was delighted, "I'll be in Oxford too, by then. I can't cook anything as adventurous as you, but I chose a cookery book as a sixth form prize, so I'll see what I can put together."

We climbed into Gerald's Mini and he drove us to admire Martin's car. It was a two-seater convertible in British racing green. The bonnet had two clips, one for each side, and Martin released the catches so that Rick and Gerald could admire the engine. I stood on the tarmac drive, whilst the men peered under the bonnet.

On the way back, I was sitting in the back of the mini with Steve. There was a heated conversation coming from the front seats.

Gerald said, "Compared to my Mini, it's a Noddy car. I wouldn't be bothered with it."

Rick protested, "I'll agree that it's different, but the engine has got it's own charms."

I smiled at Steve companionably and he smiled back, shrugging his shoulders. The conversation was way over my head, but it seemed to focus on the shortcomings of the side-valve engine.

"I think the car is superb," I announced.

The two front-seat occupants ignored my contribution.

It was soon time for me to leave, "Don't forget to phone when you're back in Oxford, and I'll cook you a meal as promised," I said to Steve.

"I'll hold you to that!"

Then, it was into Gerald's Mini for the drive to the station.

"Thank you for the lift," I said to Gerald, as I kissed Rick goodbye.

As the Birmingham train drew out I felt more unsettled than ever, but the pressures of theatre work soon drove all other thoughts out of my mind. The next time I saw Rick, he said, "Martin has become very fed-up with the car. He's offered it to me for £30. I've said yes."

"Great, that's terrific," I said.

Every waking moment now seemed to be taken up with the arrangements for the wedding. With regret, I said goodbye to The Queen Elizabeth, determined to embark on a successful married life.

The morning of the wedding dawned, promising a beautiful sunny day. Kay, my chief bridesmaid, was full of fun, "Now, you haven't forgotten who you're marrying, have you? It's not the best man, Jonathan, Michael Jones's brother, just because Michael showed us his special tool!"

"Kay, we were only five then." I was laughing.

She laughed, "Well, you don't forget these things, do you?"

We pulled ourselves together as the bridal march started; I took Dad's arm and was conscious of him limping. Clearly the gout in his left toe was playing him up again. As we proceeded down the aisle, I felt as though I was sleep walking.

The Vicar conducted the service with an air of gravity and without the warmth that his smile had brought to his features, when we'd first met. As the wedding service continued, the absence of any relationship with the church became patently clear. In the singing of the first hymn, "The Lord is my shepherd," I missed Hilary's beautiful voice singing next to me in the church choir. Hilary and John had been unable to attend my wedding, as Hilary had delivered their second baby the previous day. As we exchanged vows, the sinking of my heart was compounded by the perfunctory nature of the Vicar's address. Then, the next hymn, "Love divine," was all that I was hoping for, but I was overwhelmed by the dreaded feeling that love was absent. Nevertheless, I kept smiling as we emerged into the bright sunshine of a lovely, late summer day and, after photographs, left for the Lichfield reception. I felt too preoccupied with my fears to be aware of the speeches and, almost before I knew where I was, it was time to change into my going away outfit.

I was feeling very smart in my petrol blue woollen suit, with leg of mutton sleeves as we left for our honeymoon in the Morris 8.

I heard one guest saying, "What a wonderful future Annie is entering."

Rick's Auntie (who wasn't a real Aunt), had left him sufficient money for a deposit on a home, and we had a maisonette waiting for us in Cowley, Oxford. We stayed for two nights at a hotel in the Cotswolds, before heading for Oxford.

During the summer we had furnished the maisonette and, as the builders had decorated it, it was ready and waiting for our arrival. There was post waiting for us too. A letter from Rick's supervisor, inviting Mr and Mrs Thompson to a fork supper at his house in Cumnor. Oddly, I was taken aback by my new name.

The next day we unpacked then headed for Cumnor.

"What's a fork supper?" I asked Rick as he drove.

"A supper where you just use forks," his tone indicating that he couldn't believe he'd married anyone as stupid as me.

We arrived at the picturesque, white rendered house in its own grounds. Rick parked the car and rang the doorbell. The door was immediately opened to reveal a lovely dark-haired lady in her forties.

She introduced herself warmly, "I'm Mrs Jones, the wife of your husband's supervisor."

Then she turned to me saying, "Come and meet Doctor Parkes, the Maths Don."

I was horrified, thinking, "How could someone as stupid as me have anything to say to anyone as clever as a Maths Don?"

"David, this is Mrs Thompson, Rick's new wife," she announced and moved away.

Doctor Parkes was tall, gauche and appeared totally tongue-tied. Conversation with him needed all the skills learned in my hospital anaesthetic room apart from the handholding. As we left the fork supper I thought, "I will never be overawed by academic qualifications ever again."

As the next day was Sunday, we headed for the nearest Methodist Church at Rose Hill and received a very warm welcome.

The minister's wife asked, "What will you be doing while your husband is doing research, Annie?"

"I'm reporting for duty as a District Nurse at the East Oxford Health Centre, tomorrow morning."

185

"Good luck," she smiled.

As we walked home, Rick said, "Eight o'clock is too early for me to get up but I've got a bus timetable at home, so you'll be able to find your own way there."

As it was delivered as a statement and not a question, I didn't respond.

The following morning, I caught the number 5 bus and began my life as a temporary District Nurse. I was loaned the use of a blue district mini and a navy blue uniform, with a matching felt hat and gaberdine mack. We reported in at eight each morning, re-equipped our Gladstone bag and collected new referrals.

My new colleagues, mostly plump middle-aged ladies, were pleasant enough, but by the end of September I was driving the Mini with tears running down my cheeks. I knew that I'd made a dreadful mistake. I felt as though I'd entered a freezer, and that Rick had enslaved me rather than the given me the companionship portrayed in the fairy stories, which I had dared to hope for.

Just when I was at my lowest, the phone rang, I picked it up, a warm voice on the other end said,

"It's Steve, I'm back at College, you promised you'd cook a meal for me, do you remember?"

I smiled, "Yes, when can you come?"

Thus began Steve's Thursday weekly visits. With the *Never Cooked Before book* in hand, I learnt to cook. Steve revelled in my attempts, and he offered me the opportunity to chat, whilst making me feel my views were valid. One Thursday, I nipped into Sainsbury's to buy the provisions for the meal. I pushed my trolley to the tills.

A voice rang out, "Come to the front, Nurse."

All the queue were attempting to clear a pathway, I looked around for a nurse, before realising I was wearing uniform, and she meant me. Then, shame-faced, pushed my trolley to the front of the queue.

I muttered as I went, "Thank you, thank you, thank you."

I was thinking, "I mustn't shop in uniform again!"

The next day, as I drove along the Ifley Road to see a patient, I was musing, "Didn't Roger Bannister set his mile record on the Ifley Road, Oxford?" I was setting my own speed record, in spite of the elderly Mini. Arriving at the house I knocked on the front door and it was flung open by a plump, smiling lady. She showed me into the front room, furnished in the style of the thirties, so that I could dress a gruesome varicose ulcer oozing green puss, on the leg of a shrivelled old lady, who greeted every attempt at conversation with total silence. As I left the room, I was called into the dining room.

"Sit here, nurse," the daughter invited.

The table was laid with coffee and freshly made cakes, and the generously proportioned daughter urged me to eat not only one but at least two. They were good, but I couldn't escape. I thought, "Now I know why most District Nurses are plump."

Sometimes, when I had finished my own caseload, I'd help with other nurse's work. One day June Barton asked, "I'm a bit pushed tomorrow, could you do an insulin injection for me on your way in?"

"I'd be pleased to, June." I smiled.

At half-past seven, I drove to the house and climbed out of the Mini, Gladstone bag in hand. I opened the gate and suddenly, an Alsatian tore from the back garden, barking ferociously. Instinctively I turned and, jumping straight over the two foot wall, in seconds I was in the safety of the car. I looked around. The milkman, the postman, and the paperboy were all laughing at me. With injured pride, bag in hand, I walked back through the gate. With every step I took forward, the Alsatian barked and took a step backwards and, in what seemed perfect step, we waltzed up to the front door. I rang the bell.

"Mum's all ready for you," a cheery lady smiled.

I was just about to complain about the dog, when I looked

round and it was nowhere to be seen. I went in, gave the injection and left.

"You could have warned me about the Alsatian," I said when I got to work.

"Oh, he always does that, if there's anyone new," June shrugged it off.

Another time, in response to, "Does anyone need any help?" June said, "Yes, could you do Jolly' s antibiotics, for TB. They are in the house."

I went to the house and an elderly lady opened the door. She seemed very confused, as I gave her the injection.

Back at base, June asked, "Did you give Mr. Jolly his injection?"

I stared at her in disbelief, "I gave it to a lady, who opened the door."

Her eyes widened, "That's his mother," she grinned.

"She looked very thin and tubercular," I said defensively.

"Don't worry, it won't do her any harm," she laughed.

"I'll go back and hopefully give it to the right person this time," I said.

The next day, I hobbled in to see my GP.

"It's that old Mini, and is it only the right knee?" Doctor Abraham asked, as he tugged on his black goatee beard.

"Yes, but I'm hardly able to walk because of the pain."

"It's post-patellar thickening, due to the stiff clutch. I notice it's not the leg that you use for braking that's affected, do you ever use the brake?" he sounded amused.

"Well, I'm leaving the district to do an obstetric nursing certificate, before health-visiting," I said in an irritated tone. I was annoyed by his implied criticism of my speedy driving, though it was probably justified.

Dr Abraham just smiled.

Sandy went to live with John and Hil in Shrewsbury where brother John was a Junior Doctor, and Sandy came to live with us in Oxford when they were away. He came for his week's holiday. On the ground floor below our maisonette lived Mrs Williams. She was a quiet lady, but didn't appreciate Sandy living on the floor above her.

"The dog scratches the carpets in the night," she complained.

"I'm not sure how I can stop him, but I will try," I assured her.

Next door to Mrs Williams was Mr James, a wheelchair-bound man with multiple sclerosis.

His wife said, don't worry about Mrs Williams, she is rather bored and complaining gives her something to do."

Mr and Mrs James didn't have time to get bored, they spent their time working for DIG, the Disablement Income Group. They felt they'd achieved a great deal when the Chronically Sick and Disabled Act was passed that very year, in 1970. As a result of their comment, I shrugged off Mrs Williams' complaints.

Sandy and I spent our holiday week in The Parks, where I often watched Oxford playing cricket while Sandy slept. He was an old dog now and had gone blind. I can remember sitting in a deck chair knitting a Guernsey sweater in oiled wool for Rick, the coarse wool played havoc with my hands. I never did grasp the rules of cricket, but it was pleasant sitting in The Parks with Sandy. The engineering building overlooked the Parks and Rick drove the "8" to the engineering building each morning, so it didn't inconvenience him to drop us off.

After the holiday, I went for a three month course in Obstetric Nursing at the Nuffield Maternity home. During the course I gained a lifetime's fear of midwives, if nothing else. As a breed, they seemed so rumbustuous and sure of themselves. As I had returned my Mini when I left district nursing, I had to catch the 715 bus from Cowley Centre to the Maternity unit, which ran alongside the main Radcliffe hospital. The very idea that Rick should wake to drive me in, though I was now the bread-winner, was a non-starter, though the engineering building was only a stone's throw away. After my first arduous night duty, I discovered that the buses didn't run on Sundays. On the verge of tears, I started to walk home. An ambulance drew alongside.

The smiling driver lent out, "Would you like a lift, Nurse?"

"How do you know I'm a nurse?" I asked querulously.

"Nobody else would be walking in Oxford at this time in the morning. Hop in, we can take you as far as Cowley Road."

I was ready for a holiday, as I hadn't had a break between gaining my Obstetrics Certificate and starting the Health Visiting training. So when Rick said, "I've asked Steve if he'd like to come for a holiday on a boat with us, going down the Thames from Oxford and back up to Oxford on the canals," I jumped at the chance. Steve asked his fiancee, Paula, to come as well, and we all set off. The attention that Steve normally gave me was now lavished on Paula. I felt neglected and the realisation began to dawn on me that, as Steve had completed his final year, he would be going and I would not see him so often. It would leave a tremendous gap in my life, but I would have to come to terms with it.

Back from holiday, I started at Oxford Polytechnic. Rick didn't mind taking me there, because the time coincided with his own itinerary. Oxford Polytechnic was a tower-block building, obviously designed by an architect of the utilitarian school, it lacked any of the romance conjured up in the designs of Oxford University architects of previous centuries. Rick dropped me off and, fighting my way through the melee of other students, I reported in at the reception. I felt great sympathy for the weary receptionist, as she directed me to the lift to the second floor.

Stepping out of the lift, I followed the directions to the classroom and went into an L shaped room packed with desks. Part had been sectioned off as a staff-room. Each desk bore the name of its intended occupant, organised

190

alphabetically. As my surname was Thompson, I was near the end, by the door. It felt as though a shoehorn had been used to fit me in as an after thought. The two tutors were Miss Ridley, who was all skin and bone and overactive, and her junior colleague, Miss Cook, who was plump and laid-back. Both appeared to have tricky thyroid problems. As time went by, Miss Ridley became more anxious and hyperactive, while Miss Cook seemed to get slower and slower.

Soon I was busy coping with the complexity of new subjects, like social policy and the sociology of the family, too busy to pass comment or chuckle about the tutors increasing eccentricities. New friendships were formed. Chris, who sat in front of me, was sponsored by Cambridge Health Authority. While Oxford paid me a full first year Health-Visitor's salary, plus an allowance to buy as many books as I considered necessary, Chris, who'd been the Ward Sister of the Transplant Unit at Addenbrookes, was only paid three-quarters of her salary and £10 to spend on books. The library held just one copy of each book that was recommended by the visiting lecturers. She was unable to drive, so she was also paying out for driving lessons. Inevitably, Chris had to cover her expenses by working for an Agency on night duty, on alternate weekends. On the weekend she was free she came for Sunday lunch and very soon our friendship was established, filling the emotional gap in my life, which Steve had left. As part of the course we were placed with a Health Visitor for practical experience. This mostly involved working in the baby clinic, where mums brought their infants for weighing, vaccinations and advisory sessions. It also included a check for deafness at seven months, but it was rather Heath Robinson. With babysitting on Mum's knee, the Health Visitor, standing behind, would ring the bell. If baby turned its head, it was presumed to be hearing.

Now the winter was making the outdoors feel cold. The duffle coat had given way to Afghan coats as a uniform in the early Seventies. My mother, having bought a new sheepskin coat, gave her old one to me. It wasn't trendy but at least it was warm. However, it was useless in the rain. January was a very wet month in Oxford, and I missed my gaberdine mack from District Nursing days. We did not have a uniform for Health Visiting so, one day in January, I was walking along The Corn Market in the rain and I noticed that Richard Shops had a on and I went and bought an £18 mack for £9. I was delighted with my purchase. Strangely, Rick didn't see it quite the same way.

"How dare you?" he shouted.

"I need a raincoat for work," I said lamely.

An icy silence fell and, in response to his hostility, I indignantly moved into the spare bedroom to sleep. During the night, he appeared at my bedside.

He was puce in the face and shouting, "You're my wife, and you sleep with me."

With a vice like grip on my ankle he dragged from the bed. I fell onto the floor and he started kicking me. I cried and, shaking and dazed, I returned to the marital bed in a very dejected state.

The next morning, I could hardly put my right leg on the floor. The pain in my hip was dreadful, but there was no conversation as he drove to the Polytechnic. I felt very ashamed as I limped into the college. Could this have been what triggered my Lupus?

At lunchtime, Chris asked, "I need some groceries, shall we walk to the shops in Headington?"

"Yes," I agreed, doing my best to ignore the pain.

Gradually the pain eased and the year progressed. Dad's words about the Aldermaston peace marches, and our discussions about me being a pacifist, came to mind and I realised how right he had been. If someone has a weapon, you'll need a larger one to defend yourself. Unfortunately I didn't have any weapons in my armoury. I felt depressed, marriage had become a trap and I had blindly walked into it.

192

I had hoped that it would salve my conscience about losing my virginity but it had become my prison.

I did enjoy being a student but all too soon that status was over. I started as a Health Visitor at a surgery in the East Oxford Health Centre. Unfortunately Chris was also leaving to take up Health Visitor duties but she was leaving Oxford to begin her work in the Cambridge Health District, where she was to cover Isleham and Wicken Fen villages. I was very sad to lose the company of another friend. Chris still hadn't passed her driving test so she had to do her rounds on her bicycle, thankful that the fen roads were relatively level. She was offered accommodation in Soham with Mrs Bugg.

"Would you like me to drive you there?" I asked.

"Yes please, I don't know how I'd manage otherwise. I seem to have acquired so much stuff."

It was a break and an adventure, as Chris and I headed into the flat countryside with the big fenland skies overhead, so different from the dominant hills of my native Yorkshire. We arrived at about 1.30pm and Mrs Bugg, an ample bodied woman wearing a wrap around apron, answered the door.

Mrs Bugg welcomed us in her strong West Suffolk accent, "Come in mi dear, and would yu be likeing a nice cup of tea?"

Thinking back on it, Bugg's appearance could have been the inspiration for Nora Batty, in *Last of The Summer Wine*. As I drove home, I was worried about Chris. Would she be able to cope with the eccentric, old-fashioned country ways? It was a considerable change from the academic culture and spires of Oxford!

"My senior health visitor has an expression as if she's spent her life sucking lemons." I thought as I started work at the surgery in Cowley Road.

I asked Pat, one of the other students on my course sponsored by Oxford, "How is the work at Temple Cowley?"

Pat frowned, but answered, "The two Health Visitors are

nice, but I've been allocated Blackbird Leys so I'm not sure how I will cope with such an unruly area."

"That's good. I'm to go there as well. What about meeting once a week for lunch? Then we could discuss any problems."

"Yes that's a good idea, say next Tuesday at mine and I'll do lunch and then you can do the next week," Pat said smiling.

Blackbird Leys was a large, new council estate built on the edge of Oxford, built to accommodate the workers of Morris Cowley. Many of the occupants were Afro-Caribbean. Neither Pat nor I had any experience, or preparation in helping people of other communities. Neither of us had much post registration experience and we were ill prepared for the task in hand.

"It's that nobody else wants to do it, so they dump Blackbird Leys on us new recruits," I said.

Pat responded, "Yes, hopefully it will be good training at the end of the day."

We enjoyed our lunch times, chatting over the problems we faced as novices, and a close bond of friendship was formed. We were very similar in height and appearance and, whereas I was married, Pat had formed a relationship with a student at the Polytechnic.

The blood donor clinic was in the same building where I worked. As I remembered all the blood that used to end up on the floor during open-heart surgery, I felt obliged to offer help in any way I could. My periods were slight, and it seemed the least I could do was to offer my blood. So one day I took the plunge and went to a blood donor session. A sample was taken for analysis and I waited to get the OK and become a donor. A young doctor called me into her consultation room.

"You've got a positive V. D. test, so we do not want your blood. Never darken our door again," she announced, her dark eyes narrowing.

194

I couldn't believe it and just sat in the chair, shaking my head.

"I can't have syphilis, I really can't."

She was anxious to get on with the clinic and to persuade me out of the chair, "OK. We'll do further analysis, come back in four weeks time."

Four weeks later, nervous and very concerned, I returned. "It's a false positive," she said dismissing me and offering no other explanation.

I was in a state of confusion, when the phone rang back at home. It was my brother,

"Hi, it's John. I'm afraid Sandy has died."

"Oh no, John, how awful. How's Hilary taken it?"

He went on, "Devastated, but I've possibly got some good news too. I've bought a new car, would you like the old Husky?"

The next weekend we went to see John and Hilary and view the Husky, after we'd shared our grief about Sandy, I said, "John, I seem to have a problem. It's a funny thing, but I went to be a blood donor and I've had a false positive on a V.D. test."

Out came the textbooks. "You're going to get a collagen disease," John said. Lupus was here and would dominate the rest of my life.

As I drove away in the Hillman Husky, I thought, "I wonder what a diagnosis of a potential collagen disease is likely to mean?" Back at home, I consulted my copy of *Houston, Joiner and Trounce, Medicine for Nurses*. I turned to the Chapter on collagen diseases which started with Systemic Lupus Erythematosis.

I read, "Prognosis must be guarded. Once the acute phase has started, death is likely within a year or two." Shocked and horrified, I considered my position. I thought, "That's the worst scenario. I'll shut it from my mind and just wait and see if anything happens."

My life was grim and work didn't help either. Although I was based at the East Oxford clinic most of my clients were living in the Blackbird Leys estate. When Des Wilson from Shelter made a visit to Blackbird Leys, he described it as, "A modern slum." Oxford Social Services department' s response to this slur was to hold monthly lunches for all staff to discuss their problem families. Both Pat and I attended these meetings. I felt completely out of my depth, particularly when I was faced with instances of child abuse. I discovered my first case and, in something of a panic, rushed back to base and rang the NSPCC and the Social Services.

Pat and I met for our weekly lunch. "I feel so inadequate," Pat said.

"Yes, it's ridiculous. I bet Des Wilson would have something to say about putting the newly qualified into this situation."

We were both lost in our own thoughts but, after a while, I said, "I'm going to do family planning training in the evenings and perhaps that way I'll be more confident, when giving advice."

Pat said, "Good idea. I'll think about it too, but I'm hoping to have better things to do in my evenings!"

I was also thinking, "I'll be earning some extra money by working in the evenings."

Rick, by this stage, was earning extra money by teaching students. He used his money to buy a cine-camera and projector. I thought, "How unfair and mean, after all the violence I received when I bought a much needed mac with the money that I had earned."

Initially I was paid the basic rate for my evening's training at the family planning clinic but, on completing the training it was increased to a Sister's pay. However I just had to accept that I couldn't spend my earnings on anything for myself otherwise I would receive another beating.

We both missed Sandy and decided to buy a retriever

puppy, so Sam joined the household. He settled in happily, and walks in the nearby park were a delight. Unfortunately as Sandy had before, he tended to scratch at the carpet during the night and disturbed Mrs Jackson.

"I don't know what I can do to stop him, but I will do what I can," I assured Mrs Jackson, but I must admit that I wasn't very sympathetic.

We'd decided that we would start a family before we moved from Oxford and we were due a holiday before we embarked on that part of our lives.

Rick said, "I'd like to go sailing. What about the Norfolk Nroads first. I think I'll look into hiring a boat."

I agreed, my love of boats and being on the water overcoming my fear of being bullied. "It would be a good idea to go now, anyway. Once we have a baby, a holiday like that will be out of the question for some considerable time."

The holiday was arranged, I bought our supplies and we headed to Wroxham.

The wooden boat was forty foot long, with a collapsible cabin roof to allow for the rigging and the heavy wooden boom. Rick was in his element, never thinking to tell me what he was planning, and particularly when he was "to go about". The heavy wooden boom came across with such tremendous force, that it nearly knocked me senseless. He thoroughly enjoyed this dominance and, when on deck, I couldn't relax for a moment. I was constantly aware that he might reinforce his lesson at any time. I vowed, "Never again will I allow my head to be crashed into by a heavy pole travelling at what seems 'the speed of light', the whiplash injury that I suffered that holiday is still with me, possibly exacerbating my earlier judo injury.

Rick was nearing the end of his research and his PhD was imminent. He started to look for openings in the engineering industry. I stopped taking the contraceptive pill, and I was so excited when my next period was late. But when taking a bath six weeks later, I passed a small tadpole like shape into the water. I managed to catch and hold it and I stared at it in tearful disbelief. Then it slipped through my fingers. I was devastated. I searched the bath water but I couldn't find it again. In the end, with tears running down my cheeks, I had to pull the bath plug out while trying to come to terms with letting my "baby" flush into the sewers. My next attempt at pregnancy was similarly unsuccessful, but it ended without me seeing the aborted foetus. Then, just as I was feeling a complete failure, I had success. I started busily sewing my maternity clothes at the weekends.

Just as things were going so well with my pregnancy and I was feeling serene, in my pregnant state, the hip that had been damaged by Rick's violence collapsed and I was sent to bed for a whole month.

During that time, Rick was offered a job near to St Albans. So we would have to move and I was destined not to have my baby at the Radcliffe infirmary, where I'd felt that the obstetric care would be second to none. Instead, we sold the maisonette to a Health Visiting colleague and moved in early December to St Albans where Rick was to start work at a nearby engineering company.

The St Albans house was semi-detached and in estate agent's jargon was "in need of a little attention".

Rick said, "If you take out your six years NHS pension contributions, then we will be able to fund the renovations that are needed."

I readily agreed not realising that later in life I would regret the financial loss that this withdrawal would actually mean to me.

With the funds released, Rick was able to buy the materials needed. He demolished a wall and put in a rolled steel joint. My hip had recovered enough to allow me to strip and re-wallpaper bedrooms and the nursery upstairs. The downstairs appeared more like a building site, than a home.

While we were making an early start on these improvements, our new neighbours from across the road came over to welcome us. The lady was tall and had dark hair, her silent husband was a little shorter and swarthy looking. There was warmth in her smile as she offered me her hand, "Hello, I'm Joan, and this is Mike," she said, pointing to her husband.

"Hello, I'm Annie, and I'm pregnant," I announced, not wasting any time.

CHAPTER 7

MOTHERHOOD
AND DIVORCE

As I left The Radcliffe Maternity unit clutching my obstetric notes, I was warned that time was of the essence, and I had to find a GP to action my referral to a maternity unit without delay.

Joan said, "Doctor Paxman is brilliant. I'll draw the directions to his practice. St Albans Maternity unit is very good. It's where both my babies were born."

Doctor Paxman turned out to be a plump, gentle, single-handed practitioner. He inspired confidence, but I was still a little sceptical about the competence of St Albans Hospital compared to the Radcliffe in Oxford. I thought, "It is wiser to keep my council about whether St Albans is a good place to deliver my precious baby."

My first visit immediately put me at ease. I was impressed by the obstetrician, Miss Savage, as she exuded kindness and competence from every pore of her slim, fifty year old figure. Her smile was infectious and I couldn't believe I'd have preferred the Radcliffe. As February passed by, the pregnancy that had started with feelings of butterflies in my tummy, now felt more like a caged in heavyweight wrestler, with tiny feet and hands pummelling away, trying to find a way out. Then suddenly and without warning, contractions started during the night. Rick drove me to the hospital and I laboured away. By the next morning I'd delivered all six pounds of a furious baby girl. I cuddled her and she calmed down, looking at me with eyes of cobalt blue. For the first time in my life, I fell completely and desperately in love.

"What shall we call her?" Rick asked. I'd forgotten his presence.

"I thought that Sarah would be nice, "I said immediately. "Yes," was all he said.

Before we'd left Oxford, my Auntie Sarah died. She'd been bedridden for many years and in the end it was a kind release. The funeral, forever etched in my memory, was at Pole Moor, high up in the misty Yorkshire Moors. It was just like the setting for a Bronte novel. I told Grandad I was pregnant, I wasn't sure if he'd taken it in. Grandad was very shocked by Auntie Sarah' s death, and six weeks later Grandad also died. I'd secretly decided then to call the baby after Auntie Sarah, if it was a girl. As Rick had no objections, she was called Sarah.

I'd had prenatal classes in Oxford and equipped myself with Mavala bras for breast-feeding, but I was having difficulty and didn't feel the midwife understood. So when Mrs James, the health visitor, took over on the twelfth day, it was a relief to see someone who had the same approach as myself. "Somehow I can't get the hang of it, it's like a storm in a D cup," I confided.

Mrs James was supportive, "Don't forget, the most important thing is a healthy, happy baby. We'll weigh Sarah next Wednesday, at clinic."

I said before thinking," I'm terrified of midwives."

Mrs James smiled, "Me too, and I think it only it makes it worse when you're a health visitor."

We laughed together in professional conspiracy.

Sarah went from strength to strength, but our main problem was shortage of money as Rick' s salary wasn't enough for us all to live on. Missing emotional contact, I had taken my training as a Samaritan volunteer, but that didn't bring in any money. So realising that I was not helping with the problem of money, I suggested to Rick, "I'll apply for agency work on Saturday nights, and try the Family Planning Clinics for a weekday job in the evenings, while you look after Sarah."

Getting work wasn't a problem so I started as a Family Planning Clinic Sister within a week of telephoning. The nursing agency was also quick off the mark, I was soon in St Albans City Hospital for my first night-duty.

The Night Sister, Sister Strom, said," Can you report to the casualty reception ward."

I was horrified, "I've no experience of casualty wards," I said.

"That's alright, there's a good nursing auxiliary on that ward," she said.

I'd never heard of the rank of a nurse auxiliary. I was quite worried as I followed Sister's directions to the ward.

A Malaysian staff nurse gave her report and left.

I turned to the auxiliary, "I didn't understand a word of that, did you?"

"No, I didn't," the middle aged woman sighed.

"Well, let's hope her written English is better than her spoken English. If you don't mind, we'll put the Cardex on a trolley and go round Florence Nightingale style. My name' s Annie, by the way."

"I'm Jane," she smiled.

The layout was Nightingale style, with sixteen beds on each side. We checked the first bed on our round. The man in it had had a head injury from the Rugby field.

"How are you feeling, Mr. Roberts?" I asked, taking his hand.

"I'm fine," he smiled.

202

"So far, so good," I thought. We approached the next bed. In it was a young muddy patient, still wearing his Rugby strip. His mother, sitting by the bed, was looking anxious. I flipped over the Cardex and read suspected bleeding kidney, hourly blood pressure, and nil by mouth. I looked at the blood pressure chart at the end of his bed, and took it again, now his blood pressure was 180 over 110.

I turned to his mother; "Has Justin got pyjamas with him?" I asked.

"Yes, I brought them just in case." she answered.

I continued, "Have you had drink since you have been here?"

She responded, "No."

"Would you like a cup of tea?"

"Thank you very much, that would be lovely."

She sounded very tired and looked very distressed.

Turning to Jane, I said, "Can you settle Justin's Mum in the day room and put the kettle on, and then wash Justin's hands and face, while I bleep the Houseman?"

I bleeped the doctor. "Hello," was the tired and uninterested response. I was sure that Justin's condition was desperately serious so I had to get him interested very quickly.

"I'm an agency nurse, I don't know anything about casualty clearing wards, but I do know about kidneys. Justin Thomas' blood pressure is now 180 over 110 and rising, if you're not here within quarter of an hour, I'm going to have to start pushing fluids."

Ten minutes later, I heard the sound of running feet approaching the ward.

An exhausted looking houseman rushed in and before he regained his breath,

I said by way of explanation, "I have no experience here, and I don't know what I'm doing."

"You seem to know exactly what you're doing," he said.

I immediately felt sorry for him, "Would you like a coffee?"

"Yes please," he responded gratefully.

He replaced Jane behind the screens.

I said to her, "Can you make the houseman a cup of coffee, while you are making Mrs Thomas' tea?"

She simply said, "Yes."

Then I whispered to Jane, "By the time we've drawn breath, we'll need a brandy, not coffee."

Jane laughed.

I became friendly with a neighbour, another Jane. Her child and Sarah liked to play together and we had the opportunity of a cup of tea and a chat. She told me that she was overwhelmingly bored with her life as a housewife and mother.

Jane said, "Its not that I'm house proud, but rather I feel as if I'm married to the cupboard under the stairs!"

We laughed.

Chatting about things generally, out of the blue, she said, "My mother regards her rheumatoid consultant, Dr Verney-Wright as God. But she does see him privately."

I thought, "I must have underestimated you, you can see I'm in pain."

So I went on to ask, "What is the matter with her?"

She sounded sad, "Rheumatoid Arthritis," she replied. That was a good enough introduction for me, as I was still limping badly. I explained to Dr Paxman that I wanted to see the Rheumatologist Dr Verney-Wright, privately, and he made the arrangements. Before I'd time for second thoughts, the notification of the appointment arrived. Leaving Sarah with Joan, I headed for Dr Verney-Wright's rooms in Gower Street, London. Though nervous, I felt very amused by him. Dr Verney-Wright was a left over from the days of the British Empire. He talked as though his mouth was full of marbles, but he did inspire me with confidence.

Sadly, he confirmed my worst fears and Lupus (Systemic Lupus Erythematosis) was his diagnosis. The devastating news was that he thought that I may have only five years life expectancy. I was numb as he prescribed double doses of ibuprofen, started me on an anti-malaria drug, Plaquinil, and told me to stop taking the contraceptive pill, whilst telling me not to get pregnant. Dr Verney-Wright injected my left hip joint with steroids, suggested that I should go swimming, and referred me for electro-therapy on my hip, in St Albans hospital.

Family planning wasn't a problem for me at any rate. I was fitted for a Dutch cap.

Rick said, "I'm not having sex with you with that thing in…it will be like having sex with a washing up bowl."

So I removed it and equipped myself with condoms from the clinic.

"I've brought some condoms for you to use." I said.

"I'm not having sex wearing rubber gloves," said Rick after using one once.

He refused to use anything, and before I had time to be fitted with a coil my period was late. I went to see Dr Paxman again.

"I'm four days late and I'm pregnant," I announced decisively.

"You can't be sure after only four days," he said in disbelief.

"I know I am." I wouldn't give way.

"I'll phone Dr Verney-Wright and ask him what to do. Come and see me next week."

When I returned the following week, the first thing he asked was, "Still no period?"

"No, I'm afraid not."

He said, "Stop all medication and just wait and see what happens, is what Dr Verney-Wright told me when I rang him."

Then Dr Paxman went on to ask, "How do you feel?" His voice was oozing concern.

"I'm already suffering morning sickness, but I'm well apart from that," I assured him.

I was thinking, "I bet he still doesn't quite believe that I am pregnant."

I had to deal with these thoughts on my own as, since moving from Oxford, I missed the shared experiences of colleagues. In addition, a feeling of despair engulfed me and I decided that religion had let me down, primarily because I blamed religion for feeling soiled and seeing no escape from marriage. I was angry and betrayed and, overnight, I became a confirmed atheist. I'd pounce on Radio 4 to stop the Morning Service. All this was in spite of regularly seeing and being impressed by the Bishop of St Albans, when I went to do my weekly shopping. I would drive the Morris 8 into Sumpter Yard and, on parking, invariably I'd be greeted by Robert Runcie, with his gentle, cheerful, charismatic voice.

He never failed to say, "Hello," with a wonderfully strong humanitarian air about him.

I wasn't surprised when many years later, as Archbishop of Canterbury, he showed such empathetic care for the dead Argentinean, as well as British, soldiers.

I read an article in the Women's Guardian, which said, "New opportunities for women!" A new opportunities course for women was being run at Hatfield Polytechnic for one day each week for six weeks. I couldn't believe my luck with Hatfield being a stone's throw from St Albans. In spite of my mother's frequent reiteration of my stupidity, as I had already proved that I had some intellectual aptitude, I decided to discuss this with Jane.

She said, "I'll look after Sarah if you want to go to the open day, to see what's involved."

I couldn't believe my ears, I was so grateful,

"Thank you, from the bottom my heart," I sniffed, wiping my eyes.

During the introductory day Ruth Michaels, the tutor, explained that the course was Thursdays each week for 6 weeks, from 10am to 3pm and a nursery was available.

I immediately enrolled Sarah in the nursery, and me, on the course. The fees were covered by a grant.

"I can't believe it, I feel so excited!" I said to Jane when I collected Sarah.

I could hardly wait for the course to start. When it did, Sarah happily went into the nursery, and I went and opened my eyes to new horizons. Part way through the six weeks we were offered an intelligence test. As Mum had always claimed that I was "...as as thick as two short planks," it was with some trepidation that I agreed. When the psychologist had me in her room she said, "I'm afraid that we've given you the wrong test."

I thought, "Oh no, Mum may have been right, perhaps the test was not low enough for me."

She continued, "It's only accurate to a score of 150 and you're somewhat above that. Would you like to take a higher one?"

"No, that's fine thank you."

I was thinking, "Don't push your luck, I suspect that they have made a mistake."

I was excited when I arrived home, "They suggested I do a part time degree, with a grant pro-rata," I said to Rick.

He replied, "You'd better show you can manage, by going back to Health Visiting part time."

My heart sank, "You know how I hated health visiting in Oxford," I said.

He looked so triumphant that he had put me off but I was determined, and the next day I rang the St Albans Community Nursing Officer.

"I'd like to apply for a part time health visiting job."

"Can you come to see me tomorrow? Ask for Miss Roberts."

I went. "I've got a little girl of sixteen months," I explained.

Miss Roberts wasn't deterred by that.

She said, "I've got just the job for you at Harpenden, twenty hours a week and one of the best childminders is on

207

your way. The shops are very good, there's a Sainsbury's supermarket and its only about fifteen minutes from your house."

She was smiling at me encouragingly and, in spite of dreading health visiting; I found it too good to be true.

"I'm also pregnant," I said, on the verge of tears."

"That's no problem, when is the baby due?"

"In mid August," I replied.

"That will fit in just right, I've got a student coming to fill the post in August."

She gave me the directions to the child minder, and I went to see Mrs Lewis. There was an aura of calm around this slim, pretty lady, as five children were busily engaged on the floor with toys and games. An elderly Labrador was lying on the carpet.

"I hope Sarah isn't frightened of dogs," she said.

I started to say, "No, we have a Golden Retriever at home," but even before I'd finished what I was saying, Sarah climbed off my knee and onto Mrs Lewis' lap.

They smiled companionably at each other. I felt a pang of jealousy, whilst knowing I should be grateful that Sarah was so much at ease.

Sadly, my confidence evaporated when I took Sarah for her first day. As I left, she cried. Torn by guilt, I arrived for my first day of work in Harpenden.

"I've only come to apologise and say that I can't stay. My little girl is sobbing at the child minders."

As I sniffed this out, I was taking in the appearance of Joan Lewis, the health visitor. I'd supposedly come to work with. She was quite tall and slim and her grey hair was simply tied at the back by an elastic band. Her bare, hairy legs were in mid-calf sheepskin boots with a zip up the front. A navy gaberdine mack was hanging from a coat-hangar on the office door. I was intrigued by her; she was looking a little amused, as she greeted me with, "Just stay for a cup of coffee, now you are here."

Then she added, "While I make the coffee, why don't you phone to see how your little girl is getting on?"

I rang the number. The phone was picked up almost immediately.

A voice said, "I was expecting you to ring, don't say anything just listen."

I heard Sarah's little voice organising others to put some bricks into a box as cheerful and happy as I could hope for.

"Thank you, I'll see you at four o'clock," I said gratefully, stifling my tears.

I felt rather silly; obviously both ladies had seen it all before.

Joan went on to explain how she and I would work together sharing out the tasks of the week. It seemed that the practice had two baby clinics each week. I was to take the Tuesday afternoon clinic and she would cover the clinic on Thursday afternoon. As it turned out, working with Joan was a very good experience and bore no resemblance to my time in Oxford. She was incredibly good, though rather unorthodox, as a health visitor. Joan had been a Ward Sister on the very well-known paediatric ward of Hugh Jolly. While she was there, she looked after a tiny baby with a trachea-oesophageal fistula. The little boy had been abandoned, so she adopted him and trained as a health visitor so that she had the flexibility to look after him. He was now 17 and still at home. She was a very experienced health visitor. I remember asking her, "What is the surgery policy for a sore throat with a minor pyrexia?" She looked at me in amazement and said, "The surgery policy is to do what I tell them."

I was enjoying my work and, on Thursday evenings I continued as a Family Planning Clinic Sister. I was expanding and when I went out health visiting I'd usually be invited to sit on people's sofas, they probably thought that the low soft furniture would be appreciated. Unfortunately I was usually like a beached whale when I struggled to regain my feet. On Tuesday afternoons I ran the Child Health Clinic. One day, quite early on during my supervision of these clinics, Joan arrived carrying a carrycot with a tiny baby in it.

She said, "Just look after this baby will you, his mum needs a sleep. I'll be back at four to collect him."

The Harpenden mums were frequently people who had been in important jobs in London prior to embarking on motherhood, and were usually the anxious, high achiever types. Now confronted by six or seven pounds of a crying infant, they found it hard to cope. So gathering up their baby and taking it to the clinics in the afternoon gave an opportunity for mum to get a break. It wasn't long before I followed Joan's example and on the day that she ran the clinic, I was taking in babies for her to supervise.

All went well until late July, when I was working at a Family Planning Clinic on a Thursday evening. I lifted the steriliser out of the ground level cupboard and I felt a stomach cramp. Somehow I carried on with the evening clinic. But, when I arrived home, my contractions were coming in earnest. Although I was only 32 weeks pregnant, there was little doubt that I was in labour. Rick drove me to the maternity unit and the Midwife, Mrs Patel, anxiously tried to stop the contractions by giving me sleeping pills. I vomited them back.

The midwife said, "You didn't want to take them, and you did that on purpose. I'll show you, I'll make you sleep. I'll give you an injection of pethidine."

I did go straight to sleep, but awoke at 2.00am. At 2.20 am Mrs Patel shone a torch in my eyes asking,

"Why aren't you asleep?"

"I don't seem to able to."

Mrs Patel took a look and then sounded alarmed, "Do you feel you want to push?"

"Well now you mention it… yes."

"Whatever you do, don't push."

She'd already started taking the brakes off my bed and was wheeling me towards the delivery suite.

The narcotic effect of the pethidine prevented me from taking control of labour but, at 2.30, I delivered a baby.

"It's a boy," Mrs Patel said enthusiastically.

But the baby was flat as a pancake and he was placed into an incubator and whisked away into the special care baby unit. I didn't even get a chance touch him.

I drank a cup of tea and considered my position. I'd recently been reading feminist literature about the Amazonians, who cut off their left breast and gave their male children away. I wasn't sure about the amputation but I'd already decided, "If it's a boy, I'll leave the maternity unit without him."

Mrs Patel interrupted my thoughts; "We'll take you back to the ward, if you've drunk your tea?"

"Yes," I responded drowsily.

I was taken to a single room and the receiving midwife commanded, "You must stay in bed for at least six hours after delivery."

I settled down in the comfort of sleep induced by the novelty of my now non-pregnant state.

Suddenly I was awake, I looked at the clock. It was seven o'clock and I wasn't allowed up for another half an hour. The hands of the clock moved agonisingly slowly. At last it was time. I put on my dressing gown, and left my room.

Meeting an auxiliary nurse, I said, "I'm just going up to special care, but I can get the lift, so you don't need to worry."

She responded, "That's all right, I'll just get a chair and take you."

Wild elephants wouldn't have stopped me, somehow my maternal instincts had kicked in during my sleep. I thought, "I'd commit murder if anyone tried to stop me getting to my baby."

When I arrived he was out of his incubator, and in seconds he was greedily sucking at the breast. I thought, "Poor little thing, spending all those months growing inside me and thinking I didn't want him." While I was feeding him, the Unit Nursing Officer came in.

"He seems very well now, after the Pediatrician has checked him we'll bring him down to the ward."

I went downstairs for breakfast, and shortly afterwards a Midwife arrived, pushing a cot.

"All clear," she announced cheerfully.

I felt ecstatic as I cuddled my safely delivered little baby.

During the afternoon, Rick brought Sarah in to meet her brother, she was very excited. Rick suggested names, and we agreed to call him John. I went home two days later, and Dr Paxman came to visit the following day.

He immediately blurted out, "Dr Verney-Wright is on an extended holiday in the Caribbean holiday. Before he went, Dr Verney-Wright suggested I arrange for you to have a tubal ligation whilst you're still breast feeding. Let me know when it would be convenient for you to go into St Albans hospital, and I'll make the arrangements. In the meantime, you'll receive an appointment to see the Registrar at U.C.H. for a check-up in two weeks time "

It seemed that it was already a fait accompli, and there was nothing else for it.

I simply said, "Yes, thank you," as he left.

During my pregnancy, I'd been in a state of confusion about Lupus and I felt no worse for the absence of drugs, thinking, "It must be common sense that food has an influence on how I am."

Then and there I decided to try a dietary approach to my problem by reducing my protein intake. I decided to fast for five days and just drink water, thinking that John would get the nutrients that he needed from me. But after trying it for just one day, every time I put my foot on the floor my head ached. I reassessed my position, thinking, "Perhaps it was going too far to try five days without food whilst breast-feeding."

I stopped and introduced just one foodstuff at a time, until I worked out a diet that suited me and was low in protein.

212

I was still shopping for all the family. With John a tiny baby, Rick had removed the old bench seat from the Morris 8, replacing it with a small seat that had been taken from an old sit up and beg Ford Escort, for me to sit on and drive, leaving behind a small step with just enough room for a carrycot and space for Sarah to sit alongside. I attached a carrycot transporter on the back seat of the car with bungee straps and headed to the car park spaces in Sumpter Yard. I had always found the grounds of the Norman Abbey, built on the site of the first English martyrdom of Alban, very soothing. I was intrigued by the history but my anger, and professed atheism, prevented me from venturing indoors. On going through the gatehouse with its big, heavy fortress-like structure with stone dressings, I couldn't avoid being affected by the peace and tranquility, even if I had lost my faith in religion. I was also beginning to question my faith in medicine as well, but I knew better than to tell any doctors involved that diet was better than the drugs that they readily prescribed for the pain in my joints.

In fact, Rick responded to the increase in his family size by changing the Hillman Husky for a larger Cavalier Estate. Rick took to buying Hawkes and Greaves shirts, whilst I had to make do with sewing my clothes or buying cheap cheesecloth, with Indian sandals or clogs with socks for the winter.

Despite Dr Verney-Wright being away, I was soon back on the treadmill of hospital visits to University College Hospital, London. The appointment came for a Monday, Rick drove me to the station in St Albans and I made my way to the hospital on the train, getting out to assemble the carrycot and transporter. Sarah sat with her legs over John's sleeping body, the necessities for the day ahead in the bag hanging from the handle of the transporter. I walked to the park and, while Sarah played on the swings, I fed John as discreetly as I could. After this break, I girded my loins and found the clinic. Giving a urine specimen was not a problem as, by then, I had an abundant supply of wee.

213

I was called through to see the registrar, I trundled in, parked the carrycot, and Sarah climbed onto my lap. Dr Jones, who didn't introduce himself, was a thin, dark man. He had sweat on his top lip and looked nervous and out of his depth. Half a dozen students sat behind him.

"Now, what drugs are we taking?" he asked in a supercilious tone.

I looked around at the medical students, suddenly realising thar his boss's absence had plunged him into seniority, for which he was ill prepared, but it wasn't of my making and I had to make a stand.

I drew breath, "I'm not taking anything, and I don't intend to take any more drugs."

There was a stunned silence followed by a shuffling of notes. After a while he said, "At the very least, will you agree to attend weekly to have your blood taken, for analysis?"

"Yes, I'll come as often as you want, and you're welcome to as much blood as you'd like."

It was my attempt at humour to lighten the atmosphere; I felt triumphant and in command.

The registrar was writing phlebotomy blood test request forms, which he handed to me.

He then glared at me, saying, "Make an appointment to see me next week."

I took the forms. There was an eerie silence in the room. Sarah climbed off my knee and I steered the carrycot containing the still soporific John and left, without further comment. I made my next appointment and headed to Dracula's department. I handed the forms to the phlebotomist and we arranged ourselves. She turned to face me, her face showing a look of overwhelming pity as she read the request form with my diagnosis written on it. Dressed in cheesecloth, with cropped hair and Indian sandals on my feet, I took my seat. I felt like breaking down on the spot. Instead I bit my lip and cuddled Sarah whilst the blood was taken. John slept on.

That finished, we headed for the lift and I put Sarah back into the carrycot and she automatically put one leg on each side of her sleeping brother.

"Would you like to go to the Zoo, Sarah?" I asked brightly, drawing on the depths of self-control I didn't know I possessed.

"Yes please, Mummy," Sarah responded brightly.

I pushed my precious load up Great Portland Street and crossed into Regent's Park. John woke and started crying. As we walked through the Park I was trying to banish the tears that prickled behind my eyes. I found a quiet corner and, while Sarah chased pigeons, I fed John. We headed for the Zoo. A notice board on the gate announced the entrance fee, "Monday special rate, £1.50 per adult. Children under 5 free." As soon as we got through the gate, we saw two elephants, and one started a cascade of wee.

Sarah said, "I need a wee wee Mummy."

I found the toilets, and felt very silly when there was a mother and baby room next door. I thought, "Stupid me, of course a zoo would have a mother and baby room." Anyway, the Zoo provided a happy interlude after the hospital trip and I had a little while to forget my problems. The weather was lovely; we ate our picnics and relaxed. Afterwards, we walked to St Pancras Station to catch the train home.

For the next appointment, I parked at St Albans station and retraced the route to the hospital.

Dr Jones frowned at me, saying, "The measure of the destructive process of your disease is in blood test results, E.S.R. Last week yours was 62, the normal range is between five and ten."

He was writing the request forms for this week's tests, handing them to me without further comment. Dr Jones clearly felt that I was being foolhardy by not taking drugs but as the weeks went by my levels fell by about ten points each week, until they reached normal, at which time he discharged me without further comment.

215

The trips to the hospital and the Zoo became a happy experience. I was lucky in that by arriving four weeks early, John was eight weeks old; when I was due to start my degree. I was still feeling very tired, and Sarah had reached the stage of being able to climb into my bed clutching Richard Scary's *Best Word Book ever* to her chest. I'd open one eye to glimpse where she wanted to start and, with all the theatrical style I could muster, I'd start reciting, with exhausted eyes shut tightly. It wasn't only that I was worn out, but also that I was in great pain from my right hip. I realised that I'd have to 'bite the bullet' and face up to the diagnosis about my collagen disease. "Is it Lupus playing up?" I thought

It was a glorious summer and we'd spent much of the time together in St Albans Park. But now the summer was over and it was time for me to start my academic life at Hatfield Polytechnic.

A new system of organisation was called for. We all had to have breakfast by half past nine and arrive at the Polytechnic in time for me to settle Sarah and John in the nursery, before going to get a cup of coffee in relative comfort and draw breath. Lectures started at 10am and I soon found that, by parking on a slope, I was able to turn the crank handle on the eight and turn the engine over to start first time. This usually achieved the admiration of anyone watching my performance. I felt very smug.

It was my first week at Poly and Rick announced, "I'm going to move to a factory in Shipley, Yorkshire."

I couldn't believe it, but then he'd done such a good assassination job on one of his colleagues, claiming his incompetence and getting him sacked, that his boss obviously felt he was in line for promotion and suggested moving him to a job in Shipley. Initially he went to America for experience and then onto Shipley in late January.

I said to Ruth Michaels, "I'm afraid I won't be able to complete my degree." I was almost in tears.

Ruth looked concerned, saying, "Why not? "

"My husband's job, he's moving to Shipley, near Leeds."

She smiled, "That's OK. What about transferring to Leeds? It's a good university."

I was surprised and felt very lucky all at the same time; it was just like my luck with the health visiting situation all over again.

Shortly afterwards I applied to read Sociology at Leeds University and almost immediately I was called for interview by Professor Sigmunt Bauman. He was Polish and his accent was intriguing.

He said, "I will be writing to offer you a place to read Sociology here at Leeds."

I made my way home in a state of shock. I felt that again, people seemed to be making life easy for me.

Rick left me to sell the house, which wasn't much of a problem due to Mr. Laurence, a charming estate agent. Mr Laurence had a great sense of humour, he phoned me most evenings to report on progress.

One evening he said, "You'll never guess what happened today. I went to value a property and when I asked to see in a large shed, the lady said, 'No, you can't go in there, a tramp lives there, and he doesn't like to be disturbed.'"

With Mr Laurence's help the house was sold, and arrangements were made to move in July.

Rick, back in the UK, was organising the other end of things and had found a house in Pudsey, between Leeds and Bradford.

The moving date was set for the first of July. I'd taken Sarah and John across the road to play with Jane's children by the time the Pickford van arrived. It was all set to be a scorching hot summer day and at last, the heaving and loading of all the furniture was completed by two sweating, corpulent characters. They claimed to be named Bill and Ben, one blonde and one dark, with stomachs that looked as though they were used to holding enormous quantities of beer. Their trouser belts were slung below their bellies and the creases in Bill and Ben' s bottoms were available for all to see. A smaller van drew up for the overflow, crewed by two slimmer men, and finally both removal vans were packed, leaving just our overnight necessities for final collection in the morning. The four sweating men wiped their brows for the last time that day, downed their final mugs of tea and left. One of the vans was to return first thing in the morning to pack the last few things and head for Pudsey. Rick put Sarah John and the dog, Sam, in the Cavalier and set off for the North.

I said a tearful, "Cheerio and thank you for everything," to Jane. We gave each other a hug and kiss, she waved me off and I climbed into the "8" and departed. The sun was beating down from a cloudless sky, as I headed towards the A1 at a steady speed of forty miles an hour, hoping against hope that the distance wasn't too far for the little 8-valve engine.

As I needed to concentrate on my route, I was pleased that I did not suffer the distractions of such modern contrivances as a radio, in a car built in the 1930s. I was also grateful for the unaccustomed peace due to the children's absence. I soon fell to pondering my position. Rick and I had worked well together in organizing the move, and I hoped that it would mark a new beginning for us both. Our relationship had always been cold and distant, and, since John was born, Rick had been away a lot. He hardly had any contact with his son and he was a loving little boy of one year old ready to make a relationship with his father. Sarah on the other hand, was excited about living with her Daddy again. She'd been delighted by the pretty dresses printed with Winnie the Pooh characters that Rick had brought back as gifts from his American trip.

I said aloud, "Perhaps I'll be able to build a relationship with Rick if I focus on developing our joint parental skills."

As I passed the Letchworth turn, I thought, "I'll miss the warmth of Hertfordshire." Then, as the flatness of Lincolnshire gave way to the rolling hills of South Yorkshire, clouds began to form. I thought, "I am Yorkshire borne and I'm going home to the friendliness of Yorkshire." I smiled to myself as the miles sped by. I was getting excited and as I passed the junction of the A435 to Barnsley I started thinking about my History of Architecture course that I had taken at Hatfield Polytechnic. This had opened my eyes to building styles. I thought, "It'll be great to discover the traditional buildings of my early childhood." I'd prepared for the move by buying the *Pevsner's Guide to the Buildings of East and West Ridings*.

Six hours after leaving St Albans I finally found the A6618 to Pudsey. The weather had deteriorated and the gloomy atmosphere was reminiscent of the scenery and glumness of Auntie Sarah's Pole Moor funeral. I was feeling unsettled as I turned into the driveway of the nineteenth century house that we'd bought. It was built of Yorkshire stone blocks and had an intriguing castellated façade. All architectural thoughts were driven from my mind when I opened the front door. I faced the chaos of unpacked boxes left by the newly departed removal vans.

Sarah came running to greet me, exclaiming, "Mummy, John's done smelly poo in his nappy!"

Sam wasn't far behind, tail wagging, greeting me enthusiastically.

When the next morning dawned, it was as if we'd brought the warm weather from the South with us. I gasped as I looked out of the large picture windows at the scenery of the Fulneck Valley. I breathed in the sweetness of the fresh country air, feeling content. Our new home was at the end of a row of three Victorian houses. There was only one small single garage as an adjacent double garage had been converted into a Granny flat. The previous occupants had sold the house after Granny's death. Rick didn't waste any time before beginning the conversion. He knocked a doorway through the two-foot thick wall of stone, thus incorporating the flat into the rest of the house.

All I previously knew about Pudsey was that it was the cricketer Len Hutton's birthplace, and I was pleased at having the summer to familiarise myself with the area, before starting at Leeds University at the beginning of October. So, Pevsner in hand for my first trip into Pudsey to discover the historical buildings, I found the Church of St Laurence, built by the Yorkshire architect, Thomas Taylor in 1821. It was solid, proud and functional without frills and frippery.

"This is Yorkshire architecture," I said to Sarah.

But she was too too busy exploring to reply. Putting John on my lap, I sat in a pew and opened Pevsner. John, in the meantime, was busily occupied rearranging the hymnbooks and orders of services. I discovered that Pevsner dismissed "The usual and clumsy pinnacles" of St Laurence and thought, "Ah well, perhaps Pevsner just doesn't understand the no nonsense Yorkshire character!", as I put the hymn books back in order, opened the heavy door to exit, and Sarah came running down the aisle.

My next trip was to explore the valley that the house overlooked. Taking Sam and the children down into Fulneck, I discovered that it was home to a Moravian settlement, which now ran a privately funded Protestant school. Pevsner's description, "These seventeenth century buildings present a symmetrical and beautiful front," was true. I was relieved that the disappointment I'd felt in St Laurence's wasn't replicated. I was entranced, feeling comforted that the area had such a romantic aura. I hoped it might have the same effect on Rick.

Going into Pudsey again I came across the local antique shop, where I soon became a frequent visitor, probably affording Don, the shop owner of the normally deserted shop, a great sense of relief from potential ruin. I started by buying stripped pine furniture for the children's play room. Then I found a kneehole desk in pitch pine.

"Just what I need to write my essays on," I explained when making the purchase.

The coolness of autumn arrived early in Yorkshire and Don the antique shop owner showed me a size sixteen, musquash coat.

Don said optimistically, "Look, this'll keep cold out for ye."

I'd made some full length wool skirts to wear the previous winter. I wore them with woollen tights and wooden and leather clogs to complete the ensemble. As I had the physique of a broom handle, due to my cautious dietary attempts to reduce my symptoms of Lupus, I was only a size ten and had to admit that the oversized coat added to a rather eccentric appearance, but it was warm.

The hoped for warmth in my relationship with Rick didn't happen and my hopes of being welcomed as a returned Yorkshire prodigal were also dashed. My voice didn't display any of the broad Yorkshire accent. I spoke with more of a received English accent and was regarded with all the suspicion of an outsider. It seemed it wasn't immediately obvious to everyone that I was to be welcomed with open arms. My family had been Yorkshire born, bred and brainwashed, since records began. "There was a clog-maker on my grandfather's side some four generations back," I was ready to explain should anyone ask, but they never did.

I'd inherited Mrs Arbuthnot, the cleaning lady from my predecessor. Mrs Arbuthnot was a plain, stout, no nonsense Yorkshire woman with the biceps of a prizefighter, and oh boy, could she clean! She described her last employer as, "So lazy she'd rather break a pot, than wash it."

I asked dubiously, "Would you like a cup of tea or coffee?"

She was decisive, "I never drink coffee. But a cup of tea will do nicely, thank you."

Well, she can't think I'll poison her due to the laziness of my kitchen habits, I concluded.

Early October and time to start university. Sarah and John

made an easy transition into the university nursery. Oddly, I found the move more difficult and I was taken aback by the dominance of male teenage students, with only a handful of mature ones. It resulted in a very different atmosphere compared to that of the mature mothers at Hatfield Polytechnic. During the second week, when I'd dropped the children at the nursery and started across the road to my lectures, one of the mature students joined me, walking from a student accommodation house in the road overlooking the nursery.

He said, "Hello, I'm Bill. You're on the Sociology course too, aren't you?"

I answered, "Yes."

As we walked towards the lecture theatre together, conversation developed naturally and easily between us. We were about the same age. Bill said he was from Darlington, where he'd gone to night school to take his A levels. With thick black hair and brown eyes, he had a lovely smile and a charming Durham accent. I felt warmed by his company. Bill had a look in his eye of a punished dog, which drew me to him. He went on to explain more about his life.

"My father died I when I was sixteen, and my mother took it very badly, so I didn't feel able to get on with my life for a few years."

I didn't know what to say but thought, "How kind to put someone else's needs before your own."

It wasn't long after that I was ready for sleep, Rick moved to kneel on my chest. He was holding me down by my hair, and he forced his penis into my mouth. I struggled, but the more I tried to fight him off, the tighter he pulled my hair. I gagged and retched, though I wasn't actually sick. Rick was stony-faced. Then he became flushed and, grunting, ejaculated into my mouth. I could do nothing other than swallow his sperm. Then, suddenly gasping, he rolled off me and was soon sleeping soundly. I was left wide-awake, with my breasts, which had been crushed by the weight of

222

his knees, feeling very painful. My head was sore from Rick pulling my hair and my throat and mouth were sore from his attentions. I was shaking and shocked but eventually went to sleep. In the morning, Rick just went about his business as if nothing out of the ordinary had happened. I was upset and confused. I just couldn't understand what had made him behave in such a way. Despite my protestations this became a regular occurrence, and I couldn't do anything to prevent it.

Autumn gave way to winter and, when driving the "8", I experienced an icy blast cutting through the gap between the hood and the windscreen. It welded my frozen fingers onto the steering wheel and, for the first time, I realised the difference in temperature between the North and South. Fortunately, Sarah and John were sheltered in the back of the car, as we continued backwards and forwards to the university. Gradually the winter weather turned into springtime. But still the sexual torture went on.

It was the spring of 1971 and my grant cheque arrived. I went into Pudsey National Westminster Bank.

"I want to open an account," I explained to the girl at the till.

She wrote down all my details, got me to sign a form and told me to, "Call back in five working days."

I was confused, as I walked out, still clutching my grant cheque. I went home and the phone rang, it was Rick. He said, "The Lloyd's Bank Manager has rung me and said that you wanted to open an account at NatWest. I've told him that's rubbish and to ignore it."

That was the end of my first attempt at financial independence, and still the abuse went on.

I re-examined my situation. Clearly, the flood tide of adolescent hormones had trapped both Rick and I a decade ago. He was set to gain financially as a result of his Aunt's legacy, but the down side for him was that it involved marrying a woman he presumably considered weak and appeared to despise. I was trapped, by the shame at the loss of my virginity, into marriage with the person who'd taken my honour from me and I expected love to develop, as it did in children's fairy stories. Sitting alone, when the children were in bed, and looking at my drawn face in the mirror, I had the opportunity to ponder. The tears ran down my cheeks leaving trails in my make-up, as though snails had crawled down my face. I tried to make sense of things. Apparently Rick's father had been so controlling that it was reputed that even the pound notes in his wallet looked ironed. Was that an indication of Rick's behaviour, I wondered? Then one morning after more abuse, sobbing pathetically, I faced him.

"You can't treat me like this. I'll leave you, if you treat me like that again." I blurted out between the sobs.

With a look of utter disdain, "You'll never leave me," he scoffed.

That night Sarah woke before dawn. She was crying, and she climbed into bed with me for a cuddle. We settled to sleep, then suddenly I felt a warm wet patch spreading through the bottom sheet. Sarah had wet the bed. I lay thinking while the patch was going cold and was convinced that my despair was starting to affect her. Something had to be done. But just as it's a bad sailor that doesn't make for port when he can see a storm brewing, it's a poor health visitor who blunders along in increasing distress for her children's sake. Then, I recalled those years before. Mum' s golf partner had warned her that Rick's paternal grandmother had committed suicide. At the time we dismissed it as malicious gossip, but now it seemed to hold great significance for me and I was determined not to follow her by committing suicide myself, or was that what Rick wanted? Was Lupus another form of suicide? I asked myself. If so, I couldn't allow myself to give in to it, I'd got a child of four and a thirteen month old baby. That night my brain switched into self-preservation mode.

I was spending more time in conversation with Bill. He knew how unhappy I was but not the whole story. One morning I went to his room to exchange a book for an essay, which had to be handed in before the end of the summer term. I sat down on his bed, whilst Bill collected the book from his desk. He came over to me, books in hand and sat beside me. He started kissing me. I didn't resist. He began to lift up my turmeric yellow cheesecloth top, as if to take it off. I untied my cheesecloth skirt, and we gently had sex. It was caring and non-threatening. Afterwards my thoughts were in turmoil. I collected Sarah and John from the nursery and headed for home. Later, thinking it all through, I knew what had to be done. It was nearly the end of the summer term. I had made my decision.

The essay completed and handed in, Bill packed up his things and went home to Darlington. I found out that I missed him terribly. One evening, making a rather a feeble excuse to Rick, I left him to look after Sarah and John and went to see Bill in Darlington.

"If I leave Rick, would you be interested in living with us all?" I asked.

Bill responded immediately, "Yes, I would."

I drove to Tina's, who was another mature student on our course who lived in Headingley. Parking the car, I rang her doorbell.

She opened the door with a surprised, "Hello!"

I went in and blurted out, "Rick is abusing me. If I left him, could the children and I come stay with you?"

"Yes, I'd be pleased to have you all."

I said, stunned, "Thank you, I'll let you know when I'm ready."

I drove home in a state of shock. Rick seemed indifferent as to where I'd been.

I had a sleepless night, and after seeing Rick off to work in the morning, I went into action.

Shaking, I phoned Tina.

A drowsy voice answered, "Hello?"

I asked, "Can I come now?"

"What time is it?" she gasped.

"It's half-past eight."

"Yes, I said you could come last night. Just pop the kids in the car and drive straight here."

Tina had taken control.

Putting the children into the car, I drove to Headingley.

Tina opened the door and said to Sarah and John, "Would you like to play in the garden with Mike, Kate and Juan?"

The five children rushed into the back garden.

Then, turning to me she said, "You look as though you could do with a coffee. Come and sit down, I'll put the kettle on."

Suddenly feeling safe, I collapsed on the sofa in the sitting room.

Tina carried a tray of coffee and biscuits through, and ordered me to, "Drink this. Now, I've written a list of the things you'll need. You go and fetch the items on the list. Leave the children here."

I returned to Pudsey and mechanically followed the list Tina had drawn up, feeling too exhausted to do otherwise. The list was mostly toiletries, clothes and bedding. Whilst putting the things together, I noticed the box containing my bridal-gown and added that to the items in the car. Then I hugged Sam for the last time and closed the door on the Pudsey house, with the finality of closing a coffin-lid. I headed for the shops in the Centre of Headingley and rushed breathlessly into the Oxfam charity shop. I handed over the bridal-gown box to a startled assistant and departed without speaking. Next, I parked at the Lloyd's Bank cash machine, drawing £30, noticing that the date was the twelfth of July. That had been the date on which we'd originally arranged to get married, in 1969.

"That's a strange coincidence," I thought.

As I headed back to Tina's brick built, four bedroomed

semi-detached house, I thought, "The house, like it's owner, has the feeling of being solid and secure, and I feel safe."

As I pulled up outside Tina's house, I could hear the shrieks of excited children coming from the back garden. They were happily playing on the climbing-frame and slide. I smiled with relief as I went through the open front door into the house.

I was calling out to Tina, "I'm back, I'm back, I'm back!"

Tina came down the stairs, saying, "I didn't expect you so soon, well done. While you were away, I rang the solicitor for the rape crisis centre and made an appointment for you to see her at half past two today. We'll have lunch in a while and then you won't have to rush. I'll look after Sarah and John."

I asked, "Have they been alright?"

Tina smiled, "They've just been playing, as though they hadn't a care in the world. Sit down, you look exhausted."

I couldn't quite take it all in. Yesterday, I'd been living in Pudsey with only a vague idea of how to bring about an end to my misery and today, thanks to Tina, things were in motion. When I first met her I was struck by her aura of competence. Tina had explained how she'd ended up as a Sociology student in Leeds. Apparently, on leaving school, she'd worked at the Gas Board, where she'd met her husband, Dave. Tina and Dave had had two children and then adopted a Brazilian orphan named Juan. Both Tina and Dave questioned the idea of spending the rest of their lives working for the Gas Board, so they'd both applied to do degrees at university. Whilst Tina tried Leeds, Dave approached Bradford, to read Peace Studies. Dave was now living in student accommodation in Bradford. Although they were still the best of friends, they'd put the house up for sale, with Tina and the children staying until the sale had gone through. In appearance, they were opposites; Tina was short and auburn-haired, with a cheeky grin, and Dave was tall and fair. He took life and the universe very seriously.

Suddenly, I was brought back to the present from my reverie, as five children ran into the kitchen. At seven, Mike was the oldest, a natural leader and very like his father. He started making five drinks of squash for the others. Kate, aged six, was a younger version of her mother. Juan, on the other hand, looked Brazilian. He was five years old. Sarah and John seemed completely at ease in their company and didn't appear to require any explanation. Then, after a lunch of bread and cheese at the kitchen table, I took John for a wee-wee and he ran to join the others in the garden.

Tina, who was clearing up, refused my offer of help, saying, "You make the coffee, then it'll be time for you to go."

I headed for the solicitors in the centre of Leeds and introduced myself to the receptionist, who suggested that I should take a seat.

Although still feeling broken, soiled and defiled as I sat down, I was determined.

"Miss Sykes is ready to see you now," the receptionist called out to me, giving directions to her office.

I knocked on the door. It was opened almost immediately by a slim, grey- suited lady in her twenties. She introduced herself with a sympathetic smile, "I'm Helen Sykes, do take a seat."

I sat down and recounted my story. When I broke down in tears, she took some tissues out of a drawer and passed them across to me.

"We've got him by the short and curlies," she said with a sigh.

I left, feeling drained.

Back at Tina's, I gave my account of the interview, and we discussed the future.

Tina said, "I don't want anything for your board and lodgings while you're here. But can we arrange for you to do the shopping and cooking one-week? Then the following week, be responsible for cleaning and child care?"

"That's very generous of you, Tina. Thank you. The division of labour sounds great, and I'm sure it'll work out well".

Then I added, "I'll phone Rick at six o'clock and give him your telephone number, if that's alright?"

"Yes, I suppose you must," Tina agreed.

When I telephoned Rick to say I'd left, he simply took Tina's number without comment. I also contacted Bill explaining what had happened that day.

Tina said, "I've been thinking. The children were only off school for the day, today. They're back tomorrow at Spring Bank. It's only across the main road, why don't you arrange to see the Head and see if Sarah can start at Spring Bank in September?"

I made the appointment and, taking Sarah with me, asked Mrs Eccles, the Head, if she'd allow Sarah to start school in September.

Mrs. Eccles had an aura which suggested that the decision to become a teacher had been a toss-up between teaching and taking holy orders as a nun. Looking at me, as if she'd just realised she'd chosen the wrong option if teaching meant dealing with the likes of me, she said, "Now, let's see, Sarah will be four in March. Well, if you can't look after her properly, then Spring Bank can."

That's how I suddenly realised that in society's opinion I'd just joined the ranks of the feckless parents. But still, the school was delightful and I'd save on Sarah's nursery fees.

Sitting at Tina's large kitchen table, feeling comfortable and at ease, we discussed Mrs Eccles. The arrangements with Tina, although only temporary, worked out brilliantly. But all too soon the 'For Sale' sign outside Tina's house, was replaced by a 'Sold' sign.

Initially, Rick's response to my and the children's absence was to send me a large bunch of flowers.

Showing me the bouquet, Tina said, "Look what' s come for you."

"That's a bit late in our relationship, he's never given me flowers before. Throw them away, I don't want anything to do with them."

Tina said, "We can't let them go to waste, they're gorgeous. I'll put them in a vase."

When the gift from Inter-Flora didn't bring about my immediate return and Rick had received the solicitor s letter, he must have realised, he'd pushed me too far. Then, in the evenings, when he was home after work, the phone would ring.

Tina said after answering, "It's Rick again."

By the time I picked it up, he'd be sobbing.

The Samaritans' training I'd gone through in Watford prevented me from replacing the receiver. I just listened patiently, but felt completely numb to his apparent despair.

I shared the childcare with Tina whenever I could, particularly bath times. Rick's telephone calls kept recurring. After several days Tina said, "Isn't it peculiar that now he always seems to ring when you're bathing the children. Are you sure that you haven't arranged it that way?"

I chuckled. Bath time was a delight. It involved running just one bath full, five little bodies, undressing them, popping them in, then getting them all dried and into pyjamas. Then, the best bit of all, reading bedtime stories to an attentive audience, that hung on every word; though Mike, at seven, undressed, dried himself off and put on his own pyjamas, very conscious of the seniority of his advanced years. For me, doubling up the responsibilities of motherhood with Tina proved time effective, as well as good fun.

One evening we'd just finished our evening meal, when the phone rang. Tina went to answer it, "Yes, she's just here. I'll call her." She called to me; "It's Chris for you, Annie."

I thought as I rushed to the phone, "A voice from my health visiting course and Oxford days."

"Hello?" I said questioningly.

Chris said, "I rang you at home and Rick gave me this number. Are you all right?"

230

"Yes, I am. You've obviously heard that I've left him."

"Rick told me… Annie, in Oxford when you had so much difficulty walking, he'd hit you hadn't he?"

"Yes, he had."

"Annie I feel dreadful. When he told me you'd taken the children and gone, my response was that I said that I thought you'd take the dog and leave the children. It was just such a shock, I blurted out the first thing that came into my head."

I went on to explain, "I had to leave Sam behind. Tina has a cat, you see."

"Annie, if there's anything I can do, please makes sure you let me know."

"I will, Chris. Thank you."

I came back from the phone saying, "Tina, I've just remembered that Bill said that he's coming tomorrow, will that be all right with you?"

"Yes. When he comes, I'll take all the children to the swings, so you'll be able to have some time together."

I heard the throbbing of the red Capri's engine, before I saw Bill's car. I went out to meet him, and we kissed.

"You've actually done it then!"

I said, "Yes and if you're still game, we need to sort things out. Did you notice that Tina's house is sold?"

We went into the kitchen, and I made coffee for us both.

Bill said, "Before the end of the summer term, Eva said I could move in with her and Connor. She doesn't use the top floor in her house, hardly at all. I'll call to ask if we can all move in."

Eva was another mature student, with an eight year old son. Her husband had died in a car accident. After having some lunch, Bill went round to talk to Eva but she came back with the news that she had said no.

The following day was a Friday. Rick had arranged to collect the children for his first weekend of access visits. The children were packed and ready to go. When he collected them, I was confident that he wouldn't jeopardise this by not bringing them back. As arranged, Bill and I had the time to ourselves to look for accommodation. We had no success.

"There really isn't anywhere," I confided in Tina, after a whole day of searching.

She said, "Don't get down hearted. Why don't you try UNIPOL on Monday."

"Tina, you're brilliant, I hadn't thought of that!"

UNIPOL was the university and polytechnic student's housing office. I was feeling much more optimistic when the children came back, none the worse for their weekend away.

On Monday morning, the telephone rang; it was the probation service.

"My name is Mrs Jennings, I'm a probation officer. I need to come and call on you this week, to ensure the children's safety."

She arranged to come the next day. I found the thought of her visit unnerving and throughout the night I felt as if my heart was in my mouth. I was thinking, "I suppose Rick thinks he can get me on an unsuitable parenting order." I was in need of a diversion and said to Bill, "I'll take Sarah and John to Headingley library, to look for some new story books."

I left Bill and Tina idly passing the time of day together at the kitchen table. Having equipped ourselves with some new reading material, I asked, "Would you like some sweets?"

In unison Sarah and John sang out, "Yes, yes, yes!"

We headed for the adjacent newsagent, which doubled as a sweet shop. During the time consuming business of sweet selection, I glanced idly at the *Yorkshire Evening Post*. The headline announced, 'Death of Leeds University lecturer, Geoffrey Parkes died of stab wounds today. His wife has been arrested.' Suddenly, the world seemed to be going round. Was I going to faint? I grasped the shop counter.

"Do you need a seat? Are you okay?" The assistant looked concerned.

The sound of her voice brought me back to the present.

I said, "Thank you, but no, I've just had a shock. How much do I owe you for the sweets and Evening News?"

Settling the account, we headed home in silence.

I rushed us all out of the car on arriving home and, grasping my newspaper, went inside the house.

"Geoffrey Parkes is dead!" I announced theatrically, tossing the newspaper onto the table.

Tina pounced on it, "We've all signed up for his option. What will happen now, I wonder?"

I shrugged, "Don't know. I was relying on the Social-Psychology option. It would have been great."

Completely out of character, Bill was suddenly assertive. "We'll worry about that later, we've got housing problems at the moment."

Calling to Sarah and John to get back into the car, Bill drove the children and I to the UNIPOL office. Bill and I explained our situation to the housing officer. She looked like a thirty year old librarian. There was much sorting through of information, while Sarah sat quietly and John ran about. After a while of searching through information, the librarian said triumphantly, "Some accommodation has just been released to us in Hunslet Grange. Shall I put you down for that?"

"Yes please!"

We signed the forms, accepting tenancy without looking at the accommodation.

Later I was explaining it all to Tina, when the phone rang.

"I'm coming to collect the "8" tomorrow," Rick announced.

I felt sad. I'd enjoyed the eccentricity of driving such an old car but as Rick had originally bought it and kept it road worthy from the start, I felt I couldn't keep it. I was feeling saddened throughout the evening, but time passed quickly in the hurly-burly of caring for five children.

When the Probation Officer arrived the next morning, the children were all playing happily in the garden. She accepted Tina's offer of coffee and, while the kettle was boiling, I considered my position. "This doesn't bode well," I thought. Mrs Jones was a forty something, middle-class lady, and I could see that she lacked imagination. Once settled with her coffee, she said, "I'll come straight to the point. I visited your husband on Saturday. The children were busily helping him bake a chocolate cake. They were very happy together."

She downed her coffee and left without more ado. My heart was beating so fast, I couldn't get my breath.

"It's quite obvious whose side she's on." Tina said.

"I can't believe it. He's never cooked a thing in his life before." I was fighting back tears.

"Phone Helen," Tina advised.

Helen' s response was, "Oh, that old trick! Don't worry."

That evening, I kept a low profile when Rick collected the car. I'd left the key in the ignition and didn't want to watch the old car go. Now time wasn't on our side at Tina's. It seemed only fair that we should leave her in good time, so that she could organise her own move. Tina was going to share a house with Julie, another mature Sociology student.

UNIPOL helped us to get sufficient basic furniture together. There was a furniture Storehouse in the basement of their offices. We were taken downstairs and selected a double bed and two plastic covered armchairs. They didn't have any dining chairs or table, but we found a kitchen table and four church chairs in a second hand furniture store in Headingley. It was with great sadness that I left Tina and her children and moved into Hunslet Grange with Sarah, John and Bill.

One of the reasons I was looking forward to moving north was discovering Leed and particularly Quarry Hill flats. Pevsner sounded impressed by Quarry Hill when he conducted the survey of English architecture. He says,

"Completed in 1941, it was the largest such estate built in England, the outcome no doubt of strong impressions received from the scale of Vienna municipal housing." Apparently Quarry Hill had an integral day nursery, revolutionary in Britain in the Forties. At Hatfield, I'd become a recruit of the Women's Movement and was fascinated by the architect of Quarry Hill's forward thinking. But, some twenty years before I'd had the opportunity to see for myself. Leeds Council, in their wisdom, had demolished Quarry Hill and replaced it with Hunslet Grange. The photograph in Pevsner's book was all that I had left of the Quarry Hill concept in Leeds.

Generally demolishing old buildings and replacing them by building upwards was the Sixties' building strategy and, in Leeds, Hunslet Grange followed that general rule. Hunslet Grange didn't include a day nursery, it was simply a group of six storey buildings. The upper floors were served by lifts, although there were dark, dingy, dirty, concrete staircases as well. As you climbed the stairs, each footstep echoed spookily and an unpleasant aroma of stale urine was ever present. The smell of urine in the lifts was far worse. It was obvious that some of the tenants regularly used them as toilets, presumably this was their defiance of authority. The lift flooring was a two-inch, thick waterproof layer, that meant a pool of stale urine splish-sploshing about, as the lifts went up and down. Consequently, stout shoes or wellington boots were needed to keep dry. At least the staircases had a little ventilation from the doors opening onto them. The architect clearly hadn't anticipated the residents' apparent lack of continence or attention to hygiene, and the smell did not give a welcoming ambiance to Hunslet Grange.

The living accommodation comprised of two two bedroomed dwellings on two floors. Entry to the top floor accommodation was from the landing walkway, into a tiny hall, leading directly into the sleeping areas, and the stairs went down to the living accommodation on the floor below.

Our flat had been freshly painted throughout with magnolia emulsion and I exclaimed, "Phew! Emulsion could be marketed as a cover for stale urine."

Bill whined, "That's why they paint it all over everything in Council accommodation but it's starting my asthma."

We heard later that our good fortune in being offered the Hunslet accommodation could have been stymied. Two young children had fallen from a walkway and Leeds City Council had put an embargo on children living higher than the ground floor accommodation. It was our good fortune that their embargo did not apply to accommodation arranged by the university or we would have been homeless.

"We'll just have to make the best of things," I concluded.

Sarah and John certainly didn't consider that they had any problems as they gleefully made their way around our walkway, Sarah on her tricycle, and John on his little wooden Gault push-along. I was determined to make the best of a bad job but Rick was not impressed when he returned the children after their first weekend access visit since our move to Hunslet. Bill was busy scrubbing the lino floors in the bedrooms when he knocked on the door. I answered the door. Rick had placed my white Antler holdall containing the childrens' clothes on the doorstep. I stepped out to collect the bag and suddenly I received a terrific blow across my face. Shocked, I staggered back and screamed.

Rick said coldly, "You bitch."

Sarah immediately vomited and Rick bent to console her, but she ran and flung her arms around me

Bill came out to see what was going on, wearing pink Marigold gloves, and without speaking picked up the holdall and took it indoors. I followed, taking Sarah and John by the hand. We entered the flat and closed the door.

Rick went away with nothing else said. I was bruised and shocked. Sarah was still shaking and upset, but John seemed unaware that anything untoward had happened.

Fortunately, all the time we lived in Hunslet, nobody vandalised the Ford Capri. It was Bill's pride and joy and we were able to travel back and forth to the university in comfort. All in all, living in Hunslet didn't work out too badly. It was only a five mile car journey to Spring Bank school to take Sarah and then just a mile back to the university and the nursery for John.

We'd only been in Hunslet for three weeks but were feeling quite settled, when a letter came from my sister, Bid, in Guernsey.

"I'm coming over to England to see Mum and Dad. You can be sure that I'll put enough time aside to come to Leeds."

When she arrived at Hunslet she didn't show any surprise about where we were living, but almost as soon as she'd taken off her coat said, "Dad says you'll need a thousand pounds as a deposit on a house, and he'll be willing to give it to you."

"That would be wonderful. I don't know how to thank you enough for coming, Bid!"

We both hugged and cried. I said, "I'll go around the estate agents tomorrow, to sort out what we can afford. Give Mum and Dad my love, "I added tearfully.

Later, I said to Bill, "Actually, the first thing is to go to the bank. We've got to discuss the size of the mortgage they'd be prepared to lend us. At the moment we only have our grants as income, that is, if you're happy to have a joint mortgage?"

Bill simply said, "Yes."

Going to the bank presented some problems. Bill had been with Barclays since leaving school so it had seemed the obvious place for me to open an account with my grant cheque. There was a branch directly opposite the main entry into the university, but the Students' Union were holding a demonstration about their perception of Barclays involvement in South Africa. All day long the students had been walking up and down with their placards and jeering anyone who was brave enough to use the bank. Fortunately the bank opened at 9:30 and the students hadn't dragged themselves out of their beds so, ill at ease, I crept into the bank to commence negotiations.

Barclays were only too happy to offer a mortgage to anyone willing to run the gauntlet of protesters. Bill and I took in the statements of our grants.

The plump, bald manager smiled," I'd be happy to add £11,000 to your thousand pounds deposit against a first charge on the property that you buy."

We were both excited as we left.

I said to Bill, "Next, to Firth's Estate Agents in Headingley."

There I asked, "We are looking for properties under £12000."

The pretty blonde girl behind the desk, who'd looked as though she was trying to stifle a yawn, suddenly shot into action. She began collecting details from various racks.

"Yes, here are a few and we've just received instructions for a property in Meanwood but we don't have the leaflet yet."

Somehow it was meant to be. Even before the instructions were printed, our offer was accepted and Bill and I were about to become homeowners of a brick built Thirties semi-detached house in excellent condition in Meanwood.

I said to Bill, "Only five minutes drive away from the university. It's almost too good to be true!" But it was true, even the legalities for the house purchase went well.

Christmas time passed and with the holidays over I was waiting for Sarah outside her school. She ran over to me with a little girl in tow. "This is June and she's waiting for her Mummy," she said.

A woman who was undoubtedly June's mummy approached us.

"Hello, I'm Margaret, we arrived back from Canada last summer, and June my little girl has been bullied because of her accent. She didn't want to go back to school this term, but when I went to collect her after her first day back she was smiling and kept telling me that "Sarah's sorted it out", and subsequently "Sarah will sort it out." I'd imagined someone big and strong not someone smaller than June. So I just wanted to thank you and, of course, Sarah"

I felt some sort of reflected glory from Sarah's confidence. As Sarah and I walked hand in hand, and climbed into the Capri, I was beaming.

"You look cheerful," Bill said testily.

I said, "I know why you're feeling irritable, it's because we've got to go to buy shoes for Sarah."

Bill responded, "Isn't that reason enough to be irritable?"

I said, "I've had a wonderful experience."

And I recounted what had taken place outside the school, expecting him to be as pleased but he wasn't at all impressed and just drove to the centre of Leeds, without comment.

We were in the shoe department of the Leeds Co-operative Society. No sooner had the three of us taken seats than John, who as normal was investigating everything he could, tripped and fell over onto the sharp corner of a foot-measuring machine.

"Oww! Oww! John cried. Blood was pouring from a cut above his eyebrow.

While I picked him up and cuddled him, a very distraught, plump, middle-aged assistant produced a first-aid box.

"It's all right, I'm a nurse," I tried to re-assure her, adding, "I'm afraid it will need stitches."

She asked, "Shall I call an ambulance?"

"Yes please."

So shoes had to wait, and we had a visit to casualty at Leeds General infirmary. John was a brave little boy and didn't even whimper despite being subjected to x-raying and suturing. That night he slept well, though; I spent a sleepless night, worrying about his head-injury.

That year the Yorkshire wind in Hunslet seemed particularly cold. Bill and I were struggling with the second year of our Sociology degrees, and completing our assignments on time. Mean while our solicitors were busily working towards completion, and soon we received confirmation that we were the proud owners of the Meanwood house.

"Hurrah! Hurrah! Hurrah!" I was jumping for joy as I read the letter.

"No more going along frozen landings! We can organise our move!"

And I began hugging and kissing Bill and the children. They were all infected by my excitement.

The moving date arrived. I took Sarah to school and John to nursery then drove straight back to Hunslet. No sooner had I thrown off my heavy musquash coat, than the doorbell rang. I opened the door. It was Jim, another Sociology student. As arranged, he'd turned up with the white Students' Union van to help us move.

Jim was grinning, "Shall we start with a cup of tea? Isn't that how the professionals do it?"

I looked at his stick-insect frame and said, "No, if you want to be like a real removal man you must have the body for it. Your trousers should show the cleft in your backside!"

He shrugged his shoulders, "Shall I take my van and go then?"

We both laughed and I said, "Bill's just collapsing the children's beds. I'll put the kettle on, then we can get started."

Bill came out of the bedroom, looking as if he'd got the weight of the world on his shoulders. I was beginning to realise that Bill must have had Scandinavian ancestors, he was so completely subsumed in melancholy and his glass always seemed to be half empty.

Jim asked, "What's up with you, mate?"

Bill said, "It's all right for you."

I started to feel nervous. This wasn't how the move was supposed to be. I'd thought it would be fun.

240

I said, "It'll all look better with a cup of tea inside you."

Without waiting for a reply, I went into the kitchen, started filling the kettle and, while it was boiling, I considered my position. I asked myself, why was I living with Bill? I considered the issues that I'd thought through before making my move. If I hadn't moved in with another man, Rick would have caused tremendous difficulties, and Bill was very kind to the children. Fortunately Jim's cheerfulness was infectious, and when I appeared with a plate of shortbread biscuits and three steaming mugs of tea, both of them seemed much happier.

We stood about dunking biscuits into our tea and, in what seemed like no time at all, they were moving the first load into the lift and into the van. Then Jim and Bill drove off to Meanwood, while I washed up and organised the next vanload. When they came back, Bill said, "Well, there's one good thing about those plastic armchairs from the Student Union store, they're very light to move."

Relief at his better humour overwhelmed me, and I thought, "Perhaps I'd been unfair about Bill's moods." The next load, the kitchen table and church chairs, was the last, and Jim set off in the van whilst Bill and I followed in the Capri. My spirits lifted as Bill drew up behind the van outside our new home. We climbed out of the car and Bill unlocked the door. As I walked across the threshold, I felt I couldn't quite take in the scene that confronted me. Apart from the higgledy-piggledy furniture deposited by Bill and Jim, it was just as lovely as I remembered it, with Laura Ashley wallpaper, co-coordinating mustard coloured velvet curtains at the large bay windows in the sitting room and an open fire set into the chimney breast. Jim and Bill were carrying the plastic armchairs in through the front door. I grimaced at the thought that the plastic covered armchairs didn't quite set it off.

Jim said, "Have you got the kettle on yet?"

"Typical of you! I put the tea making equipment into Bill's car. I'll go and fetch it. But are the water and gas left on?"

"I've already checked. Yes they are," Bill said.

The kettle was boiling by the time they'd emptied the van.

Bill said, "I'm starving."

Jim said, "And my stomach feels as if my throat's been cut. So when we've drunk the tea, if you follow me, we'll take the van to the Union and on the way back, buy some fish and chips from Brian's in Headingley."

Within half an hour, I'd found and washed three plates, and we ate Brian's fish and chips greedily at the dining room table.

Suddenly I looked at my watch and gasped, "The time has flown by! It's nearly three o'clock. I'd better go and fetch Sarah and John."

I rushed to Spring Bank and collected Sarah and then raced on to the nursery for John, telling them both,

"Today's the day we've moved into our new house, isn't that exciting?"

"Yes, mummy," they chimed in unison.

I parked in the small access driveway to the garage at the bottom of our small garden and they tumbled out of the car in eager anticipation, their little legs running up the back garden path.

Bill came out to greet us, "Come and see your new bedroom."

They ran in through the open back door both shrieking with excitement. Bill led them into the bedroom, where he'd already assembled their two beds.

"Do you like it?" I heard Bill ask.

Giggling they ran round the bedrooms and then downstairs and out into the garden. I felt so happy and relieved, my eyes filled with tears as I looked through the kitchen window into the garden and said to no-one in particular, "We're going to be so happy here."

"Yes you are," said Jim behind me.

"You made me jump. I'd forgotten you were still here." I replied

The routine of university and school and nursery life was much easier from Meanwood. Bill and I managed to attend all our scheduled Sociology lectures and I felt relieved, relaxed and in control. Apart from me, the other seminar group members were all male students; they shuffled into our tutor, Tim's room, throwing themselves down into the vacant chairs. I looked at Tim, thinking he was barely older than me; a small, slight blonde haired figure, but with a Doctorate in Sociology. But what did he really know of life?

Tim was speaking, "The topic I asked you to prepare for discussion over the next two weeks was the concepts of anomie and alienation". He continued, "For some the metropolitan community may not be a place of friendly community, but rather one of anomie and of alienation, a mass culture of individual impotence in the face of industrialism, capitalism, and personal struggles against impersonal bureaucrats technocrats and the like. So, we'll start with anomie. Who's presenting today' s paper?"

"Me," said Hugh, a swarthy, plump Welsh lad.

His lilting voice began, "Well it's like this you see, you could say that anomie is the opposite of bonhomie…"

In this group barely out of adolescence, I suddenly became overwhelmed with a feeling of terror and claustrophobia. I rushed into the ladies lavatory, closed the door, locked it, and sobbed my heart out. I thought, "How can it be that now, when I feel secure at last, the delicate scar tissue holding in all the pain from my marriage has burst letting out a flood of uncontrollable emotion?" It looked as if I'd only been able to survive all the changes of the last six months by screwing a lid down tightly on my feelings. Now I was safe, it seemed the lid wasn't strong enough to hold back the flood of trauma below and it had burst forth in uncontrollable emotion, when I least expected it.

Eventually, I pulled myself together, wiped my eyes and

went back into the seminar room. As I took my seat, five pairs of eyes stared at me. The discussion about anomie continued I might as well not have been there, I was in a daze. Tim brought the session to a close, saying anxiously, "Annie, can you stay behind to see me please? The topic for next week is 'Alienation'. It must be your turn, James," he said, turning to the spotty teenager sitting next to Hugh.

James made a grumbling acknowledgement, and we all collected our papers.

"What's up, Annie?" Tim asked when the others had ambled out.

I started to cry again, "I really don't know what's wrong with me. I'm sorry," I sobbed wiping my eyes and nose with the tissues he passed to me.

Tim said no more, but watched as I collected my things and left.

The next week my troubles repeated themselves. Again, Tim asked me to stay behind. I thought, "I probably have the answer," and said, "Do you think that I could have a female tutor?"

Tim nodded, "I'll ask Professor Bauman."

The next day I was asked to go and see Professor Bauman the Leeds Professor of Sociology.

He said, "I'm afraid we don't think it advisable for you to have a female tutor, but Dr Graham Jones is prepared to offer individual tutorials to you in his room during lunch times. You must arrange to see a psychotherapist through Student Health, or I'm afraid you'll have to abandon your degree."

I left meekly, closing the door quietly. He probably knew, but somehow it didn't been seem quite right to admit to him that I had overwhelming feelings of terror and claustrophobia.

I wandered across to Student Health, wondering what on earth Professor Bauman must have thought about my pathetic state. He, his wife and family had managed to escape from Poland just as the Second World War commenced. He secured a teaching post at The University of Haifa, later moving to an

American University and onwards again to Leeds. He and his wife were well known for going to the fruit and vegetable market each Friday morning at six. I presumed they'd faced great hardships and shortages of fruit and vegetables in their home country and had continued there routine for the rest of their life. I admired the strength of character, which the Professor must have had, whilst I, on the other hand, probably looked like a wimp. Not only that, but he was also having to converse in English (well Yorkshire anyway). Professor Bauman's first language must presumably have been Polish, or Yiddish, then Hebrew for Israel, followed by English for an American post, and then the Professorship in Leeds. Whilst I couldn't even explain my distress in my native language.

It's no wonder, I thought with some humility, that I just accepted what the Professor had said. The receptionist at Student Health looked up inquiringly.

I asked, "Can I have an appointment with Dr Fraser please?"

She smiled and asked, "What about tomorrow morning at 9?"

"Yes, thank you," I sighed, and returned her smile.

I felt on my own territory in Student Health, and I was already quite impressed with their abilities. When I'd previously seen the GP, Dr Fraser, it was to complain about pain in some of my joints. He was a large, middle-aged man, dressed in Harris tweeds, who'd asked kindly, "What different foods have you been eating or drinking?"

I was amazed. No one from the medical profession that I'd had previous dealings with had ever considered my claims that diet was a contributory factor in the inflammation of my joints. In fact, they had acted as though I was a bit of a nut case for even mentioning my ideas about diet. From that moment Dr Fraser gained my complete confidence.

After making my appointment with Dr Fraser, I was looking for a sympathetic female ear. My Aunt Margaret was, by chance, working as the Professor of Education's

245

secretary in Leeds University. The Education Department was situated just next door to Student Health, so I knocked on her door.

She smiled as I walked in, "Hello Annie, how's things going?"

It didn't matter what she actually said, Margaret's smile was full of gentle warmth, and just being in her presence made me feel better. Margaret was my mother's younger sister by ten years, who in spite of coping with her husband's early stages of Alzheimer's, was still managing to work. I explained my problems.

"I've heard of an excellent psychotherapist called Lucinda Poole. Perhaps you could get Dr Fraser to refer you to her?" she suggested.

The next day I outlined this suggestion to Dr Fraser.

"No problem, I'll refer you to see her straight away," he said as he patted my hand.

The appointment to see Lucinda came through the post the following week.

I walked across the road from the university and up to her rooms with extreme trepidation. Lucinda was slim, dark and thoughtful, and she looked just as I'd imagined a psychotherapist would look. There was also an enormous box of tissues prominently positioned between us. I gave an outline of my problem in answer to her inquiry and used a copious number of her tissues during my explanation.

Lucinda said, "The important thing is for you to tell me your feelings in all the difficult situations that confront you. Then for us to work out a way for you to act in any situations where you may be behaving inappropriately due to your past. Then we'll work on new methods and a coping strategy."

By then we'd run out of time and made arrangements for an hour's consultation fortnightly.

Although I was still feeling pretty delicate, the next weekend we drove down to Shenstone, in Bill's Capri. The children were with Rick for a weekend's access visit. Dad had phoned during the week before.

"Annie, Miss Taylor has died suddenly. Her bungalow along with all its contents is up for sale. What about coming to see if you want to buy any of her furniture? Would you like to come to stay and take a look?"

"Yes, Dad that would be super!

I was chuffed at the idea. There had once been two Miss Taylors living there after they retired to Shenstone after careers in teaching at a school in Handsworth. The older sister had died after a stroke years before. The remaining Miss Taylor attended Shenstone Methodist Church, where we'd originally met and I'd occasionally visited her home.

"I'd love the sitting-room furniture," I said after taking a look around the bungalow.

Dad said, "I'll arrange to have it brought up to Meanwood."

In Leeds, the University Women's Movement had been canvassing for parental support to save the nursery, as the Student Union were threatening to remove their financial support. I was horrified by the thought of this loss so I joined the campaign with a religious fervour and became the leader of the parents' group. We went around wearing enormous badges, declaring, "Support The Nursery, the university doesn't!" Then it occurred to me that my involvement might jeopardise my degree.

"I know, I'll go and explain to the Vice Chancellor," I said to Bill.

I wandered into Senate House and found Lord Boyle's secretary's office.

In response to my knock, a muffled female voice called out, "Come in."

I pushed open the heavy oak door, and walked in.

An attractive young blonde swivelled round to face me. She looked surprised as I was wearing the musquash coat, four sizes too big, a floor-length burgundy woollen skirt and heavy brown wooden clogs. She eyed me suspiciously.

"May I make an appointment to see Lord Boyle?" I asked politely.

She opened a large diary, "Can you come tomorrow at ten o'clock?"

"Well, that was easy," I thought as I walked back to the Union.

The next day I simply gave my reason for fighting the campaign to Lord Boyle. He listened attentively, before bringing the interview to a close, saying "Thank you for coming to see me. In all my time as Vice Chancellor, I don't think that any other student has ever come to see me to explain what they're doing."

As we shook hands, I smiled, thinking, "But you see, I'd met you before when you were the Conservative party candidate for Handsworth. But then you looked much bigger, or perhaps I was smaller."

It was a serious time for me as I was having one to one tutorials with Graham and meeting Lucinda fortnightly. I was proud of myself that I had been able to stand and deliver a rallying call for support at the Students' Union AGM and speak to the thousand or so students. However the male engineering students arrived in force and voted out the motion to support for the Nursery.

"Well, that's typical of the male dominated engineers to do down the support for a nursery," I complained to Bill furiously.

Coincidentally, The Women' s Movement soon had another cause for concern and they started the movement to 'reclaim the night'.

This was in response to the horrific murders of female prostitutes in Bradford. The press dubbed him, "The Yorkshire Ripper," and as time went by the tally of murders ran into

248

double figures. Originally it was prostitutes in the 'red light district' around the Lumb Lane area in Bradford, but he gradually moved further afield and Leeds became his hunting ground.

The Women's Movement had an active campaign to "Reclaim the Night." Students refused to take police warnings seriously and, when walking home alone late at night, often ended up being curb-crawled home by police cars. No doubt wasting police time in the process. As my night time activities involved bath-time and bedtime stories, I wasn't out reclaiming the night. Just before he was caught, the Yorkshire Ripper's last victim was indeed a Leeds University student.

I noticed that several students and postgraduates were dressed in orange.

"What's that all about?" I asked Wendy whose daughter was at nursery with John.

"While you've been tied up with your nursery campaign there's been a sect recruiting for followers for an Indian leader called the Baghwan Shree Rajneesh. Its all about free love and peace, and his disciples wear orange. It wouldn't suit me with my red hair, but it'd look good on you," Wendy said.

John and Anne were postgraduate Psychology students and one day I met John, Anne's partner, dressed all in red when I dropped my John at nursery. He was delivering Timmy, John's best friend.

I asked, "What's this all about then?"

John looked bashful, "Anne' s joined the Bagwan, but as I'm not so sure, I'm wearing red."

I was amazed; they had always seemed so level headed. He look worried so wondering what was involved,

I said, "Well, what's it about"

"First," said John, "let's go to the Students' Union for a coffee."

When we'd collected our coffee, he poured his heart out to me.

249

"A month ago some followers of the Baghwan Shree Rajneesh came recruiting in Leeds. I'm not sure what to do, Anne's gone so overboard about it." He gulped his coffee and continued, "Apparently his disciples all have to approach him on their knees, which is a bit tricky as he is in Poona and Leeds being so far away. So, they have a poster of him wherever they meet so everyone can approach his picture on their knees."

At this point I bit my lip to stop myself laughing at the thought of all those orange-clad disciples, shuffling forward on their knees towards a photograph.

"What's his philosophy?" I asked.

"Well, it centres around using meditation to clear psychic channels that then allows the spirit to enter. They give you a new name and his disciples have to practice laughter. The Bagwan has instructed them to laugh for five minutes each day before breakfast. But what really makes me suspicious is that his followers have to give him most of their income and virtually all their assets. If I don't go along with it, Anne will probably take Timmy and I will lose him as well." John sighed.

I tried to lighten things by responding, "That's me out for a start. My knees aren't strong enough. Forgive me, but it just sounds like another form of male dominance to me. Though I admit that the idea of someone choosing another name for me sounds appealing at the moment."

John smiled, "Thanks for listening."

"It's not much, but it's all I can do to help," I said sadly as we went our separate ways.

I told Bill later, "I don't know about laughing for five minutes each day, the Bagwan must be laughing all the way to the bank."

Bill raised his eyebrows; "You're not becoming a follower then? That's a relief!"

I was beginning to feel stronger. Life was settling into a pattern and I didn't intend to invite more chaos by rushing off to join an Eastern religion. Both Sarah and John had adapted well to the fortnightly access visits to their father. I was still going for two-weekly discussions with Lucinda and coping with the tutorials with Graham Jones. Towards the end of our second year Bill said, "I'll get unemployment benefits during the summer vacation, so it'll be better for me to stay at home and look after the children and you can get a job as a nurse."

Accepting his logic, I worked as a staff nurse at St James' s Hospital, Leeds.

As the final year started, any thoughts of concentrating on achieving a Sociology degree were interrupted by a court case in Bradford Assizes. Things had been moving irrevocably towards my divorce settlement. It was also a difficult time for my solicitor, Helen. The drugs squad had called at her house and accused her of growing dope in the window box in her front garden.

"I bet she was set up!" I said to Tina.

Tina claimed to have more information, "They say it's grown by her teacher boyfriend. I bet he needs it, he teaches at Armley. Can you ask her for some for me, next time you see her? "

I wasn't pleased, "No, it's a nuisance. It might get in the way of her fighting for my custody."

Tina looked serious, "What's happened about that?"

I replied, "Rick has claimed that because of Lupus, I won't live long enough to justify my having custody. I've been referred to Dr Verney-Wright. He examined me, and wrote to say that my life expectancy was normal."

"What a relief!" Tina added.

My heart was in my mouth when we attended Bradford Assizes and fortunately the judge awarded custody to me. He also made a financial settlement of the princely sum of one hundred pounds and maintenance at five pounds per week. I was pleased at the custody outcome, but displeased with the miserly financial settlement. Rick left it like that until the children were 18; I sat reading the colour supplement in the Sunday Observer and came across an advertisement for a Dali print signed by Salvador Dali himself. It was £100.

"I'll send for one, then at least I have something positive," I said to Bill.

When it came, I was very pleased with my acquisition and only found out later that Dali's friends had joined in with the signing, or so it was claimed.

"Have you seen this?" Bill asked angrily.

He was showing me the announcement of the deception. He had always thought that the purchase was rather frivolous. It was no surprise to me.

I was laughing, "Salvador Dali opened an exhibition at the Academy of Arts with a loaf of bread under one arm. Of course he'd see signing prints as just a jolly jape!"

Bill didn't see the funny side.

The next time I saw Lucinda was after the court case, I said, "I feel as though I've been stung by a swarm of wasps."

"We must work on that," she said.

I was beginning to realise that I'd got rather a lot of work to do if I was to get through my finals. Sorting out my relations with men would have to be deferred.

Bill said, "I'm going to apply for a post graduate diploma in education. They offer one at Huddersfield Polytechnic."

That left me with three choices; I could go back into health visiting, try for a research scholarship being offered through the Department of Health or a post qualification in law.

The tutor, Graham Jones, who had been so supportive during my troubles, had begun a relationship with another mature student mother. Her name was Eva. Graham said, "Eva has been accepted by Leeds Polytechnic to take a postgraduate qualification in law. She thinks that it would be good for you as well."

I said to Bill, "After my experience in court, I don't think I'd be strong enough to do law. What do you think?"

252

"Just apply for everything and see what turns up," he said

When the final results were posted up in Senate House, both Bill and I had a 2:2.

My Sociology of the Family tutor said, "For your paper on the sociology of the family, you've gained the highest mark in the year of any paper...Congratulations!"

"Well, I must have done rather badly on the rest," I said despondently.

She didn't comment.

When everything was sorted out, I was accepted by the London School of Economics (LSE) for a PHD in the History of Nursing, and Bill was accepted by Huddersfield Polytechnic for a Post Graduate Certificate in Education.

I was chuffed, "That'll be great. John will be four in July, so I'll put his name down for Meanwood Primary school. If I get Sarah in there as well, we'll be sorted. The occasional days when I need to see my supervisor in London, I can easily catch the train for London and the travel between Meanwood and Huddersfield is not far by car."

Bill made no comment.

I wandered down the hill to keep the appointment that I'd arranged with the Headmistress of Meanwood Primary School. She said, "Obviously Sarah must come here. How old is John?"

"Four in July," I replied

"Then he'll be ready for the reception class in September. What a relief," I thought they had both been accepted.

Just to walk the short journey with them both each morning, seemed too good to be true.

I said to Bill, "I can't believe how wonderful it feels having finished our degrees. Mostly working from home and walking a hundred yards to school and back will be super. "

Bill wasn't so enthusiastic, "You'll be alright with the odd trip to London to see your supervisor. I've got to drive twenty miles along the grotty A62 to Huddersfield every day."

"Sorry to be so smug," I said, feeling only slightly guilty.

The phone rang. It was Bid, "Den's going to the Annual Methodist conference in England. While he's away, how about you all coming to Guernsey for a holiday?"

"Yes," I cried out at once.

I said to Bill, "It'll be great. With finals over and the opportunity of cheap rail travel courtesy of the Student Railcards, I'm sure we can afford it." I gabbled on without stopping to draw breath.

Bill frowned but rather grudgingly agreed.

I was very excited at the prospect of re-visiting Guernsey as I made the travel plans, I could almost smell the sea air. I packed two cases for us all. As we had to start our long journey by bus, it was a great help that the bus stop was just across the road from our Meanwood home. The day arrived, and we steered two excited children to the blue Leeds Transport sign. Bill carried the heaviest suitcase, I the lighter one, and Sarah and John each grasped a bag of necessities, books and toys "wanted on voyage". All went well, we clambered aboard the big red bus to Leeds station, then on to the train for Kings Cross. We passed places I'd never been to, like Newark. As we passed Grantham, Bill said, "Grantham! Isn't that where the new Prime Minister, Margaret Thatcher, comes from?"

Then on to Peterborough and Kings Cross, Bill's grim expression didn't change. Manhandling our heavy cases, each holding a child's hand, we struggled down the escalator to the underground and Waterloo, before boarding the train to Weymouth and catching the ferry for St Peter Port.

The smells of the city were left far behind and we stood at the prow, watching the gulls wheeling above the boat. I breathed deeply as the anticipated smell of the sea air became a reality. The crossing was calm, no seasickness, and then the tremendous excitement of seeing Bid waving frantically from the quay. I returned her waves enthusiastically from the deck of the boat as it manoeuvred into the harbour.

"Our journey had all the elements of going on safari," I said to Bid as she crammed us and all the luggage into her Morris Minor traveller.

Bill interjected in a grumpy voice, "The Leeds train was late. I think I must have read The Very Hungry Caterpillar about two thousand times."

My hackles rose and I rallied to the children' s defence, "John and Sarah have been brilliant throughout the long journey. I'm amazed John brought the Very Hungry Caterpillar. He hasn't read it for years. You were reading Captain Pugwash mostly. John particularly likes Master Bates," I told them with a grin.

Bid defused the situation with, "You sent Andrew The Very Hungry Caterpillar for his first birthday twelve years ago!"

Nearly all the carload broke into laughter, and I wondered whether they'd picked up the Master Bates innuendo. When we reached Bid's St Sampson's home, we tumbled out of the car into a scene set for an idyllic time. The detached five bedroomed house was just a stone's throw away from the beach.

"Haven't you all grown!" I exclaimed to Bid's children, who were too polite to say what they thought of such an inane greeting. Then I introduced Bill to them. I hadn't seen them for six years and ,at thirteen, Andrew seemed just the same though bigger. He still had the same studious expression in his dark brown eyes and wore his curly red hair short. Eleven year old Frances had grown into a pretty little girl, with blue eyes like her mother, and ten year old Robin, despite wearing torn jeans held together by blanket pins and something like a lavatory seat cover over his bottom, was still the little brown-eyed boy that I remembered. They were very tolerant and enthusiastic in the company of their young cousins. Sarah and John were excited and loved playing with Suzy, Bid's five-year-old golden retriever, whose tail wagged wildly as she splashed around on the St Sampson's beach.

I couldn't wait to re-visit Fermaine Bay, and two days later I borrowed Bid's car for the trip down memory lane. I hoped to recapture my teenage years and recounted stories about the happy times on the beach at Fermaine to Bill, Sarah and John as I drove. I parked the car in eager anticipation and Sarah and John ran to the beach. Bill and I followed, lugging bags full of swimsuits, towels, buckets and spades, sandwiches and drinks etc. But no sooner had we settled ourselves down on the shingle beach, than Bill started to wheeze, he gasped,"Sorry, asthma! We'll have to go back."

So without so much as one of the delicious ice creams I'd remembered, I collected everything together, and took him and the disappointed children back to St Sampson's. All my hopes of a glorious time smashed.

Throughout the rest of the holiday Bill continued to wheeze, with the result that he felt trapped on the island and longed for the day when we could leave. Bid, anxious to help, said to me, "You look washed out. I'll take all the children with Suzy to play in Saumarez Park. You both go to bed. Perhaps Bill will feel better after a rest."

But whatever we tried didn't seem to help, though he did cheer up a little for the Queen's visit. Bid equipped us with Union Jacks, and he came to the end of the road to wave his flag as the Queen's car swept by. Bid was going to meet the Queen, so I played lady in waiting to her. I dressed her in a kaftan of indigo-blue.

"Which matches your eyes of blue, "I told her.

Bid laughed, "I must practice a curtsy."

Without more ado, and with me playing the role of the Queen, Bid and the five children all lined up to curtsy and shake my hand. Round and round they all went with gales of laughter, until we had to stop. It had become so rumbustious that Bid nearly tore her kaftan.

Eventually the day that poor Bill was longing for arrived. The holiday was over. It was time to go. We all piled into the Morris Traveller, to head back to St Peter Port for the ferry home. I was tearful as we waved goodbye but, miraculously, Bill stopped wheezing.

"It must be the sea air," he said.

Once we were on our way home, Bill was almost cheerful, which was just as well for as we re-traced our route, John was increasingly under the weather. He deteriorated throughout the journey becoming first a grumpy little boy and then a tearful one, sobbing, "No, no, no," to every suggestion with increasing regularity. We arrived home with huge relief, like refugees from the storm.

Next day I took John to the doctors.

"Mumps," said the Doctor, confirming my suspicions.

Worried that the infection might have spread, I rang Bid regularly.

"Now Sarah's down with mumps as well," I told her.

Bid said, "Rob's succumbed too. To be honest with you, it's a help really."

"How can you possibly say that?" I laughed.

"I've got four Americans coming to stay, and with me teaching full time, it's given me the excuse to stay at home to look after Rob as well as the Americans. I'd be exhausted trying to cope with work and entertaining. Fortunately, Rob isn't very ill."

I was grateful for her response. "If they hadn't been vaccinated, I can't begin to think what a worry it would have been. As it is, it's bad enough."

Bid agreed, "Yes, think how ill they'd be if they didn't have any protection. But how are you managing?"

"Oh, all right. I'm relieved I chose the research option. The children's' illness is only putting my work back a bit. If I'd decided to do the post-graduate law qualification it would have been a real problem."

Working mostly at home made life easy, "It's a good choice," I thought. Really it was a cowardly act, but I felt too vulnerable to take Graham Jones's advice and follow the law option. The nursing profession was much safer and more secure.

I was aware that my theory about Maggie Thatcher was realised when, in the first eight weeks of her leadership, she started selling off nationalised industries. Her slogan became "Spend only what is in the Nation's purse." How long would it take before she caught up with my research fellowship?

"I blame the Unions for this," I complained to Bill.

"How so?"

"James Callaghan lost the election because of all the strikes, giving the Conservatives a golden opportunity for the slogan, 'Labour Isn't Working'."

"That's true. Hey, that cat's here again, don't let it in!" and deftly changed the subject.

Whenever we came home from school, a female cat was always waiting for us, mewing pathetically.

John recognised her, "That's Postman Pat's cat!"

I smiled, "She must be lost, I'll put a note in Meanwood Post Office window, tomorrow."

"And buy some cat food," Sarah joined in.

I wrote the note and called at the Post Office. It wasn't an inconvenience, we called in there daily on our way home from school, for child-bait, the reward for a good day at school! But getting no response after a couple of weeks, I said to Bill, "I'd better take her to the vets."

"To have her put down?"

I was astounded, "No! She's sweet. Fortunately, she doesn't have a primeval instinct, bringing in dead mice and things. She's obviously chosen the comfortable life."

Bill was scathing, "She knows who's a soft touch, more like."

Surprisingly, Postman Pat's cat didn't put up much of a struggle when I put her in a cardboard box and carried her the hundred yards up the road to the vets, though she mewed all the way. "She'll have lost her trust in me" I thought.

258

"What's her name?" the vet asked, taking her out of the box by the scruff of her neck.

I suddenly felt caught out. We'd called her pussy, but how could I admit that to this dishy young thirty year old, who was inspecting me over his trendy horn-rimmed glasses. Inspiration came to my aid. Drawing on the name of Christina Rossetti's cat, I said, "Muff," and asked, "Has Muff been spayed?"

"Giving Muff an anaesthetic and opening her up is the only way to tell," he continued.

I wasn't impressed by his answer, but decided to take a chance that she had been. I paid the bill for all the injections and left.

A few weeks later, it became clear that she hadn't been, and I discovered why a female cat is called a Queen! One morning six or more male cats were camped out in our back garden. Muff strolled out, inspecting her suitors. When she'd selected the chosen one, Muff flicked her tail at him, and they went off together. The other hopefuls patiently maintained their vigilance. She returned for a sleep, awoke, stretched, then worked her way down the hierarchy. When the first suitor returned three days later, having recovered from his excursions, he resumed his place in the queue. I was concerned that this behaviour didn't give the children a very good introduction to sex education!

The next Monday morning, as we were walking to school, Sarah said, "We're learning to write a diary now."

"So, what are you going to write?" I asked.

Sarah didn't answer, and I hoped that the sexual behaviour of cats didn't feature in it. I'd just arrived home, when the phone rang. It was the school secretary. She seemed very vexed.

"Children with head lice must be kept off school," her irate Yorkshire accent boomed down the phone.

I started to laugh, which didn't help. Recovering myself, I said, "Sarah has dandruff. She's scratching her head; I considered it advisable to treat her simply as a precaution. I'm afraid that's what comes of being a health visitor without a caseload."

The secretary seemed stunned. After a few minutes silence she simply said, "Thank you," and put the phone down.

No more was said regarding the infestation.

As it transpired, starting John and moving Sarah to Meanwood Primary School was a mixed blessing. I enjoyed the convenience of the school's closeness, and Sarah loved her teacher, Mrs. Stephens. Mrs Stephens inspired Sarah and valued her contribution apart from news for her diary. As we walked home that day, she said, "Mrs Stephens asked us to write our weekly diary. She asked, has anyone got any news? I put my hand up and told her I've got nits. But she wasn't interested, she just left the class for a few minutes. Why do you think that was, Mum?"

"Don't worry, Sarah," and I chuckled to myself all the way home.

John wasn't quite as welcome as Sarah. Having been at nursery since he was eight weeks, he was a much more self-confident little boy than the other children in his class. On the way home, he complained, "Mrs Jones picks on me."

When I went to see Mrs. Jones, I found her fat, dull and boring. Though she didn't agree with John' s interpretation of events, my sympathies were with him. Her observations were so monotonous, I couldn't remember what she said and left thinking, "She's wasted in teaching, a hospital could put Mrs Jones to better use to save money on the anaesthetics!"

The six weeks of Muff's confinement passed quickly, and I played midwife to six assorted kittens. Once they were toddling and playing, it seemed that the inquisitiveness of the entire complement of Meanwood School was stimulated. The children all turned up with their mothers in tow. I could only imagine the dialogue when they arrived home from school, "Mum, Sarah's cat has had a litter of kitchens, I'd love a kitten!" Consequently homing them didn't present a problem!

Somewhere amongst all this, I had research to do.

Bill said, "You can't go to London wearing that tatty fur coat," and insisted that I went and bought a Burberry cashmere and woollen one. "And while you're at it, you'd better get a decent wrist watch as well."

I wasn't quite so sure about that. I'd previously bought an 'H. Samuel five-shilling' watch for taking pulses, and now wore it hanging from a chain round my neck as part of my image. It had been with me for a decade, but it would be churlish to refuse, so I smartened myself up for my occasional trips to LSE.

CHAPTER 8

PETERBOROUGH

Fortunately, Bill thought he'd made the right career decision and he wanted to apply for a lecturing job at a college of further education.

"There's a job advertised at Peterborough Regional College. The job has a rented house going with it in a place called Orton Goldhay," he said.

"Down the A1 towards London," he continued.

"Yes! The train stops there, and it's only about an hour to London from Peterborough. That would be great!" I enthused.

Bill applied for the job in Peterborough, was interviewed, an offer made and he accepted. I looked Peterborough up in the *Pevsner's Pioneers of Design*. Peterborough didn't feature in the index, I thought, "So much for architecture!"

I visited various estate agents and obtained their estimations for a sale price on the house. They weren't very good, so I decided to test the market myself. I wrote a For Sale sign for the sitting-room window and also put a notice in the local Post Office. I was just contemplating expanding my efforts to estate agents and the local newspapers when the telephone rang. It was neighbours from the nearby main road and they met the asking price.

I couldn't believe our luck. When contracts had been

exchanged, I rang Pickfords and arranged the moving date for the last week of the school summer term. We set off in the Capri to move into our brand new rented house in Orton Goldhay, Peterborough, courtesy of the Peterborough Development Corporation.

"It's an adventure!" I said to Bill and the children.

We were all in Bill's Capri, as he drove us down the A1 to our new home in Peterborough. I was in the front passenger seat navigating. Sarah was sitting on the back seat on one side of Muff's box with John on the other. As we were approaching the Grantham turning, we passed a Pickford's removal van.

"There's our furniture." I said hopefully.

Bill sighed, "All I know of Peterborough is the college."

Apart from negotiating our new house, I only knew Peterborough from the train. I hoped that the Railway Station wasn't the city's most distinguishing architectural feature. "It's not one of the prettiest stations in the whole world, in fact it could be one of the ugliest. I wonder what the original looked like?" I thought.

I cried out, "That's it! Take the next turn onto the A47."

Suddenly the bleakness of the snaking motorway style road was replaced by a two-way road through lovely, undulating countryside. I caught sight of a river drifting along and consulted the map.

"The River Nene," I announced.

The A47 took us through the village of Ailsworth and then Castor, with their picture book stone cottages suggesting a cosy warmth on this sunny July day. Then the road ran alongside the River Nene and near a charming stone bridge built of stone the same colour as the cottages. I was beginning to feel better as I pointed this out. It looked as though the bridge had been built for the local gentry to access the water meadows or take a shortcut to the other side of Peterborough. As I changed the map from the *Motoring Atlas* to the *Peterborough Street Map*, I thought, "This region has a gentle feel to it. It feels more welcoming, and is different to the harshness of the Yorkshire landscape."

Suddenly the vista changed into modern, brand new roads and roundabouts! I navigated us around a confusing number of roundabouts that all seemed to look the same and was just going to say, "What on earth do they need all these roundabouts for?"

When Bill chipped in with, "Well I'm glad they built the roads first. Someone in Peterborough's got their priorities right!"

I didn't comment, particularly as I was concentrating on the route. The children were looking around and were unusually quiet, when Bill asked, "Haven't we got to go somewhere to collect the key?"

I turned to the information booklet for new tenants, nodding, "Yes, Misterton."

There were rows and yet more rows of identical new small terraced houses. I was thinking,

"We'll never find our way round all this lot," when I saw the sign "Misterton Housing Office".

Bill said, "The key'll be in my name. You stay here while I go and sign for it."

He'd left before the now bored children started whining. It had been a very long day, and Sarah and John seemed perfectly justified in moaning. They hadn't been out of the car since we stopped to hastily guzzle burger and chips at the Blyth services. That must have been at least an hour and a half previously!

"It won't be long now," I tried to reassure them, though without much confidence.

Surprisingly, Bill was soon back, "We're to meet Jill, the housing officer, at number 21 Riseholme."

He drove there. I couldn't work out how, but Jill arrived before us. We all piled out of the car and as I stood up, I took a deep breath and a lungful of the soft, fresh, Fenland air. Sarah was busy seeing to Muff while John started running around Jill, a plump dark-haired twenty year old. She smiled at John. "E's a good ole' boy," she said in a strong fenland accent. This was the first time that I had heard the use of 'ole boy' referring to young males.

She led the way into number 21, a compact, newly built house. Deftly she explained the mechanics of the heating, lighting and water services. She left, saying over her shoulder, "Peterborough' s not a bad ole' place."

I was still taken aback by the accent, when Bill said, "I'll get the tea making things from the boot. Why don't you try those shops for some milk?"

I came to, and said to the children, "Shall we go and explore, Muff will be alright for a little while."

The Orton Goldhay Shopping Centre was only about two hundred yards away, so the three of us soon collected milk and the goodies we needed. Retracing our route, we passed a primary school still under construction. The sign outside announced, "St. John's Primary School, Opening September, 81." In two months time I thought, that would mean the children could start at the beginning of the autumn term. As long as I could get them in." We seemed to be lucky again. By the time we got back, the Pickford's van was parked outside the house.

"Any chance of a cup of tea?" one removal man asked.

I put the kettle on and the business of unloading began.

As soon as the removal van had left, I rang sister Bid to give her our new telephone number.

She asked, "Don't you miss the hills and scenery of Yorkshire?"

She was a dedicated disciple of Yorkshire and Yorkshire life.

"No! The scenery here in Peterborough is the wonderful sky. In Yorkshire we lived in the hills, with mists and hard granite stone as our backdrop. Here it makes you think of the French landscape paintings of Claude Monet, especially the one of the meadows along the river near Giverny. Do you know the one I mean?"

265

I continued without waiting for an answer, "It's dry here too! I really didn't see much of the scenery in the rainy days in Yorkshire and the dampness affected my joints. While at the moment we are living beside a building site, I have the feeling that it's going to be really great and I'm going to be happy in Peterborough."

Obviously unconvinced, she nevertheless wished me luck.

Life in Orton Goldhay was in fact easy and convenient and again, with pressures reduced, my emotions surged, and I frequently burst into uncontrollable bouts of sobbing. It was September; the school opened and there was an infectious buzz of newness and enthusiasm about the area. John was particularly regenerated, and his disappointing start in Meanwood was soon forgotten. Sarah settled in very happily too. My ego was being massaged by some of the neighbours needing health visiting advice. All things considered it would have been tempting to stay put, rather than start house hunting again. But, the value of our house in Meanwood had doubled during the two years that we had lived there, so the comparatively low Peterborough house prices meant we could afford a four bed-roomed detached house instead of the three bed-roomed semi that we had in Leeds.

I started my research and asked almost everyone who might have reason to know, about the quality of the Peterborough schools.

Almost without exception the general consensus was, "We'd recommend Longthorpe Primary, followed by Jack Hunt comprehensive."

So we started to look for a house in Longthorpe and I also realised that I would need my own transport. The local garage, Marshalls, was launching a new model, the Leyland Austin mini Metro. I'd read research that yellow was the safest colour, so in I went and ordered a bright yellow one from the obsequious Mr Davenport. He took charge of the paperwork, placed the order and in due course I was able to set off in my bright yellow Metro to house hunt in Longthorpe. I discovered several problems, albeit minor ones, with the car.

"I don't expect this from a new car," I complained to Mr Davenport.

His reply, "You haven't bought a Rolls Royce, you know."

Like the washerwoman in Wind in the Willows, I puffed my chest out and, looking him straight in the eyes, said, "This car is more important to me than a Rolls Royce!"

Needless to say he did not answer but merely continued organising a time for the mechanics to sort things out.

Later I said to Bill, "I never trusted him anyway." I continued, "You see his face is constantly smiling, but his cold grey eyes never do."

With Bill at college and the children in school, my yellow mini Metro was busy buzzing between the estate agents in town, house hunting in Longthorpe, and visiting Barclays bank to arrange a mortgage.

"Come and look at a brilliant house I've found!" I said to Bill, one day.

"It's not finished yet. It's on a new estate, being built by Wates. We don't have much choice, other than to buy from new, if we're to get the best schools."

Anyway, Bill was happy enough to go along with the move. The bank accepted our mortgage request, subject to my passing a medical examination because of my Lupus diagnosis. It was arranged with a doctor at Park Road Medical Centre, a rather grand title for a reclaimed Baptist Chapel! The doctor was Irish, charming and very thorough, pointing out that I had a heart murmur. I felt insecure, as he insisted on showing me around the premises, ending with, "Fer sure they'll not turn ye down."

A little bemused, I said, "Thank you! So can we all join your practice?"

He seemed pleased, and his receptionist sorted out the appropriate paperwork for us to complete.

In October Peterborough took on a change of character. Heavily laden lorries appeared thundering along the Oundle Road to the British Sugar factory. They could be seen discharging their cargo of sugar beet into gigantic heaps ready for processing. Two enormous chimneys belched out evil smelling clouds of steam that smelt like rotting socks, the aroma pervading everything.

"What on earth, is that smell?" I asked a local shop assistant.

"Sugar beet! And it lasts until February when the campaign finishes," she replied.

I was relieved that it didn't seem quite so smelly in Longthorpe, as we signed contracts to buy the Longthorpe house. I'd visited the primary school and arranged that Sarah and John could start in January.

"They'll be very welcome," Mrs Bishop, the headmistress, said.

I felt happy. The house was progressing nicely. It was a detached, four bedroomed, with a cloakroom, study, utility room, and it had an en suite off the main bedroom.

"We'll be very posh," I said on the phone to Dad.

My next priority was to sort out my hair. Bill had been cutting my fringe so I could see, but the rest of it had been neglected for many years. When I was in the Peterborough town centre I spotted a smart looking hairdressers. On arriving home, I said to Bill," I've been very grateful to you for cutting my hair all this time but I'd like to have it professionally styled. So, I've made an appointment at Ivan Lewis."

I was so disappointed at the outcome.

"And I had been looking forward to it for so long," I wailed to Bill.

"So why don't you ask Heather who teaches hairdressing at the college? Apparently she has a salon nearby,"

I had already agreed to earn a little extra by teaching on the History of Nursing course at the college, so the next time

I was in, I popped a note into Heather's pigeonhole. It read, "Am suicidal! Haircut gone wrong. Please help and finished with our telephone number!"

Heather phoned that evening, and we arranged an appointment to visit her salon, and sort out my hair.

"When I said I was suicidal, I was only joking of course. But what a relief getting it sorted it out," I confided to Bill later.

We arranged to move into our new home on January 10th. Everything went according to plan, though in reality we only exchanged one building site for another, admittedly more upmarket, development. However, we were all very excited at the change. Longthorpe felt like a village, it had a thatched post office, a stone church and a mock Tudor pub. Despite Sarah and John having had four school moves in two years, they soon settled into their new surroundings. I thought, "Children are so resilient."

With all this going on, my research had been rather neglected, and I vowed to make up for lost time. Sitting in my study, fervently writing the early chapters, and heading off to LSE to see my supervisor, Brian Abel Smith, seemed a pleasant way to earn a living. When Brian Abel Smith constantly criticised my split infinitives, I retreated defensively to the view of Kingsley Amis that, "The people who say you should never split infinitives know nothing. The splitting of infinitives may add to the elegance of the script!" However, I thought it better to keep my views to myself on this point.

Life seemed settled and springtime was imminent. One day there came a ring at the door. I went to answer it. Abigail stood looking awkward on the step. Abigail had taken lodgings with Lucy, one of my previous neighbours in Orton Goldhay. She'd been taking her A levels in Jamaica and during the Jamaican elections she became romantically entangled with two men who were on opposite sides of the political spectrum. Her mother, realising the dangers, had rung her British friend, Lucy, requesting that Abigail should come to live in England to finish off her A levels, hoping that matters would calm down given time. At first all was going well, until Abigail started seeing an older man that Lucy considered unsuitable.

"Lucy won't let me go out! I can't take it any more! Please could I come and live with you, until I've taken my exams this summer?"

Bill and I discussed it. Abigail was a very attractive, elegant Afro-Caribbean girl. She had already risked being severely beaten or even murdered by one side or the other in the Jamaican elections, and it didn't seem fair to turn her down. In addition it was my opportunity to help somebody and show some kindness similar to that had been shown to me by so many people during my troubles.

I put it to her, "OK but I need you to help me. Will you clean the house, and if I'm away in London, would you look after the children when they come home from school?"

She agreed. So Abigail moved in, but my friendship with Lucy was irrevocably damaged! Abigail was a wonderful houseguest. She was great fun for Sarah and John, cleaned wonderfully, and could cook an intriguing line in curried goat with sweet potatoes.

When it was time for Abigail to leave, Bill realised that the cleaning may have to fall on his shoulders and suddenly started having asthma attacks.

"Muff is the cause," he said decisively.

He told his students, and one of them offered Muff a home. But still the asthma didn't improve.

"Perhaps it's the dust from the old furniture from Miss Taylor's?" I suggested.

Bill said. "Yes, it could well be that." Though Bill had practically rocked the back out of the old armchair. So we took that to the tip.

I asked, "Shall we go and choose a new leather sofa and chair?"

Bill agreed with alacrity.

We went into town and chose a leather sofa and armchair from Armstrongs. The old furniture was moved into the spare bedroom and the old armchair to the local tip. Still the asthma persisted!

I thought, "I know, I'll put an advert in Longthorpe Post Office, for a cleaning lady."

I just couldn't use a vacuum cleaner as my joints were too frail and the effort would mean days of pain. A legacy of Lupus. I had to accept that I just could not clean properly, and hence the need for a cleaning lady. Next morning there was a ring on the doorbell.

"Have you found a cleaner?" asked a young lady with purple spiked punk styled hair.

"No," I said, noticing the bicycle propped against the porch. I asked her to pop it around the back so we could discuss terms.

With that, Carole became our next cleaning lady.

Just as things were getting settled, a letter arrived, "The Department of Health regretfully informs you that as from October 1981 your research award will cease."

"Oh no," I thought, "this must be my contribution to Maggie Thatcher's cuts to get the economy back on its feet."

I went to ring Dad to let him know, but Bill said, "You can't use the phone, if you're not earning any money."

Sarah's mouth dropped open. "So, that's how it's going to be," I thought.

The next morning, I telephoned the community nursing services.

"Have you any vacancies in health visiting?" I asked the manager of the community nursing services.

The response was, "You'd better come in to see me."

I went and explained what I was doing.

She said, "I will be in touch," in a decisive tone.

I wasn't at home for more than a few minutes when the phone rang and a voice said, "Hello, it is Bob Locket here.

I'm Director of nursing services for Peterborough ... Tell me, do you really want to do health visiting?"

Before replying, I thought, "What sort of question is that to ask someone whose partner has said "no income, no phone", and has got a mortgage and two children to support?"

I prevaricated but in the end, and over the phone, he offered me a post as a research nurse, with the support to carry on with my own work, starting at the beginning of October.

As I was to find out, the community nursing division had two research projects in progress with different universities. They needed help to sort out research lingo and protocols. When I lapsed into academic jargon, Bob would counter this and say, "Annie, I don't have any academic qualifications, no O-levels or anything and I don't understand a word you are saying." He was however a very astute and kind man.

Perhaps I was just lucky to get the job, but it became obvious that despite his many skills and abilities he was very nervous at dealing with academics and particularly the professors heading up the two research projects. One project was working on the community services for the mentally handicapped, the other helping to establish a scheme for "Hospital at Home ".

Bob had arranged for me to use one of the offices at the end of the corridor in the maternity unit's GP unit. There were four rooms, one of which was the size of a four-bed ward. I had landed on my feet, and was soon happily settled.

Although none of us really felt that we missed Muff, somehow the pet free existence left a gap.

John was the first to deal with this, "Can I have some gerbils, please?"

Bill was horrified, "You'll have to look after them yourself, and keep them in your room."

When the gerbils were installed, I asked Bill, "How would

it be if we bought a Golden Retriever puppy? We'll get it properly trained." I was like a child again.

Sarah was enthusiastic, "I'll walk it!"

Bill did not object and we called the puppy Holly. She was quick to learn in terms of house training. When her injections were due I took her to the vets and while she was being checked over by Mr Smith the vet, I said, "I'm giving Holly out of date baby milk, made up with boiled water. But she's going out and drinking the water from the pond. How can I stop her doing that?"

Looking over his spectacles at me, Mr Smith sat on the window ledge and, crossing his arms, said, "Madam, treat your dog like a dustbin, and you won't go far wrong."

I walked out, feeling chastised and quite stupid.

Once Holly's quarantine period was over, I enrolled her for puppy training. Sarah and John came with Sarah's best friend Julie. Every day, Sarah and Julie would rush in straight from school, bent on walking Holly. Then when Holly's second season was due, I said, "Wouldn't puppies be a lovely idea?"

Bill seemed resigned to the proliferation of animals in the house, and I was amazed when, in 1984, he suggested that we should get married. Not really a proposal, more an arrangement!

I responded, "Haven't you heard Billy Connolly, saying, 'Marriage is a wonderful invention, but then again so is a bicycle repair kit, and I don't have a use for one of those either'."

So instead Bill bought a bike, followed by an Escort XR3i; whether there was any connection with my remark I never found out. He seemed unsettled. It never occurred to me that he might be having an affair until one day in late May, I came home at lunchtime to pack a bag for Sarah and John to go to their father's for the Whitsun half term holiday. There was something different about the house. At first I couldn't put my finger on it, but going upstairs I was shocked to see that Bill's wardrobe was empty. He had left me! In shock, I stood looking in the mirror in the en suite. A voice came back from it, "You'll be better off without him!" It was the nearest thing I'd ever had to an "out of body" experience. In a daze, I sorted out the children's holiday clothes, ready for collection by their father and kept a smile on my face. When they had left, I allowed my tears to flow. I cried a lot that week. I changed the locks and by the time they returned I'd worked out my strategy of how to cope, by us all pulling together! Sarah and John didn't seem unduly concerned by the fact that Bill had moved out.

I had been holding conferences for the East Anglian Nursing Research Group, and I usually arrived home to find the house in darkness, and Bill sitting in his chair watching television. However when I arrived home for the first time after his departure, I walked in and smelt something cooking.

Sarah said, "Would you like some spaghetti bolognese, Mum?"

I felt like crying, as I said gratefully, "Yes, please!"

Bill was having a relationship with one of his students, a 17 year old anorexic punk by the name of Helga. I needed to sort out the house so I contacted a solicitor. Then I telephoned my bank manager, whom I'd never met, so that I could sort out the mortgage and my options. His secretary put me through to him.

"Ian Hall speaking, how can I help you Miss Armitage?"

Mr Hall was very reassuring when I explained the position I was in. It seems 'even a blind sow finds an acorn once in a while! Although, it might take her time to realise what she has found!'

Very soon, I drew up a list of tasks that we should share, and sitting around the kitchen table our team of three were ready to defiantly "take on the world".

John said, "I'll cut the grass."

He was only ten, should I really encourage him to use a Flymow hover mower? I had visions of a *Peterborough Evening Telegraph article*, "Boy of ten electrocuted by cutting through the electric lead of a lawn mower."

"I don't think you're old enough for the mower," I said.

He puffed out his chest and raised himself to his full height of four feet one inch, saying emphatically, "I can."

I would do what cleaning I could manage, whilst Sarah would vacuum the house.

In a few weeks Holly whelped, there were eight puppies, two bitches and six dogs. Every afternoon Sarah and her friend Julie rushed home from school to take care of the puppies and then take Holly for a walk. Though I anticipated the answer, I said, "If you like we can keep one of the bitch puppies, but only one."

They were all very excited at the very thought of this, and the choice was easy, and Sarah asked, "What shall we call her?"

There followed much discussion, and in the end it was agreed.

"Abbey."

Puppies are a handful and we were all ready for the puppies (and that included Holly) to go to new homes when the six weeks were up. Most of them were sold to families in Longthorpe, so we still had the opportunity to see them. I had previously taken Holly to obedience classes, and now it was Abbey's turn. Both dogs, Julie, Sarah and John and I would be ready each Tuesday evening, to drive to dog training. After the basic course, I opted to train the dogs to the gun; they were exercised each evening and that task usually fell to Sarah and Julie.

With the routine of reading books each evening before eight o'clock, Sarah and John, one of them clutching a copy of Adrian Mole, would climb into my double bed. They'd take it in turns to read out what they considered to be the best bits before leaving me, and going to sleep in their respective beds.

John read, "Maxwell was supposed to sleep on the sofa, but he cried so much that he ended up sleeping between his father and Doreen, so father was unable to extend his carnal knowledge. "What's carnal knowledge Mum?" he asked.

Before I'd time to work out my answer, Sarah jumped in and my eyes must have widened as she said, "You know, it's all those things they talk about in those books that are kept back to front in the bookcase, you know, like the 'joy of sex'."

"Perhaps it was better not to say anything," I thought.

Pat, my friend from Oxford days, was now a single parent as well. She came to visit with her two children, Peter and Polly. While the children all played together in the garden, we chatted.

Pat said, "I find that doing Yoga helps me a lot. I can usually manage that when the children are in bed"

"Yes, I think I could do that," I said."

"Shall I send you the book?" Pat asked.

It wasn't long after that Pat sent the book *Teach yourself Yoga* and after the children's book reading time, and while the children settled to sleep, I started the course in Yoga, eventually settling myself to sleep.

"That's wonderful, it's having a great effect, Pat, thank you," I said to her the next time we were on the phone.

Not long after Bill had left the telephone rang. It was Lynn, the wife of one of Bill's colleagues. There was concern in her warm Staffordshire voice.

"I've only just heard about you and Bill splitting-up. How are you Annie?"

"We're alright, thank you, Lynn. Goodbye."

I was about to replace the receiver, when Lynn ended with, "I know you don't want to speak to me Annie, but I shall ring you every Thursday evening, to make sure that you are alright."

My heart warmed, I said gratefully, "Thanks Lynn."

I did feel wary about gossip at the college, and to avoid rumours that generally run rife in such places, I had chosen not to make contact with anyone from there. But when he heard it about it, Geoff, another lecturer from the college, seized the opportunity.

He rang, "Are you free any time, Annie?"

"No, I'm afraid that I'm very busy," I said warily.

He was slim, married, good looking and I was worried in case he believed that I fancied him, whereas I was so busy that I didn't have the time. I had been asked to prepare a paper for delivery in a conference at the Kings Fund Centre. It was entitled "Historical Insights into Today's Decisions". My paper was one of four and the chairperson in summary said, "Only one speaker took a courageously personal stance." I took the perspective that rather than chasing higher academic levels as entry to nursing, the need for compassion should be paramount. I further claimed that the obsession with academic entry was primarily to protect nursing's status, which in my opinion gave little thought to patient needs. These were, and still are my personal and genuinely held beliefs, but it put me at odds with the professional hierarchy. I thought I'd shot myself in the foot. During delivery of this paper I'd used many quotes regarding Florence Nightingale, and it wasn't long before I was contacted with a request to join a group of four nursing historians to work on opening the Florence Nightingale Museum at St Thomas's Hospital, London.

I was trying to finish my PhD thesis. During it's writing, I'd became convinced that compassion was an essential component of nursing care and that embracing the totality of Project 2000 seemed to involve dispensing with this concept. Indeed, the medical profession were probably grasping this change with alacrity and enthusiasm. Many doctors didn't appreciate or approve of the authoritarian management structure epitomised by the matron character, so aptly played by Hattie Jacques in the film *Doctor in the House*. Perhaps the wimpish role of Kenneth Williams as the consultant also held more than a grain of truth for some of them. In 'Project 2000', Britain was adopting the European model of nursing, where nurses were trained to be doctor's assistants. The reasoning of three great nurses that founded the UK nursing profession, Peterborough's own Edith Cavell, the often overlooked Mary Seacole, and of course Florence Nightingale herself, was that nurses prime function was to be carers of patients. This, in my opinion, was now seriously at risk. I thought, "The founders must be turning in their graves!" Was the concept of tender loving care, being an integral constituent of the vocational and professional nursing standards, about to end? Was the very reason for my entering nursing also about to end? Medicine had always held the tools to cure disease, and nursing provided the balance with personal empathetic care. Was the emphasis on medicine about to become dominant? Was I being a Luddite? I thought not and hoped that my forecasts would proved to be wrong!

Despite struggling with Lupus, and the increased need for rest that Lupus demanded, I felt that I was successfully meeting my responsibilities for the children, and my job at Peterborough Health Authority. I was becoming increasingly at odds with the nursing profession. I was receiving little input academically, perhaps academic supervision was easy money, so regrettably I accepted the inevitable and accepted an M.Phil rather that soldier on for my PhD. To be fair, I had not given my research the undivided attention it needed and I had other commitments. I was attempting to run a Nursing Research Group for East Anglia, providing contact for the Peterborough Hospital at Home Pilot Scheme, and monitoring the research into community homes for people with a mental handicap.

My tall, punk, cleaning lady who was now a friend phoned,

"Would you like to come out for a drink with me and Dennis and make up foursome?" Dennis was Carole's boyfriend

She went on, "Michael will be coming."

"Yes, I could do with a break. The children are away at their father's."

I enjoyed the evening, but couldn't quite work out how I ended up in bed with Michael. It didn't feel good. When I told her later, Carole was horrified. It turned out that John and Sarah were not impressed either. Fortunately Michael was leaving to take up a job abroad, so it was destined not to last long. He did call for me at home a couple of times before he went and whenever he was due, John would hide behind the settee, to monitor any goings on.

"It's those green leather trousers he wears, Mum. They make him look stupid. How can you think of going out with someone who wears green leather trousers?"

I didn't have an answer and just shrugged my shoulders, grateful that Michael was soon to be heading for foreign parts.

Derek Wilson was the next man to phone. He was a friend of Bill's, and had been since they were at school together.

Derek said, "Next week, I'll be driving through Peterborough. Would you like to come out for a meal?"

"That would be lovely," I said.

I didn't realize at the time that he was planning to save on his expenses by expecting a bed for the night as well. Anyway we spent the evening discussing Bill.

Derek's view was that, "Bill has always considered that life has dealt him a cruel blow!" He continued, "Bill represented the triumph of mind over morals."

I thought, "That's not very loyal from someone who's supposed to be an old school friend."

He called a couple of times, but then rang to say that the journey was too far.

I felt a bit confused. John had never considered Derek as much of a threat to his male domain, probably because he lived so far away in Darlington.

279

John's surveillance of his mother's male contacts took a back seat as he had other things on his mind. He'd reacted to the dog breeding with his own idea of making money and enthusiastically went into breeding rabbits. He chose the dwarf lop rabbit breed and I bought a buck rabbit, which he called Rambo. Then I bought four does to complete his stock and a double layer of hutches, which we housed in our double garage. When his first baby rabbits were six weeks old, he had no compunction in putting them into Muff's redundant cat box and cycling off to the pet shop. Here he was offered 50p for each baby rabbit. All went well until he became concerned that his does were lonely. He did some research, and said, "Ms Beaton's book of household management suggests that keeping guinea pigs with rabbits stops them being attacked by rats."

"I don't think they're likely to suffer from that, John," I assured him.

Then he tried a different tack, "My rabbits are lonely living in a hutch alone."

Knowing I wasn't going to win, I gave up and invested in a guinea pig for each of his does. I was impressed with his entrepreneurial spirit and often boasted about his prowess, until it was pointed out that I was supplying the investment and he was taking the rewards!

Life in early 1986 seemed pretty good to me, I was quite relaxed with my parenting responsibilities and work offered interesting opportunities, though I was probably naïve about the "Thatcher effect". The mid eighties saw the conservative government turn its attentions on the National Health Service. With an air of 'shifting the deckchairs on the Titanic' the government had decided to radically restructure the NHS and its management culture. The local elections had come round again.

"Changes are afoot," I said to Carole.

She had called and was to eat with us. I was jointing a chicken for our evening meal when there was a ring at the doorbell. John went to answer it.

"There's a man wants to see you, Mum."

"I'm canvassing for the Conservative party. Can we rely on your vote?"

"No! And I can tell you why!" I said rather forcefully and he disappeared in a hurry up the road.

I went back indoors saying, "He's rushed away."

Carole said, "I'm not surprised, look what you've got in your hand."

I looked down and realised that I had been brandishing a French cook's knife covered in blood. No wonder he moved so quickly. We had a fit of the giggles.

The Conservatives won the election again. No doubt because Labour had still not escaped from the loony left image and the winter of discontent. Consequently the NHS changes continued and my boss, Bob Lockett, the District Nursing Officer, was moved to be Chief Nursing Officer of the Prison Service. I missed him greatly, but his parting gesture was to appoint me as Quality Assurance Manager for the District Health Authority, reporting directly to the District General Manager. I was to stay working in my office at the top floor of the maternity unit. This had previously been a small four-bedded ward, so there was plenty of space. Jill, a young widowed single parent with a little boy, had come to join me on a temporary assignment whilst doing her third year research project in the Social Psychology department of LSE. Jill's research was to survey nurse's attitudes to changes in their profession. She looked at two groups of nurses. There was a general resistance to change amongst most nurses but she found that those already on the diploma route were much more amenable to the proposed changes. Jill suggested that the next ten years would bring about major changes in nursing especially with the proposal of Project 2000. I enjoyed her company, and I was also joined by Jilly, a very computer literate health visitor.

It was early days for computers in the Health Service and she was well ahead of the game!

"Annie, I am sure that modern computers can provide a third dimension to healthcare. You see that data now can be easily collected, categorised and used to inform decision making for health needs in both the community and hospital services?"

We had many similar discussions.

She said, "Both you and I know that a nursing visit can cover advice on a range of issues, and some of these require referral to other professionals, so with computerisation comes the opportunity to record this for senior managers to have a clearer understanding of patients unmet health needs, as well as staff workloads and skills requirements."

"Jilly, do you think that the senior staff have enough vision to see this?" I warned.

"No, I have to admit that the ignorance of the senior staff to the value and use of computers is staggering," she said sadly.

Unfortunately for both Jilly and the future use of computers in healthcare, the Health Authority appointed Doug Johns, a typical grey-suit, as IT Manager. He did have pressures on him, but perhaps it was his lack of vision that made him consider Jilly's ideas as whimsical! So her ideas went straight into the deleted bin. The only information that was considered to be operationally pertinent to the NHS were cost-based analysis systems. The draw back of these was that they only looked at costs and cost centres rather than patient's needs and the accountability of the local Health Authority and the Department of Health to the community that it served. Was Jilly ahead of her time? Only time would tell. Jilly left the Health Service!

As her parting gesture to me she said, "I've brought this poster for you, I hope you like it!" It was an A4 size picture of Margaret Thatcher being carried by Ronald Reagan with the caption "She promised to follow him to the end of the world, and he promised to organise it!"

"Oh Jilly that's really great!" I said laughing.

This left me with my original research projects but they were both drawing to a conclusion. One of these was "Hospital at home", which aimed an early discharge into the care of the District Nursing Service, and the other was for the mental health unit that could provide small communities for people with special needs.

My post also involved lecturing about my nursing research in the Peterborough School of Nursing and for the East Anglia Health Authority. In addition, I was travelling to London to research for the establishment of the Florence Nightingale Museum at St Thomas's Hospital. I would often sit in the British Library reading room marvelling at the wonderful domed ceiling and wondering how many famous people had sat there in the past.

It was late 1986 and after receiving information about an introductory course in quality at the Kings Fund Centre, I decided to enrol. Fortunately the course was not due to start for six months and, as I was having problems with my periods, I went to have a consultation with my gynaecologist.

Mr Hackman looked over his half-rim spectacles at me saying, "I'm not prepared to leave you any longer. This thing inside your uterus is getting larger by the minute. I'm putting you down for admission."

I felt irritated saying, "I can't come in, I've two children to look after."

He was resolute "I'm putting you on the list for urgent admission. You'd better go home and work out how you'll organise your child care arrangements."

After overcoming the initial shock I sat to think it through. When the children arrived home from school, we all sat around the table for a planning meeting.

I said, "I've got to go into hospital and have an operation."

Sarah was quick to respond, "I don't care what happens, so long as Grandma doesn't come."

Recovering from her response, I continued, "Don't worry, I won't be in there for long. I'll go into Hospital at Home so it will only be for a couple of days. Perhaps you could stay just two nights with each of your best friends. What do you both think about that? "

They were both very positive, so I began contacting the respective parents, who thankfully were pleased to help out.

Realising I'd need some flexibility with my money, I rang the bank and asked to speak to the manager. I had spoken to him only once before when I rearranged my mortgage to pay off Bill with half the value of the equity on our Longthorpe house. An arrangement that had annoyed my parents no end, as Bill had not contributed to any of the original deposit.

Mum had said, "If you keep giving away half the value of your house, you won't end up with very much will you?"

I hadn't responded to that, but I had thought it was only right to be ethical in these matters due to my divorce experience. Anyway I was feeling nervous when a voice answered, "Ian Hall here, how can I help?"

I said, "I've got to go into hospital for surgery, can you allow me some flexibility on my account until next Easter please, Mr Hall?"

We negotiated an overdraft limit until the 30th April.

He then added kindly, "I'll sort it out and confirm by letter…May I wish you all the best for your operation."

My experience as a patient, on the other side of the sheets went well. I was rather surprised to hear that my current boss had come onto the ward to visit me on the day after my surgery.

"I said that you were not well enough for visitors," Sister Beattie said authoritatively.

I smiled saying, "Thank you."

I mused about this. The ward sister certainly had the

ward under control, but I couldn't understand why my boss had considered it appropriate to see me. I was only in hospital for forty eight hours!

The children slept at friends', Sarah just nearby at Julie's, and John a few roads away at Paul's. The children came in each day to feed and walk the dogs. After a two-day stay in hospital I returned home and was looked after by community nursing working for the 'Hospital at Home Project'. I was really pleased with the success of the project, particularly as I was able to get first-hand experience for myself as a patient.

As soon as I was able, I became mobile once more. However the clutch on my Metro started to play up, so I called into the local garage.

Authoritively I said, "I'm having trouble changing gear; I think the clutch must be worn."

The owner, Les, started the engine and took it for a test drive. Stopping the car next to me he got out with a quizzical look on his face, he asked, "I don't suppose you have had any surgery lately?" I was astonished at his powers of deduction.

I said," Well yes I have actually."

"I don't think that you are fully depressing the clutch," he said.

Of course, I was not pushing the clutch pedal down sufficiently to achieve the gear change! Feeling embarrassed and rather silly at bothering him, I apologised profusely and went on my way to Sainsbury's to buy a chicken for Christmas. I'd already bought a frozen turkey, which was sitting in the freezer, but realised that after my surgery I wouldn't be able to physically lift it out of the oven, so it would have to stay frozen until a later date.

After Christmas the children went to their father's for their week's access visit. I evaluated my position. All too soon they'd be following their futures without me. "I know," I thought, "I'll put my name down for a Morgan car. Then, I'll sell the house, taking off in my Morgan to see the world."

I rang my old school friend Kay who lived in the Midlands, fairly near to the Morgan factory, to see if she wanted to come with me on a test drive.

Kay was rather surprised to hear my request, but in her normal and jolly way she confirmed her delight and willingness to help me sort out my future. I collected her from her home near Tamworth, and we turned up for our demonstration at Morgan cars as arranged, on a cool and windy April day. The Managing Director of Morgan Cars, no less, took us for the spin. It was great with the top down, the wind in our hair as we whizzed along the country roads. I could appreciate the delight and delirious excitement that toad felt in Kenneth Grahame's so eloquently detailed description in *Wind in the Willows*. Kay was sitting in the back and when I eventually turned around to see if she was as exhilarated as me, she looked frozen, so I suggested we changed seats. We did, and the even colder journey in the rear seat didn't diminish my enthusiasm.

After the test, I flamboyantly got out my chequebook and wrote a cheque for £100 as a deposit.

As I was driving her home, Kay shook her head and said,

"Well, I thought that it was very cold, but when I looked in the mirror at your face in the back seat you were beaming with delight."

I replied, "It will be about seven years before I come to the top of the waiting list, I will phone you, and you can come with me when I collect it."

I was feeling much better after my surgery and Easter holidays were approaching. I still had the frozen turkey occupying a lot of room in my freezer, so I rang my nurse training friends Gill and Eileen, to see if they and their families could help me out by coming over for a weekend to share it. Imagine my irritation on Saturday morning, when, all set-up for a busy weekend with lots of fun and laughs expected and a house full of guests, I received a letter from the bank. The post was early and my guests had not yet relinquished their beds. The letter read, "Dear Miss Armitage, at the close of business on the 15th of April your account was £1597.65 overdrawn against an agreed limit of £1500. We would also like to point out that you have a mortgage with us. No doubt you will rectify matters shortly. In the meantime we should be grateful if you would refrain from issuing further cheques until your account is, and can remain, within the agreed arrangements, Signed M. Taylor (Manager). I was incensed at the tone of the letter, how stupid did this character Taylor think I was. Of course I realised that I had a mortgage. Did he think that I was oblivious to a large chunk of my salary being gobbled up by the bank each month? So with a house-full, I indignantly scribbled a reply, ending with a postscript. Anyway where's that nice Mr. Hall gone?"

On the following Tuesday morning Mr. Hall rang me in response to my letter of complaint. He explained that he had only gone away for a few extra days over the Easter break. He suggested that I call the next day to sort out my finances. I suspected trouble, so I wrote out my accounts on sheets of A4. Actually they were a list of my outgoings and my estimation of additional efforts that I could undertake to rectify matters. Wednesday arrived and I went to keep my appointment. I was shown into Mr. Hall's office. A slim balding man with the warm smile stood up, arm outstretched, as we shook hands, and I thought, "His grey suit seems to be at least a size too large." But he was talking again.

"Do sit down, Miss Armitage."

He resumed his seat behind a large, foreboding desk. The desk and its contents were clearly designed to make you feel at a disadvantage. I sat, but moved my chair to the side away from the telephone and a large penholder that was between us so that I could put my papers down. He responded by moving his chair so that the status quo was maintained. "So that's how it is " I thought. But he was already studying the sheet of paper that I handed him to him.

"What's this withdrawal, Miss Armitage?"

"That's my house insurance." I said, referring to my copy.

He went on, "And what's this withdrawal, Miss Armitage."

"That's my house insurance."

"So are you paying two house insurances?"

"I suppose I must be," I replied, rapidly realising I was losing all my financial credibility.

He continued, "What's this withdrawal, Miss Armitage?"

"That's my mortgage."

"It seems very high. It appears to be a gross figure. Are you getting tax relief elsewhere? "

"Not that I am aware of." I replied shrinking even further into my chair.

He was speaking again, "So how are you going to clear this overdraft and manage your finances?"

I perked up, "Breeding dogs."

"How many bitches have you, and how many puppies can you expect each year?"

"I can get both whelped each year say eight puppies each, that's sixteen per year." I responded.

"And how much profit per puppy after expenses?"

"Probably £50 each" I said.

Realising that my financial competence was looking very dubious, I said, "I do get maintenance for the children from my ex-husband."

"And how much is that?"

"Five pounds a week."

I was thinking, how can I explain that I lost six years contributions of health studies pension, only received such a small amount of maintenance and a £100 one off payment for all my salary contributions, and when I was just a student! I couldn't explain the tremendous fear that I still felt about my marriage.

"Yes well," he said, obviously not impressed with the size of the income. He had moved on again, "And what about your Barclaycard bill?"

It was almost £700 and due to be paid by the end of the month, only a few days away. This was the last straw in my humiliation and I meekly discussed my profligacy with plastic. I suggested that I should cut up my Barclaycard but Mr Hall pointed out that I needed that to guarantee cheques. So, I promised never to use my plastic ever again.

"Well don't worry," he said kindly, "We will put the overdraft and sufficient funds to clear your Barclaycard on a loan and you can pay it back over two years. I can make the transfers today so that you can clear your Barclaycard."

I signed the relative papers and Mr Hall went on to assure me that he would sort out my tax on my mortgage and that future payments would be less, as they would include my MIRAS tax relief.

I hadn't known that in those days the bank could charge mortgage payments net of tax relief.

He said, "I'll sort it out." We shook hands and I left.

That evening, I'd just arrived home from work feeling exhausted and was starting to sip a medicinal gin and tonic, when the telephone rang. I rushed to answer it,

"Is that Miss Armitage? "

"Yes," I replied, recognising the voice.

I was wondering what I had done wrong now.

"It's Ian Hall from Barclays Bank here, I forgot to emphasise the need to pay off all your Barclaycard bill so that you can avoid the interest charges. I suggest that you send a cheque in the post tomorrow first class to settle it? That way you won't be penalised with the extra month's interest."

I replied," Yes certainly."

But before I could say goodbye, he continued with, "Err, err… I was wondering whether you are doing anything on Friday evening?"

Not quite able to believe my own ears, I looked with incredulity at the telephone receiver, before putting it back to my ear, and answering querulously, "No."

He continued, "I was wondering whether I could take you out for dinner?"

Again I looked at the telephone receiver in disbelief, before saying, "Yes thank you, that would be very nice."

I started to give him directions to my house, but he replied, "Don't worry I know where you live, I'll pick you up at seven o'clock on Friday."

Off balance again I said, "Thank you very much. I'll never use my Barclaycard ever again,"

I put the phone down, thinking, "I hope he doesn't think I can't even afford to eat?"

CHAPTER 9

ANOTHER BEGINNING

I was feeling strangely nervous when, on Friday evening, a grey Escort drew up outside my house at seven o'clock precisely. As he held the door open for me, I thought," I'd better watch out, this man is clearly a stickler for punctuality."

Nonetheless I said cheerfully, "Thank you, Mr. Hall," as I clambered in.

"Please, call me Ian," he responded.

As we pulled away, he asked, "Will The Black Horse at Nassington be OK?"

I thought, "I'm assuming this man is paying, as he is doing the asking!"

But simply said, "Yes."

I thought that I had been to The Black Horse before but I was confusing this with another village called Wansford. The last time that I had been there was to say "thank you" to the children's friend's parents for the offer of two nights accommodation while I was in hospital. I'd hired a boat for me, the four children and the dogs. The boat hire company was at Stibbington, and I'd planned for a weekend along The Nene. We set off but by the time we arrived at The Heycock at Wansford I felt I needed a break, so I moored up, and after spaghetti bolognese on board, I walked, without the children, to the bar for a gin and tonic. When I returned two days later in a rather dishevelled state, I was greeted by the barman with a warm, "Oh! You're back, another gin and tonic?"

I was exhausted, "Yes please!" I whispered.

So I had very fond memories of The Heycock. But I digress, suffice it to say that The Black Horse and Ian's company gave me a very pleasant and memorable evening!

This being our first date, conversation was naturally a little constrained. I was initially feeling relaxed and at home in the comfortable surroundings of The Black Horse. Soon established with a gin and tonic and studying the menu, I could see that I should be in for a splendid meal. We ordered our food and suddenly I found myself desperately compensating for my anxiety and insecurity by explaining my position in the Health Authority. I paused as I was thinking, but didn't say, "I am presently in a relationship with my boss, a married man with two children. He had started an affair with me when I returned to work after having my operation. How had I allowed this to happen? I was feeling very confused." To cover this confusion, I nervously launched into a somewhat garrulous explanation of my position in the NHS, saying to Ian, "Now I am working as Quality Assurance Manager for Peterborough Health Authority whilst at the same time, I have been taking a course in Quality in the Health Service at the King's fund. Following this course in quality, a small group of us have set up an organisation called N.A.Q.A. It is a National Association, and I am going to edit its journal, though I am still trying to complete my PhD. in nursing history. I am also a member of a small group of nurse-historians set up by the Florence Nightingale Museum trust to open a museum at St Thomas's hospital in memory of Florence Nightingale."

I stopped to draw breath, but was thinking, "And all this with the disease of lupus, I don't quite believe it myself, I wonder if this man does?"

To give him his due, Ian did seem interested in what I was saying, and was starting to respond when a pretty, young lady wearing a long rain coat approached our table, and asked, "Mr Hall?"

"Yes," he said.

Then she took off her raincoat to reveal a scantily dressed young lady in bra, panties and suspenders. A kissogram! She sat on Ian's lap and read a poem about our date. I pushed my chair away from the table, thinking, "Someone must be checking out whether Ian's date has a sense of humour."

Afterwards she kissed Ian, donned her raincoat and left. Ian was obviously taken aback but soon recovered his composure, he said, "I know who must have organised that, as I've only told two people about this evening's arrangements."

We carried on with the rest of the delicious meal a little bemused, as we got the measure of each other. Although I knew the answer, I asked if he was married.

Ian said, "My wife has been hospitalised for some time now, and she will never come home again."

Ian seemed lost in thought, so to recover the situation I asked, "Do you have time to play any sport?"

He said," Yes, I play golf"

I said rather rashly, "I've played golf all my life."

"Oh, where do you play?"

"Well I used to play at the Belfry, but that was some time ago."

Oh dear, I was beginning to regret this line of conversation. In truth, my mother had given me her old golf clubs, because as a child during the school holidays my Dad took me round the Belfrey course with him on Wednesday afternoons. I couldn't really pretend I played. My response to Mum's donation of golf clubs was to book a golf lesson the year before I had had my operation, and my skill at golf was found wanting. I didn't book any more lessons.

Somehow, it was only two days later that I found myself, clubs at the ready, with Ian in the pouring, almost horizontal rain. We were on the first tee at Milton, with the Captain looking out through the clubhouse windows. Milton was a local club, for members only, and Ian was a member. The Club Captain was waiting to follow us, I thought, "No one in their right minds would choose to play golf on a day like this." Anyway it was here that Ian found out that I was far from being a competent player at golf. Although it was May 3rd, it was very cold and, needless to say, it was not the happiest round, sloshing around in our waterproofs trying to keep warm and well ahead of the Captain's four ball behind us. I managed to leave clubs on various holes on the back nine. When Ian discovered my attempts at sabotaging the round he ran back to recover my five iron, seven iron and putter that I had scattered behind me. On the fourteenth Ian suggested that we retire to the 19th hole and I was grateful to end my suffering and humiliation. It was some time before we were to play again!

However I was gradually putting together an understanding of who this man was. Ian lived with his two children, only about 200 yards away from us. Ian's wife had been hospitalised in 1985 when she was eventually diagnosed as suffering from Huntingdon's Chorea. In 1987 she was by now in the latter stages of this terrible and terminal cerebral disease. Although we continued to see each other, I thought, "After all those years of caring for a wife suffering from advanced dementia, Ian doesn't need an involvement with someone with the diagnosis of Lupus." But nonetheless I was enjoying being taken out by him, and as the dates continued, finding him more and more delightful.

Now I realised that it was time to untangle myself from my relationship with my boss. He suggested a weekend away at a conference. I packed a particularly boring, cream cotton crochet dress. It was another gift from my mother and was an unflattering outfit. He got the message, which left the field clear for me to move on. At the end of the second month of dates with Ian I exposed myself again, this time as being

294

financially unreliable. I had arrived home very tired and couldn't quite think what to cook. It was the end of the month and the children were fractious. I thought,"My salary will be in the bank what can I do to make the situation a little easier?"

I asked, "What about going to the Fox and Hounds for meal?"

"Yeeah," they chimed in unison.

Lazily, I put my Barclaycard in the pocket of my jeans, just like the Barclaycard advert that was currently on TV, climbed into the car and drove to the local pub. The pub was in a mock Tudor style, built about 1930 on the same site of one that had burnt down. It wasn't known for its cuisine, but it fitted the bill at the time. The children had finished their beef burger and chips, and I had eaten my chicken kiev and chips, when Ian and his friend Gerry walked in.

"Oh no," I thought," I've stupidly left my bright yellow Metro on the front car park in full view of passers-by on Thorpe Road." Ian had seen my car, called for Gerry as arranged and went about tracking me down. I was taken aback as they both walked in and, on approaching our table, introduced everybody. Ian asked, "What can I get you all to drink?"

Furnished with the drinks, I looked at Gerry, thinking him to be some six inches shorter than Ian, and about 30 years older, and this was confirmed as Ian said, "Tell them what you did in the war, Gerry."

Gerry took a breath in and started, "Have you seen the film called the Dambusters?"

John was suddenly interested, "Yes," he said.

Gerry, sensing an enthusiastic audience in John, said, "Well that was my plane on that film. I was part of Barnes Wallace's team that perfected the 'Bouncing bomb' we flew up and down the Wash in mosquitoes."

Gerry stopped to take another drink of his beer, and John are asked,"What did you do then?"

"After that I went on to carry the bomb on Beaufighters, and I was part of Coastal Command, do you know about that?"

"No, not really, "said John, and Sarah shook her head too, but they were both beginning to get a bit bored.

"Please can we go now? Sarah asked.

Now I realized that I had a problem, I was stuck with no money and just the card that I'd promised never to use again.

I said, "You two go ahead, and get ready for bed, I'll come along later."

They kissed me and left me to extricate myself from the situation. Realising these guys were not going to leave before me, I faced the inevitable; I needed to pay the bill, so I sighed and, using my Barclaycard, paid the bill. I returned to the table to see Ian's amused look. I'd been caught out yet again.

However this repeat of my financial mismanagement didn't put Ian off, and John began to think that this man might become a threat to his position as "the man of the house". Several times when Ian came to call, John attempted to shut the door in his face. But Ian was too quick for him and put his foot in the doorway to stop it being prematurely closed. Soon Ian and I became "an item".

One evening we were at small NHS departmental ball in the Great Northern Hotel, a truly classic building that was a good example of a 19th century railway building. It was very smart, so imagine my horror when the man I'd chased away brandishing my bloodstained knife walked in. I whispered to Ian, "Oh no its that man," and I explained the story.

Ian responded, "That's Myers Tennyson, he's retired now but he is one of your neighbours and was David's predecessor at the Bank."

I felt awful saying, "Perhaps he won't recognise me."

Ian chuckled, "Myers never forgets a face."

With That Myers headed towards us with hand outstretched and, saying with a smile for both of us, "Hello Ian and hello again to you!"

I was overcome with embarrassment but Ian formally introduced me and no more was said about the previous incident.

Ian's friends seemed to be pleased to include me in his social engagements. We were invited to a wedding reception at The Heycock. On our way we came across two cars that had collided on the narrow road. The road was blocked and we stopped to assist. Two ladies had been thrown out of the rear doors and it looked as if one of them had travelled some way along the road on her face. There was a lot of blood coming from her head. Another car had stopped a little way ahead, and the occupants came running back. As I was trying to keep the lady who was bleeding still and calm, a passenger from the other car was wanting to lift and comfort her, calling out "Mama mia, mama mia" hysterically over and over again. Ian held her back and eventually had to smack her face to stop her struggling to get to the injured woman. She calmed down and joined the others who were wandering around in a state of shock. Fortunately it wasn't long before the police and ambulances arrived, closely followed by a fire engine. The injured were hastily dispatched to the local hospital and a policeman explained to the Italian occupants of the other car how to get to Peterborough hospital, and left as well.

I was very bloody. A kind fireman saw my plight and offered to wash me down. He turned on the water from his fire engine and Ian and I washed the blood from our hands.

I smiled and said, "Thank you, I expect you've done that a few times before!"

We all laughed, and we continued on our way to the reception, a little the worse for wear.

Ian said, "It looked as if half that woman's face was missing."

I sighed, "I didn't look, best not, I thought I couldn't do anything for her anyway."

Ian continued, "I've never hit a woman across the face

297

before you know, but it was the only way I could think of stopping her."

"Don't worry," I said.

He looked relieved, presumably thinking that I might wonder if it was the way he often treated ladies. Far from feeling at risk from his violence, I felt relaxed, and the reception went well. We thoroughly enjoyed the evening.

Back at work, I was beginning to settle into my new job, and it wasn't long before some companies were sniffing naïveté and moved into the Health Service, hoping to set up business models, increase their profits, and reduce NHS costs. It needed a fundamental change in thinking to achieve this objective! An early approach in Peterborough was to promote quality circles as a tool to improve management in the Health Authority. In fact even before had my surgery, I had been on a course in 'Quality in the Health Service' at the King's fund. It had meant my travelling daily to London. During this time I met up with a group of freshly appointed staff that, like me, were becoming involved in quality issues. We were a mixed bunch; Health Authority Directors, nurses, health visitors and some university staff. One of the directors, Delia, an enthusiastic Welsh woman in her fifties, suggested setting up a national quality interest group. Delia was appointed to the Chair and she wrote to both Margaret Thatcher and the British Standards Institute (BSI) to inform them. The BSI soon took us under their wing, and this led to heated discussions regarding the lack of similarities between healthcare and industrial standards. Once more facing industrial engineering types, the ghosts from my marriage reappeared. Despite trying, I felt that I didn't adequately express my opinion that the NHS needed tools to document and measure caring outcomes as well as setting the standards. The group eventually became known as NAQA. [The National Association of Quality Assurance in Healthcare] and I agreed to edit the journal and record conference the proceedings.

There was a lot to think about and I was very pleased when Steve, my old friend from Oxford days, invited me and the children to stay with him and his new wife in their new home in the Lake District. Steve really hadn't changed over the years and his kindness and sandy coloured hair always reminded me of my dad. I was looking forward to the break. I said goodbye to Ian and headed to Cumbria. I carefully worked out the route, and John sat beside me, reading my written instructions and looking for each junction. Sarah sat in the back with the dogs. We arrived without incident, and Steve and Sue made us most welcome. They had a male Old English Sheepdog, who was delighted by the company of two bitches. Unfortunately he was prone to substantial dribbles and you had to ensure that you were out of the zone when he shook his head, otherwise you were assaulted by quantities of unpleasant saliva! One day towards the middle of our stay I took the children pony trekking, it was some way from Sue and Steve's house, and I had to stop on the way back to fill up with petrol at Kendal. I parked by the pumps, and John announced, "That's Ian's car."

I responded, "It can't be, Ian is going to Malta tomorrow."

I went into the garage shop and sure enough it was Ian.

He hadn't spotted me so I went behind him and put my arms around him.

"Guess who?" I said.

Now both of us were surprised.

"What are you doing here?" I continued.

"I went to buy a map," he explained.

And then added, "I had to see you before I went. I couldn't wait for over two weeks until I could see you again!"

"You follow me and you won't need a map," I said. So I filled up with petrol and we went in tandem to Sue and Steve's, and after the introductions, Steve asked Ian, "How long did it take you to get here?"

Ian answered, "Oh, about five hours."

Steve's response was, "And you are planning to drive

straight back, I think that's risky. Please stay here for the night and go early in the morning."

Ian was pleased, responding, "Thanks. It's probably the sensible thing to do."

And so it was arranged, Ian later explained that he was being romantic and trying to emulate a current television advert, "And all because the lady loves Milk Tray". He was glad that he didn't have to dive off a cliff though. So he had bought a box of expensive chocolates and planned to leave them at Steve's for me.

It was very early the next morning when Ian left, heading home to Peterborough so that he could pack and with his children head to Stansted airport for the flight to Malta. While we continued with our holiday, Steve said, "That man must be very keen on you, you know."

"Yes, I do know, Steve. But it doesn't alter the fact that, after all that Ian has been through, caring for his first wife and things, he doesn't need to be involved with somebody suffering from the potential complications of Lupus."

Steve made no comment and we happily went on with our holiday all feeling cheerful and having a good time, before returning home to Peterborough.

I went back to work to find that a decision had been made to relocate the midwifery training school from Peterborough to Norwich. The Secretary of Midwifery at the school, Joan Newey, was in her late forties and was another single parent with two children. I arranged for her to join me to work in the quality department. I had been sent information about the planning of a quality circle program developed by the University of Manchester, and it seemed very good.

"Shall we give it a try?" I asked Joan.

"Yes lets go for it," Joan sounded keen.

We started up with a quality circle recruited from the catering and maintenance departments and soon the recruits were enthusiastically on board. Joan was a natural leader.

Before long we were joined in the QA department by Huw, a plump, well built Welshman. He was in his twenties and had just finished a Masters Degree in Health Service Management.

I asked him, "What do you know about standards setting in healthcare?"

Huw answered, "It was an area we covered in my degree. It's going to be very important to the changes in the Health Service."

As I felt rather at a loss in the male dominated world of the BSI, I was happy to delegate 'Standards Setting' to him.

Huw seemed genuinely pleased and he enthusiastically set about his task.

On Friday my team and I often went nearby for lunch at The Sessions House. The Sessions House, Peterborough, was built in the mid 1840's as a prison and later used as a courthouse and headquarters for the local police force. Though it was built in the Victorian era it had distinct characteristics of Norman architecture, with heavy roundness and a distinct castle-like appearance. By the 1960s, it had become engulfed by the hospital buildings and was converted into a pub and restaurant. A very convenient place for our team to take stock of what we had achieved in the week and start planning the week ahead. We produced a leaflet introducing the team at a QA exhibition in the hospital in June 1988, seeking to encourage awareness of quality in the NHS by offering visitors strawberries and cream provided, of course, by the catering department's quality circle.

Val Wright, the District Catering Manager, had embraced the quality circles program with exuberant enthusiasm. It was quite a success. So when the first edition of the journal and conference proceedings for NAQA was due for publication, we were able to publish the Peterborough work in it. Delia was still employed as Director of Nursing for Gwent, while she was Executive Director of NAQA, and both of her daughters were salaried employees.

The three of us from Peterborough worked together on our work for the Health Authority as well as publishing the NAQA Journal and Conference proceedings. Much of the first edition focused on the Peterborough work but by Issue 2 in Spring '89 and Issue 3 in Autumn '89, we were able to encourage more contributions from other people in other Health Authorities. By that time there were several universities that had developed or were planning programmes for working and researching health care and quality issues.

I was very busy with all these changes, and Ian was finding that the bank was under going fundamental structural changes as well.

One evening Ian said, "I have seen the Local Head Office Senior Director about my prospects and the rumoured changes to the bank's management structure. After discussions he confirmed that, whilst I may expect modest promotions, even he expected to be ousted within the next five years. He was able to offer me a fairly good early retirement package. I've got a month to think it over, but I'm not sure what to do. My original reason for being in the bank was to be a 'money doctor' and to help people. But now I think all that is about to change."

I replied thoughtfully, "Well you certainly helped me."

"Now the approach seems to have changed and I feel like a fish out of water. What do you think I should do?"

"If you leave what will you do next?" I asked.

"Well all I've got is an Advanced Diploma in banking. I don't want to stay in the financial industry, otherwise I may end up as an insurance salesman or even worse, a building society manager. I have been a manager for several years but I have nothing to prove this, no certificates or anything. Am I a competent manager? And I need to find myself."

"What about getting a degree?" I said

"Well I have always regretted that I didn't go to university after I left school. Ok there were good reasons at the time but do you think I could do a degree? Is it possible?"

"Yes of course!" I responded.

So Ian decided that he'd like to take the leaving package.

He said, "I'd really like to apply to universities to do an M.B.A. Do you honestly think that I could manage to do it"?

My reaction was immediate. "With all your banking experience and qualification, of course you can!"

Ian managed to suppress his doubts and applied to undertake the required GMAT (Graduate Management Admission Test). This completed, he applied to universities for a placing. His GMAT results came through and to his surprise he was substantially over the minimum threshold for admission.

The University of Nottingham gave him an interview, and we arrived on a lovely summers day. I waited for Ian whilst sitting on the grass in that super campus, knitting and consuming the occasional ice cream that I purchased at the nearby student shop. Nobody could have been more surprised than he when he was interviewed by Professor Brian Chiplin, the Principal of the Management School, who offered him a place there and then. He was still feeling very anxious; I wondered whether he'd hoped not to be accepted. I knew that he felt that it was a very large step for him to take. Could he manage it?

Then it was my turn to feel nervous when the following morning my telephone rang at work; it was the District General Manager, he said, "Tony Newton, the Minister of Health, is coming to visit Peterborough. I want you to prepare a paper on the developments in your department, and to meet with him to explain what you're doing in Quality Assurance. "

Together with Joan and Huw, I set to work on the presentation, and Tony Newton genuinely appeared interested and concerned. I was relieved how it had gone and getting back into the department I declared, "Tony Newton is a gentleman and a really nice guy."

A few days later Ian rang me at work and sounded

worried, "I have to formally accept the bank's offer, but I haven't had the university confirmation in writing."

I said, "I'll ring Brian Chiplin's secretary, have you got the telephone number?"

Furnished with the number I rang and explained the position.

"My name is Margaret and you can be sure that if Brian Chiplin says he is in, then he is in. We'll see him in October and if there is anything else that I can help with please don't hesitate to contact me."

From the tone of her voice, I suspected that we were both smiling as we said our goodbyes.

I rang Ian to reassure him and, although Ian was still unsure at the informal nature of the university's approach, unlike the specific and formal ways of the bank, he signed his resignation papers and made preparations for his life as a student.

While all this was going on, Ian's daughter, Andrea, had left school and was looking for jobs in catering as she had previously worked part time at a local "Wimpy Bar". His son, Trevor, wanted to move from the local Grammar School to take his A levels at what he saw to be a more trendy school, the local comprehensive, Jack Hunt School, where Sarah had just finished her first A level year. John, who was at the same school doing his GCSEs, said, "I want to move to Ian's house."

Feeling a bit hurt, "What about your rabbits?" I said.

"I can look after things just as well at Ian's."

Ian and I agreed and John moved in to live with him.

Changed seemed to be a regular feature in our lives. One day the phone rang at work.

A male voice asked, "Am I speaking to Annie Armitage?"

"Yes, speaking."

My name is John Tait from the Nursing Division Ministry of Health. The Minister has instructed me to contact you and ask if you would be interested in a temporary contract as

Consultant in Quality to the nursing Division at the Department of Health."

"Can you give me time to think about it please?" I responded.

I was shocked and even more so when the following day the phone rang again, and someone I knew from NAQA said breathlessly, "Please don't say anything about this conversation to anyone, but the Chief Nursing Officer is against your appointment. They will be out to discredit you."

Now I was in a real dilemma. Was it that the person who didn't want me thought that I was a threat to their position, or was it a genuine warning, and kind concern for me? Could it really be because the paper I'd given at the 'The King's Fund' conference, "The UKCC - Historical Insights into Today's Decisions", had left me as an outcast with the nursing hierarchy? Had I scored an own goal? But that was what I believed and, whatever happened, I had to be true to myself. But I was worried what to do and Ian said, "Yes it is undoubtedly a risk but if you don't do it you will possibly regret it for the rest of your life."

This was what I had said to him about Nottingham and the MBA!

"But I'll be leaving Huw and Joan behind," I said.

Ian's joking response was, "They will probably be glad to see the back of you," and he laughed.

So it was back to a family council session again.

"Go for it mum." Sarah was enthusiastic. John was non-committal; he had other things on his mind. Although, he was too young to drive one, he had managed to buy a 95cc defunct motorbike. He put it in Ian's garage.

"You're too young to drive that thing!" Ian said. John's response was, "That's alright, it isn't roadworthy anyway, so I'm just going to work on it."

I did wonder about all the changes and the children's futures,

"Is now the right time to be doing this?" But I went ahead and give in my notice.

The next morning I was still pondering my decision and, looking in the bathroom mirror, I noticed a very black mole on my left arm. It was about the size of a raisin and I thought, "I've never noticed that before." It was with a feeling of dread that I rang my GP's surgery.

"Dr Gordon can see you this afternoon at 2:30," the receptionist said.

Dr Gordon examined it and immediately said, "I'll ring Dr Hudson at the hospital".

I returned home and within the hour the telephone rang,

"Can you attend Dr Hudson's clinic on Thursday at 11.00?"

"Yes, thank you," I answered, rather overawed by the situation.

Today was Tuesday so I only had two days to wait.

I felt a bit sick when I walked into the clinic, and very soon the nurse called me through. I looked at Dr Hudson and thought; "He looks just like Mr Slope from 'Barchester Chronicle'." Then I felt guilty as he looked at me again and said kindly,"Take a seat outside, we will take that off today."

My name was called and I was prepared on the operating couch. An African doctor, Dr Mubaru, was operating that day and as he administered the local anaesthetic by injection and removed the mole and said, "These neurotic white women, I'm fed up with taking off their very small moles."

He was very black and I knew that his white wife was an elegant blond. I hoped that he was not like that with her. Anyway when I returned a few days later to get the results, Dr Hudson confirmed, "It was a malignant Melanoma it was 'insitu' and there was no evidence of spread. We will need to follow this up for the next three years just in case."

"So much for Dr Mubaru's comment," I thought.

Both Ian and I were preparing for the major changes in our lives. I was worried about leaving my friends and colleagues in the Health Authority but as I wasn't moving house and going a 1000 miles away, I felt I could cope with it. We were still seeing the catering manager, Val and her husband Geoff socially, and this included a New Years Eve break with them, our children and two of our neighbours, Trish and Paul, to the White Lion in Aldeburgh, Suffolk. We really enjoyed the time away and particularly the excellent food during the New Year celebrations at the White Lion.

After one of these New Year celebrations, as we were driving through Suffolk, Ian said, "I'll take you to the birth place of the most famous English painter."

I was baffled and said, "I didn't know Turner was borne in Suffolk," I said.

Ian said, "Constable! I didn't say the best, I said the most famous and he actually lived at Flatford in Essex, just over the Suffolk border."

That began years of a family joke with Ian pointing out every reproduction of Constable's works that he came across to prove his assertion. I was amazed at how many there were and, how few of Turner's works.

This year I felt stressed with all the changes that we were about to face and it wasn't long before Ian suggested, "I think that we need a holiday."

I jumped at the chance, because since leaving the children's father I hadn't been able to afford to pay for holidays. £5 per week maintenance was not exactly a fortune. I am sure that I could have got more, but to chase my ex-husband for extra money would have involved court intervention and I knew that I couldn't endure the additional stress that those sorts of pressures would involve. So he managed to avoid some of his financial responsibilities and I had previously relied upon friends and family offering us the opportunity to get away for a break. The children's father had regularly taken them abroad and to some wonderful places, probably to make me feel guilty. I was very excited when we decided to hire a narrowboat from the British Waterways at Nantwich on the Shropshire Union Canal. Years before and shortly after I was married I had a holiday on a narrowboat. Therefore as an experienced boater I took charge. We decided to go onto the Llangollen canal in a seventy-foot long boat so that we could accommodate both our families. The boatyard was conveniently placed just by a lock and the boatman, having demonstrated how to empty and refill a lock, returned to his boatyard leaving me and my novice crew in charge of what seemed to be an impossibly long craft. Standing at the helm and steering along a canal no more than 20 foot across was daunting. Feeling somewhat nervous I turned off the 'Shroppy' into the first flight of four locks, on the Llangollen canal. The Llangollen seemed even narrower that the 'Shroppy'.

"How on earth are we going to manage this?" I whispered quietly to Ian.

I was hoping that the children hadn't heard me. Ian just grinned rather nervously I thought, despite his knowledge and experiences in sea going boats.

When we had been packing to go on our jaunt, I had teased Ian about the size of the first aid box that he was going to take.

"It's massive!" I declared.

He just shrugged his shoulders and put it in the car. Shortly after we started out, and when we were well beyond the reach of anything other than boat transport, travelling at between three and four miles per hour or traipsing across miles of fields, I caught my right hand, middle finger in a lock mechanism. It was a severe pressure wound and it poured with blood. It needed stitches. The 'large' first aid box was brought into action and was invaluable, as Ian was able to 'sterri strip' the wound using micropore tape and gauze.

"Call yourself a nurse," Ian said laughingly.

"Okay you were right, I have to admit we needed it." I

thought. "Well when I come to think of it nurses aren't specifically trained in first aid."

He continued, "You see, my St John's ambulance training comes in handy sometimes."

Although I had to admit defeat on the issue of the first aid box, I got my own back when it came to handling a boat on the canals. Ian's previous boating experience was on the sea. Consequently whenever we needed to tie up, Ian's reaction was to jump off the front of the boat and pull the front rope very tight. I was at the back on the tiller, unable to control the boat at the stern, initially ending up with the boat diagonally across the canal.

Several times I had to say, "Don't pull the front rope, darling!"

And with increasing exasperation following my loss of control of the boat, this became, "Ian, just hold the front rope!"

At first he clearly didn't understand what I meant and eventually I ended up shouting, "Drop the fucking rope," and, as an after thought, "darling!"

Somehow our relationship wasn't destroyed by these antics and my Anglo Saxon. As our competency improved we became more relaxed in handling the boat, although it did steer rather like a supermarket trolley. We chugged through beautiful countryside and came to another lock with a narrowboat already in it, going up the same way as ourselves. A lady was at the helm and a man and two teenage girls were trying to fill the lock. It was clear that they weren't very accomplished.

"We may be some time," I said. In the traditional way of the canals, we moored up and went to help them.

"Sorry, I'm afraid that we are rather slow. We aren't very good at this boating lark," the man said in a Welsh accent.

He was embarrassed.

We all laughed, feeling rather superior as our boys showed off their newly acquired skills. Both carrying windlasses they

309

operated the lock while we introduced ourselves and chatted.

The man, whose name was Alan, said, "When we turned into the Llangollen canal, somehow we managed to turn the boat round in the first lock pound of the four, and had to do the rest backwards."

Although he was a trifle embarrassed we all laughed and teamed up. The two families worked together and followed each other, with our children showing the others how to use the windlass and operate the mechanisms. Eventually they became a good team and we spent the rest of the holiday together, the children spending the evenings on one boat listening to their music, with the parents on the other, relieved that we didn't have to share the children's music; *The Stone Roses*, etc were not our idea of relaxing music. All in all it turned out to be a very amusing holiday.

It was beautiful scenery as we went over the Pontcysyllte Aquaduct, marvelling at the sheer drop of 150ft down to the River Dee below and the wonderful smell of very fresh air. The deck of the boat was above the level of the channel of ironwork supporting the canal water and there was a path with railings on the other side. Apparently this was originally used for the horses to walk along as they pulled the boats. From the deck we appeared to be unsupported because the rim of the steel was so close to the boat that we couldn't see it. I shouted nervously and then in exhilaration, "We really must do this again!" I enthused.

"Yes, we must" Ian agreed.

All too soon the holiday was over, and though I was feeling relaxed, it was back to work for me, and Ian was working his notice out before starting at Nottingham. Joan and Huw were organising my leaving do before I went to the Department of Health and we were also getting the current NAQA Journal ready for publication. At the last meeting of NAQA we had decided to launch the NAQA Gold Award for the best implementation of quality in health care. We had received complimentary noises from the Department of Health and were anticipating that they would take an active interest and hopefully fund or part fund further development of NAQA.

For Ian and I home life was going well. John was happy at Ian's house and John and Trevor were spending most of their spare time fishing. I was relieved when John sold his motorbike before he had an accident, but my relief was short lived as he pushed home an old Mini into Ian's garage to work on.

I was anxious, "What are you going to do with that, John? It will be ages until you are old enough to drive."

John's reply was, "Don't worry, Mum, I'm just going to mess about with it, it won't go anyway."

Ian was preparing for his life as a student in Nottingham, and I started my daily train trips to London and the Department of Health. I said to Ian, "I certainly don't feel that they want me there. Perhaps I'm being paranoid, or do you think that they are setting out to rubbish me?"

"Give it time and see how it goes," was Ian's response.

I struggled on and, in October, Ian began his MBA. He was enjoying the studying when, although it was expected, his wife died shortly after Christmas. This left Ian with the shadow of his dead wife and two traumatised children, though neither of them really remembered her before her illness had taken over. Ian was left to travel to Nottingham where he had to concentrate on all that the Masters degree demanded. I was feeling rather inadequate, having to show the correct amount of compassion, whilst respecting the memory of his wife and his children's mother. Of course she was someone that they hardly knew, but I felt that one way that I could help was to do the shopping. Each Thursday I would drive from the station car park to the shopping centre in my Metro, pick up my purchases at the customer collection point, then head for home with children at each house eagerly waiting to check the goodies I'd brought them.

One day on my way home, fortunately it was a Tuesday rather than a Thursday, I arrived at Kings Cross to find that the trains to Peterborough weren't running because a tree had blown down on the line and blocked it. I went to customer services for advice, and was told, "You need to go to Leicester, and then catch a train to Peterborough."

So I caught the train to Leicester. When I got out at the station, suddenly I was met by a lot of clapping, and someone shouted, "Here's another one!"

During previous journeys to London I had felt a bit unnerved by male passengers scrutinizing the third finger on my left hand, so much so that I'd said to Ian, "I'd appreciate it if you could buy me an eternity ring." By chance the January sales were still on, so we went to buy an eternity ring, and then I felt more relaxed about my train journeys. It was some of those same chaps that had unnerved me in the past, although they'd never actually spoken to me, that now welcomed me at Leicester. I was accepted as one of their gang and, each day thereafter, they saved me a seat and chatted amiably as we went backwards and forwards on our journeys between Peterborough and Kings Cross.

Somehow both Ian and I managed with the new demands on our lives. Though I was working in the Department, I was still responsible for the editorship of the NAQA Journal, but the hoped for financial support from the Department of Health was not forthcoming. We needed money to establish the infrastructure to run NAQA in a professional manner. Unfortunately Tony Newton had moved on and Virginia Bottomley took over as Minister of Health. Her reputation that she was out of touch and a bit off a 'toff' had preceded her, and all too soon it was obvious that her commitment to quality issues were not as robust as Tony Newton's. Things were going on behind the scenes and I was soon informed that my short term contract would not be renewed.

In March my boss at the Department of Health, John Tait, arranged a meeting with myself and Ian. At the meeting it

312

was suggested, and I accepted, that I should spend the rest of my contracted time helping Deborah Harman. She was a lecturer in Quality in Health Care at the University of Birmingham and was involved with NAQA. I was very happy with this as Deborah was a very competent, gentle person, and it would be a pleasure to be developing courses alongside her. Amazingly, the courses were due to be run in buildings where my preliminary nursing training had been held, and so with some sense of Déjà Vu I set about enthusiastically preparing our lectures.

With no funding, sadly Delia and her daughters had to abandon their dreams regarding NAQA, and the organisation was doomed. The last time that I rang her Delia said, in a resigned voice,

"I'm afraid it's not going to happen is it? The Department is not going to back us, are they?"

I answered sadly, "No, there are forces working against us that do not believe in our quality approach to the quality model." Delia sounded so dispirited. I thought back to all our optimism at the foundation of NAQA. It seemed so very sad that it might become just a waste of our efforts and enthusiasm. Perhaps I was just being a pessimist. Only time would tell.

Ian successfully finished his MBA and started working for the School of Management. When he arrived home early one afternoon, he followed a beat up old Mini leaving a trail of rust, which entered his driveway. Ian stopped behind it ready to find out what the driver was doing on his driveway when John stepped out.

"Whatever do you think you are doing John?" Ian asked

"My mates were late for school so I gave them a lift. You won't tell mum will you"

"No I won't," Ian replied and John gave a sigh of relief. Ian continued, "As long as you tell her yourself within the next hour!"

Needless to say Ian immobilised the Mini and my 14 year

old son and aspiring driver was precluded from any more illegal auto activities.

Eventually Ian moved the Mini to my driveway where it rested for several weeks, prior to disposal. John did not or would not, despite requests, arrange removal. Ian sold it for scrap for £35 leaving me relieved that John had not been arrested for driving under age, lacking tax, insurance and MOT.

John said to Ian, "You owe me £10 as you only paid £25 for that Mini."

Ian replied, "Don't be so cheeky, after all the trouble we have had I should charge you parking fees, you probably owe us much more than £10." John moaned and Ian responded, "I'm afraid, John, that you have to learn the rules of business. You normally have to pay for what you get."

Back in Nottingham, The Business School offered Ian a contract to work for them on Management Research and by chance his principal project was for the Trent Area Health Authority. In reaction to my feelings of insecurity about my employment Ian said, "Don't worry, if there is a termination of your contract we can set up business together as a partnership and possibly get married?"

Although I was excited about the idea of the partnership and marriage, I really felt that with the diagnosis of Lupus hanging over me, Ian would do far better to find someone who could promise him a better future than I could offer.

So I repeated what I'd always said, "I am very happy to hold your hand while you get over your wife's death. But then I think you really should look for someone who can offer you the security of a happy healthy time."

Ian then said, "Look if I die and we are not married you would not be able to claim my bank pension and, whilst it isn't a fortune, it could be very useful in your old age. As we intend to live together for the rest of our lives, what's the difference? Anyway I would feel more secure if we were married." After a short pause he added, "Perhaps we should buy a narrowboat and move it around the canals to wherever we are working?"

Well that was the clincher and my response was immediate, "That would be wonderful but I think we should leave the marriage bit for a while!"

Then we speculated about the most suitable length for two to manage.

"50 foot long?" Ian suggested.

Was this just a pipe dream? I did hope it wasn't.

Ian now had 'the bit between his teeth' and started to research boatyards who did hirings and sales.

Ian said, "If we start a business together we could call it Lockwood Hall Associates and move the boat to wherever we are working when we are away from home." Lockwood being my grandmother's maiden name.

I couldn't quite believe it, "Do you honestly think that it would be possible?"

"Yes I'm sure it would, it could be our home from home and we would save on our hotel bills."

With that decided we hired a 55ft boat by the name of Hannah from the boatyard at Penkridge, on The Staffordshire and Worcester Canal. With the children, Sarah and John, at their father's and Andrea and Trevor going to stay with Ian's sister Moira in Helpston, we set off to Penkridge with just Holly and Abbey as company. The boatyard owner, a man called Peter, took us through the first lock just to see that we knew how to handle a boat, and waved us on our way. We were excited by the prospect as we headed up the canal towards the Trent and Mersey. All alongside the banks the flowers were lovely, and it was delightful to call in at canal side pubs for food and refreshments without the required abstinence required that went with drinking and driving. Going at three to four miles an hour we were completely relaxed without the competing demands of the children and work and without a care in the world when Ian said, "I think we should turn round."

"Do you mean wind?" I said smugly.

He grinned, but said, "I think we also need to fill up with water soon."

We went on a little further until we reached Great Haywood, the junction with the Trent and Mersey where our *Nicholsons Guide to the waterways of Central England* detailed a water point. There was a boat already taking on water so we moored up behind it to wait our turn.

On the towpath was a nice looking Blue Roan Cocker Spaniel and I went to make a fuss of it, closely followed by our dogs. Inevitably I got into conversation with the owner of the boat that was on the water point. With that he held out his hand saying, "Hello my name is Rob, and where are you off to?"

I explained that we were trying out the boat with a view to buying one. With that he said, "Well my boat is for sale, come and have a look around."

We went on board Rob. Introduced us to his wife who was at the sink doing the washing up and said, "Mo, these people are going to buy our boat." She looked very taken aback and, as we found out later, that was the first time that she knew her home was for sale. It was longer than we had anticipated at 62.5 feet but we were very taken with it. We spent a few hours thinking and then arranged to meet up and negotiate terms. The negotiations went well and we came to an agreement that we would buy the boat but we wouldn't take it over until the spring of the next year.

Returning home, work issues were destined to take over. I had received a letter from Deborah saying, "We have received some very positive comments on the pilot course! Now we need to make a start designing a more advanced and longer course."

I was relieved, Sunrise No 1 passed its survey, and all went according to plan. So we picked up Sunrise No1 at Great Haywood and took her onto her new moorings on an old, virtually disused arm of the Oxford Canal at Rugby, occupied by Willow Wren boat hire. Here it was just half an hour travelling in the car to get to Birmingham University. It was all very convenient, I said to Deborah, "We could involve Ian to lecture on the financial issues and implications of quality, and he could fit this in with his work at the University of Nottingham. Shall I send you his CV?"

Deborah agreed, so Ian was recruited to teach at Birmingham as well.

During one of the planning meetings Deborah said, "Do you think that you could go to the European Health Conference in Brussels next month to represent my department as I am not able to go myself?"

"Yes I'd like to," was my immediate response.

So the next month Ian took me to East Midlands airport for my flight to Brussels.

Unfortunately, I didn't get much out of the conference, and I was feeling tired by the time that I boarded the flight home. There was a flurry of activity at the airport as Leon Britain was ushered through the departure lounge followed by his civil servant entourage. Our plane took off soon followed by an announcement, "We are sorry to inform you that East Midlands airport has been closed due to fog and we are being diverted. We may have to land at Newcastle, Shannon or Manchester."

I said to the passenger, who sat next to me, "I'm surprised that Leon Britain's plane has been delayed."

He said in a supercilious voice, "And why are you here?"

I said, "I am a nurse attending the Health Conference representing the Birmingham University Quality interest."

He raised his eyes scornfully and said, "I am a doctor."

I said no more but was irritated at his demeaning and arrogant attitude.

Shortly afterwards another message was announced, "We have a passenger who requires medical assistance. Is there a doctor or nurse on the plane?"

I leant forward and in my most conciliatory voice said, "Let me know if you require my help."

317

"That will teach him," I said to myself as I settled back in my seat. He didn't return!

Then we had confirmation that due to the emergency we had been diverted to Stansted.

At the airport we were offered free drinks as recompense.

An announcement was made, "Could Annie Armitage come to the information desk?"

I went and was told, "Mr Hall is on his way to collect you but will probably be at least a hour before he can reach you."

Apparently, Ian had gone to East Midlands and had to drive back past Peterborough and on to Stansted. While I waited, I settled down enjoying ad lib supplies of free gin and tonic. Eventually I pulled my hat over my eyes and went to sleep. When Ian arrived I was the only remaining passenger. The lights were out apart from those on the security desk. The security staff simply pointed to where I was sleeping, but as an after thought warned him I might be the worse for wear after the number of 'G and Ts' that I'd had.

Equipped with my case Ian helped me to the car and I was asleep before he had driven out of the airport.

The next morning John was waiting to have a word with me before going to school.

"Mum I have something to tell you!"

There was a pause then he carried on, "The night before last I was arrested and taken to Thorpe Wood Police Station."

I was shocked, "What had you done?"

Then Ian took over, "I had a telephone call in the early hours, about 2:15 yesterday morning, asking for the parent or guardian of John. I was informed that he was in Thorpe Wood Police Station and my presence was required."

Ian rushed to the police station and discovered that John and two of his friends had been playing in Queensgate car park using a barrier as a seesaw. The barrier broke and they were chased to the top floor where they were apprehended. They had a particularly good telling-off and left the police station humiliated and contrite. Firstly a female police officer questioned their intelligence in a kind, but very effective way making them feel very silly, then a male officer continued and taped an interview of the offence, promising to keep it on file and use it against them should they re-offend."

John was definitely remorseful. I felt sick. Later when Sarah and John had gone to spend the weekend with their father. I said, "I really don't know what to say, if he goes on like this he will mess up his GCSEs and ruin his life."

Ian replied, "Perhaps it's time that he came to terms with your divorce and got to know his father better. What about sending him down there to live with his father during his A Levels?"

"I feel a failure as a mother, I've let John down," I said, giving way to tears.

I sobbed, "Rick has always wanted custody of the children. He had hoped to get custody when I sued for divorce, on the grounds that I was an unfit parent and I had Lupus. In fact, after my hysterectomy I wrote to him to say that there was nothing suspicious in my results. He wrote back saying he was sorry to hear this as he was hoping to increase the size of his family."

By that time Rick had remarried and he and his wife had two children.

Ian was shocked on hearing about Rick's reaction He was quiet and let me go on, "Not only that, in 1986 I had a letter from my mother and in it she wrote, "I have recently become aware of your lifestyle and I am increasingly worried about the children. They have had a chequered upbringing. In two years time you will be 40 and your charm for the opposite sex will begin to wear thin. Think seriously about this." She just signed it off 'Mum'. As always no love or kisses. She clearly thought that the children would be better off with their father, him being such a successful businessman... Do you think that she was right?" I asked in tears.

Ian took my hand and said sadly, "Well perhaps it would be better for John in the long run. He has to come to terms

319

with the issue regarding his father at some time. You must consider it very carefully. Take your time before coming to a decision. Don't rush such an important one as this. Whatever you decide you will have my support."

Eventually I decided. No matter how hard it was for me to let him go, if John was to fulfil his potential he needed to lose some of his 'mates', who I was convinced were bad influences, and try to obtain his A Levels whilst living with his father. My feeling that I had failed John was all encompassing; it was probably the most difficult decision of my life. Ian and John had become good friends and John appeared to look upon Ian as his step dad.

Ian said, "I also feel I've let John down, but we must face the unpleasant fact that John needs a change from the environment that he has collected around himself in Peterborough. So when Sarah and John came back from their father's, I put it to him, and eventually he agreed that it would be a good idea for him to go, if it was what his father wanted; needless to say, his father was delighted. "Whether his step mother will be as pleased is another issue," I thought.

"What will you do with your rabbits?" I asked.

"Sell them," John said, without a second thought.

I must admit I was not sorry about John's reaction about his lack of concern. John's rabbits had caused me problems from the very beginning. When Rambo had finished servicing his does, he would lie on his back and repeatedly kick the door to his hutch until the latch loosened and he could hop out to see what he regarded as his harem of local wild rabbits.

Early one morning, not long after I had started going out with Ian, I was woken by the persistent ringing of my doorbell. I wearily made my way down the stairs and opened the front door to find a neighbour's son cradling Rambo in his arms. I went to take Rambo from him when his father, Ronald, rushed down the drive in an intensely angered state.

His face was flushed, and, in an aggressive tone, he said, "It's like living in a council house living next door to you."

"I wouldn't know what you mean,"I said in an as much received English accent as I could muster. Then as an afterthought I followed this by saying, "Oh go and bully the girls at work."

With that he flounced away up the drive, closely followed by his son.

Later Ronald, who knew Ian from his working connections, rang Ian and said, "Don't have anything to do with the mad woman in Longthorpe." He didn't say why.

Ian rang me at work and asked, "What happened first thing this morning with you and Ronald?"

I explained and we both found it very amusing.

Later, John reacted by throwing eggs at their house. Ronald was not happy and accused John. It remained a mystery as John denied all knowledge for many years to come.

Although John's interest in his rabbits and guinea pigs had waned, he still looked after them reasonably well. Unfortunately one week when he was holidaying with his father all the guinea pigs died from a mysterious illness. John did not seem particularly concerned at the news when he returned. Meanwhile Rambo continued his amorous excursions. We would regularly find his hutch door open, the latch loosened and no Rambo. We cleaned his hutch, put in new straw and food and waited. Two or three days later he would be back, hutch door open, lying on his back exhausted but looking content. We often thought that he had a smile on his face!

In due course, when John was living with his father, we advertised Rambo's sale at the local post office, and a young girl by the name of Lucy called in response. She was very taken with Rambo, cuddled him and we had no compunction in letting her take him. But that still left the does. I rang Dee, who had supplied the rabbits in the first instance, and she was happy to take all the rabbits that were left. For some years to come, when out walking the dogs, Rambo's fertility was obvious, as many of the local rabbits had semi-lop ears. It took some time before the 'lop' eared trait had bred itself out of the wild population.

The sadness of John packing the trunk that I'd used myself when I started nurse training and leaving was soon filled with a busy time of reorganisation. Sarah's closest friend Julie from her first years at school, who had been so involved with the care of the dogs, left school after her GCSEs and their friendship just died out. Julie sent me a present and a letter saying, "You are probably wondering why I have given you a present, but I didn't think that I could show my appreciation in any other way for all the things that you have done for me over the past few years. Thank you."

I was very touched by this. I am sure that the care of teenagers is never easy, and during their sixth form days I seemed to have become a family planning advisor to many of them. I dreaded to think what their parents' reaction would be if they found out. But fortunately we all got away with it, and it was good to know that sometimes my efforts at helping them were appreciated. It was some consolation to my feelings that I had failed John. Fortunately Sarah still visited her father and could let me know how John was doing. At the start she reported back that John was finding things rather stressful but did feel that it had been the right decision for him. This made me feel a little better about it.

Also, the next time that John stayed with us he brought me a porcelain figure of a bear sitting on a trunk with all the accoutrements for a holiday, including a bucket and spade and a book entitled 'Happy Days'. The present made me very tearful. Perhaps I hadn't been such a bad mother after all!

Sarah took us by surprise when we were organising Christmas. She was 16; "I am fed up with boring Christmas days, I want to see my friends," she said decisively.

I discussed the Christmas arrangements with Ian.

"Well Christmas always seems too early for me why don't we eat in the evening and have an 'open house' from 11 o'clock so the children can invite their friends to drop in and we can invite neighbours and other local friends?" he suggested.

"Yes that way if we are late to bed on Christmas Eve and a little hung over in the morning, it won't matter. Lets give it a try this Christmas."

So 'Christmas morning open house' started and we thought it was a great success. It seemed to suit everybody. Easy to organise and folks, having got their turkeys into the oven, came over to share some mulled wine and refreshments before returning to their Christmas lunches. Friends of the children appeared and disappeared at regular intervals after indulging in a good old chat and a few, and in some instances more than a few, snacks. Possibly returning home to their lunches and being told off for not doing it justice. So 'open house' became a tradition for us on Christmas day.

Unfortunately our contract in Birmingham wasn't renewed, and Deborah left the university.

However Ian's work at the University of Nottingham not only continued but also increased. So we left Rugby and the two semi-detached canal-side pubs at Newbold that we regularly used for our "pub grub". I felt a bit sad to leave as we moved Sunrise from Rugby, through Braunston Junction, on to the Grand Union Canal (Leicester Branch) and up the Soar Navigation. At Loughborough we broke down with yards of plastic wrapper, probably from a carpet, wrapped around our prop. Up came the weed-hatch and Ian spent several hours cutting the offending material away before we could proceed. Then onto the River Trent, into the Trent and Mersey Canal at Shardlow and what turned out to be our final destination, Shardlow.

All in all our journey had taken just over a week, and we now considered ourselves to be competent boaters! After we moored up, I took in our new surroundings. The mooring was alongside the Shardlow Heritage Centre, which was a small museum of canal memorabilia.

"This is wonderful, Ian, well done!" I said and kissed him. I said, "I hope we find somewhere nice and comfortable to eat."

Ian just smiled; I suspected that he had something up his sleeve. Then we crossed the lock and went for a meal at Hoskings Wharf. It was excellent and I found out why Ian had looked so pleased with himself. The cuisine was delicious.

We hadn't arranged a permanent mooring so in the morning Ian went over to Shardlow Marina, to successfully negotiate a mooring. It was just 15 minutes away from the University of Nottingham by car and about 30 minutes from Birmingham University. I realized that Ian's cunning plan to be able to move Sunrise to wherever we were working was truly inspired!

We were now both teaching on the Nottingham MBA 'Quality for Service Industries' course and, when we began our second year, we were commissioned by the University of Nottingham to write a self study workbook for managers explaining the rudiments of quality. It gave us a welcome opportunity to work from home. Together, Ian and I prepared the workbook entitled, "Self-Study Workbook, Understanding Quality". I worked on in it in my study downstairs, while Ian worked in John's old bedroom that he had converted into his office, upstairs. Although we worked well together, it wasn't without its disputes. Working downstairs, I would rush upstairs complaining about some issue, to which Ian would say, "You can make a book out of a sentence!"

I'd retort, "Well you can reduce a book into a sentence!"

Somehow we managed to finish it, although the university hadn't disclosed the number of words required or the target date for submission. In the end we were rushed and the process was not exactly cost-effective! But it did go to two editions.

In the meantime, Sarah had been accepted by Robinson

College, Cambridge to read English providing she took a year out. Alternatively, Leeds University offered her a place that was available straight away.

After some discussion and deliberation she said, "Mum I have decided on Cambridge and to take the year out. I want to live in London and get a temporary job. My friend Dinah wants to join me so I think we should get a flat together."

"What do Dinah's parents think of all this?"

"Oh they are quite happy, providing we can get jobs," came the reply.

The next weekend Sarah went to stay with her father. His response to her plans was apparently, "You are living in cloud cuckoo land if you think that you can just move to London, get a job and a flat just like that."

Sarah was rather deflated when she returned home on Sunday evening. We said that if she really wanted to go to London, she should go for it! We thought that she was quite capable. Ian set her to work on his computer and they drafted her CV. She wanted something to do with English so that she would have experience that helped her prepare for her time at Cambridge. So she sent her CV to all the publishers and similar jobs that she could find in London. There were many 'No thank yous' and most did not reply, but she was delighted to get a reply from Little, Brown and they offered her a proof reading job for the twelve months that she required. Sarah was ecstatic. We didn't hear what her father's response was! She and Dinah moved into a flat in Fulham in the autumn of that year and were very happy.

Other changes were afoot. At the same time, Andrea moved out to share a flat with a girlfriend and Trevor was happy to be master of Ian's house on his own. Well not quite on his own, apart from Ian there always seemed to be plenty of visitors. Having completed his A levels he was accepted at Bristol University to read Environmental Science. He refused the offer; which considering the amount of stress that he had been subject to during his life, was perhaps understandable. He was having problems and he didn't know what to do with himself. Staying in bed until the afternoon, drawing the dole and drinking with his mates all night was not a situation that should be encouraged. Ian had to take control and gave him an ultimatum that he had to either have a job or move to take up a University place by the 1st of October. October 1st came and Ian had to make the most difficult decision he had ever had to face. Unbeknown to Ian at the time, this decision and Trevor's response was to cause him much sorrow and heartache. Ian confronted him. Trevor said, "All you ever think about is money!"

With that, Trevor packed his clothes in a rucksack, got on his bike and pedalled off into the sunset. Ian didn't know where he was for at least two weeks. So started a long saga of nearly five years when he would not communicate with his father. He was so hurt and confused with all the problems that they had experienced as a family. Ian was convinced that he was doing the best for Trevor, and so it transpired, but the grief that Ian suffered during that time was intense.

With the house now empty, apart from the cat (Timmy the beagle had recently died of cancer), we decided that we should live together. Ian would finally move in with me.

The last items that he brought were ten very large black bin bags,

"What's in all those?" I asked quizzically.

He grinned, "That's my compost, I'm not leaving that behind!"

Candy the cat was a more difficult issue to resolve.

Ian said, "I don't think that it would be fair to expect an old cat, of thirteen, to live with two retrievers."

They had chased her whenever they had visited Ian's house. Ian said,"She will have to be put down if we can't find a home for her. Mind you, sister Moira loves cats."

I wasn't sure if he was serious about putting her down so we mentioned it to Ian's sister, Moira, who lived at Helpston, and she was delighted to have Candy live with her and her two cats.

One dark evening we put Candy in her travelling basket and headed to Helpston. Just where the old Lincoln roads crossed the railway line we came across a GPO (Post Office) juggernaut slewed across the road. A car coming the other way had stopped. We got out and the driver of the other car said, "I've called the emergency services and they are sending an ambulance.

"So where are the injured people?" I asked.

"There's a lady half way down the dyke," Came the reply.

I scrambled down the deep, but fortunately dry, dyke. A female was laying part the way down, she was quite still and her head was twisted at a strange angle to her body. I thought, "Oh no it looks as if she has a broken neck." I took her hand, she was still alive, I talked to her and told her not to move, she squeezed my hand. I thought, "If she stops breathing or moves her head she would either die or become a paraplegic."

More and more sirens could be heard as they sped to the scene. I let her drift off for a few seconds then spoke to wake her so that she didn't go too deeply unconscious. The Magpas Doctor was the next on the scene and I thought, "Good he can take over." The patient said to the doctor, "Don't let this lady let go of my hand." After a quick examination he climbed out of the dyke murmuring as he went past Ian "This is a bad one!" Three ambulances arrived together with a fire engine and several police vehicles, all with their emergency lights continually strobing the night. Eventually they strapped the injured lady to a stretcher and six ambulance men carried her carefully to the waiting ambulance. As we knew one of the paramedics we discovered later that she did have a broken neck and eventually made a full recovery.

We left with the cat grateful, that she had not urinated in

the car despite her obvious concern at all the activities and flashing lights. We arrived at Moira's rather later than expected and relayed the night's events. On the way home Ian said, "I heard you saying Oh God, Oh God don't let this women die, don't let her die. I thought you were an atheist!"

I thought and then replied, "I have heard that there are very few atheists in the condemned cell!"

We laughed to relieve our stress.

I said, "I do hope Candy will be OK."

Ian replied, "She'll be fine hunting in the fields behind Moira's as she was the daughter of a very successful farm cat. She will be in her element!"

Sarah finished her temporary job in London and was about to start her first year at Robinson College. She packed the things she needed into my Metro, and we set off for her new life in Cambridge. Kissing her goodbye and realising that another one of my chicks had left the nest I took a long route home, and as I felt in need of some consolation by means of retail therapy I stopped off at Anne Furbank's, a very up market, ladies dress shop in Buckden, just off the A1. I was very pleased with my purchases. When I arrived home Ian had been thinking about our marriage.

Again he said, "If I die my bank pension will die with me and you won't get anything, unless we get married before that."

I thought about it and then said, "Yes, OK, but I want a quiet do, will you be happy to have a quiet ceremony at a registry office in our ordinary clothes, and just two witnesses?"

Ian smiled and simply said, "Yes, No problem."

The choice of witnesses was simple, Carole was mine, and Gerry was his.

We booked the date, March 20th 1992, and the four of us arrived. The registrar asked, "Who is the bride, and who is the groom?"

Before anyone else was able to speak, Gerry said, "I'm the groom, and I'm marrying this lady here!"

He was pointing to Carole, who was of course six inches taller, and some thirty years, his junior.

We were all grinning, apart from the registrar, who was looking very worried and confused until Ian intervened and said, "I am the groom, and this is my bride," indicating me.

Having previously been somewhat nonplussed, fortunately the registrar smiled, took our vows and we signed the register. Then she insisted on taking the four of us out into the garden, to take photos of us herself. After that the four of us went for a meal at our favourite restaurant, The Lodge Hotel, that was run by two of our friends. That night we got quite merry.

We had decided to have a reception later in the year when the weather was warmer and all our friends and relatives had time to make the necessary arrangements.

Ian said, "Perhaps we should have a reception at Hoskins Wharf in July. That is pretty central for most people."

We drew up a guest list, which in the end came to over 150.

"Let's discuss it with Margaret and David," I suggested.

Margaret and David who owned the pub and restaurant at Hoskins were very happy for us to hold the reception there.

"Is there enough space for all of us?" I asked Margaret.

"Come and look at the upstairs room," she said.

With that we went to look. The room overlooked the canal. It was a very romantic setting.

Next we had a meeting to discuss the menu with Margaret and Rudi, their corpulent Swiss chef.

Later Ian said, "Rudi told me that he met the writers of the Muppets, and he was their inspiration for the character of the Swiss Chef in their shows."

"Yes and he could double up as Father Christmas as well!" I agreed.

July approached and it was time to collect Sarah for the summer vacation. I went via Buckden and bought my outfit for the reception from Anne Furbank's. I tried it on and Sarah confirmed, "That's lovely!"

The arrangements, and nearly everyone responded to the invitation, but unfortunately not my parents. Mother had one of her upset stomachs coming on! Ian and I decided to stay on the boat, while everyone else who wanted to stay overnight booked into nearby hotels or B&B's. Rudi prepared a magnificent spread and a jolly good time was had by all.

It was a bit of an anticlimax when after a short break, it was back to work for us both.

We went back to teaching at the University, and I said to Ian,

"I am feeling fraudulent pontificating on quality in nursing, when in reality the last time that I actually did hands on nursing was 1977. I think I should go and have a look at what is really going on."

I spotted an advertisement in the local paper for "Paramed Services", looking for nurses for flexible part-time working. I sent my CV and applied. I was interviewed and accepted.

"You will need the protection of three vaccinations for Hepatitis B," the Agency Nursing Officer said.

I booked at the doctors, and after I had the first of three doses, I felt a little below par. After the second, I felt distinctly poorly and was having breathing difficulties. The deterioration happened over a period of several weeks and, though I was equipped with the uniform and, working in Peterborough Hospital and local Nursing Homes, I couldn't get myself well. I even felt too ill to gain any insight from the experience and I became convinced that Lupus was again raising its ugly head.

I went to see my GP, Doctor Gordon and said, "I was originally diagnosed with Lupus by Dr Verney-Wright in 1974 at U.C.H. He is still working, but now as a Professor at Leeds, do you think you could refer me to him?"

Ian and I went up to Leeds to see him but I really didn't feel he was able to offer me much help. He seemed to have lost touch with the recent research activities in Lupus.

The deterioration continued, and one day when I was sitting at home and feeling particularly ill, Ian said, "Why don't you go and see your friend, Don Snuggs, he may be able to help?"

Ian was helped tremendously by Don's treatments during the time that he was suffering with all the stress of his wife's deterioration, and, of course, subsequent death.

Ian continued saying, "I know that you originally sent me as a 'guinea pig', but he certainly sorted me out. Why don't you go and see how you get on?"

I made an appointment for the next day. By then I was having considerable breathing difficulties and pains in one of my kidneys.

Don said, "I can't deal with this Annie, you need to see your G.P. as soon as possible."

After examining me my GP, Doctor Caskey, said, "I want you to go into hospital straight away and see my next door neighbour."

With that he arranged an emergency admission to see Dr Guttman, the renal specialist at Peterborough District Hospital. It seemed that my kidneys were packing up and my heart was stressed due to the respiratory failure. I was in a bit of a mess. It seemed that my immune system, stimulated by the Hepatitis B injections, had gone into overdrive, and nothing would stop it from consuming me!

I was admitted to intensive care, and Dr Guttman called in my Rheumatologist, Dr Sheehan. He concluded that I had a cerebral lupus inflammation. It seemed that the 'Sword of Damocles', in the form of Lupus, was about to claim another victim. In reality I had not been taking enough notice of my illness, to the point that I had been subconsciously denying its presence! Whilst not giving up, and bearing in mind that my original diagnosis had given me a maximum of five years to live and I should have been dead seventeen years previously, I felt that I had achieved much more than they had thought possible. But now my life was in the balance as I lay there hypoventilating and sounding as though I had severe whooping cough.

Ian heard the doctors in conference, discussing whether there was any hope and whether I was worth the effort. Luckily they decided to try and sent me up to ICU (Intensive Care Unit).

Close family were called to my bedside and my slim chances of living, let alone full recovery, were discussed. After five days in intensive care and a few more days on the ward in Peterborough, I was whisked off to the neurological unit at Addenbrookes Hospital, Cambridge, almost totally paralyzed, confused and disorientated, to begin the slow process of recovery and rehabilitation.

My life of dependency had started!

CHAPTER 10

DISABILITY

Why wasn't I called into the big blue yonder? I just kept wondering why. Surely it would have been far easier, not only for me but also my loved ones, so that they could move on with their lives and be free. However it seemed that it wasn't to be. I had been discharged home from hospital with my first feelings that there was to be a life for me after my incarceration in Peterborough District Hospital and Addenbrookes. It was wonderful to be in my own home again and in Ian's loving care, but even with that security I felt as though I'd landed on another planet. At first, I really didn't grasp the level of my disability, and the enormity of the task that lay ahead in my getting to something near an independent life.

I didn't have any colour vision, and could only see in black and white. My brain damage had left me with little sight at all in my right eye. Gradually I began to realise that if anyone approached me without speaking, I didn't have a clue if they were male or female. Voices that I'd known well before I was ill didn't present a problem, but sometimes I wasn't even confident about that. When I was out and without the security and familiarity of my own home, I felt lost. I began to revisit what I guess must have been the feelings that I had when I was a baby and calling all the male faces that I came across "daddy". Though everybody's response to a baby making these mistakes is to be amused, it wasn't likely to elicit the same response towards an adult doing the same.

During this time Bid came to stay for a couple of days, and her cunning plan was to get me going again, by taking me swimming. The local school pool was where the children had both learnt to swim. It was many years since we had gone there on Sunday mornings to splash about. It reminded me of that time when John was small and I was trying to keep fit. I used to rush up and down the swimming pool to do twenty lengths at a time, thus aiming to keep my joints supple for the rest of the week. I looked over my shoulder and noticed that two boys around John's age were laughing and trying to pull John away from the rail, they had hold of him by the ankles and he was looking desperate. My maternal instinct overwhelmed me, and with no thought of what he may have done to bring about this incident and, at what for me was a superhuman speed, I swam to his aid. Placing one hand on each of the boys' heads, I dunked them under the water and held them until they released John. They let go, and I returned, to swim nonchalantly up and down. As the boys surfaced I noted the astonished looks on their faces and it had made me chuckle.

Bid drove me to the very same pool, but now I didn't know where I was. Bid helped me into the changing rooms and, like a baby, put me into my swimming costume. Having quickly changed herself, she helped me down the ladder and into the water. I didn't have a clue how to move my arms in the water and, with my left leg dragging behind, I was totally clueless about how I was meant to swim. Although well meant, I'm afraid that the whole exercise was a complete failure. How could I have expected to be able to remember swimming, when even in my own home of many years I was confused? I felt very sorry for myself, and on arriving home sat down and sobbed.

Realising that his wife had been replaced by someone with all the needs of a baby, Ian gave up working away to become my very competent, full-time carer. He saw to my toilet needs, bathed, dressed, fed me, and dispensed my complicated medications. I couldn't even hold a spoon of food and steer it into my mouth.

Regular trips to the hairdresser also became necessary so that I could disguise the large bald patches that had developed on the top of my head. I would look at the hairbrush with dismay as I saw what the ravages of Lupus continued to achieve.

Ian decided that a return trip to the acupuncturist, Don Snuggs, might be beneficial. Don tried to balance my ying and yang. He explained, "The bald areas on your head are to do with the renal failure Annie. Your hair will grow back eventually." I was sceptical but pleased that my proud locks may one day return.

Don certainly helped my breathing and I felt better that first time, and many visits thereafter.

After a few weeks I felt enough confidence to take Abbey for her walks on my own, she always seemed to understand my needs and even helped me to put on her lead. She was a well trained dog and didn't even pull as I walked slowly, dragging my left leg along. We would wander off down the road and through the pleasant naturalised area behind our house, to the River Nene. It was good to be out in the open air on my own again, and the sense of freedom and release overwhelmed me. When we met anyone they greeted me with the usual dog walker's cheery, "Good morning!"

With great difficulty I often struggled to respond, trying to form a sentence in reply, but my speech was stilted. I soon lost track of what I was saying and my vocabulary was stunted. I couldn't remember even the simplest of words.

Ian escorted me to my appointment with the cerebral injuries consultant. He explained that often my eyes were unable to focus, that I couldn't recognise what I was seeing, and I became flustered and confused. In addition, I had very little fine finger movement. Dr Neal simply shrugged his shoulders and appeared bored.

He said, "There is little that can be done, you will just have to wait for gradual improvement."

With that he discharged me, leaving me feeling crushed, written off and demoralised.

I felt relieved that my next appointment at the hospital was with Dr Guttman. When we were called through to see him, he stood up and shook me warmly by my functioning left hand and wished me well, while explaining, "I am going to retire, Annie, so this will be your last appointment with me." I felt devastated as Dr Guttman checked me over, then he said, "Dr Mistry is taking over the consultancy of Urology, I'll make an appointment for you to see him in say, six weeks time."

I felt very sad as we said our goodbyes, and left wishing him well for his retirement.

I said to Ian, "I bet Dr Mistry will be nowhere near as nice as Dr.Guttman."

Ian replied, "No, I don't suppose he will, Dr Guttman has looked after you so very well, but we will just have to see."

Dr Guttman had reduced my steroids by 5mg each month. So by the time I went for my appointment, I had decided to take the initiative by reducing my steroid dose another 5 mg. Ian could not make the appointment so hospital transport had been arranged. I went in to see Dr Mistry and the mental haze that had been obstructing my comprehension was gradually beginning to clear. He didn't introduce himself, and seemed distracted. He barked out an instruction, "Sit down."

I was compliant and sat down in the hard chair that a fat nurse indicated was for me. She then waddled away in shoes that didn't appear to fit. I looked at the doctor; I was sadly thinking how different he was to the kind Dr Guttman.

Without looking up from his notes he said, "Now let me see, you are taking 40 mg of steroids."

I replied, "No, I've been taking 35 mg during the last two weeks, as my dosage has been regularly reducing by 5 mg each month by Dr Guttman."

He frowned and his voice took on an irritated tone as he said, "You should also take aspirin."

To this order, I replied, "After taking so much Ibuprofen in the past, my stomach is rather sensitive to aspirin, so I would prefer not to."

I thought he had little understanding or interest in Lupus, and barely able to contain his anger, he then said, "Well I'll have to refer you to the anticoagulant service then!"

His voice sounded as though it was the worst possible punishment for a very difficult patient that he could think of, and with that we parted company.

As I sat patiently waiting in the ambulance transport reception to be taken home, I had plenty of time to watch the staff come and go. I felt grateful that I was now able to make sense of my surroundings. I was dismayed to note the poor posture of the nursing staff as they shambled along in their scruffy state. Most, if not all, seemed to be overweight or even obese. In my day we would go on duty, shoulders back and proudly carrying our starched white aprons, in our white short-caps. I thought, "Where has all the pride gone? Surely they couldn't be delivering the standards of care that was expected from us? Or am I being wise in retrospect?"

My musings were interrupted when the voluntary ambulance driver arrived to take me home. In spite his kindness I was still upset when I arrived home. Ian helped me inside, and I said to him, "Can we make an appointment for me to see Dr Gordon? I've decided that I must change my consultant and I want to be transferred to Dr Sheehan, if he will have me."

Bearing in mind that Dr Gordon had been my GP for

some twenty years, he knew me very well. When I explained why I wanted to change my consultant, he said, "It really would make more sense for you to be looked after by Rheumatology, I will write and get you transferred."

He smiled and we shook hands. I felt much happier.

Whether it was my request for a transfer that caused it, or possibly they were due to come anyway, in February a dietician and an occupational therapist both visited. I tried to explain to the young dietician, "I need a diet low in uric acid. I've tried to maintain this since I was first diagnosed with lupus as long ago as 1974."

She looked blank and made me feel insecure. I stammered, "You see if I eat certain foods, my joints become very painful."

But even I could see that she felt she was the professional, and as I was only a patient, what did I know? She didn't want to listen to any suggestion from me. Seeing my distress, Ian took over the conversation and eventually she left with nothing accomplished.

The occupational therapist wasn't much help either. After she examined my hands, she said, "You should play dominoes and cards."

At this instruction I really didn't feel there was any point in trying to explain that my sight and comprehension were totally inadequate for those types of activities, and I just said weakly, "Thank you."

Presumably she recorded a successful visit and left. Empathy and understanding was obviously not part of their regime of assistance.

It was many years later when I was at a private gymnasium and we were working on my general muscle tone, and particularly the movement of my wrists, that it dawned on me that fine finger movement substantially relies on the muscles in the forearm. Whether the occupational therapist knew this or just overlooked it is still a mystery. What were their working standards? How did they measure their outcomes? How did they know whether their interventions were successful?

I felt very dispirited as I dragged my left leg behind me and struggled to walk on my own. But I wasn't going to give in, so I made up my mind that I should walk the 100 or so yards to the Post Office, on my own.

The couple that ran it at that time were polite but not particularly friendly to customers, but I managed to buy some milk. I handed my purse to the man behind the counter, as I physically couldn't get the zip on my purse undone. I put the milk in my bag, feeling a little under the weather from my exertions and the stress of my disabilities, and was about to leave when Dr Guttman came in. He greeted me warmly and asked how I was getting on. I was too ashamed to say anything about being sorry for myself, so I smiled and said,"I do need to work hard to develop myself as far as I can."

"Well done," he responded, smiling.

I managed to walk home thinking that I really must not give up.

I'd just arrived back home, when the front doorbell rang.

Ian went to answer it, and I heard him say, "I'm just making a cup of tea for Annie, would you like one as well Pam?"

I was very pleased to see Pam and have some company. She lived next door to Trish from just up the road, and though I hadn't really known her very well, she had brought Trish to visit me when I was in hospital. It was super to see her again now that I was at home. Pam was a retired infant teacher; just seeing her cheered me up. After Ian had made us all a cup of tea, Pam smiled and asked me, "Would you like to come with Trish and me for tea at Haycock?"

Near to tears, I answered, "Oh Pam that would be wonderful!"

It was arranged and so, equipped with the mug that I could manage for myself, Pam, Trish and I went for what for me was my first social engagement. The mug was necessary because my control over my hands and fingers was so poor, that I couldn't get my fingers around the small handles on cups. It was lovely to be out again. "Can this mean that I'm not to be written off by everyone outside the family?"

Not long after the our trip out for tea, Pam came to see me again, she said, "When you feel fit enough perhaps I could help you to start writing again. I think that we should start you off using the methods we used for children in the reception class of primary school."

I was delighted and said, "That would be really kind of you, thank you, Pam."

Pam continued, "When you are ready to hold a pen or pencil, I can write the shape of letters in large writing for you to copy, but first we must work on those fingers so that you can hold a pen."

Ian and Pam put their heads together and worked out some simple tools that I could use to exercise the fingers on my right hand. Using squeezable shapes for ten minutes at a time, I managed to start to get some feeling into my fingers. When I felt ready to get going, Pam wrote out the shapes of letters in large sizes for me to copy. She came each week to review my progress, leaving me with my homework to have ready for her next visit.

Pam was so very considerate. She didn't make me feel stupid with my incompetent efforts and slowly, oh so very slowly, I was managing to copy the shapes and making progress.

Abbey seemed a bit sad and lonely without Holly for company. Ian said, "Abbey is not happy, I think we should get another dog to keep her company. As it is so difficult to haul such a heavy type of dog out of the canal when they go to jumping in at almost every lock, what do you think about going for a smaller breed?"

I wasn't sure about that. I had tremendous loyalty towards golden retrievers, but I asked, "Did you have any breed in mind?"

Ian had clearly been thinking it through, and said straightway, "When I was a child we had a golden Cocker Spaniel, how about that?"

My friend Kay had a lovely old cocker spaniel called Charlie. He was rather smelly but despite this he had a lovely temperament, so thinking about Charlie, I thought that was a good idea.

Ian contacted the kennel club and found a breeder who would have a Cocker Spaniel bitch puppy available in early December. The breeder was in Barnsley and had a very good reputation, so we took a chance and said yes without a primary visit. Then there was much discussion about names, and by chance Kay rang for a chat, when I put the phone down, Ian said with delight, "That's it! Kay Kay that's a different but great name!"

"Yes I think you are right but we'll have to check with Kay first, she may not like a dog being named after her." So another phone call was made. Kay was delighted and said that she was honoured to have a dog named after her, and we had named her twice! I did hope that this was true and that she was not just being polite.

Unfortunately though, almost as soon as we made the decision, Abbey developed cancer in the mouth, so we were feeling a bit sad when we went up the A1 to Barnsley to collect "Kay Kay of Snowgate".

I sat and cuddled the little blonde bundle as Ian drove us back home. She was such a comfort to me in my disabled state and she settled in very quickly.

Sadly Abbey's cancer was very aggressive, and very soon she wasn't able to eat, despite our best efforts, and she didn't want to go for walks. Walking and throwing sticks were the highlight of Abbey's life and now that she had lost total interest in both we knew that we must make the inevitable decision. The vet said, "I'm afraid there is no more that can be done, I think I should put her out of her misery. Do you want to take her home afterwards?"

"No" I said, "I think that it would be better if you looked after things"

We agreed it was for the best, and I held Abbey until she was quite dead. I then collapsed into floods of tears.

The Vet kindly said to me, "I will open the back door for you it'll save you from having to walk through the consulting room."

As we made our way home, I sobbed, "You see she was my Holly's first puppy."

Ian thought it best not to ask if she was in fact the first born in the litter of eight. Aas I sat next to him, I cried. At home, of course, Kay Kay was waiting with tail wagging to cheer me up.

In the post the next day a letter came from the Anticoagulant–Clinic giving me an appointment in December with transport that had been arranged by the hospital. The ambulance arrived in good time on the Monday morning; the driver helped me into the clinic, and registered me there.

I sat and waited, until I was called through for my thumb-prick, to calculate my clotting time. After that I had to wait outside the doctor's room. He called out, "Next!"

I walked in, and a smallish, serious looking man of about sixty stood up and greeted me saying, "Hello... I'm Dr Coleman."

I responded, "I suppose you are going to put me on rat poison."

He then said rather seriously, "I think that you had better sit down," and he closed the door

I obediently complied. He continued, his tone of voice making it very clear that he would not put up with any nonsense from me.

"I'm going to prescribe Warfarin for you, and if you don't take it and you have a massive stroke, it will be your problem. If you take it in accordance with my directions, anything that happens will be my responsibility. Take this prescription to the pharmacy, and you'll be sent a yellow book in the post tomorrow with the date of your next appointment. Goodbye," he said as he handed me the prescription for Warfarin.

Much chastened, I crept out of the consulting room to face a queue of amused looking patients who had heard my ticking off.

When the book arrived as promised, the next appointment was for me to see Dr Coleman on January the 3rd. By then having established his authority, Dr Coleman, and I were on good terms and we met regularly every four to six weeks there after. At one of my regular appointments I asked, "How long am I going to need to be on Warfarin for?"

He answered decisively, "The rest of your life."

So there it was. There was to be no argument, I had to accept a life sentence on Warfarin. I thought, "Well it's better than a death sentence." However the side effects of Warfarin causing me to bleed and the substantial bruising that I suffered from the merest of knocks was, and still is, a nuisance.

"We need to think about Christmas," Ian had said in early December.

He went on, "Although the boat doesn't have central heating, I'm a sure that we can make it warm enough for you to enjoy Christmas. What do you think?"

I was enthusiastic so Ian made, appropriate arrangements. He packed the car with lots of warm, thermal clothes, and we headed towards our mooring at Shardlow.

For Kay Kay it was her first trip away from home, she was just coming up to twelve weeks old and on Christmas day she was due to end her period of quarantine after her puppy injections. Kay Kay travelled well, and it was lovely for us to be on the boat again, particularly as we could have the luxury of Rudi's cooking at Hoskins Warf. As soon as we arrived we were met with a warm welcome from Clark, our next door neighbour. His old traditional working boat, named

Trout, had a small cabin and a tarpaulined central area used for cargo. In fact Clark still occasionally undertook trips with cargoes such as coal, clay or gravel. Tall, blond, Clark proudly introduced us to his new, pretty girlfriend, called Caroline. Clark had a large, white standard poodle called Oscar, and he was wandering around on the quayside as we climbed on board, with Ian carrying Kay Kay. Very soon Ian had the 'Squirrel' alight and it wasn't long before we were as warm as toast, despite the canal being frozen over.

"Christmas on the boat was a lovely idea!" I said to Ian.

It was wonderful, and on Christmas morning I climbed off the boat, and Ian helped Kay Kay onto the quayside for her morning constitutional. Oscar, who was proudly wearing a Father Christmas hat, came to greet us. He was a fine sight in his hat, and Oscar was the first dog that Kay Kay had seen since she was in the kennels where she was born. Naturally, Oscar came to investigate, and she yelped, took fright, jumped into the canal and disappeared under the ice.

"Was she very expensive?" Caroline asked.

But before I could answer Kay Kay reappeared, swimming to the side that was free from ice. As Ian retrieved her, Caroline started laughing. She said, "I could see twenty pound notes passing across my eyes!"

We all laughed with relief and fortunately Kay Kay was none the worse for her experience.

It was a lovely, relaxing Christmas but all too soon we had to go home and, shortly after that, I had my first appointment with Dr Sheehan. I was very pleased to see him, confident that he knew far more about my Lupus than I did and, together with Dr Guttman, had probably saved my life when I was in Intensive Care.

Before my appointment a plump nurse asked me for a urine sample. She handed me a cardboard receiver for me to wee into and instructed me to put it onto a small shelf in the toilet, from which she could retrieve it via a hatchway to test it. "That's neat," I thought.

I was shown into Dr Sheehan's consulting room and was curious to see what this doctor was really like, as, of course, I didn't have any idea when I was out cold in Intensive Care. He stood up to shake hands and clumsily I offered my left hand, my right being almost useless. He was a slim, attractive man probably in his late fourties.

He said, "It's nice to see you again, Annie, how are you feeling now?"

I wasn't sure what to say, but said, "I'm feeling much better now thank you."

He looked genuinely pleased, but then he said, "Can you get undressed to your bra and pants, and lie down under the sheet on this couch, I'll be back in a minute."

I wasn't quite sure about this, thinking this man is far too nice to look at me like that! Then I remembered the state I was in the last time he saw me, which was in Intensive Care. I was probably very smelly, and in a disgusting state. I was ready by the time he knocked on the door and came to examine me, then he took a blood sample and said, "You are doing very well, but I think you need to go to your GP so that he can arrange some more physiotherapy. Also, perhaps, if you feel able you could think about swimming? There's a class especially for disabled persons at Jack Hunt, as I suspect you don't feel able to go to a swimming pool on your own at the moment. Should I write and suggest this to your GP? What do you think?"

I felt very grateful, it was as though he knew just what I was going through, so I felt rather cheerful as I waited wait for my transport to return home.

It wasn't long before I received the information entitled 'Swimming for the disabled'. It included details explaining how to put in an application to apply to go to the Jack Hunt Pool on Friday evenings, transport to be arranged subsequent to the receipt of my application with a photograph. Ian organised everything, and on the next Friday a social service's disabled van arrived.

At the pool I found that everyone was very caring and helpful. I was in a group containing myself, two mentally handicapped people, and two ladies who were both deaf and blind. The deaf blind ladies were pretty good and sped up and down the pool. I felt humbled watching them, and how well they could deal with their problems. "Should I learn deaf blind signing so that I can get in touch with them?" I thought. The other two ladies were also making good progress. Then it was my turn and though I was offered a great deal of help, I was only able to move through the water very slowly. I became very cold despite the fact that the water temperature had been raised for this disabled swimming session. I was disconsolate and got out to dry myself. One of the helpers noticed my plight and suggested, "If you could get there, the water at the Thomas Cook pool in the Thorpe Wood Leisure Centre is much warmer."

When I got home, I explained to Ian and he said, "I know that Trish goes there, I'll ask her what she thinks."

Trish was a really good swimmer and went to Thomas Cook pool several times a week. She agreed about the temperature of the water and after a test session I joined Thomas Cook, though I was sad to leave the supportive service of the disabled swimming group.

The deaf blind people had made me realise that despite their difficulty of communication and getting around, they still felt that life was worth living. I'd always taken seeing, hearing and even writing for granted. Pam was still calling each week to help me. I certainly couldn't feel justified in feeling sorry for myself as I still had so much to be grateful for, and so many people who were seeking to help me.

We had noticed recently that dents in the kitchen floor were worsening, and the grit that we had been continuously sweeping up meant that the floor in the kitchen and dining area was in fact deteriorating and crumbling. Ian took a closer look and could scrape the so-called concrete surface with his fingernails.

346

"The concrete mix was clearly very poor when the house was built. Typical that it's lasted until the 10 year guarantee NHBR certificate has expired."

I smiled, "Never mind, we could start a nursery school, at least it would be good for a sandpit!" Ian treated this with the contempt it to deserved and when Pam came to give me a writing lesson, we discussed the state of the floor. She offered to take me to John Lewis to look at replacement kitchens. We went together, and while I was getting interested in their suggestions, Pam was elbowing me gently in the ribs.

She said, "I'm afraid we have got to go, my parking ticket is about to expire."

As we left, I thought that was a bit odd, but then she said, "In our last house we had a kitchen replaced by Tebbuts, and when, sometime later, I went back to collect some post that had been delivered to the wrong address, the kitchen still looked as good as new, despite being at least 10 years old. Why don't you ask Tebbuts to come and have a look?"

Ian gave them a ring and arranged for Brian Tebbut to come, measure up and give us a quote. I told him, "We don't need anything changed, just repair the floor and everything else to stay just as it is."

He ignored this, and carried on measuring. When he had finished he said, "We shall have to strip everything, all the units and pipes. It won't be possible to refit these." He proceeded to outline his plans. "I'll do a blueprint and a quote and I'll have it ready in a day or two." It sounded good and sure enough the blueprint and quote appeared a day or two later. The quote was within our means so we gave him the go ahead.

Next we went back to his showroom to choose the fitments and book a starting date for the messy business of breaking up the floor with a pneumatic hammer and relaying the concrete. Replacing the electrics, water and waste pipes came next, followed by fitting the units. Finally the floor was tiled. It all involved great upheaval. Brian's ideas were a great improvement. We were very pleased with result.

"That's great, thank you Pam!" I said when·she came to inspect it.

It was just about the time that the kitchen was completed, when Ian noticed that the window frames were going rotten and said, "Oh well! It probably would be best if we have double glazing as well!"

It was June and boiling hot when the men came to fit the new windows.

I said to them, "Working outside in this hot weather, you will need lots of drinks, what would you like?"

One of them said, "A cup of tea on the hour, every hour please, white and two sugars for him and no sugar for me!"

They had arrived to start the work at half past eight in the morning. So at nine I took the tea outside to them. I repeated this with two cups of tea at precisely ten o'clock and again at eleven. At twelve I noticed that Tom, the older of the two, was laughing; his lined and weathered face creased in mirth as he said, "I was only joking about tea every hour, we'll be awash with tea at this rate!"

I felt a bit silly but I laughed, "Oh no! I'm sorry, but I was worried that working in all this heat you'd get dehydrated."

As it was I was grateful that the mess in the house wasn't on the same scale as when the work was done in the kitchen, but anyway we did have Lynda, our cleaning lady. We employed her after one of Sarah's visits and she had suggested that we needed help with the cleaning, as 'Ian couldn't do everything.'

Sarah had responded to the idea of Pam taking me out for tea with her own suggestion, "How about if I meet you in London, Mum, and take you for tea at the Ritz as a birthday treat?"

"Yes!" was my immediate response.

Ian put me on the train at Peterborough and Sarah met me at Kings Cross. She helped me through the underground to Oxford Street tube station. By the time we got to the Ritz in Regent Street I was very excited. When we were safely seated at the table, Sarah reached into her bag, and produced a large white china mug. "Well done, Sarah! You think of everything! The staff at the Ritz were very pleasant, and totally understood my predicament after we explained the problems that I was having with my hands.

"This has been wonderful. I didn't think that such an experience would happen to me ever again," I said to Sarah when she put me back on the Peterborough train that evening.

When Ian met me at Peterborough station I was in tears and repeated, "It's been an incredible experience. It's something the likes of which I thought would never happen to me again," I sobbed.

Ian hugged me and said, "You look exhausted, so it's home to bed for you!"

Somehow I felt that I'd turned a corner. It didn't seem very long since I'd not been sure how to put my jumper without putting it on back to front; or was faced with confusion when attempting to put the correct shoe on the correct foot. Both had caused me great frustration!

In addition, although I'd lost some sight, I was beginning to make sense of words, able to read simple texts and colour vision had come back into my life. As I walked the dogs down the lane, I'd look at the trees or similar natural object, come home and ask Ian such questions as, "What colour is a tree?"

"Green," Ian said.

The next day I'd look at the tree thinking green, and come back and ask, "You know that blossom on the tree down the path, what colour is it?"

"Pink," Ian said.

Then I'd repeat the process. Going out walking the dog, often I was singing, although probably out of tune and fortunately only quietly to myself, "I can see clearly now the clouds have gone, I can see all the obstacles in my way, gone are the dark clouds of yesterday," I thought. "I must try to see all obstacles as opportunities."

Not long after that, Ian pointed out an advertisement he had spotted at the local library for a meeting of a Writers' Workshop. This was to be held monthly at seven thirty, Thursday evenings in the library.

Ian said, "Why don't you go and give it a try?"

So the next Thursday evening, although feeling very nervous, I was enthused about going. Ian dropped me off for the first meeting. I walked in to face a small group of about six people sitting in a circle. It was clear that the very pleasant looking, small, white-haired lady was the group leader. She introduced herself as June Counsel, and the other members of the group followed her lead and introduced themselves to me. June was sitting next to a thin man with a short grey goatee beard. He said, "I am June's husband, Alan, three pounds please."

I sat down and passed my purse to him so that he could extract the money, as he did that I listened to the proceedings.

It was all very informal and, starting from the left, everyone read out what they had written. I hadn't brought anything so I just watched and listened. At the end, June asked kindly, "Will you bring something next month Annie?"

I felt happy and relaxed in the group, and answered, "Yes I'll give it a try."

June then said, "Does anybody have any work that they want me to take away to comment on?"

With that Alan collected the work, which a majority of the group offered and slid it into a small briefcase.

Fortunately it was much later when I discovered that June had been at Bletchley Park during the war and had been one of the communications team who cracked the enigma code. In addition she had written several books for children. I was glad that I didn't know that at the time, or I'd have felt out of my depth in such esteemed company.

350

Ian was waiting to collect me, and when we arrived home I had a dilemma to face, what should I write? Most of my experience was being in hospital, either as a nurse or a patient. Thinking about it, I decided that I was desperate to write about what had been going on, including all the shortcomings, when I was a patient in hospital. After I had explained to Ian about the workshop, I said, "Unfortunately my handwriting still isn't good enough for me to write much by hand. The feeling in the tips of my fingers is so poor I can't manage to use the computer keyboard."

I felt dismayed, until Ian said, "You could use the Dictaphone, and Dawn could type it all out for you."

Ian phoned Dawn, she was a freelance secretary who worked for our business on an ad hoc basis. She was happy to take my writing on, calling to collect the tapes and later returning the typed pages and undertaking any amendments that I needed.

The process was rather tortuous and long-winded. Ian drew my attention to an advertisement in the local paper where the Regional College was advertising a course on voice activated computing. I decided to enrol. The class was due to start at the beginning of the following term so it took a few weeks before I was able to start my education.

I was feeling proud with my progress to date as I enrolled, but then, as it is said, "pride comes before a fall". Little did I know that this prophecy was to come true. Ian had taken me to the dry cleaners to collect some curtains, and we had parked the car across the road. It was an old, originally Victorian built road with a high kerb. As I followed Ian who was carrying the curtains, I tripped up on the kerb and fell heavily on my left arm. The pain was intense and I fell onto the car in distress.

The next day it was still very painful and swollen.

"I think it might be broken," I said.

"Yes." Ian's voice sounded resigned. "I think you may be right."

At Accident & Emergency in Peterborough District Hospital a young, energetic radiographer twisted my arm into a position that he thought appropriate.

I said, "In the waiting room there are lots of posters warning patients about attacking staff, but it doesn't say anything about staff causing lots of pain to patients. Its not fair because it really hurts you know!"

"Yes I do know, that's why I became a radiographer," he joked, appreciating that I was trying to be humorous.

It turned out that I had fractured the radius on my left arm and I was in plaster for three weeks. Unfortunately it was principally my left arm that I was using, although I was making efforts to get my right arm working again. I requested physiotherapy, but my request was diverted to occupational therapy. It was a rerun of my previous experience with them. Again they were going on about such things as dominoes and cards. Again they could offer little that could help me. The occupational therapist just couldn't seem to grasp that I couldn't actually see the dots on the dominoes, let alone understand my problems of comprehending what the dots meant. Instead she insisted on focusing on movement in my right hand, leaving me frustrated and on the verge of tears.

Another reason for my frustration was the inevitable postponement of my swimming. In addition I had to miss several Writers' Workshop, but at least the term hadn't started at the college, so I couldn't begin voice activation computing lessons.

I was irritated by this state of frustration, so I made an appointment to see Dr Gordon, and I said, "It's time I went back to work."

He responded, "I'm afraid you're too fragile to ever to work again, Annie." It was rather a blow to be told that you could never work again.

Then he took my blood pressure, complained that it was

too high and reached for his prescription pad. As he did so I asked,

"And what is your blood pressure Dr Gordon?"

"Point taken," he responded, smiling.

I went on, "Gone is the time when GPs died in harness."

He smiled again and, perhaps just in conversation, I moved on to the other worries I had saying, "It was as long ago as 1974, that Professor Wright injected steroids into my left hip to ease the pain. It helped at the time but it must have caused the cartilage to be loose, so I fear I'll need a hip replacement sometime in the future."

Without giving him time to respond, I added, "Also when I was in Intensive Care they had to carry out a cut-down into the veins of my left leg. I have developed varicose veins now. These will need surgery too," I added.

He was completely unfazed by this and took my hand, whilst saying, "Annie they will never operate on your body again, so the body you have now is the body will take to your grave."

He squeezed my hand very sympathetically and gave me a prescription to reduce my blood pressure. I left thinking how lucky I am to have a GP that has been so kind over the years and who knows me so well. He always told me the truth and gave me the time to share anxieties with him.

"I must keep committed to the notion that it is up to me to maximize my fitness and general health as much as I possibly can," I thought.

When Ian started driving me home, I said, "I think it's time for me to do the weekly shopping, on my own in Queensgate."

He asked, "Are you sure you can manage?"

I was determined, "Yes," I said very emphatically.

So the next day Ian wrote a shopping list for me to take on my first shopping expedition. This included a few things from John Lewis and of course Waitrose as well.

He asked, "How are you going to get home?"

353

"By taxi," I said decisively.

So taking it slowly, I set off. In John Lewis I was putting some things in a basket when I met Margaret Liliman who had worked in the Anti-Coagulant Clinic for many years and, because I was on Warfarin, I'd seen her each time I'd been in to have my blood clotting time, I.N.R. (International Normalisation Rate) checked. She greeted me and looked around, saying, "Who's with you?"

"I'm on my own," I said proudly.

It felt good to have some independence and to be able to do some simple tasks again. Having collected the things we needed, I headed towards the till and, as luck would have it, I met Dee. It was Dee who had sold John his rabbits. I was very glad she still worked there and she was happy to counter-sign the cross, which was all I could manage on the receipt.

After I'd been successful in John Lewis, I walked across the shopping mall and into Waitrose, hoping to repeat my newly achieved independence. Taking the trolley, putting my shopping into it, and then approaching the till, I was delighted to be greeted by Shirley. Shirley was the Waitrose assistant who, having noticed my absence in the shop, sent a Get Well card to me. I felt so very grateful as she helped pack my trolley, organised another member of staff to take it to the taxi rank and made sure that I, together with my shopping, went safely on my way. I arrived home and though tired; I was very pleased with myself. Ian came to help me with my shopping and pay the taxi driver.

I needed full time care so Ian had no option but to turn down any work that took him away from home. Prior to my discharge Ian had been working away from home, principally in the Nottingham area and staying on the boat for a few days each week. He began worrying about our finances. These weren't helped by the need to meet the cost of the work on the replacement kitchen and the double-glazing. Ian was able to do some work on updating the second edition of our 'Quality Workbook' from home. Unfortunately though, his other jobs, which had included working in Behavioural Assessment for recruitment at the new Toyota factory at Burnaston in Derbyshire, had been lost. Just before commercial production started the resource department was able to take the recruitment in-house, and Ian's contract was concluded. Ian then moved on to working for Professor Don Twendle in Quality Assurance, driving daily to Nottingham to start a day's work, then driving home to see to my needs. He started to suffer from stress and went to his GP. The GP said that he must have some time off work, wrote him a sick note stating stress as the cause and signed him off for two weeks. Professor Twendle's immediate reaction was to sack Ian.

Ian recuperated, but then anxiety about our income, together with the need to work locally, led him to join Peterborough Chamber of Commerce. Here Ian was making plenty of contacts but it didn't bring in continuity of work, so he was relieved when one of these contacts asked, "Could you come to work for me to help me with a contract for Railtrack?"

After discussing it with me I said, "Of course I can manage!"

This meant Ian travelling to Birmingham each day for over a year. Each day Ian prepared my food leaving me to take it from the refrigerator and popping it into the microwave to heat it through. I was delighted that I could manage, just. My reliance on others was diminishing. Though Pam said to Ian, "If Annie needs any help I am standing by!"

All went well and in due course, having concluded the Birmingham contract, Ian was asked if he would work for Servirail, a company based in Leytonstone. Ian was concerned about this because it would involve him staying away for a few nights each week.

"I'll be fine with this sort of arrangement. I can manage a microwave now, so I won't starve," I reassured him.

Arrangements were working well and my swimming at Thomas Cook was progressing nicely. Ian had been taking me, and I was able to manage by using the disabled changing room. Once when I was changing another lady walked in, she was about ten years younger than me and of medium height, but walking with a stick. She smiled, "Hi! I'm Sue Cox,"she said, extending her hand towards me.

I introduced myself and it turned out that Sue had been a nurse who was swimming because she had had a back injury caused by lifting patients. We became friendly and she started taking and collecting me in her car. One time when we were having coffee, discussing the problems I had with my balance, Sue looked thoughtful and said,

"My sister bought a tricycle which is she no longer uses and it's just lying idle in her garage. She has hardly used it. Shall I ask her how much she wants for it?"

We agreed a price, and Sue and her husband delivered it. Though it was very heavy and at the start was difficult to manoeuvre, it gave me transport independence. Another milestone!

I wasn't worried at all by the thought of Ian working in Leytonstone, in fact I was very pleased about it as he was enjoying his work, and feeling relieved from the financial worries. I was happy getting around on my tricycle, so all was going well. I didn't have any problems in getting to the Writers' Workshop; I was able to call Adams Taxi Company to take me and bring me home at the agreed time and I was enjoying the challenge of having to get something ready each month, though I was nervous when June said, "Next month we'll start with Annie."

Although I had been reading my work out as we took it in turns, somehow starting with me seemed daunting. Ian had to sit and listen to my reading without being too critical, although he was able to make some suggestions on the text of "I'm not afraid of the Wolf! A nurse's tale." The forerunner to this book.

"How did it go?" Ian asked.

"It was alright I think, but it will be so much better when I'm able to work on it on voice activation at home."

In the September I started classes at the college. We were a small group of students and Tony the tutor was very patient with me. Lizzie, another student of about my age, who was tall with lovely dark brown eyes, was suffering from glaucoma and hoped that voice activation would help her because she could no longer focus on the computer keyboard. I could see the keys, but couldn't manage to press them, and so voice activation provided help for a variety of disabilities.

Inevitably, my old computer didn't have enough memory for voice activation, so I needed a new computer.

As soon as Dad heard about this he was very keen to buy a new one for me.

"You buy the one you need and let me know how much it is," he said.

"We don't need him to pay for it," Ian said.

"It's the way he feels he can help, so he wants to," I responded.

So we bought the computer, and with the help of Tony I was making progress and feeling very excited. At last I was getting somewhere.

At first all went very well with Ian travelling to Leytonstone and staying away. Ian cut up a large bowl of melon for my lunch each day while he was away, and I ate that with grapes, fromage frais and cashew nuts, with fruit juice to drink. For my evening meal he put together individual dishes of diced up meat and vegetables from the joint that we had had on the Saturday evening. I was able to manage, and was very happy with the situation, welcoming him back when he arrived home. I was jubilant about how well I was coping with life.

Then one week, I fell as I was trying to put on my tights. I cut my face on the radiator in the bedroom, and blood was running down my face; it was very painful. As Ian was in

Leytonstone, I rang Pam and she came straight away, but said to me, "We are going to have to go to A and E for this, I'll bring the car over to you. Just lock the house up and wait for me."

It was good, because I found that by turning up with blood pouring from my face wound we were prioritised and were soon being dealt with. I was patched up, and the doctor accepted my reassurance that there was no underlying injury.

He said in a voice that didn't invite argument, "Go to see your GP in two days for the wound to be checked."

"Thank you very much, Pam, I don't know what I would have done without you!" I said gratefully.

In spite of my trying to reassure him, Ian was worried and came home. He made the appointment for me to see Dr Gordon, who said,

"Oh dear that looks sore, and now you've got two black eyes as well, but the wound is clean and I think that you will be OK."

That minor trauma was happily resolved until one lunchtime in December, blood started oozing from my gums. I didn't have a clue what made it happen and next day it was getting worse. Ian took me to see Dr Gordon who arranged a GP admission to Ward 1Z. By then the bleeding was substantial and showed no signs of stopping. I was very weak, and either fainted or had a petit mal fit. The ward staff were noncommittal about what it was.

"Perhaps they just don't care." I thought.

I rested and was transferred to Ward 2Y. I realised that they were going to keep me in for a few days to work out what the bleeding was all about. So when the menus were handed out for Sunday, "Ooh good roast beef for dinner," the patient next to me exclaimed!

Everyone else around me opted for a lunch of roast beef and Yorkshire pudding. I, on the other hand, still had the taste of blood in my mouth and I didn't have an appetite, so I chose sandwiches. Beef products were not good for my joints, resulting in joint pain, being too high in uric acid for a Lupus patient, or so I thought anyway. When the food we'd ordered came the next day, I was well enough to say to the staff member who brought the tray, "I am disabled, please could you open my sandwiches."

She was clearly irritated by this, and did it without speaking, dumped them unceremoniously on my tray and left. When everyone else lifted the lids from the roast beef dinners, they said they were cold, tough and quite inedible. I was glad I made the right choice. I watched the catering assistant as she collected the almost untouched dinners. There was no interest in the fact that the patients hadn't eaten or that they should have food to aid their recovery. No doubt the food just went back to the kitchen and was thrown away. What a waste!

How different from the sixties when the ward Sister would personally check what each patient had eaten. If a particular patient didn't fancy their lunch, Sister would ask the nurse, "Would she like an alternative, an omelette instead?"

And if the answer was to the affirmative, it wasn't many minutes before one of the kitchen staff arrived with the said omelette. Food in those days was seen as an important ingredient in a patient's recovery. It was a nursing responsibility to do all we could to ensure patients' general health, and this most certainly included food and drink.

I was still very weak, but the bleeding stopped and I was concerned about Ian needing to get back to work, so when visitors started coming to see me I told Pam about my worries and she said, "As you will need to be kept in a few days, I am happy to look after Kay Kay so Ian doesn't need to worry, he can go back to work."

"Oh! Thank you Pam, yet again," I said as I gave her my front door key.

The next day being Monday, at least we were getting some medical attention. I felt quite comfortable in the ward at first, until a very rough and ready nursing auxiliary turned up the fluorescent lights to their maximum intensity. I appealed to a nurse who was rushing by with uncharacteristic speed, I said, "Please turn the lights down." She sighed, but complied with my request and then made her way to Ward control and proceeded to chat with the other nurses who were typing away on their computers. It seemed to me that the whole purpose of her presence was to spend time chatting at Ward Control, and patient's needs were just some inconvenience that she had to suffer.

I was musing about this when the Nursing auxiliary came back, presumably from her lunch break, and switched the fluorescent lights on full again. The pain in my head was intense, and I exclaimed, "This is manslaughter!"

Immediately the screens were drawn around my bed and that did help, but then three young doctors came through the screens. One said gravely, "Are you seeing things?"

The second said, "Are you hearing voices?"

The third said, "What are they telling you to do?"

Unfortunately I felt too ill to respond, "Yes I'm seeing three adolescents with stethoscopes around their necks asking me silly questions," I thought. Instead I simply said, "Phone Doctor Sheehan…. he will explain."

They left, still leaving the screens drawn around my bed.

It didn't seem long until all the fluorescent ward lights were switched off. This left all the other patients in the dark, with just their over the bed light to see by. With the realisation that I was inconveniencing every body else, I felt unpopular, and made a decision that my stay was must come to an end. I told a nurse, "I'm going to discharge myself!"

The nurse wandered off, returning with two black plastic bags, on which was written, "patient's property".

I said, "Please can you phone Adams Taxi Company, and ask for a taxi to collect me, and can I have my watch?"

The only clothes that I had were those that I had on, satin pyjamas and a thin cotton dressing gown, which Sarah had bought me as a present from Indonesia.

I asked, "I am going to feel very cold, please could I take a blanket with me? As you cannot find my watch at the moment, my husband will bring the blanket back when he comes to collect it."

The nurse said, "Yes."

I wasn't really worried about the watch because it was one that I bought from H. Samuel for five pounds. One of the problems with having poor finger control was that I wasn't able to use the key for the locker in the swimming pool, and so I bought a very cheap watch so I didn't have to worry about losing it. Nobody wanted to steal it!

I put the rest of my belongings into the black plastic bags, and climbed into the wheelchair that she brought. Without speaking she put the plastic bags on my knees and pushed me to the lift and out the front door of the hospital, where she stood with me waiting for the taxi. Idly she kept wrapping her long loose hair around her fingers. I was appalled by this unhygienic behaviour and was glad that she wouldn't be attending to me anymore. The taxi arrived, and the driver helped me out of the wheelchair and into the taxi. He was very gentle and the nurse simply stood there waiting to take the wheelchair.

We started for home, and I opened my handbag, then I panicked when I realised that I didn't have a front door key.

"I don't have my door key," I said.

As though it was an everyday experience for taxi drivers to pick up a scantily dressed woman in December, he said calmly, demonstrating the compassion of a good Muslim, "Do you know where the key is?"

Then I remembered of course, Pam had the key to look after the dog.

"It's across the road at the neighbours," I said.

He said, "I park outside when you tell me, I keep your

361

things in taxi, you ring the doorbell, when the door opens I bring out your things."

While all this was going on, I was trying to give him a five pound note, and he was stuffing it back into my wallet. He didn't want to take a fare from somebody who was so poorly. I rang the doorbell, Pam opened the door and her face was a picture of amazement. The taxi driver came out with the property bags, Brian, Pam's husband, took them from him, and the taxi drove away.

The first thing Pam said was, "You look frozen, Annie!" Come in and have a cup of tea. It will help to warm you up! "

I went inside for a cup of tea and explained all that had happened.

Pam and Brian helped me home and saw to it at that I had everything I needed. It was very good to be there! Then Pam phoned Ian to explain.

In less than two hours, Ian arrived home. I was feeling very tired, and happily settled down to sleep.

The next day, Ian delivered a letter to Dr Gordon, explaining the situation and how badly the hospital had behaved with my discharge. By return he sent a letter back stating, "I must admit this all sounds unbelievable. I am not in the surgery on Wednesday, but I will call and visit your wife on Thursday."

It was good to see him when he came, and I reassured him that I was none the worse for the experience. It was not long before Ian, who was outraged about the situation and had discussed it with Pam, decided to enter an official complaint.

There followed six months of various correspondence and meetings between Ian, myself, the Health Authority, and the Community Health Counsel. The last of all these meetings was supposedly the official investigation. But it turned out to be a total white wash, they just were ticking boxes and it was obvious that nothing would be altered.

The chairman concluded, "I am not in a position to guarantee anything."

Later Ian said to me, "Perhaps it would be more understandable if it had been the first of April instead of today the first of May!"

When I looked blank, Ian went on, "You know April Fools' day!"

We both laughed but underneath I was a very sad, though not completely surprised about the outcome of what had been the culmination of six months of our time, energy and perhaps a considerable amount of Health Authority money. Our attempts at getting our message across had come to nothing.

Nevertheless, when Labour had come to power in May 1997, the government embarked on an ambitious program of reforms aimed at improving healthcare standards, and in 1998 produced a White Paper stating the aim of making the Health Service more responsive to its patients needs and delivering "A first Class Quality Service". I looked forward to its implementation, thinking now at last there may truly be the delivery of empathetic of care, of TLC as we used to write in our patients' notes in the 1960s. It had been the reason why I'd become a nurse in the first place, when I was given such gentle care all those years ago in the hospital on Guernsey, particularly as sunburn can really be classified as self inflicted. I could possibly have been treated with the indifference of, "You have brought this on yourself." Whereas the way they had cared for me, a silly teenager, was so gentle and considerate.

My experience in 2Y was almost the opposite, the nurses seemed completely indifferent to my pain. When I trained we were told to give patients the level of care that we would want for ourselves if we were in their position.

Although I was now seeing things from the other side of the sheets, I was still a member of the Royal College of Nursing, and I was optimistic when I was sent details of a

363

conference to be held at Addenbrookes in May that year. The conference title was in celebration of nursing and I was intrigued, especially following my recent experience in Peterborough. I wasn't able to go on my own quite yet, so I was enthusiastic when Ian suggested that he would take me. Ian took notes for me. Unfortunately his comments started with "Dull as ditch water", referring to the chairman's opening remarks. As each speaker waxed lyrical and boasted about their achievements, I became increasingly dismayed and, as we left, I asked Ian, "What planet are these people living on?

A small group of us from the Writers' Workshop regularly met informally for coffee at Costas Coffee Bar in the Queensgate Centre in Peterborough. Because I had missed one of the meetings, one of the members, Jack Alster asked, "Where have you been?"

I explained what had gone on, and Jack Alster said, "There should be a club for the survivors of Ward 1Z."

Though I was amused by Jack's words, I was sad to think that his experience of hospital care had been so similar to mine. I hoped that this was not the general consensus of opinion but I rather suspected that it was. I decided to research the matter further.

When I arrived home, I turned to a report produced by the World Health Organization in 1984, entitled 'Nursing Standards Toward Better Care – guidelines to standards of nursing practice'. The focus of this was the development of standards for administration and education. Levels of performance in quality was mentioned, but it gave no guidance towards improvement in the way I'd recently been treated. I turned to the Royal College of Nursing information, and that was no consolation either. Next I read the NHS Management Executive Study Notes "Measuring Quality." This focused on giving nurses the mechanism to measure the quality of care their patients received and when necessary to initiate improvements. The leaflet was issued in the early

'90s and it mentioned the new "Purchaser Provider" environment. It didn't seem to have any relevance to the way I was treated, and perhaps more to the wasted roast dinners that were just thrown away. I felt very sad.

Then I read an article in the Sunday Telegraph review of 25th October 1998. In this, Dr James Le Fanu writes 'Come back Sister Prune face, we miss you.' Dr Le Fanu spells out how 50 years ago John Keegan the esteemed military historian and Reith lecturer, spent a few weeks on a ward at St. Thomas's Hospital. John Keegan tells a story which recounts how in those days a patient in the bed next to him decided to die. This became a battle of wills between the patient, who had decided to die, and a ward sister who was determined she would do all in her power to ensure he didn't. The would-be corpse's bed was moved next to her office, and 50 times a day she shot out to sit him up, pummel his chest, rub his back, wash him and feed him when necessary.

Perhaps it would be wrong of me to suggest that an account in 1948, especially with it being by someone so esteemed as John Keegan, is just apocryphal, but he has some important lessons for today's nurses. Dr Le Fanu's article states that the replacement of Sister Prune Face with a computer literate nurse manager, sitting in front of her console organising the activities of the nurses on the ward has meant that something has been lost, and nursing staff must be encouraged to develop an empathetic relationship with their patients. Dr Le Fanu goes on to say that the astonishing thing about this new order is that there is no one in charge.

But now it was 1998, and it seemed that things had changed. Could the blame be due to the new "Purchaser Provider"? I thought not, I was sure that Sister Prune Face would have ensure the welfare of her charges, that they were fed, clean and had had their bowels opened!

Back at home and with Ian back at work, I felt safe being on my own and, of course Pam was just across the road. All should have been going well, but then just when I least expected it, the nightmares started up again. I awoke in a cold sweat, waiting for the fear to drain away and thinking, "Will the recurrence of terror never end! How could my first husband have treated me in this way? Was it that something in his childhood experience that left him as a complete bully, and in me he had detected someone who was too weak to stand up to him? If I understood this perhaps the nightmares might stop," I thought. I was again frightened to go to sleep. Recounting my experiences, I realised that previous panic attacks had occurred when I was beginning to feel safe and in control of my life. One of the times was when I left the marital home and Dad had given me the money for a deposit on a house that my panic attacks started. Then I was pleased to accept the Leeds University offer of cognitive behaviour therapy to enable me to stay on at the university. Now I decided that cognitive behaviour therapy was simply like a sticking plaster trying to heal a broken arm, and wasnot able to heal the real damage lurking deep in my sub-conscious. When Ian arrived home I explained all this, and said, "By now I should be able to meet the children's father again. Especially when you think there may be such things as weddings and christenings in the future when it would be important for us all be there together."

Ian's response was unequivocal, "They didn't have a condition like Lupus. You'd be crazy to risk it, and I don't know what Dr Sheehan would say. I sincerely doubt whether there is anything that can be done."

The discussion of my idea was to be closed forever.

CHAPTER 11

RECUPERATION

Now I owed it to Ian and all these people who had loved and cared for me to try very hard to look to the future, and not to let these experiences from the past blight it. Not think about what might've been but think of my life as a game of cards, "It's not the cards you are dealt in life, but the way you play them!" I must concentrate on this as my maxim, and "I must go out with all flags flying!" There must not be a question of could I do it, I had to find a way. It wasn't going to be easy and I knew there was a long way to go.

I remembered that, when I was a teenager, I was often down and my mother's response to this was to give me a book by Norman Vincent Peel, outlining the Power of Positive Thinking. This book stated that you could do all things by believing in the power of God. OK though now I was still claiming to be an atheist, whilst accepting the words of Peter Lipton, the Professor of Philosophy at Cambridge, who when he was 53 said, "You don't have to believe in God to see the value of religion."

So I returned to the feelings of confidence that the words that Norman Vincent Peel had given me as a teenager and resolved to look to the future!

As part of my rehabilitation, I had already gone back to

reading the Yoga book that Pat had sent me years before. The title of this book was "Teach yourself Yoga" and this helped me to get some flexibility into my body, although some of my movements were very limited. Gradually it was helping me gain some flexibility with my hands. I was also relying on Don Snuggs to keep my Ying and Yang in balance through his skill in the use of acupuncture, and he said, "There's going to be a new procedure in nursing care, and all patients are going to have a named nurse to take responsibility for their care in hospital."

I was pleased, and suggested, "Well at least someone will be taking some responsibility for looking after patients properly."

"We will see," Don said sceptically.

I was thoughtful but said, "At least it will not be like the putrid state I was left in when you came in to clean me up and give me a blanket-bath. It certainly wouldn't have been allowed for a patient to be left in such a grotty condition in my day. A patient's personal hygiene was seen as the nurse's responsibility and the nurse then saw to it that any patient who wasn't sufficiently mobile to go for a daily bath on their own were either supervised in the bath or given a blanket-bath, anything else would have been unthinkable."

Don agreed, and I left feeling better for having got that off my chest and, as usual, thanks to Don's treatment my breathing improved.

I was able to maintain the optimism that I'd had as Ian took me home. I was smiling and said, "The new idea in the recent patient's charter is for a named nurse, so perhaps at last I can hope to be properly cared for, if I need to go into hospital again!"

Changing the subject, Ian said, "Have you forgotten that Don said that he thought that perhaps you should get your ESR checked to make sure that the Lupus is not out of control?"

Of course I hadn't even remembered Don saying that, I

was thinking acupuncture would have been enough to sort me out. But I was compliant and rang the surgery.

In response to my request to see Dr Gordon, the receptionist, Martina, said in her warm Irish accent, "Doctor Gordon has gone on holiday, would you like to see Doctor Thompson instead?"

The previous time when I'd been to the surgery, I'd noticed an attractive, dark haired, young doctor; I thought that I might as well see what she's like. I went for my appointment and she was efficient as she took my blood, and suggested I went for my results the following week.

"Your ESR is 58," she said.

But before she had a chance to say anything, I bit her head off saying,"I don't want any steroids."

Then I felt guilty knowing that it should really be under 10, and said, "But you are the doctor, and I will take your advice."

She responded, "It's your body, we will try it again next week. "

I left thinking, "Well, if she's going to be like that she will be stuck with me when Dr Gordon retires!"

Fortunately, a week later my ESR was lower, so I felt relieved that I had been so adamant about not taking any steroids again. Leaving the surgery, I was feeling quite fit as I was walking along to do my shopping in the Queensgate Centre. As always all the staff there were very helpful. It was great and gave me the feeling of some independence as I wandered about. Previously it has been warm, but now it was winter and the weather was cold. Although they seemed quite happy as they pushed my trolley to the taxi rank, the Waitrose staff looked frozen in their light cotton uniforms. One week when it was particularly cold, I said to Ian when I arrived home, "There must be a better way to organise the taxi transport home."

He thought for a while, and then said, "Here is the Adams taxi number, have a word next time you're in and see if they will ring for a taxi to collect you and the shopping from

369

Waitrose customer collect. Do you think you can manage to walk through the bus station to meet the taxi there?"

I smiled enthusiastically. "Yes of course I can," I said gratefully.

So the system of Waitrose ordering a taxi to collect both me and my shopping from Waitrose customer collect was set up. It was to work very successfully for many years to come. Trevor, and later Bill, the Waitrose employees at customer collect, together with the Adams taxi driver, would ensure that all my shopping was in the taxi before we started for home. Once back home the taxi driver would put it on the doorstep and I was very relieved by what a difference this made to my independence. It ensured that I would become a Waitrose shopper for life. Even if I hadn't been before, I was now a confirmed disciple.

For ten years my hairdresser had been Heather Roberts, and even when I was in hospital, she had come in to wash my hair. So I suppose that it was inevitable that at some stage Heather would sell her shop and retire. I did ask her, but Heather wasn't sure where to recommend. So the next time my hair needed cutting, I took a chance and booked an appointment with another salon in the town, although it hadn't been recommended by anyone.

But after my hair appointment in the new salon I looked in the mirror and I felt very dispirited, I thought, "I'm just about bald." I didn't say anything, and needless to say didn't book any more appointments.

By chance, I'd arranged to meet my dear and trusted friend, Val. She was now retired but retirement hadn't changed her a bit, she bustled into Queensgate, threw her arms around me and we hugged. I felt very warm and pleased to see her, and then she stepped back in astonishment, saying, "Annie what have you done to your hair?"

"I've changed my hairdresser, and they've scalped me!"

I explained, and then Val said, "I think you'd be better off going to Michael Johns in future!"

With that she marched me straight out of the back of John Lewis and next door into Michael Johns Hair Salon. A slim, blonde lady was at the desk calmingly organising all the comings and goings of what was a very busy Salon.

She looked up and said, "Hello, I'm Sally, can I help you?"

Val said, "This lady wants an appointment with Helen."

They were looking at me quizzically and I was quite uncomfortable as they stared at me as though I was a specimen to be examined. I smiled to cover up my embarrassment. It was as if I was not quite involved in what was happening, until one of the Stylists suggested, "Perhaps it would be better to leave it for six weeks, before attempting a re-style."

So I made an appointment with Helen for six weeks time. She was dark haired, young, slim and pretty, and seemed pleased to meet me. I was very relieved when Helen showed me the result. During the appointment, I explained about my last experience and how, since I'd moved to Peterborough, Heather Roberts had been my hairdresser. Then Helen told she had trained at Heather's. So much for me thinking that my hairdresser didn't really matter compared to my doctors. I realised that perhaps it may seem superficial, but a good haircut can made me feel like all's well in the world!

Sadly, my change of GP came sooner than I'd anticipated, and the next time I went to see Dr Gordon he said, "I am going to retire, so you won't be seeing me again, Annie."

Before I'd really taken this in, I moved onto my reason for coming, which was to see if he would give me authority to go on holiday abroad and sign my travel insurance certificate.

Dr Gordon said, "There are lots of places in the UK, so why not try them for the time being?"

I was a bit disappointed, but went on to ask,"Can I give you a hug and a kiss and say thank you for all the care you have given me over all these years!"

He smiled and said, "Yes! It won't matter if they cross me off now!"

We exchanged a hug, and as I left I was a bit tearful about losing him. At least I had confidence in his replacement Dr Thompson, and I still had my consultant, Dr Sheehan. So all in all, I was very happy with my medical supervision.

Planning for my next appointment with Dr Sheehan, I decided that I wanted his reaction as to whether I could have a hip transplant and whether I was alright to travel abroad. I printed out a draft letter to my travel insurance company letter for him to sign, endorsing the view that he could see no objection to my going on holiday to Europe. Dr Sheehan examined my hip joint, and said,"The cartilage is a little loose, but it doesn't mean that it will result in wear and tear to your hip joint."

I was relieved at that, and went on to say, "Our neighbours have invited us to their house in South Africa, but I assume I would need vaccinations for that, so I couldn't go. But I wouldn't need vaccinations for Europe, so could I holiday there?"

"Yes, that should be alright, as you probably know there is an overall agreement between the European states for mutual health care."

So I gave him the letter I'd prepared. He signed it and put the hospital stamp by his signature. I was really pleased with myself when I left his consulting room, although I really hadn't made any plans to go abroad as yet, but it did give us the opportunity to make them. That felt really great!

When I arrived home from my appointment with Dr Sheehan, I said to Ian, "As Dr Sheehan has given the authority to go to Europe and signed a letter of authority, I would really like to go to Paris. Do you remember when I was in intensive care, Saskia lit a candle for me in Notre Dame? I would like to go there and see it for myself."

Ian said, "Shouldn't be a problem, what about going by Eurostar? I'll see what I can organise."

I was feeling healthy, and was happily going swimming

with Sue Cox. She was calling in to collect me and, afterwards, driving me home. One day when we were drinking a coffee, she said, "I have got to have an examination by a doctor from the social services to verify the damage to my back. Do you mind coming to give me some advice and moral support?"

I felt very pleased that she asked me, it made me feel that I was still of some use, and I had no hesitation in responding, "Yes, of course I will be pleased to."

The examination went well, and I was delighted to use my professional training again.

One day when we were getting changed after using the pool, Sue either passed out, or was possibly having a petit mal fit. She was lying on the floor quite unconscious. I pulled the alarm cord, and members of the pool staff arrived. After some discussion, we all decided that she needed to go to hospital. An ambulance was called and I agreed to go with her. She regained consciousness and was immediately saying, "I don't want to go into hospital, I don't want to go into hospital!"

But the decision had been taken and Sue, still protesting, was loaded into the ambulance, with me trailing behind carrying the two gym bags. The gym staff phoned Sue's husband, and before too long he arrived at the hospital. I explained what had happened, and he arranged for a taxi to take me home.

Fortunately Sue soon recovered, but she did stop coming to Thomas Cook swimming pool. So I started using the tricycle to go there and back.

It was only a short distance, but getting there meant going up the steep incline to the bridge over the Parkway. It was quite an effort and the tricycle was heavy so, with a sense of achievement, I zoomed down the other side of the bridge to the gym. On my return journey my hands got cold, I just couldn't grasp the brakes. On the downside I went faster and faster and, out of control, tried to take the bend at speed. Over went the tricycle, with me lying on the ground underneath it. I couldn't manage to turn it back over. I thought, "Oh well, I suppose at least I'm able to recover from the shock of it, but if I'm still here three weeks next Wednesday, I'll be very cold by then!"

But luck was with me, and it wasn't long before an elderly gentleman, out for a walk and minding his own business, came along. I don't think he could quite believe his eyes as he looked down at me.

He said, "I've never seen anything like this before, are you all right?"

Very relieved, and lying prostrate under my tricycle, I smiled and asked, "Do you think you will be strong enough to turn my tricycle over?"

It wasn't an easy job for him, but he put his walking stick up against a garden wall and managed to turn the tricycle the right way up. He helped me to my feet, and I recovered my gym kit. The gentleman said, "Are you injured?"

"No, I'm fine, thank you very much indeed!" I said, as he dusted me down. We both went on our way, and I giggled all the way home. I was thinking, "I bet he had a story to tell." Unfortunately, I never met him again. None the worse for the experience, I took much more care when going down the hill over the parkway after that!

My sole purpose for going to Thomas Cook gym was to get fit by learning how to swim again, and I was making some progress when one of the lifeguards, whose name was Lisa, said, "I want to see you in the gym."

Lisa wouldn't listen to my protestations my left foot dragging along behind me or that brain damage had left me feeling weak or the difficulties in keeping my balance. Lisa just kept repeating, "Next time you come, I want to see you in the gym."

My excuses were just ignored, so I arranged to meet Lisa in the gym the next Tuesday.

I was feeling very nervous as Lisa said, "Come on, lets get you on the treadmill."

Lisa didn't take any prisoners, there was nothing else for it but to comply.

I stood on the treadmill, I held onto the handrail very tightly. Lisa set the speed at one mile an hour with an incline of 15%.

We were off! Each time I moved my left leg, Lisa said, "Lift your left heel!" Repeating it over and over again.

After ten minutes, I was feeling very tired, and Lisa pushed the stop button.

She said, "That's enough for now! Next time I will add some more exercises for you to do. Do you feel alright?"

"Yes thank you, but I do feel tired!"

As the weeks went by, I was grateful to see the improvement I was making and wondered why no one in physiotherapy had put these types of exercises in motion for me.

Periodically I was still tripping up and falling over. Every week after doing the shopping in town, I would head across the market square for lunch at Beckets, the Cathedral Café, where the staff were helpful and the lunches good. Often I would meet either Lizzie or Val and we would eat our lunch in the upstairs room overlooking the Cathedral. It was a lovely view of the cathedral, and it made me feel very peaceful and spiritually content. One day as I was heading towards Beckets, I tripped and fell and, as I lay on the ground, two young men approached me. I opened my eyes to see arms covered in tattoos. One man handed a snooker cue to his companion, he asked, "Are you alright mi dear? Can me and me mate lift you up?"

These two skinheads were very strong, but so gentle as they lifted me onto my feet and dusted down my clothes. I was fine, and continued on to Beckets. I met Val, and explained about the skinheads.

"Isn't it amazing that when you are in trouble, it nearly always brings the kindness out in people and it so often happens that these people are the ones you would be wary of meeting on a dark night."

After Val and I had finished our toasted cheese sandwiches, Val handed me a cutting from the Daily Mail written by Trisha Holden. In the article, Trisha described Lupus as "That terrible illness that has robbed me of my career".

I did feel sad for Trisha, and having Lupus has certainly meant changes in my life, but it has also bought experiences that change the way that you look at things. Like being lifted up so gently by those two skinheads. This had opened my eyes and I was grateful for an opportunity that told me not to be so judgemental, there is probably good in almost everyone. Thinking about this on the way home, I remembered the opera singer, Mary Boomer. She had had an accident in which her nose was broken by a hockey stick, and consequently was no longer able to sing professionally. Mary became a successful comedian. I thought, I must learn from Mary and try to see the changes in my life positively!

That evening I went to June's Writer's Workshop, and she announced that she was going to retire. Most of the group's members had already realised that this was on the cards because unfortunately June was becoming increasingly forgetful and reliant on her husband, Alan, to chair the workshops. It was the early symptoms of Alzheimer's. Before her retirement announcement a member of the group, whose name was Dr Jack Alster, had been working with June to produce a collection of contributions from the group members. The idea was to publish them under the title "Wise Counsel". I submitted my contribution and decided to call it "Annie is not afraid of the Wolf". In this I outlined my experience of Lupus since 1974 when I was first diagnosed with the autoimmune condition of Systemic Lupus Erythematosis, or Lupus for short.

I was very grateful for the opportunity that the publication offered as it gave me the opportunity to put my thoughts together in the form of a short article. It was published by Moira Wilmot of the Peterborough College of Adult Education and while I wrote about Lupus, Jack Alster's contribution was his life experiences to date, starting as an eight year old refugee from Hitler's Germany. Jack's role in assisting the production of "Wise Counsel" led him to self-publish two books. The first of these was *Once we had the country*, and so Jack was moving on. I was very impressed that Jack was able to move on so purposefully after June's retirement. As for me, the thought of losing June, with all the invaluable help that she had given me, left me feeling lost and without direction. It was suggested that the Writers' group could transfer to The Adult Education College, where there was a creative writing course being led by a teacher called Jeremy. Application forms were completed and sent in.

Meeting Lizzie at Beckets, I said, "I'm feeling a bit more positive about the transfer of the Writers' group to Peterborough College of Adult Education. I will start there next term.

"You see, at the end of each session June Counsel always asked if anyone would like to give her their work. When she returned it she had written lots of really helpful comments on it.

This gave me the burning ambition to tell the world about the shabby treatment meted out to me in both hospitals, when my life hung in the balance. The workshops opened up the hope of some future achievement for me, and gave me the belief that I could add value to the world. Gone were the times when I sat on a bench opposite the rowing lake, overwhelmed by the feeling of futility in my life and I was only able to see in black and white, I was subsumed in a fog and thinking, "I'd rather be dead than disabled...and why did they bother to resuscitate me?" Then due to the workshops, I could see a future goal. Sorry Lizzie, I seem to be on my soap box again"

Lizzie said, "Good for you! Someone has got to tell them!"

As I made my way home I was thinking about how wonderful June had been to me each month and how, when she returned my contributions to the workshop, the comments she had written on the text had been helpful and positive. If June's response, in those early days, had been negative and deprecating and that I didn't stand a chance of getting published, I would have given up.

Fortunately when I was at the point of my greatest vulnerability, she steered my work into what she considered to be a more readable style, with good humour that kept me going. I hoped that the people at the College of Adult Education would be half as good, but that remained to be seen! I had a lot to be thankful for; Ian's encouragement when he found the advert for the classes in voice activation at Peterborough Regional College just when it seemed that I would never be able to get my hands to type, and my father's insistence that he wanted to pay for a computer system to use Dragon Dictate, which lifted me from feeling pretty useless. Having a positive goal for the future made me impatient to start the next term at The College of Adult Education.

In the meantime, I was still going to the gym on my tricycle, and Ian was feeling able to leave me to work away for a few days each week. After that first Christmas on the boat, I had accepted that the difficulties caused by my disabilities meant we were unlikely to make much use of the boat. By chance, John, having graduated from Aston University, had his first full time job in London. He asked, "Could I take the boat and live on it in London? You see I can't afford the costs of accommodation."

Ian and I discussed it and, as we weren't likely to need it before the summer, it seemed a good idea. John and one of his friends collected the boat from Shardlow and moved it down to a mooring in Little Venice. We were amused at the vision of John cleaning down the outside of the boat and polishing the brasses on warm sunny days. Though perhaps it wasn't quite so idyllic on cold and wet days, it certainly provided a cheap place to live in central London and allowed him to save a little money towards a deposit for a flat.

It was a good decision.

The next, more difficult decision came as a result of an unexpected phone call. I picked up the phone and a voice inquired, "Miss Armitage?"

"Yes," I responded cautiously.

"It's Morgan Cars here, you have reached the top of the waiting list. Can I ask you for further details, of model and colour you require?"

I thought for a while and then said, "I'm married now."

He responded, "I thought you would be!"

I then explained that due to illness I wasn't able to see well enough to drive. Then he said, "Just let me know when you are ready. I will keep your place on the list."

We discussed the prospect of having a Morgan in our garage and me not being able to use it. I realised that it really had been just as a pipe dream. Although I enjoyed the idea of driving a Morgan car, Ian had always considered that a car was just a necessary form of transport, though he did have to admit that when he changed the Escort for a top of the range, fuel injected, 4x4 Scorpio, it was a wonderful car to drive. It was a car to enjoy and be noticed in. Unfortunately the criminal fraternity also noticed it and, after enjoying it for many years, it was stolen from a car park one evening. Whilst seeking a replacement, it was back to relying on my old yellow Metro until he was able to buy a Toyota Carena E, which, as it turned out, was a car that was built at the Burnaston factory whilst he was working there.

Kay Kay had had a litter of puppies, and we kept one. After much controversy, we called her Flo. I wanted to call her Flush after Elizabeth Barrett Browning's dog of the same name. Ian refused to go around calling Flush. He said it sounded like an instruction for a toilet! I said, "With all the difficulties we've had naming dogs, it's a good job we didn't have children together, we would never have managed to agree about names!"

Flo was a good puppy, and she was not much of a problem

as she grew up, until one day she found a rabbit carcass, and one of the bones of the rabbit became stuck in her teeth. She could only manage to eat soft food and fortunately I had a piece of Quiche left over from the weekend. Flo was able to eat that, but at a cost of 99p from Waitrose, it was an expensive way to feed a dog, and anyway I only had one slice left! I rang the vet and made an appointment. Ian was working away and, as I wasn't sure when both dog's vaccinations were due, I decided to walk with both of them to sort that out as well. The vet had no difficulty in extracting the rabbit bone. He checked the vaccination certificates, and I started to walk home. I was just congratulating myself on my achievement, when I tripped and lay on the ground like a stranded starfish, one lead in each hand. I realized that I couldn't manage to get up without letting go of at least one of the leads. Cars were rushing by, and I was still trying to work out what to do, when a car stopped and two people got out.

The man said, "We recognised the dogs, are you alright?"

With that his wife took the leads from me, and he sat me up against his legs, explaining, "I am a paramedic, just rest for a while, but you are going to need stitches on that cut you know."

All the time, he was pressing a dressing pad on my forehead.

I said, "I can't possibly go to hospital, I've got the dogs to look after!"

I had hardly got the words out, when two people from one of the adjacent houses arrived and were looking at me. When they saw the state I was in, the man said, "You have to go into Accident and Emergency to have this cut stitched!"

I was still leaning against the paramedic's legs while protesting that I couldn't go into hospital because of the dogs. Then that man's wife joined in saying, "My husband is a retired Orthopaedic Surgeon, and I'm afraid this cut is going to need stitching. We have had dogs, so we can look after them until you get yourself sorted."

Now I was completely outnumbered. From the way the surgeon's wife was speaking, it suggested that she was a nurse, and probably trained in the late fifties or early sixties. Clearly there was to be no argument! I had to accept my fate. The surgeon's wife took the dog leads, and the paramedic's wife helped me into his car. I can recommend being in paramedic's hands as a good way to arrive at a hospital. The paramedic obviously knew just where to find a wheelchair; he pushed me into the hospital and checked me in.

I was very grateful to him as I said, "Goodbye, and thank you!"

The doctor and staff nurse took some persuading that, apart from the cut, I didn't have any other symptoms, then the doctor said, "I have put four stitches in the cut, you won't have to have them removed because they will dissolve. If you feel all right, with no headache, you are ready to go home."

"Oh thank you, I do feel fine," I replied.

I sat in the discharge area and tried to work out what to do about getting home. The majority of the taxi company's staff are Muslim, and no matter how anglicised they are, they tend to dislike and are cautious about dogs. However, I had no alternative but to ask the staff to call a taxi for me. Again I was very lucky, because when the taxi arrived, it was driven by my favourite driver. An ex-cockney, he had often picked me up previously and we chatted about his arrangements for his holiday in Cuba. On one previous occasion, when he collected Sarah and myself from the railway station, he kissed me on the cheek. Sarah was amazed and when we arrived home on that occasion, told Ian, "Well, I've never seen the like, my Mum being kissed by the taxi driver!"

When I explained the situation, and how the dogs were being cared for at a house in Audley Gate, he was quite happy to collect the dogs and take us all home. Apart from a rather sore head, I was relieved that Flo was OK. As I felt rather exhausted I just rested for the remainder of the day.

That weekend Sarah came to stay and after a delicious roast meal we all retired for the night. I was asleep quickly, but then I woke during the night with something wet and sticky at the back of my head.

I went into the bathroom to use the toilet, and passed out. Ian was woken by the sound of the crash as I fell. He shot up in bed and rushed to help me. I regained consciousness very quickly, and Ian asked, "Are you all right? The pillow is covered in blood."

He bent over to help me, and then he said, "Sorry, I am very dizzy, I'm going to have to lie down again. I'll call Sarah."

Sarah came and took over, but when she examined me she passed out and laid across my body. I lay there for a while trying to make sense of the situation and then called out, "Can you hear me, Ian?

"Yes," came the response.

"Do you think you could just press 999 and get down the stairs to open the front door?"

I heard him on the phone, and then going down stairs very gingerly, before coming back to sit with me. Sarah was still lying sparked out, across my body when the ambulance arrived.

I heard them at the door and called out, "I'm lying on the bathroom floor, can you come upstairs?"

Footsteps on the stairs, and two paramedics, one male and one female, were peering at me.

I said, "I am quite comfortable lying here for a while. This is my daughter and this my husband, by the way." I added as an attempt of some sort of an explanation. I suppose they must have been amused, because the ambulance woman said, "We are off duty in two hours, so you really need to be taken in."

With that, they helped Sarah back to her bed and me onto a chair to take me downstairs. Ian, in the meantime, had managed to get himself dressed and was ready to come with me in the ambulance as well.

We were still very amused when we arrived at the hospital. The ambulance crew was smiling, and kindly wished me all the best!

Whether it was because Ian and I were still chuckling, or perhaps he had just had a very busy night, and didn't appreciate our amusement, the doctor really seemed quite irritable. He pulled my hair as he stitched me up and was very rough in the way he handled me. The lights were very bright and, as a result, caused me a lot of pain, although I did my best to keep my eyes closed, the general amusement of the evening was soon dispelled. Both Ian and I were relieved when it was time to go. Tersely the doctor's said, "You will need to go to your general practitioner in three days to have the stitches removed."

Fortunately, the stitches were removed without further problems, and I was soon back at the gym none the worse for my recent encounter with the pavement. Ian continued working in Horsham and staying away for three nights a week. Meanwhile I was confidently traveling back and forth to the gym on my tricycle, whilst taking care not to tip it over again. As I was still unable to hold a cup, the gym kindly equipped me with a mug so that I could have a coffee after my workout. As I was progressing well, Lisa included stretches and some floor exercises to help stretch the muscles in my abdomen. As a reward for my efforts I considered it appropriate to award myself a doughnut with my coffee.

I was sitting and enjoying my break whilst watching a little boy of about four years old with his grandmother and her friend. Seeing me watch her, the slim blonde lady came over to me. Hand extended she smiled, and said, "Hello, I'm Margaret, and this is my grandson Anthony, and my friend Margie. Would you like to come and join us?"

I was charmed by her and said, "That would be nice, thank you."

I enjoyed drinking my coffee with these nice people and

having a chat, before I climbed onto my tricycle and headed for home.

Once when we were talking, I mentioned that I was hoping to go on a John Clare trip to Helpston to see the house where the poet was born.

Margaret said, "I'd like to go to there to."

So Stan, her husband, collected us and off we went to Helpston. The old house was very atmospheric, and I thoroughly enjoyed the visit, and was very grateful for the good company and the transport both ways.

My trips to the gym were going well until one day, when I arrived home from the gym after a good work out, I was feeling a bit strange. I had pains in my back, around the area of my kidneys. I thought it best to just go and lie down in bed for a rest.

Apparently, I lost consciousness, and when Carmen from across the road noticed, she said to her husband, Geoff, "There is something wrong at Annie's. The house lights are not coming on as normal."

Carmen and her husband had five children to look after, as well as both having full-time jobs. At the time Carmen was working as a teacher in Computing Studies at Peterborough Regional College, somehow she wasn't too busy to notice and be concerned about what was happening across the road. She went next door to her neighbour, Pam's. But Pam was out and there was no reply. In the meantime, Ian was very worried when I didn't answer his regular pre-arranged 4pm phone call. This had been set up so that he could check each afternoon that I didn't have any problems. Ian kept trying, with no success, and in the end he rang Pam's number. There was no answer there as well, and so he left a message on her answer-phone.

At 9.30 that evening, when Pam and her husband, Brian, arrived home from their evening out, they were to find Ian's anxious answer-phone messages, and Carmen on the doorstep asking, "Have you got a front door key to Annie's house? I think there must be something wrong." With that, Pam collected the key and they came over the road to check. They let themselves in and found me upstairs wandering about, the bed sheets soiled. I was completely disorientated and didn't know where I was or, in fact, who I was!

Pam rang for an ambulance and then Ian. Ian checked out of his hotel and headed for the station. The ambulance arrived, and Pam accompanied me to the hospital. In the meantime, Carmen stripped the bed and took the sheets home to wash them. Unfortunately, Ian just missed the train and had to wait another hour for the next one. Pam, having just arrived home after a good evening out, stayed with me in the hospital, patiently waiting for Ian to arrive. For some reason, I kept trying to climb off the trolley, with Pam valiantly ensuring that I came to no harm.

The Accident and Emergency staff, having appraised the situation, contacted Dr Sheehan, who suggested setting up a drip of one gramme of steroids. It was 2.30 am when Ian eventually arrived at the hospital to relieve Pam. He had returned home by taxi with his suitcase and then driven to the hospital. Ian stayed with me for at least three hours until 5.30, when I was moved to the admissions Ward 1Z. Apparently all this time I was still endeavoring to climb off the trolley.

Once I was in the ward Ian went home, no doubt exhausted.

But I remember very little about it, except a vague memory of thinking, "I don't think much of these commodes in John Lewis's these days." The day after my admission, Ian rang Sarah and John. I was aware of John coming to my bedside, holding my hand and crying.

CHAPTER 12

REFLECTIONS

Slowly I became more and more aware of what was going on, and was able to get to the toilet and shower on my own. One afternoon, when Ian came to visit me he said, "What are these tablets in your locker?"

I answered, "I didn't notice they were there. They must have been put there when I went to the toilet."

Ian said, "I had better check they are meant for you before you take them."

With that he went away and eventually came back with a nurse.

She said very crossly, "You should've taken these this morning."

I was on the verge of tears as she stalked off.

I said to Ian, "Honestly, I had no idea they were there."

He responded, "Surely it isn't your responsibility to make sure you take the pills, isn't that what nurses are for? It must be up to them to see that you take medication. Don't say it, in your day it was definitely the nurse's responsibility to ensure all patients take their pills on time!"

I cheered up at that and just nodded.

Dr Sheehan decided that I needed one gramme of steroids intravenously every three days, presumably checking my blood results after each treatment. Consequently, I spent the next nine days with increasing awareness of what was going on around me, and little else to do except watch. Perhaps it goes without saying that I wasn't very impressed with what I saw. Almost without exception they seemed to have an attitude of indolence. I did try to be objective rather than judgemental, but I was amazed as I watched them moving about. When we were trained, one of the first and most important things we had to learn, even before going near a patient's bedside, was how to lift without putting undue strain on our backs. I was horrified as I saw the overweight nurses completely ignoring even the most rudimentary approach when lifting a patient, not that they did much of that! It led me to wonder how many nurse's back injuries were simply a result of not being taught manual-handling techniques. But then the nurses who were shuffling about on 1Z had such dreadful postures that I doubt whether anything would have helped.

Just then my attention was drawn to two nurses who arrived with bedding. A patient in the bed opposite had been discharged. Chatting to each other, and with no attention given to what was going on in the rest of the ward, the nurses simply changed the sheets as if in a domestic household. I remember that when I was a nurse and a patient was discharged two nurses, working in pairs, stripped the bed, wiped the mattress down with spirit of chlorhexidine, turned the mattress over, and re-made the bed. Then, when one of the nurses returned the linen trolley to the sluice room, the other nurse cleaned the locker out, again with spirit of chlorhexidine. I wondered whether all this had been found to be pointless in reducing hospital acquired infection, or if it had simply been forgotten about in their race for academic qualification. I certainly wasn't aware of any reported incidence of M.R.S.A. or C. difficile when I was a nurse.

I noticed what appeared to be a bloodstain on the floor and decided to monitor how long it would take them to remove it. I was sure that it had been there when I arrived and I was particularly observant when the domestic supervisor, with her assistant, arrived on the ward, both of whom I recognised from many years before. In spite of contracting out, they both appeared to be employed in the same roll. They went around the ward ignoring the blood stain and, as the supervisor wiped her finger along a windowsill and showed it to her deputy, I thought, "If this was a quality audit, shouldn't it include taking note of the bloodstain?" The years had taken their toll on the supervisor; she had put on so much weight.

At one of the visiting times, Ian remarked, "I think that in the NHS has let the nursing-staff down, because most of them seem to be obese, if not very obese."

I laughed, "Perhaps being overweight is a criterion for employment in the current NHS."

Then I became thoughtful, "Well you see nowadays they hardly seem to move, they spend most of their time by the computers ostensibly working but as far as I can work out it is mainly chat.

Sometimes there are as many as three or four of them together. If I wanted to be charitable, I could say that they were discussing the condition of their patients, but whenever I go past on my way to the toilet, they seem to be talking about things like what they did last night."

Ian just shook his head without saying anything, and I continued, "Just this morning, as a nurse was making my bed on her own I said to her, 'It takes two and a half times as long for a nurse to make a bed on her own...' Do you know what she said? She said there isn't anyone else, it's staff shortages."

I added, "Then another nurse wandered along and said that she was going for her break. When she came back she stank of cigarette smoke. What I can't understand is the seemingly complete lack of structure and organisation. I can remember time and motion experts being employed to study the nurses and evaluate the most efficient ways to do things."

Ian interjected, "I don't suppose there would be much point in studying nurses time and motion these days, there doesn't seem to be much motion amongst them."

I laughed and carried on, "Surely it can't just be a shortage of staff. No matter how many nurses are employed they seem to always say there aren't enough. Nurses have the power of emotional blackmail; political parties just can't risk alienating them as this would lead to public outcry. Nurses hold the country over a barrel, that nurse just went out for a smoke, came back and sat at a computer consul to chat about what she did last night. It breaks my heart to see it."

Ian's response was, "It doesn't surprise me at all."

I was feeling very dispirited, despite Ian having heard it all before I continued, "In the 1960s the staffing levels were four nurses to a ward of 34 patients. With the ward sister and possibly a senior staff nurse as well if we were lucky. The most senior nurse supervised the meal trolley while the rest of us stood by, each holding a tray to take the meal to the bedside, and ensured that the patient had enough to eat."

Ian said, "When you were in Addenbrooke's you wouldn't have had any food if Sarah hadn't come in to feed you at lunchtimes, and I hadn't come in to feed you in the evenings, and clean your teeth. As it was, when you were discharged, you only weighed six stones."

I said, "I bet my Iliac crests stood out like chapel hat-pegs!"

Ian said, "What ever are they?"

"My hip bones"

Ian laughed and kissed me goodbye, leaving me deep in thought.

I lay in bed watching the goings-on. I had all the time in the world to think and wonder. I felt sad as I thought, Am I looking through rose tinted spectacles?" No! Definitely not. I accept that the strict militaristic routines of the old training hospitals would not be acceptable in this current era of human rights equality etc. But gone are so many important responsibilities; ensuring that a patient has enough to eat, that a patient's environment is scrupulously clean, and the tender loving care, even when all hope of recovery was lost. Surely that is the very least that should be offered. It was depressing to see how so called progress had lead to the loss of these healthcare essentials.

There was lots of time to reflect about the nurses who had gone before, and I wondered what Florence Nightingale, or Edith Cavell would have made of what was happening now. In my time we were expected to be role models, proud but considerate, kind but efficient; this was not my perception of the present. The very idea of a nurse going out for cigarette would have been preposterous, and none of my group smoked anyway. I was never involved in the selection process nor aware of those that failed, but how were they selected now? I can only remember one nurse leaving for a different career, now I gather that the attrition rate is around 40%, that must mean that things are not right. Their deportment also left a lot to be desired, they moved with very poor posture. Was the wastage largely due to back injuries? What were the costs to the Health Service for treating the injuries, and the cost of wasted recruitment and training of nurses that left before qualification?

As I settled down to sleep for the night, I was remembering that the minimum qualification entry to our preliminary training school was just three O levels. We spent six weeks in the preliminary training school split into groups of three, and under strict guidance by the tutor had various lessons in physical nursing activities; we took it in turns, for example, to blanket-bath each other. In that way we were able to understand how a blanket-bath felt. We had to lift and move a patient without putting undue strain on our backs, by bending our knees. We had to carry ourselves with pride, whilst our hair was fastened under caps, so that when we moved about our hair didn't actually move.

I was deep in thought but before I actually went to sleep the night nurse had come on duty on 1Z. I noted her dreadful posture and gait, her hair was loosely tied back, and she frequently and absentmindedly twisted her hair around her fingers. I wondered why, if even the local pub or the gym had specific requirements for catering staff to have their hair secured under their hats, shouldn't nurses be the same? How can it be that the nurse's uniform no longer includes hats? I couldn't understand this conundrum as I fell asleep.

The next day I felt much more cheerful. At visiting time, Pam came to see how I was getting on. It was lovely to see her. We chatted about what was happening to me and discussed how, together with Carmen, she'd found me, and the sorry state that I had been in.

Later I was thinking that I fully appreciated that times had changed, but somehow I thought that the powers had perhaps thrown the baby out with the bath water. In the past it was perhaps a bit silly that we had to make sure that the open side of all pillowcases were placed facing into the ward and away from the window, to avoid any chill draughts from it. Clearly this practice was not appropriate in days of double- glazing, it was the culture of structure and discipline that was so important. Now I watched the nurses shuffle about, often with their hair loose and long, giving the general appearance of an unmade bed. They wouldn't go for a night out looking like that.

I was still melancholic, lost in thought about days gone by, when Val and her husband, Geoff arrived. After we had exchanged kisses, Val said, "I bet that you aren't giving you enough to eat, so I've cooked some egg custard tarts for you. They'll be very nutritious and help to build you up."

I smiled, "Oh thank you Val, you know they are one of my favourites!"

So, equipped with a cup of tea in a holder, I was able to

make the most of my teatime treat. Those egg custards were the most delicious that I'd ever tasted!

Even the patients didn't seem to want to mix, and any appearance of a nurse was not only very fleeting but also quite officious. I was concerned when an African lady was admitted; she seemed lonely and confused by the goings-on. As the other patients ignored her, I went over to her, held her hand, and introduced myself. She didn't respond to me, so I returned to my bed somewhat crestfallen. Dr Sheehan came to tell me that if my next blood results were OK I could go home.

When I got home and was able to look in the mirror I realised what a peculiar sight I must have presented. The effect of the huge doses of the steroids had caused my face to swell and I had developed the classic moon face that is caused by heavy doses of steroids. The black lady and the other patients must have thought that I was very odd.

His comments left me feeling very pleased with myself. As Lupus is such a complex disease with many and varied symptoms, I had taken it upon myself to write an annual report each time that I had seen Dr Sheehan. I had always tried to restrict myself and keep these to one side of A4, allowing myself to put just three questions at a time.

In this way and with just annual routine appointments with Dr Sheehan, I could be focused on the important problems that I had. Each year I took in two copies, one for myself and one for Dr Sheehan, and together we worked through my notes. My memory was still quite poor, so I decided that if I just approached each appointment trying to remember 'off the cuff' how things had been and how I felt, I was bound to forget something important. Not only that, it would take much longer and be an inefficient use of his time. So I was very pleased that he had taken my reports seriously and maintained them in my file. I knew that I could always arrange an ad hoc appointment should I need it.

Ian walked in as usual. I couldn't wait to tell him my news, so even before he had given me a kiss, I said, "I can come home straight away."

Ian responded with, "I had better go and see if I can find anyone at Ward Control."

And without further ado he set off in search of a member of staff. He actually found the Ward Sister and came back to say, "They have made two hospital appointments, one for the Anti-coagulant Clinic on Monday morning, and one to see Dr Sheehan two weeks on Thursday. Apart from that you just have to carry on as normal. I'll bring the car around the front entrance if you can empty your locker. I collected some plastic bags from a nurse."

As I emptied my locker, I discovered some bed socks at the back of a lower shelf. They weren't mine. I wondered how long they'd been there and whether they'd still be there if I ever came back to the same bed again.

"How long do you think they've been there?" I asked Ian as we drove home.

He laughed, "Probably until they demolish the hospital," he replied. As for me it was great to get home, and the dogs were very excited to see me. I felt well, and no worse for my hospital stay, though still sad about what was happening to my profession.

The dogs were as enthusiastic as always when I was able to go out to walk them, but apart from that and the hospital visits I just rested whilst Ian took care of me, and I slowly recovered. I kept my appointments at the Anti-Coagulant Clinic and the hospital provided the transport. After one such visit, I said to Ian, "Do you know, there is something different about the hospital? When I sat waiting for my lift home in ambulance transport, two really smart, uniformed women marched in. They were slim and well presented, and they even took off their hats and tucked them under their elbows before they strode off into the hospital. Do you know what they were doing?"

Ian said, "I think that they are RAF personnel, I heard that the RAF hospital at Ely had transferred some staff to Peterborough Hospital."

I was intrigued, "I wonder if that will have an effect on Peterborough Hospital."

Ian said, "Well it could do with improving."

I was thinking about this. The RAF personnel looked so smart and walked as if they meant business. Certainly it was better than the general air of being scruffy and sloppy that the Peterborough nurses usually displayed when they shambled into work.

Ian accompanied me to my review appointment with Dr Sheehan at Edith Cavell Hospital. Dr Sheehan looked tanned and relaxed. He examined me, and then said, "I'm pleased that you are making such good progress."

Both Ian and I were reassured, and when I asked, "Do I still need to keep my October appointment next month?"

Dr Sheehan replied, "Yes, I think you should."

As we drove away I admired the large stone at the entrance to the hospital site, the name 'The Edith Cavell' beautifully carved. I thought, "The stone must give the visitors and patients a feeling of permanence and confidence as they arrive at the hospital." In fact I knew the commissioning Nursing Officer, Mary Stone and how hard she worked to get the Edith Cavell up and running. Later she was appointed Chief Nursing Officer. Mary was quite short in stature, but she had a commanding presence and was a nurse of the 'old school', my school! She was very strict, but fair in achieving a high level of care in her nursing team. Now retired, I could still see vestiges of the pride, caring and efficiency that she had endowed. So my view of nursing care wasn't totally all dismay and despondence.

Back at home, Ian asked, "Do you think you'll feel ready next week for me to return to work?"

I responded, "I will be fine, you go back. I'll be alright if we go back to things as they were before I was admitted."

The doorbell rang. On the doorstep stood Margaret, my friend from the gym.

I heard her say, "We wondered if Annie was all right because she hasn't been to the gym for quite a while."

Ian said, "Come in, Annie is in the kitchen."

Margaret said, "Stan, my husband, is waiting in the car for me."

Ian's response was, "Well why don't you both come in for a cup of tea?"

Stan came in and explained that they couldn't phone as the gym had said that they were not at liberty to give out member's telephone numbers. But of course as they knew where I lived, they decided to call and see how I was. The tall, slight figure of Stan looked concerned that they were imposing, whereas I was delighted to see them both. Ian came in with the tea, and I explained what happened since I last went to the gym.

Then Stan looked thoughtful and said, "If you want to come back to the gym but you're not fit enough to ride your tricycle, we could pick you up on Tuesdays and Thursdays, if you would like."

I felt like crying with gratitude and said, "Thank you!"

Ian asked, "Are you sure that you feel ready to go back and start on your fitness again?"

"Oh yes I do, definitely!" I replied.

This genuine act of kindness from people I barely knew was exactly what I needed. The concern for other people that Margaret and Stan demonstrated was admirable. After a work out in the gym it had been great to recover by sharing a cup of coffee, whilst chatting to Margaret and her friend, Margie. So my delightful keep fit routine was re-established on Tuesdays and Thursdays. While I did my exercises, Margaret and Marjorie were in the 'Over 50s Aerobics' class. They both found this exhausting, so they appreciated a restorative cup of coffee afterwards as well!

The gym again provided the opportunity for me to build up my general health and stamina, and this was a particular relief after my incarceration in hospital. Lisa, the fitness trainer, reviewed my training programme and again set out to strengthen the muscular support for my joints, without causing undue stress. My right hip greatly improved by working with her on the treadmill; my drag leg became virtually unnoticeable and my walking was restored back to almost normal again, as the muscles in my right hip strengthened to support the weakened ligaments. Lisa moved on to working on my right hand fingers and right arm. My fine finger movements started to improve as well. I said to Lisa, "I don't quite believe it, I have been to Occupational Therapy several times, they worked on my fine finger movements and I religiously did the exercises that they suggested, but they made little difference. You come along and immediately work out that I actually need to strengthen the muscles in my forearm in order to use my fingers properly. Why couldn't they see that and avoid all that waste of time and money?"

Lisa smiled and didn't comment. I wondered about all the people who couldn't afford a gym membership and just gave in to their disabilities because their OT was ineffectual.

I didn't mention all this to Dr Sheehan at my appointment in October, but we did discuss the worries I had with my 'hitchhiker effect', a condition where the ligaments and muscles pull the thumb into a permanently raised position so it looks as though one is hitch hiking particularly on my right hand. After examining my hands, he showed me how to stretch my thumb joints, whilst encouraging me to do it regularly. He was sympathetic when I explained how difficult it was for me to chop up anything as tough as an onion successfully, but he had no solution for that problem. We moved on to discussing the pills I was taking, and I explained that after the stress of my father's terminal illness and subsequent death, Dr Thompson had been concerned about my blood pressure and increased my dose of Lisonopril. I understood that this was a temporary measure, and asked, "Can I leave it off?"

"Not just yet, I suspect that you will have to keep taking it for some time to come," he said. I knew that he meant forever but he didn't want to totally disappoint. I then mentioned my discussion with Dr Thompson, when she had decided that I should keep some Uri sticks at home together with a course of Cephalaxin, so that if my urine was high in Leucocytes I could start taking the antibiotics straight away, thus hopefully avoiding the repeat of my last admission that had been due to an infection in my kidneys.

I told Dr Sheehan that Ian had taken me on holiday in Europe for a long weekend in Paris, though I didn't use up his valuable time by telling him what we'd done there. In actual fact we thoroughly enjoyed ourselves. We had had a delicious meal in the Eiffel Tower restaurant overlooking the Seine, enjoying the lovely view; it was magic. I had said to Ian at the time, "It is so wonderful to have the opportunity to come here, and especially because it is somewhere that when I was so ill I'd never dreamt it would be possible for me to go to. Thank you!"

Ian had smiled as he squeezed my hand, and said,

"Come on we are going to Notre Dame next." As we stood in the Cathedral, people were buying candles to light and dedicate their prayers, I remembered how Sarah's school friend Saskia had lit one for me when I was so ill. I couldn't get over how someone, although barely in her twenties and just at the age when students are often accused of being self obsessed, had been so thoughtful. In spite of being in such a beautiful city as Paris and with so much to just see and experience, she had thought of her friend's mother. I felt very humbled.

I was fortunate that Margaret and Stan were still collecting me for the gym twice a week, and I felt that I was making great progress as Lisa had incorporated pelvic floor exercises in response to my saying, "I have a horror of being an old lady who wets my knickers." In addition she added sitting twists, back stretches and back rises. I was quite content until she gave me bad news, said, "I am leaving the gym."

I was a bit down when I arrived home and Ian tried to cheer me up.

He said, "Shall we book another holiday? Where do you think you would you like to go?"

Straightaway I said decisively,"I've always wanted to go to Barcelona to see the Gaudi architecture!"

The next day we went to the travel agents and the tall, bronzed Jacquie said, "At such short notice, Barcelona is very expensive, how about booking Barcelona early for next year, it will be almost half as cheap, and booking Amsterdam this year?"

We agreed and confirmed the bookings. I was particularly pleased to be moving on without the threat of further hospital interventions and I was optimistic that I could leave most of the problems with my Lupus behind me.

We enjoyed the long weekend in Amsterdam and were amused by the fact that the bicycle ruled the streets. Sitting in the café of the Anne Frank museum with tears pouring down my cheeks, trying to enjoy the delicious lemon cheesecake after the tour of the house, I said to Ian, "I've always thought that I should go to a Nazi concentration camp like Auschwitz or perhaps Treblinka, but after the emotional feelings I have experienced here I don't think that I could cope with the stress of seeing all those little children's shoes in a great big pile. I don't think that I need to see it first hand now."

Ian wasn't crying but was obviously affected by the sombre atmosphere, he said, "Yes, it seems that this house conjures up the very presence of Anne Frank. I'm quite glad you don't want to go to a concentration camp after this."

"But I am very glad that we came," I said.

"Yes, it does put things in perspective," Ian agreed.

Though the Amsterdam holiday did put me off experiencing any further horrors of life under the Nazis, afterwards I said to Ian, "When I joined the pacifist movement in the sixth form, Dad sat me down and explained the fact that so many people gave their lives to fight the Germans in the Second World War so that we could have the freedom that we now enjoyed, but after his wartime experience in Egypt, he said, if we ever take on the Arabs we will never win. Remember that you have freedom because you have a bigger stick than the other fellow."

Ian said, "Its strange that you feel so strongly that the reason that the nursing profession was so good in your days was because it was formed by Florence Nightingale during the Crimean war, and you a closet pacifist!" My response was, "I know I'm a bore about how bad things are, but it's just as well that I can't go back to nursing as I expect that they would try to sack me for boring them to death when I keep on about the 'old days'."

Back home life returned to normal, Ian to work and I back to the gym. I missed the help that Lisa had given me and, although other fitness instructors took over, it wasn't quite the same. I was also missing June Counsel's help now. I was going to the Writers' Group classes at Brook Street. At Brook Street though we still took it in turns to read out our contributions, the tutor, Jeremy, seemed to be there under sufferance. There wasn't any positive feedback from him as far as I was concerned. When, in response to Jack's reading his work, I read mine, he commented, "I find these life stories boring. Nobody is interested in these sort of stories."

I was so dispirited, and decided that after the summer break I wouldn't go back for the next term, although I still met up with the group at Costas in Queensgate.

Jack asked, "Why haven't I seen you at the class recently?"

I responded, "Oh, I gave up writing when Jeremy said it was boring. I decided that there didn't seem much point in carrying on with it."

Jack looked surprised, but before he had a chance to reply one of the group having coffee, said, "You mustn't let that put you off, would you like me to read what you have written so far?"

I felt very grateful saying, "If you wouldn't mind, thank you, Anne. "

As it turned out the lady's name was Anne Elphick, and she had moved to Peterborough from London where she had previously been a teacher in Brick Lane School. I regularly delivered my work with a prepaid envelope for its return. She sent it back quickly with many helpful comments.

Now at least with the help of my voice activated Dragon Dictate and Anne Elphick's support I was able to pick up where I left off. But then I faced another obstacle, trying to keep the house clean. As time went by, various cleaning ladies came and went and I wasn't quite sure why it was that they never stayed very long. So when I needed to find another one, I went to our small, thatched Post Office to get the number of the cleaning ladies who had advertised in the window. Back at home I rang one of the numbers and it was answered by a lady with a strong Scottish accent.

She said, "Hello, Janette speaking."

I explained the reason for my call, and we exchanged details. Janette came the next week, but unfortunately her approach to cleaning was more like 'a bull in a china shop'. She didn't show any concern or respect for the things around her. From the start she didn't approve of 'Henry', our tried and tested old vacuum cleaner, and she demanded we buy a new Dyson instead. Reluctantly we complied with her wishes but in her hands the Dyson proved to be a much heavier weapon, as she bashed around our house. I said to Ian, "I could understand it more if she was young and careless, but she must be near to retirement age."

Ian replied, "Hopefully she will retire soon."

Items were frequently broken as she left a trail of devastation. When she broke an antique plate she said, "Well you shouldn't have left it in out on show if it was so valuable should you? You should keep it safely in a china cabinet. Then I wouldn't have dropped it."

I didn't seem to have any answer to this admonishment, and we just continued on as before. I really should have given her the sack but I was worried about replacing her, as good cleaners seemed like 'hen's teeth'. I dreaded her coming.

When Ian arrived home, he took to saying, "What has she broken this time? When are you going to get rid of her?"

But luck was with me when Janette announced, "We have decided to go back to live in Scotland near my daughter."

Instead of breathing a huge sigh of relief, I simply said, "Oh but when are you going?" feigning disappointment.

I was very grateful when she said next week and I sat back with relief, knowing that my weekly torture was about to end. For a while we struggled without getting a replacement.

Eventually I went back to the Post Office. This had recently changed hands and was now being run by Linda and Steve, a Yorkshire couple from Doncaster. The small, smiling, blonde Linda ran the Post Office counter, whilst Steve, who had retired from his previous job as a lorry driver, ran the shop. Coincidentally the previous manager had also been a lorry driver, but he hated the job and consistently displayed a lack of patience towards his customers. The grey bearded Steve appeared to take a delight in his new role, especially ensuring that all the little children who peered into the glass fronted counter to choose their penny sweets were happy with their purchases.

The older customers didn't seem to mind the delay caused by the children The atmosphere in the Post Office was quite convivial, generally one of a community at peace with itself. Steve and Linda didn't just settle into running a village post office, but under their management the post office again became the hub of the community. This included Charlton Court, which was a small close of Sheltered Housing just a short stroll from the Post Office. The residents, often supported by their walking frames or other walking aids, were able to travel the short distance to buy their groceries and keep in touch with the rest of the village. Steve hired Myra, a standby assistant and one of our neighbours. The post office became the centre of the community and principal information centre. If perhaps there was a death or someone was taken into hospital one would ask, "Have you told Steve at the Post Office?"

So when Steve noticed me looking at the adverts for a cleaning lady, he said, "You want to ring Val's number."

I had no hesitation in taking his advice. Val duly arrived and we agreed terms. She came with Natasha, more often just called Tash, and they worked together chatting and laughing as they went efficiently around our house. They left me feeling very pleased with the results after the first visit. When they were due to come for the second time, I realised that I was short of milk and the eggs were getting low, so I hurried up to the Post Office just before they were due to arrive. As I made my way home alongside the tennis courts, and across some very old crooked and uneven flagstones I tripped and fell heavily face down. I lay for a while getting over the shock. The blood was pouring down my face. I turned over checked my purchases and thought, "Well at least the milk and eggs havn't become a massive omelette." I was feeling very shaky and I got home and lay on the bed. After a while, I got up and looked in the mirror. I looked a terrible mess and thought, "If Val sees me like this she will probably just go away." So, when she arrived, I hid behind the door. When I opened it and revealed my state, instead of turning tail, Val said, "Annie sit down, now what have you done? Tash put the kettle on. Annie, where is your first aid kit?"

Val gently and expertly cleaned and dressed my wounds, while I sat and drank my tea. Val and Tash then got on with cleaning the house, but before they left, Val asked, "Have you told any of your neighbours Annie?"

I replied, "No, I'll be alright, I'll just have a rest."

Then Val said, "I'm not leaving here until you tell someone."

"Tash, watch Annie from the study window as she goes across the road, until someone opens their front door. Otherwise she'll just go around the corner and pretend she's told someone".

It was a done deal, and as I made my way across to Pam's I was thinking, "It's a good job I trust Val more than she trusts me."

I rang Pam's doorbell, Pam opened the door and she said, "Annie what have you done? Sit down, Brian put the kettle on."

I explained the situation, Pam asked, "Why didn't you come and tell me straight away?"

I responded, "Ian has got a very busy week, so the last thing he needs is to have to come home because I've done something silly."

Pam looked thoughtful, and then she said, "I will do you a deal, if you come into A and E with me, I won't tell him."

There was nothing else for it and, as Pam went across the road to tell Val what was happening, Brian got his new, black Mercedes out of his garage and I obediently got into the back seat. Pam came back and off we went to A and E. She checked me in and, after a short wait, the housewoman drew the screens around the trolley that I was lying on. After a discussion about the circumstances and my medical history, the House woman said, "I think you need to come into the observation ward overnight."

I replied, "Can I just discharge myself for five minutes, so that I can inform my husband?"

She looked surprised, but agreed.

I went out with Pam, explaining, "If Ian hears the strength in my voice he'll be reassured that I am allright really, and he doesn't need to rush home."

So Pam being happy to take care of the dogs overnight, and Ian accepting the situation, I changed into a hospital gown and was taken to the observation ward.

I spent a comfortable night but was awake at six am, listening to the ward sounds. I was grateful to have a wristwatch, and it seemed to be ages until the screens of my bay were drawn back at eight am.

A pleasant voice asked me, "Would you like two slices of toast for breakfast?"

I replied enthusiastically, "Yes please."

She went away, and it was so long before she returned with the toast, that I had decided that she'd forgotten. Anyway, the toast was very nice, she put butter on it and helped me to sit up comfortably, so that I could drink my tea and eat my breakfast before she went on to the next bed. When I heard the next patient say she would like toast, I sneaked a look at my watch to see how long the toast making procedure actually took. It was nearly 15 minutes later when she returned with it. I was still musing about the length of time taken, when the housewoman came to examine me and agree my discharge. I washed, put my clothes on and Pam arrived to take me home. The dogs apparently had been good, and they were very pleased to see me.

The following month, feeling pretty fit I rushed about doing the weekly shopping in the town. I was booked in for an appointment to get my eyes tested. There were two small, side pedestrianised roads off the principal road that lead towards Queensgate. The opticians, Smith and Hamilton, was in one of them; I took the wrong turning, panicked, and when I realised my mistake and that I would be late, rushed towards the other, turned, tripped and fell face down, glasses bent at peculiar angles. I lay there with blood trickling down my face, feeling silly and cross with myself but aware that I would be late for my appointment. Two smart ladies in suits were peering over my prostrate body.

One asked kindly, "Are you alright?"

I turned over and said, "I just need a plaster, I'm going to the opticians, I'm sure they will have one."

But before I could finish my assertion, a group had gathered around me.

One lady said, "I am a nurse .She needs go into hospital for this, it's going to need stitches. Has anyone got a mobile phone?"

One of the first ladies on the scene said, "We called an ambulance as soon as we saw her trip."

I protested, "But I'm going to the opticians, I will be late."

Then I heard the ambulance siren and there was no escape!

Two traffic wardens were next on the scene, one asked, "Have you got a car in a car park?"

I smiled, "No I haven't thank goodness. "

One of the suited ladies offered to call in at the opticians to explain what had happened.

An ambulance man picked up my belongings, carefully wrapping a lens that had fallen out of my spectacles in a sterile dressing, and without more ado I was put into the ambulance and we headed to the hospital. I was feeling guilty for not having thanked the suited ladies, who were the first on the scene, and wondering again at the kindness of strangers. I was soon in the Accident and Emergency Department. A very kind and efficient nurse was examining my wound.

A doctor set to with stitches, and there was a lot of enquiry about whether I'd passed out and if I needed to stay in observation overnight.

I said, "I have to get home to look after the dogs, and they will need a walk."

"What sort of dogs are they?" the nurse asked.

"Cocker Spaniels, and there is open space for me to exercise them not far away."

405

She obviously knew her breeds, because she was happy that I could handle their walk bearing in mind the state I was in. The doctor managed to put the lens back into my frames. Thanking him, I asked jokingly "And what do you do the rest of the time, when you are not mending spectacles?"

He laughed and said, "I work part-time as a general practitioner."

I thought, I bet he's a good one, and then remembered that I had a hair appointment the next day and asked, "I have a hair appointment tomorrow, will it be alright to have my hair washed?"

He responded, "That'll be the best way to get the blood out of your hair, with a backwash."

They ordered me a taxi, and I went home thinking, "Well that was the best of treatment, I certainly couldn't complain about that trip to the hospital!"

Arriving home I rang the opticians to apologise about my missed appointment. They already knew, the suited ladies had been as good as their word and stopped by to explain what had happened. I re-made the appointment, but it wasn't until I was walking the dogs the next morning that I realised how shaky I was still feeling. I was thinking, "Cocker Spaniels are good dogs to have in this situation!" The dogs rushed around in the bushes and didn't need much input from me. I blew my whistle when we got to the corner where I habitually put them back on their leads. Fortunately they came back straight away, looking expectant. This was simply because of the good performance biscuit I gave them as a reward for their prompt return, all to do with my system that I'd trained into them. If either of them didn't come straight away, the recalcitrant dog didn't get their biscuit. I wouldn't be conned by the baffled and hurt spaniel expression in response to a no biscuit situation.

After the walk, I was able to rest and recover for a little while before calling a taxi to go for my hair appointment, despite still feeling a little groggy from my exploits the day before. It was such a relief to have all the dried blood washed out. They didn't seem to mind, and Helen joked, "I don't know, you're not fit to be let out on your own!"

My hair done, I headed for Waitrose and, as usual, Pat was covering the till by the entrance. The normally cheerful blonde looked concerned and she asked,

"Are you all right Annie? You don't look very well. Would you like somebody to come round with you?"

Suddenly realising how weak I felt, I was very grateful, saying, "Yes please, I think that I could do with some help."

So before I knew where I was, another assistant took my list, attached it to my trolley, and we made our way around the aisles. "That's service!" I thought, feeling very relieved.

By the time Ian arrived home, and I'd had a rest, I felt much better.

Ian said, "Don't forget we're going to Barcelona the week after next. Are you sure you will be fit enough to go? After Barcelona, we will try to book early for Venice so we can get a good price."

I had almost forgotten, but I cheered up and got started with my packing and planning what I should take.

The stitches were dissolving and the bruises subsiding by the time we left for Gatwick Airport, and I was definitely on the mend. We stayed at the Hotel San Agusti for six nights.

Map in hand, we started exploring the city. The weather was perfect for sightseeing as we sat on the top deck of an open top tourist bus in the warmth of the early spring, Spanish sunshine. Were both very relaxed, and then suddenly I started to cry, "I can't believe how wonderful the Gaudi architecture is!"

I was looking at the architecture and the fantastic swirls of the metal work on the balconies on La Pedrera

"This is fantastic!" I said, then I added, "Is this Gaudi's interpretation of the influence of Art Nouveau adapted to suit Spanish culture?"

Ian grinned. He was used to my intense delight for

407

architectural excellence. He paused, laughed and said, "Can I take this architectural anorak to Casa Batllo tomorrow. The guidebook says that it is, 'Antoni Gaudi's masterpiece with an outstanding façade and the very fantastic chimneys are a sight that must not be missed by the visitor'."

The next day, I felt that it didn't quite belong to the real world; it was magic and of course that was what Gaudi had intended. I said to Ian, "I have wanted to come here to see this for 20 years, ever since I did the history of art and architecture at Hatfield Polytechnic. Is there anywhere you have always wanted to go?"

Ian immediately said, "Well, I've always wanted to go to the Galapagos."

CHAPTER 13

THE HOLIDAY

It was Ian's 60th coming up and this was the ideal surprise. The next time that Ian was staying away I went to see Jacquie at 'Going Places'. I couldn't see Jacquie so I was tentative as I asked, "Can you book a holiday to the Galapagos Islands from here?"

The lady at the desk looked doubtful. Then the tall, dark-haired Jacquie came out from somewhere at the back and said, "Hello Annie, yes we can arrange bookings for the Galapagos."

"You see Ian has always wanted to go to there, so I want to book the holiday for his 60th birthday which is in 18 months' time."

Jacquie said, "We don't have the brochure in for that year yet, but I can give you some guidance of the cost; it's around £2300 per person."

I said thoughtfully, "Perhaps it's a bit early to book."

"No, if you are sure about going, you need to book as soon as possible. The Galapagos trips gets booked up very quickly as the numbers of visitors each year are restricted. I will need £200 per person as deposit."

Clearly there was no time to lose, but I was left with several problems. I knew that I wouldn't be able to travel that far myself, and I knew that vaccinations would be required, thus ruling me out on both counts. I wanted the holiday to be a surprise but I thought he'd enjoy it more if he had someone to accompany him. There was quite a lot to think about. Ian's son, Trevor would be the obvious choice, particularly as he was a qualified ecologist.

I would have to contact Trevor to see if he was up for it and after that I would have to find the money. How could I manage to raise £4000, the estimate for two persons, without Ian, who scrupulously checks our banking accounts each month, finding out? I thought, "Sarah's good with money, she'll have some ideas." I rang Sarah to explain my dilemma, "I'm going to need to borrow about £4,000 for six weeks without Ian finding out, where can I get it on the cheapest rate of APR." She said, "No problem, I can let you have that Mum."

I was flabbergasted and said, "I did say £4,000."

Sarah responded, "Yes no problem it's exciting, and I want to be involved." Once I had recovered from my amazement that Sarah was able and prepared to lend me the money at such short notice, I rang Trevor to ask him, "Would you like to go to the Galapagos with your dad, and share a twin bed cabin with him?"

Trevor sounded surprised, "Are you really asking me if I want to go to the Galapagos? That's a holiday of a lifetime! Yes, of course I'd love to go the Galapagos with Dad."

Now I was anxious that if I didn't act quickly to deliver the deposit, I might miss the opportunity. I rang Sarah's number, no reply.

Fortunately and by chance Pam called in to see how I was feeling after the trip to Spain. I said, "I'm like a shaken up lemonade bottle waiting to go pop!"

I explained what was happening, Pam said, "If you gave me the travel agents number, I will put it on my credit card until you can pay me back." I managed to pay her back in dribs and drabs of cash so that Ian didn't notice the deficit in our cash flow

During the planning and deception I realised that I'd

never make an undercover agent or spy, as I was so stressed trying to keep things under wraps. A few months before the planned surprise Ian said, "If you haven't you got anything on tomorrow, why don't we go to the travel agent, and book a holiday in Venice?"

"Yes, that's a good idea," I said weakly, whilst I was dreading the thought of it in case somebody let the cat out of the bag. I suspected that my blood pressure was dangerously high as we walked in. Fortunately, Jacquie was there, and she acted as though she hardly knew me. Thanks to her apparent concentration on the computer screen, she was able to book Venice in good time for mid-spring of the following year and after the secret Galapagos trip.

So with nothing lost, and while Sarah was organising such things as ideas to decorate The Fox and Hounds with a Galapagos theme, I booked a table for 20 people on the Saturday evening before Ian's birthday. I then went about surreptitiously inviting friends and swearing them to secrecy. Next I went into Ian's General Practice to make an arrangement to see the practice nurse, and make arrangements for his injections. We both attended different practices, but fortunately the receptionist was very understanding, giving me an appointment for the following week. When I returned the next week, a different receptionist said that I didn't have an appointment. I produced my card. She looked bemused but directed me to an upstairs waiting room. It wasn't long until I was called in. The practice nurse said, "I wish someone would organize a trip to the Galapagos for me! But when will it be the best time for his injections?"

I thought for a bit, and then said, "On his actual birthday, it will probably be the only day that I can guarantee that he won't be working."

Then off I went to the travel agents and explained my arrangements to Jacquie, "We will be having a birthday

411

celebration for Ian at the Fox and Hounds on the 5th September would you like to come and bring a guest with you?"

Jacquie looked really pleased and said, "That's my local, I'd love to come!"

Not long after making the arrangements with Jacquie, she came into the Fox and Hounds with a female friend. Ian and I were sitting at a table having a drink.

Ian said, "Look there's the lady from the travel agents, I can't remember her name. Can you remember what it is?"

I tried to look blank whilst saying, "No, I've no idea. Sorry."

I was still desperately trying to look vague, when Jacquie came to our table and, as though she'd been primed, she said, "Hello, it's Jacquie from 'Going Places'."

After we both said "Hello" I added, "So, do you live round here?"

Jacquie said, "Yes, I live with my husband and children in Netherton."

I was very grateful when she went returned to her friend, leaving me thinking, "I have decided, I'm never ever going to do this business of a surprise again." Feeling even more stressed than I thought possible, I couldn't really believe that I would able to keep the deception up without Ian finding me out before his trip.

Other arrangements were necessary. I had to make sure that Trevor's passport was still in date, and check that he was arranging to have the injections that he needed. In addition, I decided that I should arrange to have my hair and nails done, and perhaps buy a new dress for the occasion. I went to John Lewis to see Val Ingram, because I knew from past experience that I could trust her to find something that would suit the occasion. Val was about my age, colouring and height, and together we choose a dress. She helped me into it, folded her arms and took a step backwards. She was clearly pleased with the result. She said,

"That would go really well with a pair of black ankle length boots."

"Yes, and I have already got a pair."

I was feeling very pleased with myself, as I went to pay, and I think that Val was too.

The following night when Ian was back at home, my gums started pouring with blood.

Ian said, "I'm going to have to phone for an ambulance."

In spite of the fact that I was thinking, "Oh no, this is just what I didn't need right now," I reluctantly agreed. At least the ambulance arrived quickly and the ambulance man gently but efficiently placed an oxygen mask on my face. I was soon in Accident and Emergency thinking, "Why do these sort of things always happens at the most inconvenient moments, its just two weeks before Ian's birthday party!" I resigned myself to the fact that I would probably have to have another hospital admission. I was surprised when my thoughts were interrupted by a doctor lifting my oxygen mask, she smiled at me and introduced herself. She was young, slim and exuded competence as she undertook my assessment, and said, "I think that you need to be admitted to Ward 1Z."

I accepted the situation with as much good grace as I could muster and while she packed her instruments away, I asked, "How long have you been working in Peterborough?"

She replied, "About four months, I am an RAF doctor."

She smiled encouragingly and now I realised just who these smart people were that I'd seen whilst I was waiting in ambulance transport after my outpatients appointments.

The hospital porter was now pushing me towards the dreaded Ward 1Z. I just hoped I wouldn't need to be in there very long. But then as soon as I arrived on 1Z I realised that something was different. The ward was in darkness as the nurse who was at my bedside actually took my hand. This gesture was very reassuring. It was the first time in all my inpatient experience that any nurse had taken me by the hand.

The nurse said, "Let me know if there is anything that you need, just press the bell."

She placed the bell in my hand, and then said,

"I have put some water on your locker, can you reach it?"

I simply said, "Yes thank you."

She said, "I will leave you to get some sleep now."

I did get some sleep, and when I opened my eyes the patient opposite me removed her earphones and came over to see me.

She said, "Oh! Good morning, I do apologize but I didn't see you arrive. I was concentrating on the radio; I work for Radio 4. My name is Amanda by the way."

I introduced myself, and then said, "I thought you could only get television on the ward."

Amanda said, "No you can receive the radio and it's free."

I couldn't believe that all those times I'd been in hospital I hadn't known about it, it would've been such a help to pass the time.

Amanda came over, connected my earphones and tuned in the radio.

"That is great, thank you very much!" I said.

As it happened, Amanda was due to have a gastroscopy, and she advised me that should I ever have one, to have it under general anaesthetic. She'd had it once before without and it was very unpleasant, it was far better to be knocked out.

For the first time in all those years of being in and out of hospital, I felt relaxed and confident about the nurses as they showed professionalism and care in whatever they did. For instance, when the drugs were given out, the nurse helped me take them. I still had the taste of blood in my mouth and I didn't much like eating, but a nurse was on hand to ensure that I was able to open the plastic food containers they were in. Previously it was just dumped on the locker by the contract caterers, and if I hadn't been able to attract anyone's attention to help me open the packet they would be removed, leaving me hungry and irritated by their abrupt manner.

I was amazed by what was going on. These nurses appeared fit and smart and set out to make sure I had everything I needed. Unlike my previous experiences, when any tasks were grudgingly performed. Now as I made my way back from the lavatory, pushing the drip-stand with its bag of blood hanging, there was one nurse at the computer, and she looked up and asked me in a kind voice, "Are you allright?"

"Yes thank you," I said.

As I trailed along, I was thinking, "That's the difference, if she had been an NHS nurse she wouldn't have stopped chatting with the other nurses, and if she did it would probably have been a question of well, "I am not your named nurse, so you are nothing to do with me!"

I was confused by the difference until I asked a nurse, and she explained, "I am an RAF nurse."

Then I asked her, "Where did you train?"

She explained, "I did a degree in nursing at the University of Nottingham and then applied to join the RAF."

I was left contemplating that perhaps I had been wrong all this time, blaming the university system of training for the breakdown in care I'd received over the past years. It wasn't necessarily the degree training, but there was perhaps something in the RAF selection process that ensured both empathy and fitness. As they went about their ward duties their posture indicated confidence and competence. "I bet they don't nip out for a smoke." I wondered about how their incidence of wastage and back injuries compared to the NHS nurses.

Then I remembered James Le Fanu's article, "Come Back Sister Prune Face, we need you". No, I thought, the reason why Sister Prune Face was able to care for her patients in the way that she did was surely due to the ethos of the nursing

415

administration in the hospital. I was sure that a disciplined approach to nursing was the answer. So why, and when did this hierarchy disappear? In my opinion, this is the crux of the matter. As a closet pacifist, I was amused to think that the Armed Forces still held onto a code of care for the patient. So it is not lost and gone forever!

I was just asking myself this when I was interrupted by a flurry of activity caused by a ward round. The Consultant, Dr Jonathan Rowlands, stood there surrounded by his acolytes. Previously, as Quality Assurance Manager I had quite a lot of contact with him. In due course he came and took the notes from the container at the foot of my bed and read them. I was thinking, "He was still slim and business like, but looked about 10 years older than we last met, but then I suppose it must have been about 10 years ago." Then he looked up saying, "Annie, it's you!"

With that he turned to the four or five people accompanying him, saying, "Do you know who this lady is?"

They all looked blank, and then he turned to me and said, "You haven't told them who you are, Annie, have you?"

I replied, "No Jonathan, I'm a patient on this ward."

Dr Rowlands then said, "This lady and I are old friends, we go back quite a long way. She used to be this hospital's Quality Manager."

I was proud that he still thought of me in such a professional way. He got down to business and asked, "Have you got any unusual symptoms?"

I had been a bit concerned that since I'd been in hospital my poo was black, so I replied, "Well I have had melanin stools, but I have swallowed quite a lot of blood, so I suppose it is quite understandable."

Clearly Jonathan wasn't happy with my self-diagnosis, and he said, "I will arrange for you to have a gastroscopy."

I really didn't think I needed one, but I did think it would be rather foolhardy to refuse, just in case. So I agreed in spite of being anxious to get on with Ian's birthday party arrangements.

I couldn't really judge whether I was treated any differently after the ward round, but I doubted it. During that time I'd been visited by Dr Sheehan, given two a blood transfusions and I was beginning to feel much better, but of course I'd agreed to a gastroscopy.

Fortunately I didn't have to wait long, and the very next day I was told to have only water. I had a shower, dressed in a theatre gown and lay down to wait. With a clanking sound, a trolley was pushed to my bed by two nurses dressed in theatre greens. "At least some things never change," I thought as I transferred myself onto the trolley. The two nurses were full of good humour as they pushed me through the ward, into the lift, then into theatre, and were continually making pleasant conversation. It made the whole process really quite pleasurable, and I relaxed. Then the anaesthetist approached me. He wanted to know all the details of my professional career; clearly Jonathan had filled him in about my background. It turned out that he had been working in Leeds General Infirmary when I had been working there during my vacations from Leeds University, he asked, "Would you like an anaesthetic?"

I responded, "Well it's like this, we have tickets for the Rolling Stones in London at the O2 arena this evening, so if I have an anaesthetic will it stop me from going?"

He asked, "What time are they on?"

"8 o'clock, " I answered.

He said, "I'm afraid whether you have anaesthetic or not, you won't make it. But I finish at 4 o'clock. so I could use your ticket."

I laughed, and said, "I'll have an anaesthetic then please."

With that, I floated away, and that was the last I knew about it, until I woke up back in bed on the ward.

Apparently, Sarah used my ticket, and went with Ian. So as she had a jolly good time, the ticket didn't to go to waste! The lady from Radio 4 has been discharged, and there was now a very confused old lady in her place. She kept calling out in the night, and however hard the nurses tried they could not pacify her. I'd always been dismissive about my risk of becoming addicted to anything. I'd never smoked a cigarette, or for that matter anything illegal. After having had too much alcohol and being ill, the idea of "the hair of the dog" the next day would be the last thing I'd consider, but I might vow, "I'll never do that again, until the next time". It was time to eat my words about not being susceptible to drugs, because after the experience of floating away in a haze of Valium, and facing a night disturbed by the constant demands of the old lady, I felt a desperate craving for just one more dose.

Fortunately I had no way of getting hold of any, and eventually I went to sleep. The next morning I was very relieved when Dr Rowlands came to tell me that there had only been some minor changes in my stomach lining. However he thought that I should have regular six monthly gastroscopies under the Barrets Surveillance follow up scheme. Apart from that, my blood results were fine and I was ready for discharge.

I was relieved to get home so that I could catch up with the birthday planning. Back in the gym the following week when Ian came to pick me up he said, "I've just checked our Passports, they are out of date."

With my heart in my mouth, I tried to be as casual as possible saying, "How long does it take to get Passports renewed?"

Ian's response was, "Oh about three months."

With that I started to panic saying, "That seems a long time, can't we do it quicker?"

He said, "Perhaps we can do it by express, but it would cost more."

"Lets do that then just in case we need them," I said.

My attempts at secrecy had been exposed and I was sure that Ian knew that I must have been planning something that involved foreign travel. I was left feeling very cross with myself, and even more so when it dawned on me that, with the passport offices being in Peterborough, it couldn't take three months! Had Ian set a trap? I couldn't ask him, but at least I was confident with the arrangements for his birthday and his present.

All seemed to be going well with my plans. Sarah and her husband, and John and his wife, had booked to stay at the nearby Holiday Inn. I had reserved a table for 20 at the local Fox and Hounds in Longthorpe, whilst swearing Steve, the landlord, to secrecy. Though I suppose it wasn't anything new to him he did seem to be amused at the idea. I asked him how early we could have access to the room to decorate it.

"Six o'clock," he responded.

My next task was to contact Sarah and all the other guests to give them the details and reiterate that they must keep it a secret. When I was in town, I called at the travel agents to see Jacquie. She confirmed that she would bring the tickets with her and present them to him when he arrived at the Pub.

All was going well, so I said to Ian, "Trevor would like to take you for a meal on the Saturday before your birthday. As I couldn't book a table, I said to Trev that we really need to be there by half past seven, is that alright?"

Fortunately Ian agreed, and everything was falling into place, but then perhaps I made my next mistake or omitted something.

With all my personal arrangements, nails hair etc, Ian must have realised that there was a bit more to the evening than just Trevor coming to take his Dad to the local for a meal. I got myself ready, and Trevor took us to the Pub in his car.

We walked in and the first thing we saw was a large Galapagos flag and twenty people standing up and singing

419

'Happy Birthday'. The room was decorated with lots of symbols of the Galapagos including fake palm trees, a life size land iguana, a large plastic porpoise and bunting etc. Jacquie handed Ian the tickets, wished him a super holiday and the other guests proffered their gifts. I felt an overwhelming sense of relief that everything was now in the open and everyone seemed to have a great evening.

I was concerned that his actual birthday was rather an anticlimax, especially when I said, "I'm sorry Ian, but I'm afraid that on your actual birthday, I've booked you in to have your injections because it was the only day I could really be sure that you wouldn't be working!"

Despite this news Ian replied, "Well it was the best birthday I've ever had, so a little discomfort is nothing to worry about!"

Ian and Trevor had a tremendous holiday and we both enjoyed looking at all the wonderful photographs that he took. "What lovely memories," he said.

CHAPTER 14

COME BACK SISTER PRUNE FACE, WE MISS YOU

Shortly after Ian's Galapagos trip, we booked to go and stay overnight at a bed and breakfast in Kesgrave, near Ipswich, so that we could visit some of Ian's old friends. We checked in and went to lie down for a short snooze. I became aware that my mouth was full of blood, and rushed to the en-suite to spit it out, but the blood kept coming, I said to Ian, "Please check that there isn't any blood on the sheets."

He said, "No, fortunately there isn't, but I think that we ought to get you home."

Ian phoned his friends, paid the bill and helped me into the car. Taking the roll of paper towel that we kept in the glove compartment.

"Try to stem as much blood as you can we won't be too long," he said.

As we drove past the signs for Ipswich Hospital, Ian asked, "Are you sure we should make for Peterborough rather than here?"

In spite of all the blood that was pouring from my mouth,

I said through the blood and paper towel, "If we go to Ipswich hospital it would just cause confusion, so carry on as quick as you can!"

We continued on the two-hour journey, the roll was almost used up and the front of the car was knee deep in blood soaked paper towelling.

As we neared home Ian said, "It would be a good idea for us to stop and collect another roll of paper towel. I'll help you to take off your good clothes and jewels before going into hospital."

With that we parked and Ian carefully helped me out of my clothes, avoiding the blood. But, on my way back to the car I collapsed in the front doorway, and he was unable to move me. He rang 999.

Apparently they sent a paramedic in a car and, immediately he saw my condition, placed an oxygen mask over my face and called for an ambulance. Paramedics are normally diplomatic, but he was clearly irritated by my condition. He told Ian that we'd been very silly in driving home and we should have gone to the Ipswich hospital.

In due course, the ambulance arrived, and I was taken into Accident and Emergency. The doctor lifted up my facemask and she said, "Oh it's you again!"

There was a pleasure and warmth in her voice, and I smiled, secure in the knowledge that I was in good hands, and then she said, "Its back to 1Z for you, and another transfusion"

I smiled as I said goodbye, and the hospital porter pushed the trolley back to 1Z. I was taken into a single room, the transfusion was hooked up, and I asked suspiciously, "What am I doing in here?"

The slim male nurse who was making sure I had everything I needed said, "It's the only empty bed available on the ward."

Of course, without access to the bed occupancy details, I

had no way of checking if this was true or if I was getting preferential treatment. Being in a single room meant that I couldn't watch everything that was going on in the ward, but it was lovely to be on my own in relative peace and quiet. Just before I settled down to sleep, I said to the nurse, "I appreciate, it's not exactly your job to sort out the radio, but it would be a tremendous help for me to listen to Radio 4 through the night."

He said, "I am doing something at the moment, but I will be back shortly to see if I can manage it, although I haven't actually done it before."

It wasn't long before he came back and he soon worked out how to get the channel tuned in. I was able to relax and listen to Radio 4 until it closed down for the night and then I could listen to the World Service until it transferred back to Radio 4 the next morning. I lay and snoozed, luxuriating in the simple act of kindness that the RAF nurses seem to consider as part of the job. I thought, "I wonder how these RAF nurses are selected because, unlike their NHS counterparts, they give a quality, Rolls-Royce type of service!"

I felt so fortunate to be cared for by them.

After a bag of blood and then breakfast the next morning, the nurse asked how I was feeling. I was much better so she suggested that perhaps I should just have a bowl of water at my bedside to re-fresh myself today, rather than a bath or shower and the complication of the transfusion paraphernalia. She came back with a bowl and found the things from my toiletries bag that I needed to have a wash. I sat on the side of the bed and commenced my ablutions. Suddenly there was a crash and apparently I collapsed unconscious onto the floor, knocking the bowl of water and everything else over. The nurse returned, rang the crash alarm and, when I regained consciousness, the resuscitation team were around me. One member of the team jokingly said, "We've just run a long way to see you, and all the time it's just a faint. Don't do it again!"

The group around my bed all smiled, I smiled too and said, "Thank you for coming!"

The reason that I'd collapsed was probably due to a fit, Lupus again! I had discovered that when my body was under undue stress or I became overtired, I could have several fits in just one night. I am not aware of them but when I get up in the morning I simply feel totally exhausted, as if I haven't had any sleep. Poor Ian is usually very tired as well having supervised me, being anxious in case I choke on my tongue, fall out of bed or hurt myself in some other way. So in the morning he is worse for wear as well. It seems that these fits could be put down to the damage to my brain tissue during my cerebral lupus crisis. Of course I wasn't sure on this occasion but after talking it over with the nurses they agreed that it was probably what had happened. I was still feeling weak from the experience and was grateful that two of the nurses stayed with me to help with my ablutions. After they had finished, they left me to settle down and rest.

It was quiet and peaceful in my single room, and I realised that the advantage of being on my own was I was that I was able to rest and recuperate from the fit. In the quietness of the single room I was also able to think things through.

When one of the nurses came back to see how I was and to put up another bag of blood, I took the opportunity while she was busy with her task, to enquire, "I understand that you do the same graduate training as the NHS nurses, but how are you selected for the RAF?"

She responded, "We have to take a psychometric test and pass a medical fitness examination every six months while we are in the service."

I simply said, "Oh, yes I know about psychometric testing."

When she left, I thought, "Of course that's it!'

At one stage in my professional life I had completed training in psychometric assessment with the LIFO scheme. I was very impressed by its value as an assessment tool, although at the time it was regarded as 'the flavour of the month'. While I'd been involved with that, Ian was running behavioural assessment for the applicants who applied to work at the new Toyota factory at Burnaston in Staffordshire. Anyone who wanted to work for Toyota had to be evaluated at these psychometric based assessments, to test to their attitude to work and record the skills that they possessed. The intensive and expensive recruitment process was seen as an essential component in Toyota becoming 'World Class'. So it wasn't only Toyota that believed in psychometric testing, but the armed forces as well. I was disappointed that, just when I was well into my research regarding the suitability of psychometric for the NHS, I was unfortunately interrupted by my decline into my cerebral lupus crisis. However, all was not lost, as the armed forces recognised the value and importance of attitude as a factor in the recruitment of their nursing and medical personnel.

I then considered the armed force's requirement for its personnel to pass a medical examination every six months. To my knowledge this was not available or apparently desired by the current NHS nurses. I remembered that, as a theatre staff nurse in the 1960s, I was expected to be fit enough to run up the five flights of the back stairs in the theatre block without becoming breathless. I was young and I thought nothing of it! We had to train for major emergencies. An accident in the tunnels of Birmingham New Street station was regarded as a major local hazard. We trained on those stairs wearing a hard hat that had a large spotlight on the front, and a very heavy battery box was strapped to our waist to give us the power that we would need in the dark. I was grateful, and a little bit ashamed that I was grateful, that I was in Oxford when the Rotunda, Birmingham was actually bombed.

The current forces uniforms are close to the approach of the 1960s NHS policy regarding uniforms. Nurses' uniforms

425

were measured so that the hems were 14 inches from the floor. It was important that we should look neat, tidy and proud of our profession, when we stood in line awaiting inspection by the sister or matron. Today, nurses generally look scruffy and unkempt as they stand outside the hospital having a smoke. What examples are they to the patients? I often see nurses in hospital uniform in the shops. It would have been a disciplinary matter if we had been caught in our uniforms outside of work. What about hygiene and cross infections? Are changing rooms not provided in the hospitals these days?

Then I started thinking about the time and motion studies that had been applied to most of our duties. I amused myself thinking that the current NHS nurses could be tested on how quickly they could open a packet of cigarettes, eat a cream bun, or a packet of crisps. It is sad to think that the disciplines introduced by Florence Nightingale so long ago had survived into the late 1960s but now have almost disappeared. I ruminated about how the training that Florence Nightingale initiated was a result of her experience in the military at Scutari, and how successful this had been in turning around the Sarah Gamp image of nurses portrayed so eloquently by Charles Dickens. Would the military nurses of today be successful in changing the attitude of their NHS colleagues, as Florence had been in changing the culture of nursing in the Crimea?

Fortunately before my train of thought went any further, it was interrupted by the arrival of Dr Sheehan at my bedside. He smiled as he looked at me, and I felt warmed through to the core by his diligence in coming to see me. Before he had the opportunity of saying anything, I said, "I'm sure, I am allright, but thank you as always for coming!"

He was always reassuring, and after he checked me over and read my notes, he said, "It looks as though your blood results will be back to normal after you have had another pint of blood and so, all being well you'll soon be ready for discharge. But as I'm going away on holiday, I have asked Dr Williams to verify your discharge."

I did think that Dr Sheehan looked very tired, and so I said, "I do hope that you have a very happy and restful holiday. Thank you once again for everything!"

Then as an after thought, I remembered to say,

"When Ian rang 999 and the Paramedic arrived, he said that I should have gone straight into Ipswich Hospital, rather than coming back here."

Dr Sheehan said, "They would probably have had to send you back to Peterborough in an ambulance, if he'd done that your recovery would have been substantially delayed."

I responded," Ian will be pleased to know that you think he made the right decision about that. Oh, my next routine appointment is in about a month, shall I still keep it?"

Dr Sheehan's response was, "Yes leave it as it is and I'll see you then."

All did go well with my recovery and Dr Sheehan went on his holiday. It wasn't many days later until Dr Williams, the other Rheumatology Consultant, came to see me. He looked down from under his mop of grey hair, saying, "I've read your annual reports, and they were very useful. Your blood results are OK, and so I think you are ready for discharge."

Now I just had to wait for the letters for my discharge to be organised; I lay down thinking through my situation. When, as a young mother with a toddler, I was given the Lupus diagnosis; it had been an all-consuming blow to me, particularly when I was predicted an early death. Perhaps inevitably, I went into a state of denial whilst trying to accommodate the symptoms that undoubtedly I had.

Some twenty years later, Ian's reaction to my becoming poorly and subsequent admission to hospital, was to search for information about the disease. He found out about the Lupus Society and joined. It hadn't existed when I was first diagnosed, but fortunately other people facing the same situation had been more proactive and not followed my ostrich like approach!

Having survived a cerebral lupus crisis, I was fortunate for all the Society's hard work in raising funds to support research and provide information to the medical profession that was instrumental in my recovery.

The RAF staff nurse arrived at my bedside, smiled and said, "Your husband has phoned and he will be coming to collect you in an hour, but I just need to remove the cannula from your arm, so I will go and get a trolley."

I said, "Oh yes, thanks, the site is feeling very sore."

"I won't be long," she said

Just after that I heard the crash alarm. Afterwards when heading back to my bed I noticed that the screens had been drawn around our beds, thus allowing privacy whilst the mortuary trolley was wheeled out of the ward followed by tearful relatives. Poignantly, one of them was carrying a small suitcase.

Eventually the nurse returned and I said, "I know that I am not a priority and you've been busy but this does hurt."

She looked concerned saying, "You are all priority."

I replied, "To be honest I'm glad not to be priority on this occasion!"

She looked sad as she squeezed my hand, and we shared a moment of understanding for the situation that had just occurred. She was quiet as she removed the connection, cleaning the site and placing some plaster over the wound.

I simply said, "Thank you."

I smiled at her sympathetically as she went out, emptied my locker, and waited for Ian.

Ian said, "Are you all right?"

"I was singing the NHS nurses anthem."

Ian's response, "What are you on about, I thought you were moaning?"

"All right, I realise that I've lost my sense of pitch, and I was probably singing out of tune, but I was attempting to sing 'busy doing nothing, working the whole day through, trying to find lots of things not to do!' Honestly, Ian, being in hospital and this time being cared for by the RAF has opened my eyes. I think that the dominant attitude of 'don't care about patients' is causing the damage, not the introduction of computers!"

Ian smiled and said, "Oh, come on, enough of that, let's get home, the dogs need reassuring that there is nothing seriously wrong with you. Don't forget that you have the 'co-ag' clinic on Monday."

On Monday, a small, dark-haired, smiling volunteer driver fro hospital transport came to pick me up for my appointment. He helped me into his car, and said, "Can you manage all right?"

He looked concerned, as I explained what had happened with my bleeding and hospital admission. David is one of the small group of wonderful volunteer drivers who transport patients to hospital outpatient clinics.

I walked into the outpatient clinic and was greeted by Mollie, another volunteer, whose job was to check in the arrivals. Mollie was white-haired, plump and always cheerful, sorting out those just for a thumb prick, and those who need to see the doctor. The regulars dutifully hand over their precious yellow record books and take a seat whilst waiting their turn.

As I, like many others, have to take Warfarin for my anti-phospholipid syndrome, or 'sticky blood syndrome', for the rest of my life, the Anticoagulant Clinic becomes rather like a club. Meeting regularly gives a pleasant opportunity for us catch up with the news.

The reason for my mystery haemorrhaging was still unresolved. My theory was that Dr Coleman's original suggestion for maintaining my INR at 2.6 to 2.8 was correct although Dr Hughes at St. Thomas's, who was considered the authority in sticky blood syndrome, had said that Lupus suffers should be 3.6 to 3.8.

Unfortunately on this occasion they weren't able to get enough blood from my thumb prick. After a discussion with

Jackie, the senior phlebotomist, it was suggested that I should go upstairs to the haematology department and see if they could get a blood sample. Fortunately they succeeded. I was to telephone my GP the next day and the all-important yellow book would follow as normal, by first class post.

Next morning I followed instructions and rang the surgery.

Martina, the receptionist, said, "They are all busy at the moment so I will get the duty doctor, Dr Oxley to phone you at 2:00."

Of course, although I trusted Martina, I was sceptical that this would actually happen, so I was very surprised when at 2p.m precisely, the phone rang, and a male voice said, "It's Dr Oxley here, you are very anaemic, so I want you to go straight into Accident and Emergency for another 2 pints of blood."

I thought, "Oh no not again, I've only just come out," but I actually said, "Do you think we can do this a bit more conservatively? I am happy to take iron tablets, and come in for frequent blood tests."

I suppose that I took him by surprise, but he reluctantly agreed, and the pharmacy delivered Ferrous Sulphate tablets that afternoon.

The next morning I was glad that, despite my anaemia, I was well enough to walk the dogs. Thinking it through I was amused with the notion, "My blood results are unstable but then again surely the most stable result comes from the patient who is dead, and at least that's not me yet." Making my way through the tunnel on the path under the Parkway, and down to the rowing lake, with the dogs ferreting in the bushes and me in a world of my own, someone called out, "Hello Annie, it's Jilly."

I was very surprised because we hadn't seen each other for several years. We hugged. Still small and blond she didn't look any older, I said, "Jilly, it's great to see you, but I thought you'd moved to Leicester!"

Jilly's response was, "Annie, I thought you'd moved to live to somewhere near Nottingham."

It really was good to see her again, and clearly we had a lot of catching up to do. Jilly said, "I had heard you'd been ill but that was some time ago. You look well, how are you really feeling?"

I replied, "Well I do the best I can with poor materials!"

Jilly grinned and we chatted as we walked along with my dogs and hers, contentedly following their doggy activities.

She explained, "These two dogs belong to my daughter Josie, she has gone away for a couple of days. I do so enjoy the opportunity to get out for a walk, but I always feel that there should be a good reason for taking a walk, so I'd be really pleased to come with you sometimes, or walk yours, if ever you wanted me to."

I responded, "It's great to have your company, Jilly!"

So, with that we arranged to meet regularly for dog walking and chatting.

I could see that Jilly was analysing my movements, so I explained, "Since we last met I have lost a lot of brain tissue. At first I was almost paralysed, I could hardly walk and often tripped and fell. Luckily Neil at Thomas Cooks gym took an interest in helping me. He scrutinised me with his languid eyes and worked out the exercises I needed." We laughed at my languid eyes comment. I continued, "He paid for his own training, as the gym wouldn't pay, and qualified for helping and developing the disabled. He was really great but it did emphasise the sad waste, as far as I was concerned, of NHS money that goes into occupational therapy and physiotherapy. I do hope that some people somewhere get real benefits from their efforts.

I felt very lucky to meet Jilly again and renew our friendship that offered me so much comfort and understanding, a rare compassion that should be treasured.

Jilly relayed her healthcare experiences and explained

that she had taken a job with the community in Leicester because there wasn't any community healthcare work nearer home, However she decided not to move to Leicester because her mother became very ill and was admitted to Ward 1Z after having two strokes. Working away made it very difficult for Jilly to get in to visit her mother. Her mother was unable to sit up and wash or feed herself and soon became quite neglected. Surprised and disappointed with the first few days care in hospital, Jilly went in to sort things out. The staff nurse refused to admit her because it wasn't visiting time, so she stood in front of Jilly to block her path. Jilly ignored her and marched in. The Patient Services Manager was called and informed her that she was not allowed to see her mother outside visiting hours. Naturally Jilly was incensed, but she was unable to alter the intransigence of Ward 1Z. Shortly after this encounter Jilly's mother was moved to another ward, where sadly she died.

I told her all about my dreadful hospital experiences particularly in 1Z, but was able to reassure her that as 1Z is now staffed by the RAF, the care was much improved and almost wonderful.

Jilly said, "Pops, my stepfather, will be pleased, he was in the RAF, and very proud of it."

Many of our conversations focus on hospital life, Jilly agreed, "Yes, when we were nurses we were proud of our profession, now it seems that NHS nurses have lost that pride. However its good to hear that at least the RAF are maintaining the tradition."

I added, "Yes we all knew our responsibilities and who we answered to, the ward sister was in charge of her ward and the theatre in its entirety belonged to the Theatre Sister. It was her theatre and hers alone."

I told her my story about an incident that I had in theatre. We were waiting for a frozen section result to say conclusively that a breast lump was cancerous. The medical staff were rude about the size and shape of the woman's breasts. So I pushed the instrument trolley towards the sluice room, saying, if you wish to continue with those rude remarks, you will have to manage without a scrub nurse.

Jilly said, "Yes, and do you remember how we had to count all the instruments before surgery? And the scrub nurse, with the assistance of the runner, would count them all after surgery before giving the surgeon permission to start sewing up!"

I laughed, saying, "Do you remember counting out the swabs, and hanging the used ones on the rack so that they could be counted before sewing up as well. I wonder if that still happens?"

Jilly said, "I bet it doesn't, I know how many deaths after surgery are due to instruments and foreign objects left inside the patient's body."

I said, "Ian says that key-hole surgery is brilliant, so long as they remember to take the key out afterwards. You remember Val, the catering manager, well Val and I meet up in the town for lunch quite often. Unfortunately, Geoff, Val's lovely husband, died of MRSA. He caught it in Peterborough Hospital. While his health was compromised by diabetes, he shouldn't have died. It was very sad and traumatic for Val."

Jilly asked, "How is she managing?"

"Well you know, as expected Val keeps herself busy working for a charity, but it shouldn't have happened. The hospitals seem so dirty now that the cleaning and catering are contracted out. Nurses are no longer responsible for cleaning or making sure that patients are able to get their meals. Honestly Jilly, I've been in a hospital where there were old bloodstains on the floor when I was admitted and they were still there when I was discharged several days later. When I was ill my relatives had to feed me! I'm not sure about this 'named nurse' business either, it seems that they are looking through the wrong end of the telescope. Gone are the days when the ward sister took responsibility for everything. Do you know, when I was in Addenbrooke's, and Ian wanted to give me a mouthwash after cleaning my teeth, he went and found the ward sister. Eventually she found the mouthwash in a five litre jar in the storeroom and poured him out a glassful. Ian asked, how much should it be diluted. She said it was ready to use. Back by my bed he was decided that he was not satisfied it seemed to smell so strong. He found a nurse and got her to check, she found the bottle and he consulted the label, it instructed dilution at ten to one. Can you imagine that? It would have burnt out my tongue, mouth and oesophagus."

Jilly, shaking her head, said, "That's dreadful, I can hardly believe it."

Again I was in full flow and continued, "My friend Lizzie went into Papworth Hospital to have a pacemaker fitted. When she was admitted she was assessed as needing, and was placed in, an orthopaedic electronic bed. When she returned from her operation, as she also had advanced glaucoma, she fumbled for the control and after much stressful searching found out that her bed had been replaced by an ordinary one. So she asked the sister for her bed to be returned. The sister responded, "Beds are not my responsibility."

Jilly said, "It begs the question, what is a ward sister responsible for in the NHS these days?"

I said, "I don't expect the RAF nurses would think that a patient's comfort and personal care is not their responsibility. I wonder why NHS nurses don't see it that way as well? Two nurses were essential for drug rounds and they checked to see that the patients took them. Now the named nurse just puts the pills by your bed and lets you get on with it."

Jilly confirmed, "I worried about that when my mother was in."

We walked for a while and then discussed how, unlike the NHS nurses, the RAF nurses take psychometric tests and have to pass a medical examination every six months to ensure their fitness.

When we got back, after our walk, I found Dr Le Fanu's

article for Jilly to read. While she was reading, I said, "We can only hope that the RAF will have the same effect on modern nursing that Florence Nightingale originally had on the development of nurse training! For good or ill, it's the culture of authority, and deference to it, that has been lost by the NHS nursing profession. Perhaps it is time for the nursing to stop bleating on about shortages of staff and develop a scheme that will actually achieve total patient care."

We both agreed with Dr James Le Fanu 'Come back Sister Prune face, we miss you".